Globalizing International Human Resource Management

Globalizing International Human Resource Management sets out to cover as a wide range of regional and national cultures, as well as perspectives, as possible, in order to explore how these might shape both theory and practice in this field.

In attempting this, it focuses on key concepts within it, such as

human resources (HR)

HR management (HRM),

international HRM (IHRM),

strategic HRM (SHRM),

human capital and talent as they relate to foreign direct investment (FDI)

These are discussed in a range of spatial and organizational settings, including multinational corporations (MNC), international joint ventures (IJV). The book covers a wide range of countries and cultures in North America, Europe and and Asia. Next, we have a set of nationally-based cases that represent exemplifications of many of the conceptual points made by contributors, who include scholars based in a wide variety of countries around the world, in universities and business schools.

This book was previously published as a special issue of *The International Journal of Human Resource Management*

Chris Rowley is at the Cass Business School, City University, London

Malcolm Warner is at the Judge Business School, University of Cambridge

Globalizing International Human Resource Management

Edited by
Chris Rowley and Malcolm Warner

LONDON AND NEW YORK

First published 2008 by Routledge
2 Park Square, Milton Park, Abingdon, Oxon, OX14 4RN

Simultaneously published in the USA and Canada by Routledge
270 Madison Avenue, New York, NY 10016

*Routledge is an imprint of the Taylor & Francis Group, an Informa
business*

Typeset in Times 9.5/11pt by the Alden Group, OxfordShire
Printed and bound in Great Britain by MPG Ltd, Bodmin, Cornwall

British Library Cataloguing in Publication Data
A catalogue record for this book is available from the British Library

Library of Congress Cataloging in Publication Data
A catalog record for this book has been requested

ISBN 10: 0-415-44001-7 (hbk)
ISBN 13: 978-0-415-44001-1 (hbk)

CONTENTS

Notes on Contributors

Mike Bendixen is at Nova Southeasten University, Florida, USA.

John Benson is at the University of South Australia, Adelaide, Australia.

Allan Bird is Eiichi Shibusawa-Seigo Arai Professor of Japanese Studies, College of Business Administration, University of Missouri-St Louis, USA.

Chris Brewster is at the Henley Management College, UK.

John Child is Chair of Commerce at the Birmingham Business School, University of Birmingham, UK.

Chan Yan Chong is a member of the Faculty of Business, City University of Hong Kong.

Philippe Debroux is at Soka University, Tokyo, Japan.

Marianela Fornerino is at Groupe Grenoble Ecole de Mnagement, France.

M. Khasro Miah is at North South University, Dhaka, Bangladesh.

Jacobo Ramirez is at the ITESM-Management Dept, Monterrey, Mexico.

Rosoava Rijamampianina is at the University of Witwatersrand, South Africa.

Chris Rowley is at the Cass Business School, City University, London, UK.

Randall S. Schuler holds positions at Rutgers University, New Jersey, USA, and GSBA, Zurich, Switzerland.

Ashok Som is at the ESSEC Business School, Paris, France.

Paul R. Sparrow is at Lancaster University Management School, UK.

Ibraiz Tarique is at Pace University, New York.

Rosalie L. Tung is at the Simon Fraser University, Canada.

Malcolm Warner is at the Judge Business School, Cambridge University, UK.

Albert Wocke is at the University of Pretoria, South Africa.

Yanni Yan is a member of the Faculty of Business, City University of Hong Kong.

Masae Yuasa is at Hiroshima City University, Japan.

Ying Zhu is at the University of Melbourne, Australia.

Introduction: globalizing international human resource management

Chris Rowley and Malcolm Warner

Introduction

This book on 'Globalizing International Human Resource Management' sets out to cover a wide range of regional and national cultures, as well as perspectives, as possible, in order to explore how these might shape both theory and practice in this field. In attempting this, we focus on key concepts within it, human resources (HR), HR management (HRM), international HRM (IHRM), strategic HRM (SHRM), as well as human capital and talent as they relate to foreign direct investment (FDI) in a range of spatial and organizational settings, including multi-national corporations (MNCs), international joint ventures (IJVs), *vis-à-vis* the growing phenomenon of globalization (see Warner, 2002).

HRM, as opposed to Personnel Management (PM), is essentially a post-World War II development, has North American roots and has increasingly spread worldwide in recent years. It is now well entrenched in management theory and practice. As Price (2004: 673) points out:

> Regardless of the rationale or the nature of its practice, HRM has become a common label for various forms and functions of people management. In British-speaking countries, the term has replaced 'personnel management' in many contexts. For example, academic courses, journals and textbooks formerly labelled as 'personnel management' are now described as 'human resource management'. However, and particularly at practitioner level, re-labelling does not mean necessarily that either the approach or the content have changed.... The diverse interpretations of HRM are apparent when we compare practices in different countries and organizations ... [and] 'personnel' and 'human resources' can co-exist and many organizations throughout the developed world follow North American practice, using the terms interchangeably.

With increasing globalization, some say you will get more and more HRM, or IHRM, of this genre, in a wide range of business organizations around the world, some of them employing large numbers of employees, in many very different locations spread across the world (see Warner, 2005). Size matters here and formalization/standardization that often characterize say, HRM practices, are associated directly with, say, the number of employees in a firm. The bigger the firm, the more likely it is to be a global player. The more this is the case, the more IHRM predominates. How can we make sense of this phenomenon? Is IHRM now on an inexorable track? What is the evidence for this?

First, we look at *perspectives on HRM and IHRM in different parts of the world*: namely, in *North America*, in *Asia* and in *Europe*. Here we have a sequence of three chapters (Schuler and Tarique; Ying *et al.*; Brewster). Next, we have a set of nationally based cases that represent, we believe, exemplifications of many of the conceptual points made by contributors to the Special Issue. The central foci of these valuable contributions may be seen within the following *analytical* groupings, which we have used to organize this part of the Introduction: (1) *strategy/level*, e.g. Yan *et al.*, Som, and Wocke *et al.*; (2) *practice/function*al/*level*, e.g. Sparrow, Tung, and Benson *et al.*; and (3) *macro/theoretical/level*, e.g. Miah and Bird (cultures) and Ramirez and Fornerino (neo-contingency).

The above categorization does not preclude alternative ways of looking at the material, as many chapters cover, in a varying range of explicitness, more than one area and make numerous contributions; so one may possibly also note that they cover a range of issues and areas regarding the impacts on IHRM of globalization, FDI and so on. These could, say, in terms of the above offer in more detail: (1) *Strategy* (Yan *et al.*; Som, Wocke *et al.*); (2) *HRM function, style, practices and issues*, e.g. HR resourcing (Sparrow; Tung; Benson *et al*; Miah and Bird; Ramirez and Fornerino), development (Benson *et al.*; Miah and Bird; Ramirez and Fornerino), rewards (Benson *et al.*; Ramirez and Fornerino), participation (Miah and Bird), gender and internal labour markets (Benson *et al.*); and (3) *theoretical issues*, e.g. varieties of micro/neo-contingency (Sparrow; Ramirez and Fornerino; Som), divergence (Ramirez and Fornerino), Dunning's eclectic paradigm, convergence (Wocke *et al.*), vertical integration (Yan *et al.*), in passing on monopolistic advantage, internalization, international technology gap, competitive diamond (Tung) research-based view of the firm, relational and social capital, institution theory (Sparrow). However, since the above schema seems a little over-elaborate, we have stayed with the earlier categorization.

A wide set of *organizational* sizes, types and forms, locations and sectors is also exemplified using a range of research methods and analysis. For example, MNCs (indigenous and subsidiaries), IJVs, domestic companies, and so on, are investigated in great detail. They also cover a wide range of *regions* and *countries* (both developed and developing) within the articles in Asia, Europe and North America, taken broadly in the Perspectives section and in the Nationally Based Cases section, for example Bangladesh, France, India, Pakistan, Japan, Malaysia, People's Republic of China, South Korea, Taiwan, Thailand, South Africa, UK and Vietnam. A diverse range of *sectoral* settings and examples are in turn also covered, including, manufacturing, automotive, chemicals, petro-chemicals, brewing, pharmaceuticals, fast moving consumer goods, telecoms, fast-food retailing, hotels, electronics, IT and software, public sector, finance, and so on. Another diversity that should be emphasized concerns the *authors* themselves, who are known HRM scholars based in a wide variety of countries around the world, in universities and business schools, including those in Australia, Canada, France, Hong Kong, Japan, Mexico, South Africa, UK, US and so on.

We should further note that the subject of IHRM is evidently a highly flourishing one these days. For example, The International Journal of Human Resource Management now comes 12 times a year and publishes well over 100 refereed articles annually. There appears to be no shortage of papers at hand and it is only one leading journal amongst many others, most now getting increasingly internationally oriented submissions. The number of textbooks proliferates by the year equally as more and more courses in business schools and similar university level institutions offer either full-time HRM degrees at different levels as well as teaching the subject within an undergraduate management degree course or MBA/DBA programmes and courses in the area of IHRM. It is also an important area of other subjects, such as International Business. To enrich the content of what is taught, new knowledge must be sought and it is the function of research to do just this. We seek in this book to present 'cutting-edge' research to help achieve this goal.

Perspectives

North America

Schuler and Tarique.   In their key-note contribution, Schuler and Tarique note that the past 15 years have witnessed important advancements in the research and practice of IHRM. The field of IHRM, they argue, is about understanding, researching, applying and revising HR activities in their internal and external contexts as they have an impact on the processes of managing HR in organizations throughout the global environment to enhance the experience of multiple stakeholders. In this review of the field, the authors offer a perspective from North America to describe how IHRM has evolved since the framework by Schuler *et al.* (1993). They present a thematic framework of IHRM that organizes and updates the existing IHRM literature within five thematic areas: (1) Strategic MNC Components; (2) Exogenous Factors; (3) Endogenous Factors; (4) IHRM Issues, Functions, Policies and Practices; and (5) MNC Effectiveness. Within each thematic area, the authors describe several sub-themes that reflect important changes in, and evolution of, IHRM issues. Taken as a whole, the thematic approach describes the contributions of previous models of IHRM and identifies key scholars and their contributions to understanding and advancing IHRM.

Next, the authors significantly build on and extend the thematic framework by discussing in detail one of the increasingly important sub-themes in the 'Strategic Management Components' theme, namely, cross-border alliances (CBAs). Including this sub-theme provides the opportunity to discuss the impact of the phenomenon of complexity which is significant for MNCs as well as CBAs. The authors describe the several forms of CBAs and argue they all share varying amounts of complexity, which in turn can serve as road-blocks to common needs (for learning, economies, efficiencies, control) shared with all MNCs. Thus, because these conditions are amenable to IHRM activities, as the form of CBA goes from relatively simple to more complex, the importance of IHRM increases (Schuler and Tarique, 2006a, 2006b). Similarly, as the complexity for MNCs grows, the importance of IHRM increases. The authors then focus on the most complex form of CBA, the IJV, and develop a typology as a way of illustrating their complexity and the challenges of crafting an effective sets of IHRM activities.

Finally, the authors offer 20 avenues or topics for future research and investigation in IHRM. This is done by organizing the suggestions according to the five thematic areas in the basic framework of IHRM. This is based on a presentation of the realities of MNCs and their implications for the field and profession of IHRM. Overall, the authors believe that the nature of IHRM in North America is changing rapidly as the twenty-first century gets under way and this seems consistent with the rest of world (Sparrow and Brewster,

2006). Increasingly, IHRM is being recognized as central to strategic planning and strategy implementation in MNCs, leading some to call for re-labelling the field as 'global' rather than IHRM (Brewster *et al.*, 2005).

Asia

Zhu *et al.* The central theme of the next chapter, by Zhu *et al.* is to illustrate the similarities and differences of people management systems among key economies in Asia and more specifically in East Asia. The chapter not only identifies what elements exist in such systems, but also examines other, new elements being adopted with influences from the US and Europe à la IHRM. The authors analyse information on the shifts in people management, factors causing the changes and time. The common phenomenon is that when there is a crisis then that may provide some opportunities for drastic changes.

The authors conclude the chapter by pointing out that HRM is in a reforming process towards a more hybrid people management system in East Asia. However, this reforming process is not one-way only but rather triangular with influence between Asia, Europe and the US. In addition, multiple factors are shaping the outcome, identified as foreign influence, the State's role, the stage of social and economic development, and the national and organizational historical path. Given all of the evidence and argument in this chapter we can see that it would be foolish to define an 'Asian HRM Model' as such. However, the implications of this study are manifold. The purpose of this study is not about showing who has a more 'superior' people management system than others, but identifying what elements exist in East Asian people management, what other new elements have been adopted into the existing system and then what factors are determining such changes. Therefore, future changes may go ahead along the lines of shaping factors and influences presented in this article. Also, other economies, no matter whether in East Asia or other parts of the world may draw some lessons from this study as can the field and practice of IHRM.

Europe

Brewster. Brewster argues in his chapter that the US-originated notion of HRM has been commonly accepted across the world – but it has also been widely criticized. The underlying features of the economies of *Europe*, or the European Union (EU) more specifically, are different from those of the US and these have led to other and more critical approaches to HRM being developed. This critique explores the concept from a 'European' viewpoint (inevitably involving generalization). It examines the nature of the concept as it has come from the US and the universalistic 'scientific' paradigm that is widespread and is the focus of most leading journals there. The study points out that Europe is different, both in terms of culture, with less individualism, and institutions, with a greater role for the State, employment legislation, trade unions and consultation and different patterns of ownership of organizations. These have led to a different concept of HRM amongst European researchers and practitioners.

The chapter explores the contested nature of HRM (what it covers – and in whose interest); the variety of levels at which HRM is studied in Europe (from European through country and organizational to strong workplace traditions); and the different focus of HRM, with more concern with understanding, than assisting, companies (some of which can be see in this book itself). The result has been that HRM is more often studied in Europe not from a universalistic but a different ('contextual') research paradigm: where the aim is not to find some universally applicable truths but to understand the range of HRM practices and the impact of a series of contextual antecedents that explain them. Hence, a different and more critical approach to HRM has developed.

On the basis of these conceptual differences, the author briefly examines some of the comparative variations in practice within Europe and with the US in: the nature of work and the extent of contingent or flexible working practices; training and development; HRM function's role, including its integration into senior management decision making and the role of line managers; and the nature and extent of communication and consultation. Finally, the author argues that the challenge to the standard US perspective on HRM is to emphasize its complexity and the absence of universal truths. In reality, HRM is always embedded in a complex and more or less integrated network of institutional arrangements and cultural assumptions and legitimacies. National institutions and cultures are not the only layer of complexity but they are amongst the most powerful and need to be taken into account in attempts to understand IHRM.

Nationally based cases

Strategy/level

Yan *et al.*   The chapter by Yan *et al.* directly addresses the requirements of international firms in terms of the application of firm-specific assets and HRM needed for the implementation of vertical integration decisions. This empirical investigation is based upon a sample (136) of IJV hotel firms in the People's Republic of China (PRC). This highlights how the vertical integration of corporate management acts as a catalyst for the emergence of a structural approach to strategic orientation, contractual control and formalization. The significant findings suggest that the IHRM literature can be extended to take better account of the inner connection of a firm's structural properties in the vertical integration of its corporate management. The results offer valuable insights into both how the process of the vertical integration of corporate management positively influences the establishment of strategic orientation to achieve long-term development and also how contractual control guides the development priorities of IJVs.

The study of vertical firm-specific asset boundaries has received considerable attention due to the issues of asset heterogeneity, the imperfect mobility of resources and the effective utilization of organizational capabilities. The vertical integration of a firm's management is importantly related to the synergistic benefits that result from the introduction of HRM as an institutionally supported package. It follows that studies on corporate management have become critically important in the process of strategic management, especially when the vertical integration of human assets specificities involves significant organizational changes. Scholars assert that an efficient HRM function can exert a positive influence on people-related competencies and management endowments.

Studies of the effects of vertical integration on corporate management concentrate on one of three areas. First, strategic orientation is increasingly employed to guide businesses as it provides a method for planning the coordination of business development activities. Second, contractual control is seen as pivotal to ensuring that service qualities are well managed. Third, organization and formalization establish the specific rules, regulations, procedures and authority relations that characterize operations. The empirical analysis of the vertical integration of corporate management has increasingly captured the interest of many academics and practitioners. There has been an increasing interest in the effective use of vertical firm-specific assets and HRM in national or global business surroundings when organizations are predominantly constrained by their heritage of administrative traditions. The authors attempt to uncover whether corporate managements differ in their vertical integration processes.

The IJV hotels exhibit contrasting asset specificities and distinct HRM practices that provide a broad organizational setting for investigation. It highlights how the method of vertical integration of corporate management that is employed influences the nature of a firm's management properties, such as strategic orientation, contractual control and organization formalization. The authors analyze vertical integration using three integration variables to explore the differences exhibited when these are implemented individually or in combination to ensure a full exploration of the vertical firm-specific assets and HRM practices of each firm.

Som. In the next chapter, Som looks at adoption of innovation in SHRM in a liberalizing country – India. Though the liberalization process started in 1991, it took a decade for organizations to respond to such structural adjustments. Drawing from SHRM literature, five main propositions of the adoption of innovative SHRM practices in Indian organizations are made.

Consistent with prior research the study finds that institutional pressures influenced the adoption of SHRM practices and that organizations adopt SHRM practices for a variety of reasons. The antecedents include national environment (extent of unionization and sector characteristics, technological sophistication), organizational restructuring and ownership structure, legitimizing driver (use of international consultants), organizational culture, and the role of HR departments. The study's propositions are close to those found in the developed economy literature and, therefore, may be relevant to most sectors and industries anywhere in the world wherever there is a competitive market or movement towards it. The theoretical contribution of this chapter is that it analyses drivers of adoption due to changes occurring in the macro-environment through a contingency-based framework. Adoption of SHRM practices represents a strategic choice. The adoptions are contingent upon the strategic and systemic organizational responses of firms and takes place at a slow and varied pace. Potential payoffs, cost of adoption, power relations and social factors hinder the adoption process, and more so in a liberalizing economy. The generalizability, applicability, acceptability, and the diffusion of practices are also discussed.

Wocke *et al*. With global expansion now ongoing, Wocke *et al.* (looking at South Africa specifically) note that MNCs are under pressure to find an appropriate balance between global and local HRM practices. The standardization of HRM practices across MNCs, they argue, helps to smooth the transfer of competencies across organizations but local conditions may require affiliates in host countries to adopt their own context-specific practices. This proposition is the primary focus in the coordination of activities across a MNC. Indeed, much IHRM research is from the perspective of MNC affiliate differences or the degree of isomorphism between the HRM practices of parents and affiliates.

This 'cross-case analysis' study describes four approaches for configuring and implementing corporate HR strategy by four MNCs (Nando's International, MTN International, Sasol and SABMiller) from South Africa, a market characterized by high levels of societal change, uncertainty and diversity. These MNCs vary in the scope and level of abstraction of corporate HR strategies primarily due to differences in business model used, need to accommodate national culture and type and role of organizational culture in the MNC. These factors, the authors argue, all impact on the level of convergence of HRM practices.

Thus, the level of abstraction varies from policy-type HR strategies to detailed operational-level procedures and is closely aligned to the type and role of organizational culture in the MNC. Variation in scope is evident with one MNC focusing on three key HR programmes, while another provides a comprehensive list of HR practices affiliates/subsidiaries are expected to follow. Additionally, the authors find that the evolution of the MNC is likely to lead to a higher degree of standardized HR practices, which enhance capability to allocate scarce skills, consistency in performance management and associated reward and remuneration, and the building of a strong organizational culture.

The research in this piece makes an important contribution to the centralization/decentralization debate and highlights the role of MNC corporate HR strategy and organizational culture in the isomorphism debate. Additionally, the authors show that flexibility is an important element of any MNC-wide HR strategy in the continuous debate about how much control the centre needs to apply to host-country affiliates/subsidiaries. HR practitioners in MNCs need to consider the two dimensions of level of abstraction and scope when designing an IHRM strategy. These are important when designing systems for the transfer of firm-specific advantages or MNC competencies across national borders while retaining a stable, but flexible, organization. In short, the authors address the development requirements of MNCs in terms of the application of firm-specific assets and HRM needed for the implementation of vertical integration decisions.

Practice/functional level

Sparrow.   A series of changes, Sparrow argues in the next chapter, is being wrought on a significant range of IHRM functions – recruitment, staffing, management development and careers, and rewards – by the process of globalization, highlighting the differences between globally standardized, optimized or localized HR processes. This study of functional realignment within globalizing organizations in a UK-based setting, examines the driving forces within business functions as they seek to co-ordinate (develop linkages between geographically-dispersed units of a function) and control (regulate functional activities to align them with the expectations set in targets) their activities across borders. The interesting and unusual examples of a number of key UK-based cases are used in this study: namely, the BBC World Service, a Strategic Health Authority in London, Save the Children and Barclaycard International.

International resourcing now covers prosaic groups, ranging from: contract expatriates; assignees on short-term or intermediate-term foreign postings; permanent cadres of global managers; international commuters; employees utilized on long-term business trips; international transferees (moving from one subsidiary to another); virtual international employees active in cross-border project teams; skilled individuals working in geographically remote centres of excellence serving global operations; self-initiated movers who live in a third country but are willing to work for MNCs; immigrants actively and passively attracted to a national labour market; and domestically based employees in service centres but dealing with overseas customers, suppliers and partners on a regular basis. In addition to this, fragmentation of international employees, some labour markets have themselves globalized.

Arguing for the need to study international resourcing based on populations other than expatriates this research is based on four case studies, each examining a specific context: international recruitment from overseas countries for employment in the home (UK) market; resourcing specialist skills for use in home and overseas markets; recruitment in the context of an internationalization strategy; and devolving responsibility for international recruitment. The chapter examines the process of functional realignment due to globalization within the international resourcing function in these contexts in order to identify: indicators that evidence globalization at the functional level; patterns or strategies within the activity of organizations at this level; and if these patterns can be explained by existing theory and what new directions would be helpful.

The HR function is shown to be realigning itself in response to a process of *within-function globalization* (building new alliances with other functions such as marketing and information systems). This is creating new activity streams, roles and skills that carry important implications for the study of IHRM. The author shows that although the field of IHRM has traditionally drawn upon core theories such as the resource-based view of the firm, relational and social capital, and institutional theory, once the full range of resourcing options now open to IHRM functions are considered it is evident that they need to incorporate both more micro theory as well as insights from contingent fields in order to explain some of the new practices emerging.

Tung. In the next contribution, Tung notes that the continued influx of FDI into the People's Republic of China – the world's top destination for this kind of investment since 2002 – and the growing desire by indigenous Chinese companies to invest abroad have created an unprecedented demand for people who possess competencies to compete successfully in a global economy. This phenomenon has resulted in a paradox of 'scarcity among plenty' whereby the most populous nation in the world has a shortfall of talent. Indeed, without this pool of talent, economic growth will slow and outward FDI aspirations will be thwarted. To address this situation, the Chinese government has embarked on a two-prong approach to develop managerial talent: first, massive expansion of MBA programmes at home, including satellite campuses from abroad and IJVs with business schools from other countries; second, attracting those with the necessary skills to work for Chinese companies either in China or abroad. Indeed, since the 1990s many foreign-educated Chinese nationals, referred to as ex-host country nationals (EHCNs) or *haiguis*, have returned to work in China. A growing number of non-Chinese is also attracted to work in China because of the career developmental opportunities in that country.

This chapter presents two inter-related studies to shed light on China's ability to meet this HR challenge. The first study pertains to the intention of a sample of Chinese university students in Canada to return to work in China upon graduation. The second study examines the willingness of non-Chinese university students to work for Chinese firms overseas or in China. In general, most Chinese students are receptive to returning to work in China, albeit to start up their own businesses or work in foreign-invested enterprises. Furthermore, many Chinese respondents are cognizant that the conditions for EHCNs now are not as they were earlier. Some of the *haiguis* have become *haidais,* that is, encountering difficulties in finding high-paying positions upon return. Despite general negative perceptions of China, non-Chinese students were more willing to work for Chinese companies overseas than in China. These surveys were supplemented by interviews with Chinese who have returned to work in China and those who chose to remain overseas. The interviews with some Chinese who remained in Canada revealed a disturbing phenomenon of 'brain waste', whereby highly educated and qualified Chinese work in menial jobs that do not require their advanced skills.

The implications of these findings on IHRM, both practical and theoretical, are discussed. From the practical standpoint, there are implications for the burgeoning phenomenon of 'brain circulation' and the looming 'war for talent'. From the theoretical perspective, the need to refine existing models of IHRM to incorporate the concepts of 'boundaryless careers' and 'brain circulation' and for greater cross-fertilization of research on cross-national and intra-national diversity are argued.

Benson *et al.* The rapid economic growth of Japan in much of the second half of the twentieth century, Benson *et al.* argue has served to widen the gap in wages and employment conditions between men and women workers and their role in HRM. While women's participation rates in the labour force increased greatly over this period, this was due to rapid growth in the manufacturing and service sectors. Yet, unlike male colleagues who enjoyed permanent employment, seniority promotion and extensive on-the-job training, women workers occupied a peripheral position in the labour market. The male-dominated nature of enterprise unions served to reinforce these practices. More recently, however, the aging of the population and the globalization of the economy has brought significant economic and social change that, when coupled with the traditional employment practices, have contributed to a shortage of skilled labour. This deficiency may provide the impetus for increasing employment opportunities for women and even participation in mainstream employment.

The authors' exploration of the prospects for women's employment and HRM begins by outlining the current state of employment in Japan, paying particular attention to the state of the peripheral labour market and employment conditions. Next, the authors explore the changes in the internal labour market. A variety of issues is considered, including the erosion of the grading system and lifetime employment, performance-related pay, and the mainstreaming of atypical workers. From this analysis, it is clear that the decline in the internal labour market has reduced some of the key structural employment barriers for women. Yet, as the authors show in the next section, women are also disadvantaged by the gender bias inherent in the work organization in enterprises which are continually reinforced by company HRM practices.

What does all this mean for gender diversity in Japanese employment and HRM? While a major constraint on employment equality was the internal labour market, its erosion has not provided the expected opportunities for women. This, the authors argue, is primarily due to the gender bias inherent in Japanese company work organization. In particular, lack of objectivity in assessment, continued use of length of service as a key promotion criteria, bias in the allocation of tasks and in recruitment for certain jobs, lack of female role models and entrenched male-dominated culture that exists in many Japanese companies all serve to restrict the opportunities available to women.

The authors conclude by arguing that employment prospects will ultimately be determined by the contest between the forces that have worked to erode the internal labour market and those that continue to maintain discriminatory forms of work organization. The outcome of this contest between these contradictory forces is not clear or pre-determined. The growing skill shortages in Japan may have an important effect on reducing gender biases in their HRM policies, although this will depend on the degree that Japanese companies are prepared to embrace globalization and government policies designed to reverse declining birth rates.

Macro/theoretical level

Miah and Bird. The authors here, Miah and Bird, investigate national and organizational cultural influences among managers in three types of companies: Japanese companies in Japan (JC), South Asian (India, Pakistan, Bangladesh) local domestic companies (SACO) and Japanese subsidiaries and IJV in South Asia (JVC). The main objective is to explore and assess national cultural influences on the choice of participative HRM style (PHRMS) and firm performance. The authors propose seven hypotheses relating to the use and efficacy of different types of HRM systems and their relationship to performance. The authors measure each firm's managerial system on an autocratic-participatory continuum. Firm performance was measured using an 8-point scale. In addition, HRM functional areas of hiring and recruiting, training and development and employee turnover were measured by obtaining responses to items assessing the extent of use of specific HRM practices using a 5-point scale.

Results showed that a participative HRM style consistently affects firm performance positively across each of the three managerial groups. Regression analysis showed that merit-based hiring and training and development consistently influenced PHRMS positively across the three managerial groups. On the other hand, employee turnover consistently affected the PHRMS negatively across the three managerial groups. *ANOVA* results indicated that JC have the most PHRMS among the three managerial groups. By comparison, JVC have a moderate level and SACO showed the least PHRMS.

In conclusion, the author's findings suggest that a Japanese parent company's culture tends to have a much stronger influence with JC. Japanese parent company culture tends to have less influence than South Asian national culture in shaping the HRM styles and practices in JVC. While some SACO are in the initial stages of learning about PHRMS from foreign companies, most still tend to maintain their national culture and traditional ways in the operating systems of their organizations.

Ramirez and Fornerino.   For many decades, as Ramirez and Fornerino in their chapter on their paper on firms in France compared with those in Britain point out, scholars have noted that technological, economic and institutional forces provoke homogeneity in practices and even may reduce cultural differences between nations. There is also a long tradition of work affirming that nations' cultural and institutional idiosyncrasies outweigh the significance of any similarities in the formal structures and processes of organizations. These studies have reported considerable differences between organizations operating in similar task environments but different societies, which have been underpinned (implicitly or explicitly) by contingency or divergence paradigms (Rowley and Benson, 2003, 2004). This study continues this by examining how a firm's level of technology and country of operation shape certain HRM policies and practices. This perspective supports the neo-contingency approach, which does not claim primacy for either technological or national cultural factors shaping HRM. The principal question discussed is whether there are consistent patterns of differences and similarities in recruitment and selection, training and compensation in firms with the same level of technology (163 high-, mid- and low-tech firms) operating in France and Britain. The contingency variable chosen is technology. Divergence theory is specifically illustrated by the national education approach.

The authors found support for the neo-contingency approach. The moderator effect of national culture on the relation between the level of technology and HRM was validated for two variables: (1) recruitment technical policies; and (2) long-term approach to training. However, only France showed a significant statistical difference between technology-intensive and low-tech firms for the recruitment technical policies variable. On the other hand, France and Britain present a statistically significant difference between the technology-intensive and low-tech firms for long-term approach to training. Finally, the moderator effect of national culture was not supported for compensation based on performance.

A key implication of the findings is that employees working in technology-intensive firms need a creative and adaptive HRM approach, which would better enable them to cope with the challenges of the business environment. Additionally, the strong influence of educational systems on managers' behaviour emerges. French firms seem to prefer higher levels of control and formalization in recruitment and selection and training than the British ones, a reflection of educational systems. However, it is important to highlight that national culture and technology factors cannot be the total 'determinants' of organizations. At most they are important features that, along with others, 'influence' organizations' internal operations. Future neo-contingency studies using other organizational characteristics as moderators would be useful to gain further insights into the neo-contingency approach proposed.

Concluding remarks

In this book, which we have called 'Globalizing International Human Resource Management', we present a selection of chapters incorporating ongoing 'state-of-the-art' research at various levels in the field. Many people in the past have found HRM and IHRM to be a rather vague and indeed elusive notion – we must admit – not least because it seems to have a variety of interpretations. We have tried to remedy this in the set of chapters we set out. As already pointed out (Warner, 2005) there are too many assertions in the literature (in general) that may require qualification and caveats. First, MNCs have been seen as more important, *grosso modo*, in the share of business generated than they deserve to be globally (see Rugman, 2003) but only employ a small minority of the world labour force worldwide *directly*, after all (although more and more are being included *indirectly* if we add in links via supply chains). Also the state retains its influence across a swathe of countries, as recent events in Thailand show – and others in this book exemplify (see Zhu *et al.*; Brewster) – MNCs may be the main drivers of international business but are rather a *special* case analytically, if one takes the widest set of firms both local and global that exist across the myriad of economies across the planet. Second, IHRM as such is a fairly recent conceptual topic in the literature and its roots are not explicitly accounted for and fully explained. Third, IHRM appears to be *exceptional* in business practice rather than the rule in how people are managed.

Many critics of HRM, often coming from a 'left of centre' perspective, were perhaps more comfortable with the older Industrial Relations (IR) frameworks (see Hyman, 2001, for example). Others, however, saw the two approaches as compatible and indeed that HRM did co-exist with IR practices in many firms. However, we have tried to clarify many important questions here and illuminate matters a step further *vis-à-vis* IHRM. As well as providing empirical evidence and cases, the chapters presented in this book we believe, importantly contribute to developments in the area of theory that may better elucidate matters, such as contingency, supporting the work of others, such as Rowley *et al.* (2004), Rowley and Benson (2004), and so on, as well as the need for greater disaggregation of analysis such as levels and degrees of acceptance, etc., such as Rowley and Benson (2002), etc.

The collection makes valuable contributions to many other parts of IHRM. These include (re)confirming important areas. We find, for instance, a magisterial presentation of the challenges to conventional wisdom in the field (Schuler and Tarique) The long-contested and different nature of HRM, and by implication IHRM, in the 'blind rush' to publish in US journals with their own perspectives and aims, is reconsidered (Brewster). The importance of trade unions and employee relations to IHRM is also recalled (Ying *et al.*; Brewster; Benson *et al.*; Som). The continuing specificity of IHRM also comes out in many of the papers, at both national level, such as environment, the state and country of operation, culture, social and economic development stage, etc.; and organizational level, such as structure and cultures. This includes the impacts (along with some other factors) on shaping HRM policies and practices (Benson *et al.*; Ramirez and Fornerino), HRM function and style (Sparrow; Miah and Bird).

Going one step further, we must finally ask some questions. 'What' is really going on in terms of global, as well as organizational resource allocation in this debate about IHRM? 'How' is such scarcity-resolution playing itself out in IHRM? 'Why' is this globalization of IHRM in MNCs diffusing so fast? Of course, here we would go on to argue that Labour Economics might help us see a little further and should go 'hand in hand' with HRM, as it can help elucidate further the globalization debate. Labour supply now more than ever shapes the international division of labour that underpins contemporary MNCs' activities in the context of globalization. The 'name of the game' has now changed significantly in the last two decades. Half the world's labour supply has now entered the global labour market only in the last 15 years – as Freeman (2006) has argued – as the giants of Asia, namely China and India, with their vast armies of workers, are now increasingly linked via a web of supply-chains with the wider world-wide economy, by virtue of World Trade Organization (WTO) entry (see Zhu and Warner, 2003).

To paraphrase Adam Smith, the international division of labour is dependent on the extent of the market. This market has now been globalized beyond recognition (see Root, 2001). The HRM implications of WTO entry have not however been really examined in the literature, nor the impact of the latter on HRM - let alone IHRM, although some work has been done on employment implications (see Bhalla and Qiu, 2004). India has had WTO status since 1995 and China since 2001. Many others are 'knocking at the door' and some have now just signed up, like Vietnam in 2006. It is a phenomenon that many HRM academics and other experts have not yet fully taken on board. This demarche has fundamentally changed the rules of the game; HR, or putting it more bluntly 'labour', is now being 'commoditized' on what critics say are increasingly disadvantageous terms. WTO entry makes it easier for MNCs to spread their wings. In any event, IHJRM is not merely about procedures, it is about *power*.

With WTO entry by more and more countries, the neo-liberal economists (the so-called 'Washington Consensus' not withstanding, as criticized by Stiglitz, 2006) see employment growing as trade expands; all are supposed to gain from this. There are clearly 'winners and losers' from globalization, it would seem (see *The Economist*, editorial, 20 January, 2007: 11):

> These are the glory days of global capitalism. The mix of technology and economic integration transforming the world has created unparalleled prosperity. In the past five years the world has seen faster growth than at any time since the early 1970s. In China each person now produces four times as much as in the early 1990s. Having joined the global labour force, hundreds of millions of people in developing countries have won the chance to escape squalor and poverty. Hundreds of millions more stand to join them.

Yet, we must note that much of the new employment is created in firms controlled by inward invested firms, most of them giant MNCs. The terms of employment for the newly hired workers are set out by the HRM policies of these large global corporations, not by the local state-owned enterprises; they also influence the conditions in small and medium-sized firms as sub-contactors in the supply-chain. Lifetime employment, policed by PM of the 'old school', has now gone out of favour in the former Soviet Union (see Ashwin and Clarke, 2002) as well as in China (see Chiu and Frenkel, 2000); something similar had already happened in South Korea and Japan (see Ying *et al.* in this book).

There is considerable pressure on both nations and enterprises to maintain a 'competitive advantage' (see Garelli, 2006). Such developments may help Western consumers of course. Granted, low wages out there are now feeding into lower prices for imported manufactured goods in advanced economies, balancing to a degree at least the current rises in the price of many services in high wage countries. Immigration, legal as well as illegal, may temper the rise in the costs of services at the low-skilled end as it has done in the US and UK, however. Whether it will contain inflation remains to be seen, only time will tell here.

Many broad macro-economic questions not widely discussed in the literature impinge on the IHRM debate but are largely not confronted in it. Yet, as it proceeds, manufacturing jobs in advanced economies, a politically sensitive issue in may countries, increasingly leach outwards and service jobs, even some lower or middle-managerial ones, are more and more out-sourced 'eastwards' (Engardio, 2006). Call-centres abound in India (e.g. for UK companies) and the Philippines (e.g. for US companies), for example. The IHRM literature needs to encompass these broader questions. Will all this significantly boost unemployment levels in advanced economies? Will real wages of the workers in the West grow more slowly? *Cui bono* – in the final analysis, we may well ask? There are more and more issues that spin out of the IHRM debate than can be encompassed in this book. We can only emphasize here that the 'WTO' debate has to be linked up with the 'HRM' or 'IHRM' one in our future research – to make sense of what we are facing in the wind of globalization, which few as yet have done.

References

Ashwin, S. and Clarke, S. (2002) *Russian Trade Unions and Industrial Relations in Transition.* Basingstoke and New York: Palgrave.

Bhalla, A.S. and Qiu, S. (2004) *The Employment Impact of China's WTO Accession.* London: RoutledgeCurzon.

Brewster, C., Sparrow, P. and Harris, H. (2005) 'Towards a New Model of Globalizing Human Resource Management', *International Journal of Human Resource Management*, 16: 949–70.

Chiu, S.W.K. and Frenkel, S. (2000) *Globalization and Industrial Relations and Human Resources Change in China.* Bangkok: ILO Regional Office for Asia and the Pacific.

Engardio, P. (2006) 'The Future of Outsourcing', *Business Week*, 30 January: 50–64.

Freeman, R. (2006) 'What Really Ails Europe (and America): The Doubling of the Global Workforce'. *The Globalist*, 3 June. Online at http://www.theglobalist.com/StoryId. aspx?StoryId = 4542

Garelli, S. (2006) 'The World Competitiveness Landscape in 2006', *IMD World Competitiveness Yearbook 2006.* Lausanne, Switzerland: IMD, pp. 46–51.

Hyman, R. (2001) *Understanding European Trade Unionism.* London: Sage.

Price, A. (2004) *Human Resource Management in a Business Context*, 2nd edn. London: Thomson Learning.

Root, F.R. (2001) 'International Trade and Foreign Direct Investment'. In Tung, R.L. (ed.) *The IEBM Handbook of International Business.* London: Thomson Press, pp. 366–81.

Rowley, C. and Benson, J. (2002) 'Convergence and Divergence in Asian HRM', *California Management Review*, 44(2): 402–28.

Rowley, C. and Benson, J. (eds) (2004) *The Management of Human Resources in the Asia Pacific Region: Convergence Revisited.* London: Frank Cass.

Rowley, C., Benson, J. and Warner, M. (2004) 'Toward an Asian Model of HRM: A Comparative Analysis of China, Japan and Korea', *International Journal of Human Resource Management*, 15(4/5): 917–33.

Rugman, A. (2003) 'Regional Strategy and the Demise of Globalization', *Journal of International Management*, 9: 409–17.

Schuler, R. and Tarique, I. (2006a) 'Alliance Forms and HR Issues, Implications and Significance'. In Shenkar, O. and Reuer, J. (eds) *Handbook of Strategic Alliances*. Thousand Oaks, CA: Sage.

Schuler, R. and Tarique, I. (2006b) 'International Joint Venture System Complexity and Human Resource Management'. In Björkman, I. and Stahl, G. (eds) *Handbook of Research in IHRM*. Cheltenham, UK: Edward Elgar Publishing.

Schuler, R., Dowling, P. and DeCieri, H. (1993) 'An Integrative Framework for Strategic International Human Resource Management', *International Journal of Human Resource Management*, 4: 717–64.

Sparrow, P. and Brewster, C. (2006) 'Globalizing HRM: The Growing Revolution in Managing Employees Internationally'. In Cooper, C. and Burke, R. (eds) *The Human Resources Revolution: Research and Practice*. London: Elsevier.

Stiglitz, J. (2006) *Making Globalization Work; The Next Steps to Global Justice*. London: Penguin.

The Economist (2007) 'Rich Man, Poor Man', *The Economist*, editorial, 24 January: 11.

Warner, M. (2002) 'Globalization, Labour Markets and Human Resources in Asia-Pacific Economies: An Overview', *International Journal of Human Resource Management*, 13: 384–98.

Warner, M. (2005) 'Whither International Human Resource Management?', *International Journal of Human Resource Management*, 16: 870–4.

Zhu, Y. and Warner, M. (2003) 'HRM in Asia'. In Harzing, A.-W. and Ruysseveldt, J.V. (eds) *International Human Resource Management*. London: Sage, pp. 195–220.

International human resource management: a North American perspective, a thematic update and suggestions for future research

Randall S. Schuler and Ibraiz Tarique

Introduction

The past 15 years have witnessed tremendous advancements in the research and practice of international human resource management (Brewster *et al.*, 2005; Sparrow and Braun, 2006; Sparrow and Brewster, 2006; Taylor *et al.*, 1996). Broadly speaking, the consensus is that international human resource management (IHRM) is about the worldwide management of human resources (e.g. Brewster, 2002; Brewster and Suutari, 2005; Briscoe and Schuler,

2004; Harris and Brewster, 1999; Poole, 1999). More specifically, the *field of IHRM* is about understanding, researching, applying and revising all human resource activities in their internal and external contexts as they impact the processes of managing human resources in organizations throughout the global environment to enhance the experience of multiple stakeholders (Schuler and Jackson, 2005; Schuler and Tarique, 2003; Sparrow and Braun, 2006; Sparrow and Brewster, 2006; Stahl and Bjorkman, 2006).

The purpose of IHRM is to enable the firm, the multinational enterprise (MNE), to be successful globally. Because observations about large multinational enterprises (MNEs) are also applicable to small and medium-sized enterprises (Sparrow and Brewster, 2006), the singular term MNE refers to both throughout this article. Being successful globally entails being: (a) competitive throughout the world; (b) efficient; (c) locally responsive; (d) flexible and adaptable within the shortest of time periods; and (e) capable of transferring knowledge and learning across their globally dispersed units (Sparrow and Brewster, 2006). These requirements are significant, and the magnitude of the reality is indisputable. IHRM for many firms is likely to be critical to their success, and effective IHRM can make the difference between survival and extinction for many MNEs (Briscoe and Schuler, 2004).

In this article, we attempt to offer a perspective from North America to describe how IHRM has evolved during the past 15 years since the framework by Schuler *et al.* (1993) was introduced. Although those authors actually described the framework as one for 'strategic' IHRM, for consistency with the IHRM field more broadly defined, we incorporate the strategic perspective and use the term 'IHRM'. We use 'strategic IHRM' as a critical component of the broad field of IHRM. We start by presenting a thematic framework of IHRM that organizes and updates the existing IHRM literature within five thematic areas: (1) strategic MNE components; (2) exogenous factors; (3) endogenous factor themes; (4) IHRM issues, functions, policies, and practices themes; and (5) MNE effectiveness themes. Within each thematic area, we describe several sub-themes that reflect important changes in and evolutions of IHRM issues.

Next, we build on and extend the thematic framework by discussing in detail one of the increasingly important sub-themes in the 'strategic management components' theme, namely, cross-border alliances (CBAs). Including this sub-theme provides the opportunity to discuss the impact of the phenomenon of *complexity* which is significant for MNEs as well as CBAs. We describe the several forms of CBAs and then argue that all forms of CBAs share varying amounts of complexity, which in turn can serve as a roadblock to the three needs common to all forms of CBAs, including the needs for learning, economies and efficiencies, and control, needs shared with all MNEs. Thus because these conditions are amenable to IHRM activities, as the form of CBA goes from relatively simple to much more complex, the importance of IHRM increases (Schuler and Tarique, 2006a, 2006b). Similarly, as the complexity for MNEs grows, the importance of IHRM increases. We then focus on the most complex form of CBA, the international joint venture (IJV), and develop a typology as a way of illustrating the complexity of IJVs and the challenge of crafting an effective set of IHRM activities.

Finally, we conclude with 20 avenues or topics for future research and investigation in IHRM. This is done by organizing the suggestions according to the five thematic areas that are illustrated in our basic framework of IHRM. This is based on a presentation of the realities of MNEs and their implications for the field and profession of IHRM.

Thematic framework of IHRM

Within North America, the development of IHRM has been a significant trend during the past quarter century (Briscoe and Schuler, 2004; Reynolds, 2001; Schuler, 2000; Schuler and Jackson, 2005; Stahl and Bjorkman, 2006). Clearly, the field of IHRM has become substantially more important in every way because of globalization. Broadly speaking, we conceptualize *globalization* as being about movement and change: *movement* in goods, information, knowledge, people and service across borders facilitated and accelerated by *changes* in economic, social, legal, political, cultural, technological, educational and workforce conditions. It is the characteristics of these conditions that are important for MNEs and IHRM, so they are incorporated throughout this paper.

As a result of the globalization of industry, many firms now must compete on a worldwide basis rather than on the regional basis that was previously favoured (Bartlett and Ghoshal, 1998). It must be noted, however, that some argue quite persuasively that the majority of MNEs do and should compete strategically on a regional or even local basis, rather than on a global basis (Ghemawat, 2005; Greenwald and Kahn, 2005; Rugman, 2003). Nevertheless, all MNEs need to be concerned on an operational basis with human resource management issues on an international or global platform (Sparrow and Brewster, 2006). Human resource management in this international context requires developing an understanding of the issues facing multinational enterprises of all sizes (Briscoe and Schuler, 2004; Evans *et al.*, 2002). In turn, this requires an understanding of the environmental realities these enterprises confront. These are presented in a later section of this article.

Models/frameworks of IHRM

In an effort to understand the role of human resources in MNEs, scholars have suggested several IHRM models or frameworks (e.g. Brewster *et al.*, 2005; De Cieri and Dowling, 1999; Schuler *et al.*, 1993; Sparrow and Brewster, 2006; Taylor *et al.*, 1996). Each of these has some very useful and interesting contributions to the field to IHRM, but the thematic framework of IHRM we use in this article is based on the framework offered by Schuler *et al.* (1993) (shown in Figure 1) because it draws on Sundaram and Black's (1992: 733) definition of a MNE as: 'any enterprise that carries out transactions in or between two sovereign entities, operating under a system of decision making that permits

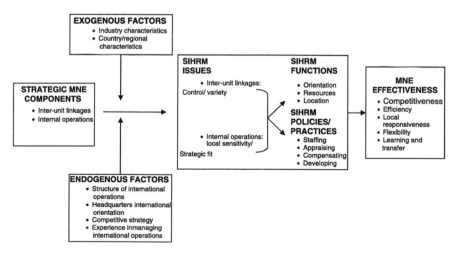

Figure 1 *Integrative framework of strategic international human resources management in MNEs (adapted from Schuler et al., 1993)*

influence over resources and capabilities, where the transactions are subject to influence by factors exogenous to the home country environment of the enterprise.' This definition serves to highlight the differences between managing global firms and domestic firms and thus establishes the basis for conceptualizing IHRM as substantially more encompassing than domestic HRM (e.g. Bartlett and Ghoshal, 1998; Black *et al.*, 1999; Briscoe and Schuler, 2004; Roberts *et al.*, 1998). In addition, the framework provides an overarching structure to utilize five thematic areas and highlight sub-themes that reflect several changes in and evolutions of key IHRM issues during the past 15 years.

As shown in Figure 2 (as well as Figure 1) there are five major themes: (1) strategic MNE components; (2) exogenous factors; (3) endogenous factors; (4) IHRM issues, functions, and policies and practices; and (5) MNE effectiveness. Taken as a whole, the thematic approach describes the contributions of previous models of IHRM, and identifies key scholars and their contributions to understanding and advancing IHRM. Use of this framework also enables us to present and discuss the changes in and evolutions of sub-themes efficiently and to organize our suggestions for future research.

Strategic MNE components

SHRM systems

Because a number of aspects of strategic human resource management (*SHRM*), as well as human resource management (*HRM*), research have influenced IHRM, it is useful to review this field and its key concepts of alignment and systems. At this time, it appears that scholars have not yet adopted a common definition of SHRM, but most would probably agree that it covers research intended to improve our understanding of the relationship between how organizations manage their human resources and their success in implementing business strategies (cf. Schuler and Jackson, 2005, 2007; Snell *et al.*, 1996). As a focal topic for HRM research, SHRM began to emerge approximately 25 years ago (Dyer, 1985; Fombrun *et al.*, 1984; Galbraith and Nathanson, 1978, Niniger, 1980; Schuler and Jackson, 2005; Schuler and MacMillan, 1984). Since then, it has

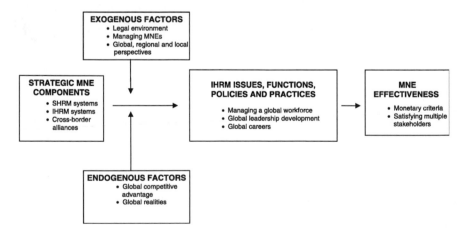

Figure 2 *Thematic framework of international human resources management in MNEs: 2007 update and extension (adapted from Schuler* et al., *1993. While consistent with the original, entries in this version highlight important sub-themes that have emerged in IHRM literature over the past 15 years)*

evolved to include several streams of theoretical and empirical investigations. More detailed reviews can be found elsewhere (e.g., see Becker and Huselid, 1998; McMahan *et al.*, 1999; Schuler and Jackson, 2005).

An element that differentiates the *strategic* HRM approach from earlier approaches is a focus on the *system*. *Horizontal alignment* among HRM policies and practices is a hallmark of an SHRM system (Schuler *et al.*, 2001; Schuler and Jackson, 2007). Higgs *et al.* (2000) provide an example of how adopting a systems perspective can influence the practice of HRM. They note that the traditional HRM perspective treats selection primarily within the context of hiring decisions. They further explain that adopting a systems view of selection reveals that a large number of HRM practices that were previously considered as distinct activities (e.g. hiring, training, performance evaluation, special assignments, career development) can all be considered selection processes (Schuler and Jackson, 2005). Begin (1997) used the systems approach for examining how sets of IHRM policies and practices fit together and then used these sets in making cross-national comparisons in the management of human resources.

Another key element in the strategic HRM approach is *vertical alignment*. The main aspect of this alignment is linking the HRM policies and practices with understanding and knowledge of the organization, including all its internal contextual factors, such as its strategy, leadership, vision, values and culture, and all its external contextual factors, such as the political, social, culture, competitive and legal environment (Jackson and Schuler, 1995). Vertical and horizontal alignments that are distinctive in strategic HRM systems are also found in IHRM systems, although attaining them in IHRM is considerably more challenging.

IHRM systems

As is true for firms operating in a single country or region, MNEs strive to develop IHRM systems that fit the contours of the realities of MNEs, their present context – a context that is much more complex, multifaceted, uncertain and even chaotic than ever before (London, 2006). Consequently, effectively managing human resources in MNEs also requires a strategic and systems approach for managing human resources globally (Briscoe and Schuler, 2004; Evans *et al.*, 2002; Sparrow, 2007). This implies that the practice of strategic *international* human resource management involves an under-standing of the environments of MNEs and the management of the MNE's *inter-unit linkages* as well as the concern for horizontal and vertical alignment (Bartlett and Ghoshal, 1998). Understanding the environments requires that IHRM continually monitor the external and internal contextual factors. Managing inter-unit linkages is needed to integrate, control and coordinate the units of the MNE that are scattered throughout the globe (Ghoshal, 1987; Galbraith, 1992). Concern for alignment includes concern for how the IHRM policies and practices fit together and for the way the MNE and its units operate in concert with the laws, culture, society, politics, economy, and general environment of particular locations (Ballon, 1992; Tung and Thomas, 2003). This is developed further in the discussion under the 'Managing MNEs' sub-theme.

Cross-border alliances

In our review of the past 15 years of literature and research on IHRM, an important sub-theme that has emerged in this thematic area of 'strategic MNE components' is that of cross-border alliances. The recent work in this sub-theme has demonstrated the significant interdependence between CBAs and international human resource manage-ment (Schuler *et al.*, 2004). Because this sub-theme is so important to incorporate into our current framework, an extensive review and update of the CBA literature is warranted. This is undertaken in a separate section later in this article.

Exogenous factors

There is a variety of environmental conditions that can influence the approaches organizations use to manage their human resources. These conditions include exogenous factors such as the legal environment, industry dynamics, institutional pressures, economic and political conditions, and country cultures (see the work of Hofstede, 2001; House *et al.*, 2004; Sparrow and Brewster, 2006; Trompenaars, 1993). Thus, it seems apparent that international human resource management needs to include a constant scanning and understanding of these factors (see also Barney and Wright, 1998; Dowling *et al.*, 1999; Gooderham and Nordhaug, 2006).

Legal environment

In North America, particularly the US, the practice of human resource management has long been shaped by legal regulations, which provide to employees a variety of rights and protections against unfair and unsafe employment practices (Florkowski, 2006). Monitoring the legal and regulatory environment to ensure that a firm's HRM policies and practices comply with this aspect of the organization's environment has long been a primary responsibility of HRM professionals. In addition, because an organization's pay practices must take into account the pay practices of other organizations competing for the same labour, HRM's role has traditionally included monitoring the HRM policies and practices of competitors in the external environment. Likewise, because an organization's planning for future recruitment, staffing and development is affected by supply and demand in the external labour market, HRM's traditional role generally included tracking labour market conditions. In recent years, however, the evolution of IHRM has meant that HRM's responsibility for monitoring the external international environment has grown (Sparrow and Braun, 2006; Sparrow and Brewster, 2006).

Managing MNEs

North American HRM professionals are becoming more sensitive to cultural and institutional variations. In doing so, they are recognizing that there are important differences in the cultures and institutional environments of North America and other countries (e.g. Madhok and Liu, 2006; Rousseau and Schalk, 2000; Sparrow *et al.*, 1994; Tung, 1990). Understanding and using these cultural differences, however, are a necessary challenge to meet for North American MNEs, particularly in aligning their HRM systems with other elements of the external environment – the laws, economic conditions, and political trends in each country of operation (Madhok and Liu, 2006; Schuler and Jackson, 2005; Von Glinow *et al.*, 2002).

Global, regional and local perspectives

Another related challenge facing HRM professionals in North American MNEs is developing a global approach to managing human resources that embraces a few universal principles that give the entire global system consistency while also allowing local and regional autonomy. Achieving the right balance between *consistency* and *autonomy* requires continual evaluation and discussion about which policies and practices can be global and which can or should be regional or even local (Gupta and Govindarjan, 2001). It appears that many North American MNEs that adopt local HRM practices find it difficult to develop global HRM systems that demonstrate consistency throughout the entire MNE (Boudreau *et al.*, 2003b; Schuler and Jackson, 2005; Schuler *et al.*, 2002). This results in part from the reality that local conditions relevant to HRM practices vary so greatly. Thus, as local units align their practices with local conditions, and attain horizontal and vertical linkages and alignment with themselves, they invariably find themselves having different HR practices across local and even regional units globally. Some companies such as General Electric, Bell, Cisco and Morgan Stanley, in attempting to get consistency across all units in how they manage their employees, either develop a common set of values that can guide development of local HR practices or develop a multi-level set of HR practices, some of which are common globally, e.g. performance appraisal, and some of which are unique locally, e.g. labour relations.

Horizontal and vertical linkages and alignment in a global context thus may occur under a broader umbrella of *IHRM policy*, whereas in a domestic context, this occurs under a more narrow umbrella of *IHRM practice*. This is expanded upon in the following discussions on 'Global Competitive Advantage'. Some of these issues have been discussed extensively in a special issue of *Human Resource Management* (Spring 2002, Vol. 41, No. 1), which focused on whether and under what conditions there are 'best practices' that can applied in a global, regional or local situation. Making this determination can be a rather significant challenge for most IHRM professionals and MNEs, but one that is worth addressing (Pfeffer and Sutton, 2006).

Endogenous factors

Global competitive advantage

It might be noted here that gaining competitive advantage through human resource management can be pursued in several ways (Schuler and MacMillan, 1984). One approach is to adopt broader HRM policies that have been shown to be effective across many types of organizations. An example of an IHRM policy that has been shown to be effective in a wide range of organizations is linking pay to performance. Organizations that effectively link pay to performance can be expected to outperform their competitors, all else being equal. Adopting HRM policies and/or practices that have been identified as among the 'best' can be useful for moving the organization into a competitive position. However, if such policies or practices are widely known and easily adopted by others, they are not likely to be a source of long-term, sustainable competitive advantage (Barney, 1991; Schuler and MacMillan, 1984). But even if such practices are widely known, there is no assurance that they will be or can be easily adopted. As Pfeffer and Sutton (2006) have pointed out, power and politics may prevent rationale activities from being pursued. In addition, it may not always be so easy for HRM professionals to identify the appropriate conditions under which to implement best practices. They may be unaware of those conditions or be unable to actually implement all the details that are part of those 'best practices' (Webber, 2000). This situation may be even more challenging in a global context and with the conditions that are used for gaining global competitive advantage.

While a great deal of the earlier discussion of competitive advantage was most applicable to a domestic context, a more recent discussion of gaining competitive advantage in the global context has emerged (Gupta and Govindarajan, 2001). To achieve global competitive advantage, a firm may need to develop HRM practices that are appropriate for its specific context (Gupta and Govindarajan, 2001). For example, a North America manufacturer competing on the basis of cost might adopt the policy of performance-based pay and then develop an individual piece-rate pay system that specifically supports that strategy and fits within the context of the North American culture of individualism. Our interpretation of the academic and professional literature/practice is that several approaches to gaining competitive advantage may exist, but that 'lasting' *global* competitive advantage from human resource management comes from developing HR practices that are appropriate for an organization's specific context including its culture, legal and political systems. Additional bases of global competitive advantage come from: effectively using economies of scale and scope; relocating operations around the world; and transferring learning and knowledge across operations worldwide (Boudreau and Ramstad, 2002, 2003a; Gupta and Govindarajan, 2001). All these bases of gaining global competitive advantage have distinctive implications for IHRM that are developed more explicitly in the suggestions for future research.

Global realities

A significant aspect of international human resource management in being strategic is that the IHRM practices be linked with the needs of the enterprise. These needs in turn are driven by the global realities of MNEs. Therefore, IHRM needs to understand these global realities and then develop the implications of these for IHRM. A possible listing of these realities of MNEs is shown in Exhibit 1. Because of the importance of the realities of MNEs for IHRM, it is important for IHRM researchers to explore them further and understand their implications for IHRM practices (Evans *et al.*, 2002; Sparrow and Brewster, 2006). While conditions or realities were important to the IHRM field over the past 15 years and were incorporated into the Schuler *et al.* (1993) article, they have increased in their number and in their importance. In contrast to the 1993 presentation, the realities shown in Exhibit 1 are more now explicitly linked with MNEs, followed by an discussion of their explicit implications for IHRM. These realities of MNEs and the implications for IHRM help form the bases of the 20 suggestions for future research later in this article.

Exhibit 1: Global realities of MNEs*

Economic characteristics

- Globalization and free trade are the biggest realities and have many supporters and critics
- There are huge disparities in income and standards of living worldwide
- The biggest markets for products and services are increasingly global
- There are increasing demands on energy, raw materials and infrastructure
- Concern by societies for worldwide competitiveness and job creation
- Growth in foreign direct investment (FDI)

Social characteristics (geopolitical, cultural and technological)

- More integration and expansion within the EU, ASEAN, WTO, COMESA, NAFTA, GCC
- Increased recognition of relationship between government efficiency and business efficiency
- Greater concern by societies for sustainability
- More complexity, volatility and unpredictability
- Still many local and regional legal and cultural qualities
- Technology is making the world flatter, more accessible and less costly

Strategic (enterprise) characteristics

- An increasingly larger number of MNEs and SMEs
- Consolidation through increased merger and acquisition activity
- Opportunities for growth and expansion are in the emerging markets
- Global competitive advantage attained through scale, scope, local adaptation, knowledge management and optimal relocation
- Costs, risks and uncertainties are high, so greater need for alliances such as IJVs
- There is a need to change business and organization models constantly

Workforce characteristics

- There is a huge potential labour force that is more highly educated and growing
- There is a greater awareness of worldwide disparities in income and lifestyles
- Workers can be adaptable to workplace styles and human resource practices
- Emigration flows will accelerate in some areas; reverse in others
- Workers need not move: work can move to them through offshoring and outsourcing

---

*Based upon R.S. Schuler, I. Tarique and S. E. Jackson, 'International Human Resource Management', Presentation at the 7th IHRM Conference, Limerick, Ireland, June 2004; Schuler and Jackson (2005: 11–35); D. Briscoe and R.S. Schuler, *International Human Resource Management 2 edn*. London: Routledge, 2005; PriceWaterhouseCoopers, *9th Annual Global CEO Survey: Globalisation and Complexity,* New York: PWC; *Trade and Development Report 2005; Trade and Development Report 2006* (Geneva: UNCTAD); R. Schuler, 'Globalisation: Realities and Trends: Implications for IHRM, MNEs/SMEs and Employees', keynote presentation at the 9th IHRM Conference in Tallinn, Estonia, 12–15 June 2007 ©R. Schuler, 2007; and Garelli (2006: 46–51).

IHRM issues, functions, policies and practices

Managing a global workforce

Managing a domestic workforce can be significantly different and more complex than managing a foreign workforce (Tarique and Schuler, 2007). Yet, many North American organizations operating internationally for the past 25 years adopted the human resource practices of the parent country to the local conditions (a few adopted the local HR practices). In addition, they used their expatriates as a major means of staffing the senior management cadre of local subsidiaries. By staffing with expatriates, the North American parent attempted to exercise control over the foreign operation (Jaussaud and Schapper, 2006; Tarique and Caligiuri, 2004). Because this ethnocentric approach was widely adopted by North American MNEs as they began to internationalize, most of the early practice and research in IHRM focused on expatriate selection and compensation (Mendenhall *et al.*, 2002; Schuler and Jackson, 2005; Tarique and Caligiuri, 2004).

While managing expatriates continues to be a significant practice and an active area of research, it no longer dominates IHRM in North America. With the enhanced pace of globalization and rising costs associated with expatriates, North American MNEs have decreased their reliance on the traditional expatriate (Tarique *et al.*, 2006). They have turned to third-country nationals and host-country nationals as vital sources of staffing, for both non-managerial and managerial positions (Pucik *et al.*, 1993; Reynolds, 2004; Schuler and Jackson, 2005). In doing this, the MNEs shifted their staffing focus from one primarily driven by the parent country to one better described as 'global'. In addition to thinking about and managing this new *global workforce (GWF)*, MNEs also shifted to thinking about and managing the *regional workforce (RWF)*. This fits the MNEs, which pursue a more regional strategy rather than a more global strategy (Rugman, 2003). No doubt, however, local staffing conditions and considerations are also important to MNE staffing strategies (Ghemawat, 2005; Scullion and Collings, 2006).

Global leadership development

The study of global leadership development has received considerable theoretical and empirical attention during the last few years (e.g. Brewster and Suutari, 2005; Conner, 2000; Morrison, 2000; Suutari, 2002). The evidence, thus far, suggests that that there has been a positive trajectory of growth with respect to the number of organizations identifying and developing leaders who are capable of functioning effectively on a global scale and with a global perspective. For instance, in the early 1990s, Adler and Bartholomew (1992) surveyed organizations headquartered in the United States and Canada and found that most organizations had taken a global approach to overall business strategy, financial systems, production operations and marketing but lacked globally component managers. Recently, the *1998 Global Leadership Trends Survey Report* indicated that senior managers and HRM executives identified developing leaders as the most important HRM goal for global effectiveness (Csoka and Hackett, 1998). Similarly, Gregersen *et al.* (1998) found that among US *Fortune* 500 firms, 8 per cent of companies reported already having comprehensive systems for developing global leaders, 16 per cent had some established programmes, 44 per cent used an ad hoc approach, and 32 per cent were just beginning. Overall, it is clear that the strategic preparation of global leaders has become a major component of IHRM's contribution to MNE effectiveness.

Global careers

The concept of global careers has been the source of a great deal of recent research attention (Thomas *et al.*, 2005). Several journals have devoted special issues to this topic (see *The Journal of World Business,* 2006; *Personnel Review,* 2005; *The Journal of Management Development,* 2004; *Thunderbird International Business Review,* 2004). Within the context of global careers, researchers have examined issues related to *knowledge transfer* within MNCs (e.g. Lazarova and Tarique, 2005; Minbaeva, 2005; Riusala and Suutari, 2004), *work–life balance* (e.g. Harris, 2004), *boundaryless careers* (e.g. Lazarova and Tarique, 2005; Stahl and Cerdin, 2004), careers of global leaders (Suutari and Taka, 2004), top leaders' national diversity (Caligiuri *et al.*, 2004), and self-initiated overseas experience (Richardson and Mallon, 2005). On the whole, this stream of research has shown that the global career phenomenon has important implications both for individuals and for the MNEs that employ them (Thomas *et al.*, 2005).

MNE effectiveness

Monetary criteria

While the goals and concerns of MNEs shown in Figure 1 of the Schuler *et al.* (1993) article are still applicable today, there has been an increased attention on the use of monetary criteria (Becker *et al.*, 2001; Huselid *et al.*, 2005). Early efforts to demonstrate effectiveness in monetary terms usually employed utility analysis (e.g. Schmidt *et al.*, 1979) or cost accounting (e.g. Cascio, 2000). Regardless of the technical merits of such approaches, they have not been widely adopted by organizations (Becker *et al.*, 2001; Pfeffer and Sutton, 2006). Undoubtedly, there are many explanations for the slow adoption rate of utility analysis and cost accounting methods, including the fact that these measures may not reflect fundamental strategic objectives or the concerns of a broader set of multiple stakeholders (Boudreau and Ramstad, 2003a, 2003b; Donaldson and Preston, 1995; Jayne and Rauschenberger, 2000; Pfeffer and Sutton, 2006; Webber, 2000).

Nevertheless we believe that assessing IHRM effectiveness primarily in monetary or economic terms is likely to continue to evolve in the future, as organizations improve their understanding of and competencies related to the underlying drivers of long-term organizational success (Huselid *et al.*, 2005; Kaplan and Norton, 2004).

Satisfying multiple stakeholders

Not explicitly incorporated into the 1993 framework were the interests of a wide variety of stakeholders. The importance of developing IHRM systems that address the concerns of all key stakeholders is now becoming recognized in North America. Certainly, the *organization* itself including all its subsidiary units, is a primary stakeholder, so it is appropriate to assess the impact of the IHRM system against objectives such as improving productivity, improving profitability, sustainability and capability, and ensuring the organization's long-term survival in a multiple-country context (Sparrow and Braun, 2006; Sparrow and Brewster, 2006).

Employers also recognize that organizational strategies that depend on total quality, innovation and customer service cannot be met unless *employees* are willing to strive for the same goals on the organization's behalf. Perhaps this attitude is best captured by Larry Bossidy's (former CEO of Honeywell International) who was famous for saying: 'Don't bet on strategy, bet on people'.

The effectiveness of an IHRM system can also be assessed by showing its effects on *customers*. HRM practices can influence the quality and variety of products available to customers, the price at which those products can be purchased, the service received and so on. In a multiple-country context, analysing and responding to customers' needs in several environments can constitute a successful competitive strategy in being local and global at the same time (Gupta and Govindarajan, 2001).

Other major stakeholders who can be affected by an MNE's HRM practices include *suppliers and alliance partners* in a multiple-country context. Through various forms of cooperative alliances, a company seeks to achieve goals that are common to all members of the alliance. Although organizations may understand that these stakeholders can all be affected by IHRM, alliance partners are seldom included when organizations assess the effectiveness of their IHRM systems. This is developed more fully in the following section.

Finally, within North America the effects of an MNE's IHRM practices on the *local community and the broader society* are being taken into account when assessing the effectiveness of IHRM, moving beyond the sole concerns embodied in laws and regulations (Florkowski, 2006; Florkowski and Nath, 1993). Numerous revelations of unethical and corrupt business practices serve as a reminder that a variety of IHRM practices can contribute to such problems. An organizational assessment of IHRM effectiveness that fails to consider its ability to reduce or prevent unethical or corrupt business practices in a multiple-country environment is negligent (Florkowski, 2006;

Paine *et al.*, 2005; Schuler and Jackson, 2005). Similarly, assessment of an MNE's impact on the broader community when it opens a facility in one country and then relocates it to another country is also being called upon by some, especially with the International Labour Organization (Rogovsky, 2005).

Cross-border alliances (CBAs): major extension of the IHRM field

CBA forms and HRM issues

As shown in Figure 2, an important 'strategic MNE component' is *cross-border alliances*. Because this area is so significant and relatively new in the IHRM literature, we are treating it in this separate section (Schuler *et al.*, 2004). This discussion also provides the opportunity to illustrate the significance and role of complexity, a phenomenon that is increasingly important for MNEs.

An important challenge for MNEs is developing and managing CBAs. CBAs in general involve two or more firms agreeing to cooperate as partners in an arrangement that is expected to be 'mutually beneficial' (Hagedoorn, 1993). Such an alliance can take the form of a complete merger or a creation of a third entity, an *international joint venture* (IJV) (Gulati, 1998; Koka and Prescott, 2002; Schuler *et al.*, 2004).

As suggested earlier, all types of CBAs share varying amounts of complexity, which can become a barrier to the three needs common to all forms of CBAs; the needs for organizational learning, economies and efficiencies, and control (Schuler and Tarique, 2006a). Prior research suggests that organizational learning is a key building block and major source of developing and sustaining a competitive advantage for MNEs as well as CBAs (Gupta and Govindarajan, 2001). CBAs provide partner firms with access to the resources such as knowledge bases, and organizational cultures of the entire network or system. This access can be a powerful source of new knowledge-based capabilities that would not have been possible without the formal structure of a CBA. As such, CBAs are no longer a peripheral activity but a mainstay of competitive strategy and competitive advantage (Gupta and Govindarajan, 2001).

Another important need for CBAs is to develop and maintain managerial and organizational efficiencies and economies. These economies and efficiencies can result from combining operations, building upon the experiences of existing management, and taking advantage of the latest in technologies, e.g. when establishing a new facility (Luo, 2002; Newburry and Zeira, 1997). Finally, the third significant need for CBAs is to develop the ability to exercise control. In the absence of control, it can be challenging for partner firms to build conditions that maximize learning for itself, and its partners (Schuler and Tarique, 2006a).

All three needs (e.g. organizational learning, economies and efficiencies, and control) are important to MNEs and are important to IHRM activities (Schuler *et al.*, 2004), and as the form of CBA goes from relatively simple (equity alliance) to much more complex (non-equity alliance) the importance of IHRM increases (Schuler and Tarique, 2006a) (see Figure 3). There is an inflection point, however, with CBAs involving only two separate companies that do form a separate third entity, an International Joint Venture (IJV) (Schuler and Tarique, 2006a).

An IJV alliance involves two or more legally and economically separate organizational entities that collectively invest financial as well as other resources to pursue certain objectives. Consequently, the levels of complexity and complications increase and so also the potential for conflict, uncertainty, and instability that is likely to be much greater than in CBAs in which there are only two organizations (Schuler and Tarique, 2006b) as illustrated in Figure 3. In addition, the international dimension adds more complexity

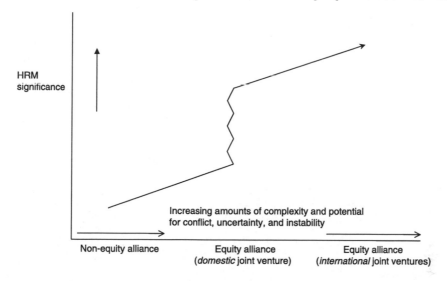

HRM
significance

Increasing amounts of complexity and potential
for conflict, uncertainty, and instability

Non-equity alliance   Equity alliance   Equity alliance
(*domestic* joint venture)   (*international* joint ventures)

Figure 3 *IHRM significance and cross-border alliance forms (adapted from Schuler and Tarique, 2006)*

and complications and thus potential for conflict, uncertainty, and instability (Briscoe and Schuler, 2004; Luo, 2002; Mallik *et al.*, 2004; Schuler *et al.*, 2004).

Next we discus the challenges of developing an effective set of IHRM activities in the most complex form of CBA, the IJV. By discussing these we would hope to encourage future research focusing on IHRM issues in all forms of CBAs, thus benefiting MNEs in managing themselves as well as any CBAs they may have (Schuler and Tarique, 2006a, 2006b).

IJV complexity and IHRM significance

Schuler and Tarique (2006b) argue that an IJV system can be differentiated on the basis of three important dimensions: the number of partners, the number of countries represented in total by the IJV system and the extent of country culture differences represented by partners in the IJV system (e.g. Beamish and Kachra, 2004). These dimensions can lead to complexity and potential for conflict; all of which can serve as barriers to three needs common to all forms of CBAs, including IJVs (e.g. organizational learning, economies and efficiencies, and control) (Schuler and Tarique, 2006a).

Figure 4 illustrates the relationships between IHRM significance and IJV complexity. There is a significant distinction between IJVs that have multiple country cultures and multiple partners and those that have only two country cultures and two partners. As the IJV form moves from a simple two-country, two-partner, two country-culture IJV to a complex multi-country, multi-partner and multi-country cultural IJV, the amount of differentiation, complexity, and conflict increase and the potential for further conflict, uncertainty, and instability also increase (Bouchet *et al.*, 2004; Luo, 2000; Osborn and Hogedoorn, 1997; Schuler *et al.*, 2004). IHRM policies and practices have the ability to provide clarity, and structure to manage these complexities. IHRM policies and practices can contribute to the three needs for managing the learning processes, gaining and retaining efficiencies and economies of scale, and exercising

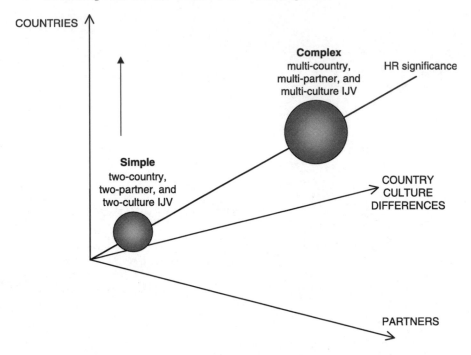

Figure 4 *IJV complexity and IHRM significance (adapted from Schuler and Tarique, 2006)*

control over the IJV system activities. Therefore, as the IJV system moves from simple to complex, the implications for and significance of IHRM will increase (Schuler and Tarique, 2000b).

Overall, the above discussion of CBAs highlights three important issues: (1) CBAs are inherently complex organizations where IHRM's role is critical to achieve success; (2) in IJVs, complexity is a function of number of partners, number of countries and magnitude of cultural differences; and (3) the greater the IJV complexity, the more salient IHRM's role will be in achieving MNE success (Schuler and Tarique, 2006a, 2006b). Indeed, the greater the complexity facing an MNE, the more salient will be IHRM's role (Bryan and Zanini, 2005).

Suggestions for topics for future IHRM research

To allow for more flexibility in the use of the research that has been done in IHRM over the past 15 years, suggestions, rather than explicit propositions, for future research are offered here. Similar to the Schuler *et al.* (1993) article, we offer some suggestions for topics to explore in IHRM research organized around the five themes depicted in Figure 2.

Strategic MNE components

1   There are many implications for IHRM based on the global realities of MNEs (Friedman, 2005; Garelli, 2006). For example, because of the rapid environmental

changes, MNEs need to rely more on people than organizational structure for co-ordinating and controlling their global operations (Evans *et al.*, 2002). While this is a very important topic, research might still investigate the ways MNEs are doing this, and determine the ways for co-ordinating and controlling through people that are most effective. This is just one example of a global reality of MNEs and an implication for the strategic MNE component for IHRM (Figure 2). Researchers may wish to develop many of the other realities, as well as add or revise the realities suggested in Exhibit 1. These realities of MNEs have many implications for the field and profession of IHRM as shown in Exhibit 2.

Exhibit 2: The implications for IHRM of the global realities for MNEs*

Implications for IHRM: societal level

- Globalization will open new markets and create new economies to enter
- CEOs will be concerned about multiple stakeholders
- There is a need to consider the issues of multiple stakeholders, e.g. the environment, ethics, providing jobs, the impact of relocating and restructuring as well as profits
- When doing relocating and restructuring, there is a need to be socially sensitive
- Need to think/act globally, regionally and locally
- Need to think about workforce equality worldwide

Implications for IHRM: strategic level

- Gaining global competitive advantage depends upon effective IHRM practices
- Need to consider the context of all IHRM policies and practices: legal, cultural, socio-political, religious, economic, etc.
- Need to systematically link IHRM policies and practices horizontally and vertically to the MNE, that is, IHRM has to be strategic
- Need to cross-border alliances, so need to know and manage the many IHRM issues in IJVs and IM&As
- Greater need for learning, knowledge transfer and knowledge management
- Greater need to rely more on people than structure for co-ordinating and controlling global operations
- Offshoring and outsourcing will continue to be strategies for MNEs
- MNE expansion will be greater in the developing markets than the developed markets

Implications for IHRM: workforce level

- Greater need for transnational and diverse teams, global leadership, and borderless careers
- High-quality managers, those that can motivate employees to innovate, will be in big demand
- High-talent individuals, those who have skills and are flexible and innovative, will be in big demand
- Need for global mindsets and cross-cultural competencies
- Need to think of IHRM policies and practices in terms of the global workforce but *also* in terms of regional and local workforces and *how* to mesh them

- Need to prepare employees to deal with complexity, volatility and change
- The challenge of managing employees of an MNE will increase as MNEs get larger

Implications for IHRM: HR professional and MNE level

- All companies need to think of themselves as MNEs and act accordingly
- HR professionals (leaders and staff) can play a major role in all this
- All employees need to think of themselves as part of the global workforce

Based upon R.S. Schuler, I. Tarique and S.E. Jackson, 'International Human Resource Management', Presentation at the 7th IHRM Conference, Limerick, Ireland, June 2004; Schuler and Jackson (2005: 11–35); D. Briscoe and R. S. Schuler, *International Human Resource Management 2nd edn.* London: Routledge, 2005; PriceWaterhouseCoopers, *9th Annual Global CEO Survey: Globalisation and Complexity,* New York: PWC; *Trade and Development Report* (Geneva: UNCTAD, 2005, especially Chapter V); R. Schuler, 'IHRM: Realities and Trends for MNEs: Implications for the IHRM Field and IHR Professionals,' Presentation at the Rutgers Business Conference, Rutgers University, New Brunswick, NJ, 24 March 2006. ©R. Schuler, 2006; ____*The Global Competitiveness Report 2006–2007,* World Economic Fourm: Davos, Switzerland, 2006; and and Garelli (2006: 46–51).

2   A very major and recent phenomenon for MNEs is complexiy (Gottfredson and Aspinall, 2005; PriceWaterhouseCoopers, 2006). It appears that MNEs are just beginning to manage complexity (Bryan and Zanini, 2005; Lane *et al.*, 2004), which might be a very appropriate time for IHRM researchers to begin to explore what MNEs are actually doing to manage the complexity. After that, they may wish to develop the implications of these activities for IHRM practice. Another area of special investigation might be international joint ventures because they are so important for MNEs today in their efforts to expand into emerging markets and remain competitive (London, 2006). In this article, complexity in IJVs was explored and several possibilities for research were offered which could prove helpful in IJV management (Schuler and Tarique, 2006a, 2006b).

Endogenous factors

3   The IHRM field needs to be aware of and aligned with the global realities of MNEs. For example, MNEs today are seeking to gain global competitive advantage through such means as economies of scale and yet be sensitive to local conditions (Garelli, 2006; Gooderham and Nordhaug, 2006; Gupta and Govindarajan, 2001; Sparrow and Brewster, 2006). IHRM researchers may want to investigate how IHRM practices can help the organization achieve economies of scale, such as through shared service centres, yet also stay sensitive to and reflect local conditions (Brewster *et al.*, 2005). Of course, as MNEs get larger, as predicted (Bryan and Zanini, 2005; Davis and Stephenson, 2006), an IHRM challenge will be to keep employees engaged and committed to an increasingly larger and perhaps distant organization (Bryan and Zanini, 2005; Friedman, 2005).
4   As suggested by Gupta and Govindaranjan (2001), MNEs can gain global competitive advantage if they do an effective job of maximizing learning and knowledge transfer. So IHRM may wish to understand why individuals give up knowledge and how can trust be developed (Jackson *et al.*, 2003). In addition,

there are several other related inquiries here including the extent to which there are country and cultural differences in the extent to which individuals are willing and able to learn and share knowledge. Another inquiry for IHRM involves the most effective IHRM practices to use to help achieve this needed learning and knowledge sharing (Jackson *et al.*, 2003).

5   Just as MNEs may need economies of scale and scope to help achieve a global competitive advantage, they may also need to choose optimal locations for operations, and yet be sensitive to local conditions (Gupta and Govindarajan, 2001). And, as conditions change, optimal locations will change as well. This implies that individuals and organizations will need to change and move. IHRM might make a major contribution here by understanding the most effective practices to enable individuals and organizations in making these changes. IHRM might investigate ways to also help communities make adjustments to these massive changes in socially sensitive ways (Rogovsky, 2005; Sparrow and Brewster, 2006). Because the importance of this *'economic footprint'* that MNEs can make on communities (both those they are leaving and those they are entering), the International Labour Organization (ILO) has designated this topic to be of major interest to them. They are undertaking several projects that seek to identify, examine and understand what MNEs do in their activities associated with what is broadly labelled as 'socially sensitive enterprise restructuring' or simply, SSER (Rogovsky, 2005).

Exogenous factors

6   If MNEs need to be sensitive to local conditions yet be global and regional at the same time, IHRM needs to craft practices for the entire MNE and also adapt their IHR practices to multiple countries and regions, each with their own special and unique cultures (Begin, 1997; Sparrow and Brewster, 2006). IHRM might wish to investigate the ways MNEs can be most effective in making global policies, and then tailoring IHRM practices in order to be sensitive to local or regional conditions in efficient ways. A related issue of investigation here is the extent to which local and regional conditions can accommodate to a broader range of IHRM practices than might otherwise have been expected or predicted (Gannon and Newman, 2002; Hofstede, 2001; Von Glinow *et al.*, 2002). Alternatively, investigations may wish to analyse a country's culture more closely. The result may reveal multiple cultures within a single country, some more compatible with an MNE's global IHRM practices (Gannon and Newman, 2002; House *et al.*, 2004; Sparrow *et al.*, 1994). Alternatively, it may also reveal that a country's culture is no longer the same as it had been described at an earlier time due to forces of convergence. Of course, the culture may be even more different from what it had been described due to forces of divergence (Brewster *et al.*, 2005).

IHRM issues, function, policies and practices

7   If IHRM needs to be more related to the realities of MNEs, IHRM may need to think about their workforces to reflect these realities. For example, if the realities for MNEs are to be *global* and *local* at the same time, MNEs may think about their employees in at least two separate groups: a global workforce and a local workforce (Greenwald and Kahn, 2005). IHRM researchers need to think if and how MNEs can do this and still operate as a single entity with employees around the world learning, and transferring

their learning as well as knowledge, activities vital for global competitive advantage (Gupta and Govindarajan, 2001; Jackson *et al.*, 2003; Scullion and Collings, 2006). The difficulty of doing this, however, is exactly why the organization can gain the global competitive advantage (Gupta and Govindarajan, 2001; Schuler and MacMillan, 1984). But this may be even more complex and challenging if there are more than two separate workforces, i.e. global and local.

8   Yes, it is still important to think and act global and local, but researchers are seeing the importance of thinking and acting *regionally* as well (Ghemawat, 2005; Rugman, 2003) so, if MNEs are thinking and acting globally, locally *and* regionally, IHRM researchers will need to consider not only two separate workforces but three (Tarique *et al.*, 2006). Then they may wish to conceptualize the need for multiples sets of IHRM policies and practices and the need and challenge for co-ordinating them and moving employees in and out of these groups. Again, as mentioned in suggestion 5, it will be necessary for MNEs to attain co-operation across employee groups if they expect to be competitive (Gupta and Govindarajan, 2001).

9   With the greater need for co-ordinating and controlling with and through people across a wide variety of countries and cultures, there is some evidence that MNEs are trying to create *global mindsets* (Evans *et al.*, 2002). Further study might investigate the more effective ways of doing this and the specific IHRM practices that can be used. A similar investigation might be done into the practice of global career development and career systems (Thomas *et al.*, 2005) That is, IHRM may wish to learn how to most effectively construct them (viz, a global workforce), again, in a global context, and yet be sensitive to regional and local differences (Adler and Barthlomew, 1992; Gregersen *et al.*, 1998; Gooderham and Nordhaug, 2006).

10   As MNEs globalize themselves, and thus need to co-ordinate themselves more closely than ever, MNEs may increasingly rely transnational teams (Brewster *et al.*, 2005; Evans *et al.*, 2002). This area appears to offer an important opportunity for IHRM researchers. More knowledge on how MNEs can develop cross-cultural teamwork competencies could be very helpful. It appears that IHRM practices should contribute greatly to this competency build-up, but more research could offer helpful details on exactly how organizations can design IHRM systems that support and facilitate the utilization of knowledge-intensive teamwork (KITwork) to develop and sustain a competitive advantage (see Jackson *et al.*, 2007).

11   Because MNEs have a willingness to relocate operations in order to gain global competitive advantage, IHRM can investigate the impact on and reaction of those in labour relations (Morley *et al.*, 2006). This movement may have a significant impact on wages and working conditions in existing locations, an impact that may significantly affect the bargaining relationships, not only in the existing locations but also in anticipated locations (Morley *et al.*, 2006). For labour relations, the trend for MNEs to conceptualize their workforces in global terms may result in greater bargaining power for MNEs. How unions respond may be very important to the success of the labour movement, both within MNEs as well as within the countries to which work might be established or relocated. It has been suggested that a worldwide federation of unions across sectors and industries representing as many as 15 to 17 million people be formed in order to provide more bargaining power to the workers (Mendonca, 2006). Such a formation is likely to present interesting challenges to MNEs that may require new strategies in dealing with each other as well as a global union.

12   Leadership in MNEs will continue to be important, especially with heightened complexity, chaos and uncertainty (Brewster *et al.*, 2005; Bryan and Zanini, 2005;

Gratton, 2006; Lane *et al.*, 2004). A related issue of investigation here is the development of global leaders. Recent literature reviews (e.g. Morrison, 2000; Suutari, 2002) suggest that research global leadership development is still scarce and future research opportunities abound in a variety of areas. Researchers can describe trends and cross-country differences in global leadership development (e.g. Barrett and Beeson, 2002; Dickson *et al.*, 2003), determine what type of individuals benefit most from participation in developmental programmes (e.g. Caligiuri and Tarique, 2005), examine competencies needed to work effectively in a global environment (e.g. Bartlett and Ghoshal, 2003; Dalton *et al.*, 2002), and analyse the impact of specific cross-cultural developmental activity (e.g. global assignments, assessment centres for leadership development) on performance outcomes (e.g. Suutari, 2002).

13   The use of expatriates and the repatriation processes, especially by MNEs in developed economies, appears to be a likely topic for review and revision (Harzing, 2001a, 2001b; Tarique *et al.*, 2006). Two major forces, somewhat contradictory in nature, seem to be at work in causing this. One is the concern these MNEs have for cost and the need to reduce unnecessary expenditures. Because the cost of expatriates is considerably higher than the use of local or third-country nationals, MNEs may be more tempted to shift to this staffing strategy in the near future. On the other hand, MNEs can also gain global advantage through effective use of knowledge and learning transfer (Harzing, 2004; Riusala and Suutari, 2004). This may well be achieved more efficiently through the effective management of a cadre of expatriates. In either scenario, however, it would seem that a common concern is a more effective process of managing the repatriation and reassignment events for the expatriates who are used (Lazarova and Tarique, 2005; Scullion and Collings, 2006).

14   With the reality of highly educated labour pool worldwide, MNEs can locate virtually anywhere. For IHRM, an important investigation can be in trying to understand the extent to which MNEs can use common staffing practices for the highly educated segment of the global workforce of the MNEs (Scullion and Collings, 2006). A related inquiry could look at the whether common practices might be more effective at a regional rather than global level. Another related inquiry here is the impact on MNEs of using other forms of global employment such as offshoring and outsourcing, for example, on the headquarter employees. This issue has the potential to continue to become even more important as MNEs move their operations outside the headquarter country (Aron and Singh, 2005; Engardio, 2006). Another related issue here is the increasing reality that the labour pool within some countries may not be totally unlimited. For example, in India and China there is growing recognition that there is a shortage of qualified and skilled workers, not just for MNEs, but for local companies as well (Bryan and Zanini, 2005; Budhwar, 2004; Sengupta, 2006). One consequence of this for individuals is that wages and employment opportunities are increasing, so job mobility is enticing, which is leading to high rates of employee turnover. So MNEs are having to concern themselves with being an attractive place to work and to stay (i.e. becoming an '*employer of global choice*').

15   Yet, as MNEs recognize the value of and need for retaining employees, they appear to be encouraging a contradictory policy. This policy encourages employees to be responsible for their own careers and success within organizations. Put simply, it is a policy of '*Me, Inc.*' that conceptualizes individual learning and mobility as positive and necessary. The result of this policy may be employees leaving an organization and moving to another one, even though the present employer is wholly acceptable, just because the individual is led to think about mobility in very positive career terms. Thus as MNEs conceive of IHRM policies and practices that might facilitate becoming an

employer of global choice, they may need to assess the potential contradictory effects of other IHRM policies and practices that are actually harmful to the organization.

16 Related to the above issue of investigation is whether MNEs can embrace the reality of the GWF or at least RWFs, and develop appraisal practices that are identical for all. While some MNEs attempt to practice a common global performance management system (e.g. Morgan Stanley or Booz Allen Hamilton), some still believe that there are too many significant cultural differences that suggest they need multiple systems (Greene, 2005). In this scenario, IHRM researchers might investigate the extent to which employees might accept a new appraisal system and/or how employees could be assisted in adapting to new systems (Brewster *et al.*, 2005; Lane *et al.*, 2004).

17 A final issue of investigation related to IHRM policies and practices addresses compensation or remuneration. If MNEs embrace the reality of the GWF or at least RWFs, they may desire to create more equality in their remuneration schemes. IHRM researchers and practitioners may wish to investigate here such things as whether or not money is more important to some members of the GWF, and whether or not some forms of payment are fungible and so equal compensation schemes could actually be composed of different specific forms of compensation (Reynolds, 2001).

MNE effectiveness

18 Looking ahead, we anticipate seeing further evolution in the approaches organizations use to assess themselves. Here, more theory-driven research may be needed (Schuler and Jackson, 2005). The result might be research that traces the causal chain that explains how particular HR practices or policies influence intermediate outcomes (e.g. motivation, productivity turnover) and how those outcomes, in turn, are related to specific indicators of financial performance (Becker and Huselid, 1998; Rogers and Wright, 1998; Wright and Gardner, 2002), or other indicators of organizational effectiveness as described in the next point (Boudreau *et al.*, 2003a; Jackson and Schuler, 2006; Johanson and Hansson, 2006).

19 Research is needed to consider outcomes of concern to multiple stakeholders. To date, most HRM research in North America has focused on financial performance and emphasized outcomes of interest to investors. Whether other stakeholders also benefit from these practices is not yet clear (Boudreau *et al.*, 2003a). The model in Figure 2 certainly reflects the importance of multiple stakeholders as well as monetary criteria because there is evidence that some companies are embracing them because they see it as necessary and appropriate and because it does benefit the bottom line of profitability, in the short and long term (Jackson and Schuler, 2006). Of course, all this becomes much more complex when considering the cross-border alliances, especially international joint ventures. In this situation, it is possible that the multiple stakeholders of the two parents and the IJV itself become important to IHRM and as such have to be assessed and evaluated.

20 Looking ahead, we anticipate seeing further evolution in the approaches organizations use to assess the effectiveness of their IHRM systems (Boudreau *et al.*, 2003a). Investors are among the most important stakeholders for a business because without their capital, the business could not continue. Thus, more sophisticated approaches to understanding how IHRM systems influence investor satisfaction is one likely focus of future efforts (Beatty *et al.*, 2003; Nikandrou *et al.*, 2006).

As with the propositions that were offered 15 years earlier, we hope that these suggestions for topics may guide future research in the field of IHRM. The research done during the past 15 years has certainly contributed significantly to the development of the field and we anticipate that the next 15 years will do the same.

Conclusion

There has been a tremendous growth in globalization over the past 15 years (Friedman, 2005). With globalization has come a wide variety of new global realities of MNEs. Some of these realities include increased complexity, chaos, uncertainty, bigger and better educated global labour pools, more risk, more unpredictability, and greater demands for equality and fair treatment. The implications of these realities of MNEs are significant. For IHRM, these realities have many implications and offer IHRM many opportunities.

Many of the implications of these realities have been reflected in the discussions in this paper. Some of them have been incorporated into the updating of the work in the five thematic areas here using the framework proposed by Schuler *et al.* (1993) nearly 15 years ago. Others have been reflected in the suggestions for future research and investigation in IHRM. No doubt, for IHRM to seize the opportunities to make a significant contribution to MNEs, for example, in helping gain global competitive advantage, it will need to be strategic and know the realities of MNEs and their implications for IHRM.

The nature of international human resource management in North America is changing rapidly as the twenty-first century gets under way, and this seems consistent with the rest of world (Sparrow and Brewster, 2006). Increasingly, IHRM is being recognized as central to strategic planning and strategy implementation in MNEs, leading some researcher to describe the field as 'global' rather than 'international' human resource management (Brewster *et al.*, 2005; Sparrow, 2007). The implications for the change in label for IHRM is reflected in all 20 suggestions for future research. Mostly these changes are about staying linked and aligned with the nature of MNEs as they operate in a hyper-competitive and rapidly changing world and offering the IHR practices that will help deal with and manage issues related to complexity, chaos, change, uncertainty, need for leadership and co-ordination, and the need to be sensitive to many sets of multiple stakeholders the world over (Sparrow, 2007).

All 20 suggestions offered here are based on the realities of MNEs and their implications for IHRM. In no way are these realities or their implications for IHRM meant to be exhaustive, but rather to serve as a basis for highlighting the importance of the future of IHRM. And as MNEs evolve to deal with the current realities, it is likely that the realities will evolve as well and so will the implications for IHRM. Continual assessment of the evolving realities for MNEs and their extrapolation for IHRM implications will then become an integral component of IHRM. An investigation of these implications, as well as the suggestions offered here, can be guided by the continued use of a variety of theoretical perspectives, including those focusing on human capital, resource dependence, transaction-costs, resource-based, behavioural, leadership, career development, learning, cross-cultural, institutional and agency theories (Jackson and Schuler, 1995; Schuler and Jackson, 2005, 2007; Sparrow and Braun, 2006; Wright and Gardner, 2002).

Acknowledgements

In this paper, the authors have presented a succinct update on the research around thematic developments in IHRM from a North American perspective over the past 15 years. This update and the research, however, have been heavily influenced by scholars throughout the world and, as such, their work is gladly acknowledged and utilized throughout. In particular, we wish to express our thanks to S.E. Jackson, P. Sparrow, D. Ricks, C. Reynolds, D. Briscoe, J. Begin, C. Dexter, M. Langbert, P. Budhwar, M. Poole, S. Tyson, P. Stonham, M. Morley, V. Pucik, C. Brewster, C. Cooper, H. Scullion, M. Warner, C. Scholz, M. Hilb, R. Alas, C. Rowley, J. Boudreau, M. Saxer, N. Rogovsky, B. Staffelbach, R. Griffin, A.-W. Harzing, P. Dowling, H. DeCieri, D. Welch, W. Mayerhofer, H. Larsen, P. Gooderham, O. Nordhaug and three anonymous reviewers.

References

Adler, N. and Bartholomew, S. (1992) 'Managing Globally Competent People', *Academy of Management Executive*, 6: 52–65.

Aron, R. and Singh, J. (2005) 'Getting Offshoring Right', *Harvard Business Review*, December: 135–43.

Ballon, R. (1992) *Foreign Competition in Japan*. New York: Routledge.

Barney, J. (1991) 'Firm Resources and Sustained Competitive Advantage', *Journal of Management*, 17: 99–120.

Barney, J. and Wright, P. (1998) 'On Becoming a Strategic Partner: The Role of Human Resources in Competitive Advantage', *Human Resource Management*, 37: 31–46.

Barrett, A. and Beeson, J. (2002) *Developing Business Leaders for 2010*. New York: The Conference Board.

Bartlett, C. and Ghoshal, S. (1998) *Managing Across Borders: The Transnational Solution*, 2nd edn. Boston, MA: Harvard Business School Press.

Bartlett, C. and Ghoshal, S. (2003) 'What is a Global Manager?', *Harvard Business Review*, August, 101–8.

Beamish, P. and Kachra, A. (2004) 'Number of Partners and JV Performance', *Journal of World Business*, 39: 107–20.

Beatty, R.W., Huselid, M. and Schneier, C. (2003) 'New HR Metrics: Scoring on the Business Scorecard', *Organizational Dynamics*, 32(2): 107–21.

Becker, B. and Huselid, M. (1998) 'High Performance Work Systems and Firm Performance: A Synthesis of Research and Managerial Implications'. In Ferris, G. (ed.) *Research in Personnel and Human Resources Management*. Greenwich, CT: JAI Press.

Becker, B., Huselid, M. and Ulrich, D. (2001) *The HR Scorecard*. Boston, MA: Harvard Business School Press.

Begin, J.P. (1997) *Dynamic Human Resource Systems Cross-national Comparisons*. Berlin/New York: de Gruyter.

Black, J., Gregersen, H., Mendenhall, M. and Stroh, L. (1999) *Globalizing People through International Assignments*. Boston, MA: Addison-Wesley.

Bouchet, G., Soellner, F. and Lim, L. (2004) 'Check Your Mindset at the Border', *Worldview*, 3: 57–67.

Boudreau, J. and Ramstad, P. (2002) 'From Professional Business Partner to Strategic Talent Leader: What's Next for Human Resource Management?'. Working paper 02–10, Cornell University, New York.

Boudreau, J. and Ramstad, P. (2003a) 'Strategic I./O Psychology and the Role of Utility Analysis Models'. In Borman, W., Ilegen, D. and Klimoski, R. (eds) *Handbook of Psychology*. New York: Wiley, pp. 193–221.

Boudreau, J. and Ramstad, P. (2003b) 'Strategic HRM Measurement in the 21st Century: From Justifying HR to Strategic Talent Leadership'. In Goldsmith, M., Gandossy, R.P. and Efron, M.S. (eds) *HRM in the 21st Century*. New York: Wiley.

Boudreau, J., Hopp, W., McClain, J. and Thomas, L. (2003a) 'On the Interface Between Operations Management and Human Resources Management', *Manufacturing and Service Operations Management*, 5: 179–202.

Boudreau, J., Ramstad, P. and Dowling, P. (2003b) 'Global Talentship: Towards a Decision Science Connecting Talent to Global Strategic Success'. In Mobley, W. and Dorfman, P. (eds) *Advances in Global Leadership*. New York: JAI Press.

Brewster, C. (2002) 'Human Resource Practices in Multinational Companies'. In Gannon, M. and Newman, K. (eds) *Handbook of Cross-Cultural Management*. London: Blackwell.

Brewster, C. and Suutari, V. (2005) 'Global HRM: Aspects of a Research Agenda', *Personnel Review*, 34: 5–21.

Brewster, C., Sparrow, P. and Harris, H. (2005) 'Towards a New Model of Globalizing Human Resource Management', *International Journal of Human Resource Management*, 16: 949–70.

Briscoe, D. and Schuler, R. (2004) *International Human Resource Management: Policies & Practices for the Global Enterprise*, 2nd edn. New York: Routledge.

Bryan, L. and Zanini, M. (2005) 'Strategy in an Era of Global Giants', *McKinsey Quarterly*, Fall(4): 25–36.

Budhwar, P.S. (2004) *Managing Human Resources in Asia-Pacific*. London: Routledge.

Caligiuri, P. and Tarique, I. (2005) 'International Assignee Selection and Cross-cultural Training and Development'. In Bjorkman, I. and Stahl, G. (eds) *Handbook of Research in IHRM*. Cheltenham: Edward Elgar Publishing.

Caligiuri, P., Lazarova, M. and Zehetbauer, S. (2004) 'Top Managers' National Diversity and Boundary Spanning: Attitudinal Indicators of a Firm's Internationalization'', *The Journal of Management Development*, 23: 848–59.

Cascio, W. (2000) *Costing Human Resources: The Financial Impact of Behavior in Organizations*. Mason, OH: South-Western Publishing.

Conner, J. (2000) 'Developing Global Leaders of Tomorrow', *Human Resource Management*, 39: 147–57.

Csoka, L. and Hackett, B. (1998) Transforming the HR Function for Global Business Success, (Report No. 1209-98-RR). New York: The Conference Board.

Dalton, M., Ernst, C., Deal, J. and Leslie, J. (2002) *Success For the New Global Manager: How to Work Across Distances, Countries, and Cultures*. San Francisco, CA: Jossey-Bass.

Davis, I. and Stephenson, E. (2006) 'Ten Trends to Watch in 2006'. *The McKinsey Quarterly*: The Online Journal of McKinsey & Co., January.

De Cieri, H. and Dowling, P. (1999) 'Strategic Human Resource Management in Multinational Enterprises: Theoretical and Empirical Developments'. In Wright, P.M. and Dyer, L.D. (eds) *Research in Personnel and HRM*, Supplement 4. Greenwich, CN: JAI Press.

Dickson, M., Hartog, D. and Mitchelson, J. (2003) 'Research on Leadership in a Cross-cultural Context: Making Progress, and Raising New Questions', *The Leadership Quarterly*, 14: 729–68.

Donaldson, T. and Preston, L. (1995) 'The Stakeholder Theory of the Corporation: Concepts, Evidence, and Implications', *Academy of Management Review*, 20: 65–91.

Dowling, P., Welch, D. and Schuler, R. (1998) *International Human Resource Management*, 3rd edn. Cincinnati, OH: South-Western College Publishing.

Dyer, L. (1985) 'Strategic Human Resources Management and Planning'. In Rowland, K.M. and Ferris, G.R. (eds) *Research in Personnel and Human Resource Management*. Greenwich, CT: JAI Press.

Engardio, P. (2006) 'The Future of Outsourcing', *Business Week*, 30 January: 50–64.

Evans, P., Pucik, V. and Barsoux, J.-L. (2002) *The Global Challenge. Frameworks for International Human Resource Management*. Boston, MA: McGraw-Hill Higher Education.

Florkowski, G. (2006) *Global Legal Systems*. London: Routledge.

Florkowski, G. and Nath, R. (1993) 'MNC Responses to the Legal Environment of International Human Resource Management', *International Journal of Human Resource Management*, 4: 305–24.

Fombrun, C., Tichy, N. and DeVanna, M. (1984) *Strategic Human Resource Management*. New York: John Wiley & Sons, Inc..

Friedman, T.L. (2005) *The World is Flat*. New York: Farrar, Straus and Giroux.

Galbraith, J. (1992) 'The Value Adding Corporation', Center for Effective Organizations, University of Southern California.

Galbraith, J. and Nathanson, D. (1978) *Strategy Implementation: The Role of Structure and Process.* St Paul, MN: West Publishing.

Gannon, M. and Newman, K. (2002) *Handbook of Cross-Cultural Management.* London: Blackwell.

Garelli, S. (2006) 'The World Competitiveness Landscape in 2006'. *IMD World Competitiveness Yearbook 2006.* Lausanne, Switzerland: IMD, pp. 46–51.

Ghemawat, P. (2005) 'Regional Strategies for Global Leadership', *Harvard Business Review*, December: 98–108.

Ghoshal, S. (1987) 'Global Strategy: An Organizing Framework', *Strategic Management Journal*, 8: 425–40.

Gooderham, P. and Nordhaug, O. (2006) 'HRM in Multinational Corporations: Strategies and Systems'. In Larsen, H.H. and Mayerhofer, W. (eds) *Managing Human Resources in Europe.* London: Routledge, pp. 87–106.

Gottfredson, M. and Aspinall, K. (2005) 'Innovation Versus Complexity: What is Too Much of a Good Thing?', *Harvard Business Review*, November: 62–73.

Gratton, L. (2006) 'Connections and Conversations Provide the Fuel for Innovation'. Mastering Uncertainty Series Part 4: *Financial Times*, 31 March.

Greene, R.J. (2005) 'Effective Performance Appraisal: A Global Perspective', Alexandria, *VA: SHRM White Paper*: 1–11.

Greenwald, B. and Kahn, J. (2005) 'All Strategy is Local', *Harvard Business Review*, September: 95–104.

Gregersen, H., Morrison, A. and Black, S. (1998) 'Developing Leaders for the Global Frontier', *Sloan Management Review*, 40: 21–33.

Gulati, R. (1998) 'Alliances and Networks', *Strategic Management Journal*, 19: 293–317.

Gupta, A. and Govindarajan, V. (2001) 'Converting Global Presence into Global Competitive Advantage', *Academy of Management Executive*, 15: 45–56.

Hagedoorn, J. (1993) 'Understanding the Rationale of Strategic Technology Partnering: Interorganizational Models of Co-operation and Sectoral Differences', *Strategic Management Journal*, 14: 371–86.

Harris, H. (2004) 'Global Careers: Work–Life Issues and the Adjustment of Women International Managers', *The Journal of Management Development*, 23: 818–32.

Harris, H. and Brewster, C. (1999) 'International Human Resource Management: The European Contribution'. In Brewster, C. and Harris, H. (eds) *International HR.* London and New York: Routledge.

Harzing, A.-W. (2001a) 'Who's in Charge? An Empirical Study of Executive Staffing Practices in Foreign Subsidiaries', *Human Resource Management*, 40(2): 139–58.

Harzing, A.-W. (2001b) 'An Analysis of the Functions of International Transfers of Managers in MNCs', *Employee Relations*, 23(6): 581–98.

Harzing, A.-W. (2004) 'Composing an International Staff'. In Harzing, A.-W. and Ruysseveldt, J.V. (eds) *International Human Resource Management.* London: Sage.

Higgs, A., Papper, E. and Carr, L. (2000) 'Integrating Selection with Other Organizational Processes and Systems'. In Kehoe, J.F. (ed.) *Managing Selection in Changing Organizations.* San Francisco, CA: Jossey-Bass, pp. 73–122.

Hofstede, G. (2001) *Culture's Consequences: Comparing Values, Behaviors, Institutions and Organizations Across Nations.* Thousand Oaks, CA: Sage Publications.

House, R., Hanges, P., Javidan, M., Dorfman, P. and Gupta, V. (2004) *Culture, Leadership, and Organizations: The Globe Study of 62 Societies.* Thousand Oaks, CA: Sage.

Huselid, M., Becker, B. and Beatty, R. (2005) *The Workforce Scorecard.* Boston, MA: Harvard Business School Press.

Jackson, S. and Schuler, R. (1995) 'Understanding Human Resource Management in the Context of Organizations and Their Environments'. In Rosenweig, M. and Porter, L. (eds) *Annual Review of Psychology.* Palo Alto, CA: Annual Reviews.

Jackson, S. and Schuler, R. (2006) *Managing Human Resources Through Strategic Partnerships, 9e*. Mason, OH: Southwestern Publishing.

Jackson, S., Chuang, C., Harden, E. and Jiang, Y. (2007) 'Toward Developing Human Resource Management Systems for Knowledge-intensive Teamwork'. In Martocchio, J. (ed.) *Research in Personnel and Human Resource Management*. Amsterdam, The Netherlands: Elsevier.

Jackson, S., Hitt, M. and DeNisi, S. (eds) (2003) *Managing Knowledge for Sustained Competitive Advantage: Designing Strategies for Effective Human Resource Management*. San Francisco, CA: Jossey-Bass.

Jaussand, J. and Schaaper, J. (2006) 'Control Mechanisms of Their Subsidiaries by Multinational Firms: A Multinational Perspective', *Journal of International Management*, 12: 23–45.

Jayne, M. and Rauschenberger, J. (2000) 'Demonstrating the Value of Selection in Organizations'. In Kehoe, J.F. (ed.) *Managing Selection in Changing Organizations*. San Francisco, CA: Jossey-Bass, pp. 73–122.

Johanson, U. and Hansson, B. (2006) 'Measuring HRM: The Acid Text for Managing Intangible Resources'. In Larsen, H.H. and Mayerhofer, W. (eds) *Managing Human Resources in Europe*. London: Routledge, pp. 151–76.

Kaplan, R. and Norton, D. (2004) *Strategy Maps: Converting Intangible Assets into Tangible Outcomes*. Boston, MA: Harvard Business School Press.

Koka, B. and Prescott, J. (2002) 'Strategic Alliances as Social Capital: A Multidimensional View', *Strategic Management Journal*, 23: 795–816.

Lane, H.W., Maznevski, M.L., Mendenhall, M.E. and McNett, J. (eds) (2004) *The Blackwell Handbook of Global Management: A Guide to Managing Complexity*. London: Blackwell.

Lazarova, M. and Tarique, I. (2005) 'Knowledge Transfer Upon Repatriation', *Journal of World Business*, 40: 361–73.

London, S. (2006) 'High-growth Economies Make a Siren Call to Multinationals', *Financial Times*, 8 February: 8.

Luo, Y. (2002) 'Contract, Cooperation, and Performance in International Joint Ventures', *Strategic Management Journal*, 23: 903–19.

Madhok, A. and Liu, C. (2006) 'A Coevolutionary Theory of the Multinational Firm', *Journal of International Management*, 12: 1–21.

Mallik, A., Zbar, B. and Zemmel, R. (2004) 'Making Pharma Alliances Work', *McKinsey Quarterly*, 1 (4 November): 12–18.

McMahan, G., Virick, M. and Wright, P. (1999) 'Alternative Theoretical Perspectives for Strategic Human Resource Management Revisited: Progress', *Problems and Prospects'*, *Research in Personnel and Human Resources Management, Supplement*, 4: 99–122.

Mendenhall, M., Kuhlmann, T., Stahl, G. and Osland, J. (2002) 'Employee Development and Expatriate Assignments'. In Gannon, M. and Newman, K. (eds) *Handbook in Cross-Cultural Management*. London: Blackwell.

Mendoca, L.T. (2006) 'Shaking up the Labor Movement: An Interview with the Head of the Service Employees International Union', *The McKinsey Quarterly*, 1.

Minbaeva, D. (2005) 'HRM Practices and MNC Knowledge Transfer', *Personnel Review*, 34: 125–44.

Morley, M., Grunnigle, P. and Collings, D. (2006) *Global Industrial Relations*. London: Routledge.

Morrison, A. (2000) 'Developing a Global Leadership Model', *Human Resource Management*, 39: 117–31.

Newburry, W. and Zeira, Y. (1997) 'Implications for Parent Companies', *Journal of World Business*, 32: 87–102.

Nikandrou, I., Campos, E., Cunha, R. and Papalexandris, N. (2006) 'HRM and Organizational Performance: Universal and Contextual Evidence'. In Larsen, H.H. and Mayrhofer, W. (eds) *Managing Human Resource in Europe*. London: Routledge, pp. 177–96.

Niniger, J. (1980) 'Human Resources and Strategic Planning: A Vital Link', *Optimum*, 11: 33–46.

Osborn, R. and Hagedoorn, J. (1997) 'The Institutionalization and Evolutionary Dynamics of Interorganizational Alliances and Network', *Academy of Management Journal*, 40: 261–78.

Paine, L., Deshpande, R., Margolis, J.D. and Bettcher, K.E. (2005) 'Up to Code: Does Your Company's Conduct Meet World-class Standards?', *Harvard Business Review*, December: 122–33.

Pfeffer, J. and Sutton, R. (2006) *Hard Facts: Dangerous Have-truths and Nonsense*. Boston, MA: Harvard Business School Press.

Poole, M. (ed.) (1999) *Human Resource Management: Critical Perspectives on Business and Management*, vols I, II, III. London: Routledge.

PriceWaterhouseCoopers (2006) *9th Annual Global CEO Survey: Globalisation and Complexity*. New York: PWC.

Pucik, V., Tichy, N. and Barnett, C. (1993) *Globalizing Management*. New York: John Wiley and Sons.

Reynolds, C. (2001) 'Compensation and Benefits in a Global Context'. In Reynolds, C. (ed.) *Guide to Global Compensation and Benefits*. San Diego, CA: Harcourt.

Reynolds, C. (2004) 'A Short History of the Evolution of IHRM in the US: A Personal Perspective'. In Briscoe, D.R. and Schuler, R.S. (eds) *International Human Resource Management*, 2nd edn. London: Routledge.

Richardson, J. and Mallon, M. (2005) 'Career Interrupted? The Case of the Self-directed Expatriate', *Journal of World Business*, 40: 409–20.

Riusala, K. and Suutari, V. (2004) 'International Knowledge Transfers Through Expatriates', *Thunderbird International Business Review*, 46: 743–70.

Roberts, K., Kossek, E. and Ozeki, C. (1998) 'Managing the Global Workforce: Challenges and Strategies', *The Academy of Management Executive*, 12: 93–106.

Rogers, E. and Wright, P. (1998) 'Measuring Organizational Performance in Strategic Human Resource Management: Problems, Prospects, and Performance Information Markets', *Human Resource Management Review*, 8: 311–31.

Rogovsky, N. (2005) *Restructuring for Corporate Success*. Geneva: International Labour Organization.

Rousseau, D. and Schalk, R. (2000) *Psychological Contracts in Employment: Cross-national Perspectives*. Thousand Oaks, CA: Sage.

Rugman, A. (2003) 'Regional Strategy and the Demise of Globalization', *Journal of International Management*, 9: 409–17.

Schmidt, F., Hunter, J., MacKenzie, R. and Muldrow, T. (1979) 'The Impact of Valid Selection Procedures on Workforce Productivity', *Journal of Applied Psychology*, 64: 627–70.

Schuler, R. (2000) 'The Internationalization of Human Resource Management', *Journal of International Management*, 6: 239–60.

Schuler, R. and Jackson, S. (2005) 'A Quarter-Century Review of Human Resource Management in the US. The Growth in Importance of the International Perspective', *Management Revue*, 16: 11–35.

Schuler, R. and Jackson, S. (2007) *Strategic Human Resource Management: A Reader, 2e*. London: Blackwell.

Schuler, R. and MacMillan, I. (1984) 'Gaining Competitive Advantage through Human Resource Management Practices', *Human Resource Management*, 23: 241–55.

Schuler, R. and Tarique, I. (2003) 'International Human Resource Management: Thematic Discussions'. paper presented at the 7th Conference on International HRM, Limerick, Ireland.

Schuler, R. and Tarique, I. (2006a) 'Alliance Forms and HR Issues, Implications and Significance'. In Shenkar, O. and Reuer, J. (eds) *Handbook of Strategic Alliances*. Thousand Oaks, CA: Sage.

Schuler, R. and Tarique, I. (2006b) 'International Joint Venture System Complexity and Human Resource Management'. In Björkman, I. and Stahl, G. (eds) *Handbook of Research in IHRM*. Cheltenham: Edward Elgar Publishing.

Schuler, R., Budhwar, P. and Florkowski, G. (2002) 'International Human Resource Management: Review and Critique', *International Journal of Management Reviews*, 4: 41–70.

Schuler, R., Dowling, P. and DeCieri, H. (1993) 'An Integrative Framework for Strategic International Human Resource Management', *International Journal of Human Resource Management, 4: 717–64*. Published concurrently in the *Journal of Management*, 19: 419–59.

Schuler, R., Jackson, S. and Luo, Y. (2004) *Managing Human Resources in Cross-border Alliances*. London: Routledge.

Schuler, R., Jackson, S. and Storey, J. (2001) 'HRM and its Link with Strategic Management'. In Storey, J. (ed.) *Human Resource Management: A Critical Text*. London: Thomson Learning.

Scullion, H. and Collings, D. (2006) *Global Staffing*. London: Routledge.

Sengupta, S. (2006) 'Skills Gap Threatens Technology Boom in India', *The New York Times*, 17 October: A1; A6.

Snell, S., Youndt, M. and Wright, P. (1996) 'Establishing a Framework for Research in Strategic Human Resource Management: Merging Resource Theory and Organizational Learning', *Research in Personnel and Human Resource Management*, 14: 61–90.

Sparrow, P. (2007) 'Globalization of HR at Function Level: Case Studies of the Recruitment, Selection and Assessment Processes', *International Journal of Human Resource Management* (this issue)

Sparrow, P. and Braun, W. (2006) 'Human Resource Strategy in International Context'. In Harris, M.M. (ed.) *Handbook of Research in International Human Resource Management*. Mahwah, NJ: Lawrence Erlbaum's Organizations and Management Series.

Sparrow, P. and Brewster, C. (2006) 'Globalizing HRM: The Growing Revolution in Managing Employees Internationally'. In Cooper, C. and Burke, R. (eds) *The Human Resources Revolution: Research and Practice*. London: Elsevier.

Sparrow, P., Schuler, R. and Jackson, S. (1994) 'Convergence or Divergence: Human Resource Practices and Policies for Competitive Advantage Worldwide', *International Journal of Human Resource Management*, 5: 267–99.

Stahl, G. and Cerdin, J. (2004) 'Global Careers in French and German Multinational Corporations', *The Journal of Management Development*, 23: 885–902.

Stahl, G. and Bjorkman, I. (2006) *Handbook of Research in International Human Resource Management*. Cheltenham: Edgar Elgar.

Sundaram, A. and Black, J. (1992) 'The Environment and Internal Organization of Multinational Enterprises', *Academy of Management Review*, 17: 729–57.

Suutari, V. (2002) 'Global Leader Development: an Emerging Research Agenda', *Career Development International*, 7: 218–33.

Suutari, V. and Taka, M. (2004) 'Career Anchors of Managers with Global Careers', *The Journal of Management Development*, 23: 833–47.

Tarique, I. and Caligiuri, P. (2004) 'Training and Development of International Staff'. In Harzing, A.W. and Van Ruysseveldt, J. (eds) *International Human Resource Management*. Thousand Oaks, CA: Sage Publications.

Tarique, I. and Schuler, R.S. (2007) 'Staffing, Developing and Composing the Global Workforce'. In Werner, S. (ed.) *Current Topics in Human Resource Management in North America*. London: Routledge.

Tarique, I., Schuler, R. and Gong, Y. (2006) 'A Model of Multinational Enterprise Subsidiary Staffing Composition', *International Journal of Human Resource Management*, 17: 207–24.

Taylor, S., Beechler, S. and Napier, N. (1996) 'Toward an Integrative Model of Strategic International Human Resource Management', *Academy of Management Review*, 21: 959–85.

Thomas, D., Lazarova, M. and Inkson, K. (2005) 'Global Careers: New Phenomenon or New Perspectives?', *Journal of World Business*, 40: 340–7.

Trompenaars, F. (1993) *Riding the Waves of Culture*. London: Nicholas Brealy.

Tung, R. (1990) 'International Human Resource Management Policies and Practices: A Comparative Analysis', *Research in Personnel and Human Resources Management*, Supplement 2: 171–86.

Tung, R. and Thomas, D. (2003) 'Human Resource Management in a Global World: The Contingency Framework Extended'. In Tjosvold, D. and Leung, K. (eds) *Cross-cultural Management: Foundations and Future*. Aldershot, UK: Ashgate.

Von Glinow, M., Drost, E. and Teagarden, M. (2002) 'Converging on IHRM Best Practices: Lessons Learned from a Globally Distributed Consortium on Theory and Practice', *Asia Pacific Journal of Human Resources*, 40: 146–66.

Webber, A.M. (2000) *'Why Can't we Get Anything Done?' Fast Company*, June: 168–9.

Wright, P. and Gardner, T. (2002) 'Theoretical and Empirical Challenges in Studying the HR Practice – Firm Performance Relationship'. In Holman, D., Wall, T., Clegg, C., Sparrow, P. and Howard, A. (eds) *The New Workplace: A Guide to the Human Impact of Modern Working Practices*. Chichester: John Wiley and Sons.

Human resource management with 'Asian' characteristics: a hybrid people-management system in East Asia

Ying Zhu, Malcolm Warner and Chris Rowley

Introduction

The concept of Human Resource Management (HRM) was developed initially in the US in the 1960s and 1970s (Brewster, 1995). However, the formation of this concept was influenced by the increasing competition of manufacturing production predominately in East Asia, including Japan and the so-called 'Four Asian Tigers', namely Hong Kong, Singapore, South Korea and Taiwan. By adopting new management initiatives, such as HRM, the US firms might develop certain competitive advantages in order to survive in the face of global competition (i.e. Porter, 1990). In fact, some of the aspects within HRM paradigm were based on the Japanese management practices that had a profound influence not only in Japan, but also in entire East Asia in the 1960s and 1970s. The elements of cohesiveness and collectiveness, such as harmony, information sharing, loyalty, on-job-training, teamwork, etc., were key dimensions of the 'new' HRM paradigm, but had existed in East Asian organizations for a long time. By combining the predominate American-oriented, in other words, the individualistic elements of management practices with East Asian (particularly Japanese) management practices, the HRM paradigm was expected to improve the competitiveness of organizations and the well-being of both individuals and organizations (Schuler and Jackson, 1987).

Therefore, the conceptual formation of HRM was not a purely 'Western' notion, but a combination of both 'East' and 'West' conceptualizations. However, for many years, there has been a misleading view that the HRM has been seen and interpreted as a Western concept, then re-introduced into other part of the world. Such misunderstanding generated a lot of confusion and frustration among scholars and practitioners dealing with HRM issues. One of the obvious contradictions within the paradigm is the conflicting meaning between individualistic-oriented dimensions such as individual performance evaluation and rewards vs. collectivistic-oriented dimensions such as harmony and teamwork. People have tried to work out a certain balance between these two extremes in their research projects and routine HRM practices with profound difficulty. Clearly, there was both a logical, as well as empirical contradiction involved in conceptualizing this synthesis.

Another confusion concerns the notion of adoption of HRM dimensions among organizations outside the US. Under the influence of the universalistic model of 'best practices' of HRM in the US, there has been a trend for organizations outside the US to try to adopt these so-called 'best practices'. Two problems at least arise from following this trend. First, the 'best practices' in the US may not be the best practices in another country, given that the cultural and value systems as well as institutional and structural factors are very different between countries and organizations (Aycan, 2005). Second, the notion of adoption is about taking on something new. However, given the background of the formation of the HRM concept in the US, some of the key dimensions already existed in organizations in East Asia. Then, it is misleading to claim that, for example, the Japanese organizations adopt these HRM dimensions, but in fact they had institutionalized many of these dimensions before the formation of the 'new' HRM paradigm in the US. Therefore, there is a confusion among many researchers regarding which elements of HRM belong to the East Asian tradition and which elements are adopted from the West.

Then, what is the point of conceptualizing HRM with 'Asian' characteristics? First, we want to compare and contrast the current paradigm of HRM in the US and Europe and to identify the characteristics of their HRM systems. Second, we can use the same logic to illustrate the similarity and difference of HRM systems among the key players in East Asia, as well as between East Asia and the US and Europe. The process of the illustration can not only identify some of the key aspects of HRM being practiced initially in East Asia or others being adopted from the West and transformed into the current practices among organizations in East Asia, but also explore the factors that influence the development of people-management systems in East Asia. Finally, the theoretical and empirical implications can be drawn through comparing and contrasting the characteristics of HRM transformation and practices in East Asia and other part of the worlds, namely Europe and the US. The eventual goal is to illustrate the relationship between HRM systems and the factors and processes determining the development of these systems in East Asia and, consequently, some common phenomena can be drawn as HRM with 'Asian' characteristics. This new synthesis may be seen as both cross-national and even cross-cultural but contained within defined boundaries.

Therefore, this paper has the following sections. The second section compares and contrasts the dominant paradigm of HRM in the US and Europe, namely the 'Matching

Model', the 'Harvard Model', the 'Contextual Model', the '5-P Model' and the 'European Model' (Budhwar and Debrah, 2001). By using the outcome of these comparisons, we can identify the key aspects of HRM systems in East Asia in the third section by reviewing the historical evolution and current practices of HRM in Japan, South Korea and Taiwan as developed economies, Malaysia and Thailand as newly developing economies, and China and Vietnam as socialist market transitional economies. These three groups represent the majority of East Asian economies as developed, newly developing and transitional economies. The fourth section discusses the factors that influence the evolution process and determine the current HRM practices in East Asia. Finally, the fifth section highlights the finding by developing the concept of HRM with 'Asian' characteristics in comparison with European and US systems.

Dominant paradigm of HRM in the US and Europe

In the West, namely the US and Europe, the concept of HRM experienced a process of evolution from traditional model to a more concurrent one. The initial development of the HRM concept was based on the 'resource' aspect of HRM and that effective utilization of human resources could lead to the realization of business strategy and organizational objectives (Fombrun *et al.*, 1984). The so-called 'Matching Model' links different personnel functions to an organization's strategy and structure (Galbraith and Nathanson, 1978), and it emphasizes a 'tight fit' between organizational strategy, organizational structure and HRM system. The further development of this model is along the lines that the successful implementation of different organizational strategies requires different 'role behaviours' on the part of employees, who must exhibit different characteristics (Schuler and Jackson, 1987). This model may be said to represent a typical US oriented unitarist approach towards people-management system that emphasizes managerial autonomy and legitimizes managerial control over employees (Boxall, 1992). Such an approach has been challenged by both pluralists and more extreme critics such as those emphasizing the 'labour process' (Hyman, 2001).

To complement the 'hard' oriented 'Matching Model', another analytical framework was developed, namely the 'Harvard Model' with certain 'soft' variances. It pays attention to the 'human' aspect of HRM and is more concerned with the employer–employee relationship. This model highlights the interests of different stakeholders in the organization and links their interests with the objectives of management. By identifying four HR policy areas, such as HR flows, reward systems, employee influence and works systems, organization can achieve positive outcomes such as commitment, competence, congruence and cost effectiveness (Budhwar and Debrah, 2001). This model reflects a certain degree of awareness of both the European context that emphasizes 'co-determination' as well as East Asian values based on the human relations tradition (Boxall, 1992).

The 'Contextual Model' was based on the 'Harvard Model' by developing an understanding of strategy-making in complex organizations and related this to the ability to transform HRM practices (Budhwar and Debrah, 2001). Based at Warwick Business School, Hendry *et al.* (1988) and Hendry and Pettigrew's (1992) research claims that organizations may follow different pathways to achieve positive results due to the existence of a number of linkages between the external socio-economic, technological, political–legal and competitive environments as well as internal factors such as organizational culture and structure, leadership, task technology and business output. These linkages form the content of an organization's HRM and see past information of management changes and organizational development as essential to identify unique HRM practices (Sparrow and Hiltrop, 1994).

The theoretical debates on HRM among academics intensified in the early 1990s and the general trend was to explore the relationship between strategic management and HRM (Boxall, 1992; Guest, 1991). The emergence of the term 'strategic HRM' is an outcome of the effort to integrate HRM into business strategy (Schuler, 1992). In this view, SHRM has multiple components such as HR policies, culture, values and practices. Schuler (1992) developed the so-called '5-P' model of SHRM: philosophies, policies, programmes, practices and processes. This model brings interrelated activities together in achieving the organization's strategic needs (Budhwar and Debrah, 2001). It also demonstrates that the influence of both internal and external characteristics on the strategic business needs of an organization. However, this model suffers from being over-prescriptive and too hypothetical in nature so that is difficult to implement in practices (*ibid.*). It may be of interest to scholars but is less so to management practitioners.

In contrast to these so-called mainstream HRM approaches, a European-based model was developed in order to reflect the reality of European organizations and their surrounding environments with restricted autonomy (Brewster, 1995). By the 1990s, the European Union (EU) had developed a large market rivalling that of the US. Brewster (1995) identifies both external and internal factors that influence the formation of HRM in European organizations. The external factors are in the form of the legalistic framework, vocational training programmes, social security provisions and the ownership patterns (public and private). The internal factors such as organizational culture, union influence and employee involvement in decision-making through workers' councils have had a profound impact on management policy and practices and business operation (Budhwar and Debrah, 2001). Therefore, the 'European Model' highlights the influence of national cultures, ownership structures, role of the State and trade unions on HRM in different national settings within the context of increasing EU integration and the adoption of common EU labour legislation. In addition, Brewster (1995) emphasizes the need for a more comprehensive understanding of the role of different players in developing the concept of HRM and testing its international applicability.

From the review of these different HRM models, we can see that the evolution of the HRM concepts is essentially an inductive process. In particular, the earlier stage of HRM development, such as the 'Matching Model' and the 'Harvard Model' has a profound influence on the formation of later the 'Contextual Model' and the '5-P Model'. In fact, the 'European Model' has strong elements of both the 'Contextual Model' and the '5-P Model'. These findings provide a certain direction for the following research exploration by identifying the evolution and transformation of HRM in East Asia. By reviewing the development of people-management systems in a number of East Asian economies, we hope to illustrate certain patterns of formation and development of the HRM paradigm in East Asia.

The development and transformation of HRM in East Asia

We select three groups of East Asian economies to represent the general trend of development and transformation of both economic changes and people-management, namely developed economies such as Japan, South Korea and Taiwan, newly developing economies such as Malaysia and Thailand, and socialist market transitional economies such as China and Vietnam. Table 1 demonstrates the key indicators of their economic development and labour market situation. Generally speaking, most economies recovered from the shock of the Asian Crisis and experienced positive growth in recent years. In 2005, both China and Vietnam had remarkable economic growth with above

Table 1 *Real GDP growth, labour force (aged 15–64), labour force participation and unemployment in case study economies*

Economy	Real GDP growth (2005)	Labour force (2005) ('000)	Labour force participation (2004)		Unemployment rate (2004)
			Male	Female	
China	9.3	785,945	88.8	79.2	4.3
Japan	2.4	66,660	73.4	48.3	4.7
Korea	3.9	24,072	79.9	59.7	3.4
Malaysia	5.2	10,682	81.4	51.9	3.6
Taiwan	4.1	10,127	76.2	51.2	5.0
Thailand	4.6	37,119	89.7	77.7	1.5
Vietnam	7.7	44,027	83.5	77.3	1.7

Source: National Statistics of China, Japan, Korea, Malaysia, ROC and Vietnam (all 2006); ADB Key Indicators (2005) and ADB Annual Report (2005).

7 per cent of real GDP increase. Even Japan after many years of negative growth, it had positive 2.4 per cent GDP growth. Labour force and participation indexes show that there were more than 70 per cent male labour participation rate among the case economies and female participation was also very high in China, Thailand and Vietnam with more than 70 per cent. We are aware that the unemployment rate was not real reflection of the unemployment situation in East Asia due to many reasons such as lack of registration system and employment agencies, floating population between rural and urban regions, and serious underemployment situation. Based on the official figures, the overall unemployment rate was relatively lower in East Asia compared with other part of the world, in particular other developing economies.

Now we turn to the specific cases in terms of their development and transformation of HRM. In Japan, three 'pillars' have been identified as the foundation of the traditional Japanese HRM model, namely lifetime employment, seniority-based wage system and promotion, and enterprise labour unions (Sano, 1995). The management pattern in post-war Japan has been defined as paternalist and the company is seen as a 'family' with harmony, hierarchy, and group-orientation (Zhu and Warner, 2004a), but interestingly enough has Taylorist influences (see Warner, 1992). These management characteristics have a significant cultural background rooted in Confucianism that emphasizes a system of well-defined networks of mutual obligations as developed in modern enterprises (Koizumi, 1989): management emphasizes long-term recognition of the economic and social needs of its employees and their families. In return, the employee is expected to have high commitment and acceptance of rapid organizational and technological change (Moore, 1987).

However, increased global competition, the poor state of the Japanese economy and demographic pressures related to an ageing workforce have built up the pressure to reform the Japanese management system, including HRM reform (Benson and Debroux, 2004). The major changes include: (1) introducing a more flexible employment system in order to adjust labour costs according to short- and long-term economic trends by breaking employees into three groups, namely the 'first world' of core employees with regular and full-time employment, the 'second world' group of contractors and specialists, and the 'third world' group of temporary and part-time workers; and (2) a gradual shift towards an economically rational merit-based appraisal system for wages and promotion to replace the traditional seniority-based (age and tenure) system (Zhu, 2004). In almost a decade of economic stagnation, the structural adjustment and enterprise reform programme has been painful and achieved with significant human cost.

In general, human resource development (HRD) becomes an important element for upgrading skills and matching employment with industry's needs (see Zhu, 2004). In addition, the HRM system is undergoing transformation in Japan and a process of considerable experimentation. The characteristics of a new HRM system can be reflected in the areas such as where employees are provided with more flexibility in recruitment, work conditions and payment systems; a more individualized employment system where performance determines remuneration and promotion; an increase in the importance of HR managers' role to introduce new recruitment, evaluation and remuneration strategies; and increasing contract employment within the norm of permanent employment system (Benson and Debroux, 2004). In the process of reform, experimentation is a crucial aspect. Given the trends of the reform towards a more individualized employment system, it often has had a reverse effect as individual workers' attempt to improve their own performance at the expense of collaborative efforts, such as losing information and lower productivity (*ibid.*). Therefore, re-introducing a collectivist management approach is sometimes inevitable (see Suzuki, 2001). This demonstrates that certain 'new' HRM elements may clash with national and organizational cultures and could be counter-productive.

As Benson and Debroux's (2004) research demonstrates, there is a number of factors influencing the process of HRM changes in Japan: (1) the increasing mismatch of traditional HRM and business needs; (2) the increasing needs to shift from a seniority and skill-grading system towards meritocracy; (3) the changing attitude towards the organization and work by younger Japanese; and (4) downsizing and retrenchment, as well as the inability of unions to protect jobs leading to the loss of faith in the traditional model of HRM. However, other factors generate some resistance towards changes and certainly slow down the speed of HRM changes: (1) the nature of reform with experimentation created uncertainty in some leading companies and subsequently rejection of many of these changes occurred; and (2) the legal framework, such as dismissal laws that protect employees from dismissal, remains deeply entrenched and dramatic changes cannot be expected in the foreseeable future (*ibid.*). The evidence in Japan therefore demonstrates that, as one of the leading economies in East Asia, Japanese HRM is in a transitional and experimental stage and appears to be developing a *hybrid* model at this stage.

Another example of developed economies in East Asia is that of South Korea. Korea was one of the 'Four Asian Tigers' that experienced a long period of economic growth since the 1960s. The traditional value system was based on Confucianism, which has a profound influence on family and social life, as well as on business (Rowley and Bae, 2003). Japanese influences in Korea are also strong due to its colonial history and post-war economic ties with Japan. Some Japanese HRM practices could be found in Korean firms such as lifetime employment and seniority pay and promotion (Bae and Rowley, 2004). Loyalty was important like in Japan, but it was focused on individual personal relationships rather that of than individual towards organization (Kim and Briscoe, 1997). In addition, US military and economic support was important for the survival of South Korea and, consequently, the impact on managerial, business and academic outlook and views was overwhelming in the post-war period (Bae and Rowley, 2004). Due to the military confrontation with the North Korea, most male employees and managerial staff experienced military training and naturally brought many army training principles into enterprise management (*ibid.*).

The significant changes, both in terms of economic development as well as management practices, occurred after 1997 Asian financial crisis. The Korean economy was negatively influenced by the crisis but recovered quickly after adopting some drastic changes by the government and the business community. In recent years, the management practices in general, HRM in particular, have been subject to systematic reform. For example, the core ideology of the traditional Korean HRM system has changed from a collective orientation such as 'organization first', 'collective equality' and 'community orientation' towards individualistic and market orientation like 'individual respect', 'individual equity' and 'market principle adopted' (Bae and Rowley, 2001). The fundamental aspects of Korean HRM system such as lifetime employment and seniority based pay and promotion have been gradually replaced, it is argued, by the employment flexibility model.

Bae and Rowley's (2004) study identifies four key areas of HRM under transformation:

1 Recruiting competencies – patterns have changed from mass recruitment of new graduates to recruitment on demand, and from generalist orientation to specialists with general creativity
2 Reinforcing competencies – de-emphasize seniority while increasing the importance of performance and ability
3 Retaining competencies – using training and development mechanism to upgrade skills and retain capable employees while adopting new job design to divide core employees from poor performers and contingent workers in order to retain core HR competencies
4 Replacing competencies – introducing employment flexibility and outplacement to replace lifetime employment.

The key factors influencing the HRM changes in Korea include environmental turbulence, strategic choice and institutional influence (see Bae and Rowley, 2004). The most important influence on changes is the 1997 Asian Crisis. 'IMF' intervention and consequently changing government policy and business activities created an environment that flexible labour market regulation and firm-level employment relations became more easily institutionalized than before. In addition, the business community adopted a strategic choice approach by introducing policies on labour-cost control and autonomy to hire and fire employees.

Generally speaking, as another developed economy in East Asia, South Korea has experienced dramatic changes in terms of economic development and management practices. The economic crisis led to firm-level restructuring through downsizing, early retirement, performance-based incentives and employing contingent workers. Institutional contexts also have changed. As Bae and Rowley (2004) claim, it seems that a new era of Korean HRM has arrived with traces of past practice and continuity and uncertainty regarding the future.

The third case of a developed economy in East Asia is Taiwan. The Taiwanese management system is rooted in the traditional Chinese culture and values and includes predominantly small-sized family businesses, coupled with strong family control and an extensive subcontracting business network (Chen, 1995). In the first half of the twentieth century, Taiwan, like South Korea, was also colonized by Japan and Japanese influence was widespread, including its management system, even during the post-war period. The key characteristics of Taiwanese management system can be identified as hierarchy, paternalist beliefs, personal loyalty, harmony, and the tendency to cultivate individuals into a family- and group-oriented and socially dependent being (Zhu and Warner, 2004a).

Since the 1960s, Taiwan's economy had experienced sustainable growth until the late 1990s. Even during the 1997 Asian Crisis, Taiwan's economy still maintained a level of moderate growth, without the negative outcomes experienced in other Asian economies (Zhu, 2003). However, it does not mean that there is no problem within the Taiwanese economy. In fact, many potential problems exist and could lead to a crisis. In recent years, the introduction of a flexible and progressive management system has been seen as an important factor for the survival and success of individual firms and the economy as whole.

As Zhu's (2003) research illustrates, these changes occurred as part of a response towards the Asian Crisis as well as economic restructuring within Taiwan and economic regionalism in East Asia:

1   After the crisis, the key economic indicators showed the trend of changes from high economic growth and demand for extra labour (including foreign labour) to low economic growth and increasing unemployment. In that sense, the labour market environment has changed being from demand-driven to over-supply of labour. Therefore, downsizing, early retirement, performance-based wage and promotion and employing contingent workers became important aspects of new HRM practices.
2   MNCs have had a profound impact on adopting international standardized HRM practices, e.g. European- or US-owned firms or JVs have more individualist values. Foreign-owned enterprises (FOEs) are more likely to have individual-based performance evaluation and rewards systems and also significantly influence the HRM practices among local firms (also see Chen *et al.*, 2005).
3   Most firms applied such HRM practices as adherence to rules, common values and norms, 'transformational' management roles, importance of line-managers and freedom of personnel selection.

The changes in the macro-economic environment, due to the 1997 Asian Crisis, have been an important stimulus to HRM change in Taiwanese enterprises that have since implemented strategies towards enhancing individual firms' competitiveness. Economic restructuring within Taiwan and in East Asia has led to relocation of some of the production processes from Taiwan to other Asian developing countries such as mainland China, Cambodia, the Philippines, Malaysia, Thailand and Vietnam (Zhu and Warner, 2001). Nowadays, many MNCs carry out regional production strategies and see Taiwan as only one site of their regional production. Re-organization and restructuring of production systems between Taiwan and other Asian countries by MNCs has now become more important than ever before. Other changes among Taiwanese firms, such as state-owned enterprises (SOEs) and private-owned enterprises (POEs), include giving up low value-added products and moving to high value-added products, reducing business scale and business products, by concentrating the core-business sector on competitiveness, outsourcing some of the business and only employing new employees where they are casual workers (Zhu and Warner, 2001). Lifetime employment has been phased out among a majority Taiwanese firms and even the SOEs will end it soon (Zhu, 2003).

Based on the review of these three developed economies in East Asia, some common trends can be identified. However, in order to achieve a wide range of representation in East Asia, we now turn to the examples of two newly developing economies, namely Malaysia and Thailand.

Malaysia is distinguished by its multi-ethic social structure consisting of Malay Muslims, Malaysian Chinese and Indians (Smith and Abdullah, 2004). In the past three decades, Malaysia has been highly dependent on foreign direct investment and has achieved rapid economic growth until the 1997 Asian Crisis. As Smith and Abdullah (2004) claim, the crisis had significant impact on both national economic development and firm-level HRM practices. Three aspects must be addressed here: (1) global pressures on foreign MNCs to drastically change their staffing policies; (2) both informal level of local/traditional 'culture' that work together with the formal practices of modern HRM systems (*ibid.*); and (3) the state retaining a fulcrum role in employment relations (Bhopal and Rowley, 2002).

Some common Malaysian cultural values, regardless of ethnic identity, emphasize harmony, respect for elders, acceptance of hierarchy and group oriented interests over individual interests (Asma, 2001). A large number of overseas Chinese (*nanyang huaqiao*) family businesses followed the traditional Confucian value system and adopted paternalist management systems. Both effective external and internal relationships (*guanxi*) are key factors for business success. Seniority is important for reward and promotion. Basic training is provided to majority employees and the government also pays attention to develop the national HRD plan with a focus on lifting local Malay Muslims' employability. Employers are normally hesitant to dismiss employees due to considerations of maintaining harmony at the level of workplace and local community.

However, the 1997 Asian Crisis had a fundamental impact on management practices. The major change was to introduce 'hard' HRM measurement, such as retrenchment and so on. In the post-Asian Crisis period, majority companies adopted retrenchment policy (see Smith and Abdullah, 2004). In addition, by introducing new technology and automation systems, the requirement for new employment was also reduced. Short-term fixed contract systems were adopted by not only MNCs but traditionally family-owned businesses. The consequence was that the management team became less loyal to the family owners and short-term cash gain was the major attractive factor for both managerial staff and employees. The so-called 'survival is the best motivation' influences both senior management teams and grass-root production teams. The reward systems were linked with the outcomes of performance. Both group-based and individual-based performance systems were adopted among majority companies and individual oriented factors such as skills and performance became increasingly important determining factors for rewards, in contrast to the traditional seniority-based pay systems. Furthermore, most companies used multi-skilling to cope with the 1997 Asian Crisis. They did not cut training budgets, but placed a higher emphasis on training and up-grading existing employees and their skills. MNCs and big national companies continued to utilize sophisticated international HRM consulting and training firms (*ibid.*).

The case of Malaysia shows that more 'hard' HRM oriented policies and practices have been adopted among the majority companies since the 1997 Asia Crisis, no matter whether MNCs or national big companies and family-owned businesses. The new initiatives emphasized HRM with the so-called 'flexible' orientation, such as the managerial rights to hire and fire, short-term contract, individual performance-oriented pay and promotion, and downsizing and retrenchment. The 'soft' part of HRM has been maintained along the lines of key aspects of Malaysian cultural and value systems, such as managerial concern to help employees and employee compliance with new managerial measures (*ibid.*).

Thailand is another newly developing economy that saw substantial economic growth in the 1980s and most part of 1990s. Thai culture is rooted in Theravada Buddhism, which differs in many respects from the type of Buddhism in East Asia. It promotes a more passive acceptance of life events and fatalism (Lawler and Atmiyanandana, 2004). Unlike the Confucianist approach, a strong preoccupation with personal accomplishment is not particularly central to Thai identity (*ibid.*). However, some commonalities with other East Asian nations do exist in Thai culture, such as humility, deference to superiors, loyalty to the group, reliance on social networks and preferential treatment of network members, pursuit of harmonious relations and avoidance of conflict and maintaining face (*ibid.*). Quality of life and the concept of 'having fun' are important factors that influence Thai people's work and social life.

The Thai economy had experienced sustained growth since the 1980s with a large amount of foreign direct investment (FDI) in labour intensive, low value-added and export-oriented industries. The investment from Japan was one of the major sources of FDI and subsidiaries of Japanese-based MNCs tended to utilize many Japanese management practices (*ibid.*). Economic development in the 1990s was mainly positive with double-digit growth and low inflation until the 1997 Asian Crisis. The crisis started in Thailand initially and then moved to many other Asian economies. Large external debts, a significant real estate 'bubble' and misconduct of business management were the key triggers for the crisis occurred in Thailand. External support such as IMF intervention and internal restructuring led to economic and social stability by 2002 (*ibid.*). A reform agenda of business operations and management practices was one of the key aspects of entire restructuring package.

Lawler and Atmiyanandana (2004) identify three types of enterprises in Thailand, namely family enterprises, Thai-owned corporations and foreign-owned enterprises (FOEs). Family enterprises are smaller or medium-sized and rely on the conventional management practices of Chinese-style family business. HRM practices are simple and informal, with personal relationships being very important in hiring, the determination of wages and promotions. Seniority is an important factor for reward and promotion rather than either the external labour market or internal equity (*ibid.*). Thai-owned corporations were formed out of family business or through privatization of SOEs with widespread ethnic Chinese investment. Although there are increasing numbers of professionally trained managers working for this type of organizations, the core Thai cultural values such as collectivism and intra-group harmony, deference to authority, humility, self-restraint, and consideration for others still dominate management practices. Therefore, it is difficult to implement the Western-based model of 'high performance work systems' (HPWS) in these organizations. However, foreign MNCs, in particular among US-based and European-based MNCs, apply rationalistic and systematic approaches to HRM, based on notions of international 'best practices' (*ibid.*).

Lawler and Atmiyanandana's (2004) work demonstrates some shifts in HRM practices after the Asian Crisis and these changes include: (1) moving towards performance-based pay at both the individual and group levels; (2) increasingly viewing training as an 'investment' rather than a 'cost'; (3) adapting a 'core-peripheral' approach to workforce management; and (4) a more strategic role of HR field. This research also provides an explanation of the factors influencing the changes. Key aspects such as global competition and the Asian Crisis have led to a greater call for accountability and transparency, reforming commercial law and corporate governance. These pressures have pushed both locally-owned and MNCs towards benchmarking management practices against international 'best practice' (*ibid.*). The general trend of HRM practices in Thailand tends to transform towards a more flexible HPWS rather than the traditional approach, although MNCs are generally ahead of locally-owned enterprises.

The last group of East Asian economies we have chosen includes China and Vietnam. Both of these have similar traditional cultures that are predominately Confucianism, and in recent years, they have been transformed themselves from centrally planned socialist systems to a more market oriented one but still with the so-called 'socialist characteristics'. Economic reforms and an 'open door' policy have led to significant changes in the society and the emergence of new interest groups, the inflow of foreign capital and the diversity of ownership of enterprises, and a large and floating population, moving from the countryside to the cities, have accentuated conflicts of interest and require a more relevant employment relations policy at macro-level, as well as HRM strategies at micro-level to cope with these challenges.

China is the birthplace of the ancient philosophies that have long influenced the East Asian region, such as Confucianism and Daoism (see Zhu and Warner, 2004a). The 'Liberation' in 1949 imposed an ideology of Marxist–Leninism, coupled with Maoist ideas. It lasted until Mao Ze-dong died in 1976. In 1978, Deng Xiao-ping introduced economic reform as the central task for the Party/state and people. In fact, reforming employment relations systems was part of the reform agenda since the early 1980s (Warner *et al.*, 2005a).

The transformation of people-management systems towards HRM started in the middle of the 1980s (see Child, 1994; Warner, 1995, 1999, 2000, 2004). Initially, HRM as an academic concept was introduced by joint teaching-arrangements between Chinese and foreign universities as well as in management practices in foreign-owned enterprises, mainly from Japan, the US and Europe (Warner, 1995). The translation of HRM into Chinese is '*renli ziyuan guanli*' (with the same Chinese characters as in Japanese) which means 'labour force resources management'. But in fact, some people now use it misleadingly as a synonym for 'Personnel Management' (*renshi guanli)* and indeed often treat it as such (Warner, 1997). This older form of PM practice is still very common in state-owned enterprises (SOEs) and a fair degree of conservatism continues to pervade the administration of personnel in such enterprises. Certainly, it is still very far from the concept of HRM as understood in the international community (Poole, 1997). We have coined the phrase 'HRM with Chinese characteristics' to accommodate the character of transformation (Warner *et al.*, 2005).

The term HRM is in fact mostly *de rigueur* in the more prominent Sino-foreign JVs, particularly the larger ones (Ding *et al.*, 2002; Warner *et al.*, 2005). Even in these types of firms, management seems to be more inward looking, with a focus on issues like wages, welfare and promotion as found in the conventional personnel arrangements, rather than strategic ones like long-term development normally associated with HRM (Zhu and Warner, 2004a).

The empirical research study of Ding *et al.* (2002) shows that MNCs and some joint ventures both adopted more international standardized HRM policies and practices. In contrast, SOEs remained more conservative regarding changes with their 'iron rice bowl' (*tie fan wan*) policies. In addition, township and village enterprises (TVEs) and other domestic private enterprises (DPEs) had much more autonomy in their people-management compared with SOEs. Regarding the changes of HRM in SOEs, Benson and Zhu's (1999) research identifies three models of transition: (1) a minimalist approach, where organizations have made little attempt to adopt a HRM approach; (2) a transitional stage between the old and the new forms of people-management; and (3) an innovative attempt to adopt the HRM paradigm. The fact is that liberalization of economy and the introduction of foreign investment have created the opportunity for Chinese domestic enterprises to adopt some of the widely used Western and Japanese HR practices. The SOEs that are involved in JVs or contracting arrangements with foreign companies are more likely to have adopted the 'new' HRM. Therefore, globalization, more business-oriented beliefs and a stronger customer-oriented strategy are crucial determinants whether enterprises engage in HRM practices (Benson and Zhu, 1999).

Overall, the major changes started in the mid-1980s when the 'labour contract system' was introduced (Warner and Ng, 1999). Two important aspects are associated with the introduction of the 'labour contract system': (1) adopting individual labour contracts with fixed-term (one to five years) to replace the old 'life-time' employment system; and (2) 'individual' contracts were supplemented by 'collective' contracts in the mid-1990s, and that provided opportunity for trade unions to be involved in signing 'collective' contracts at firm level and set up a 'framework agreement' for the myriad individual contrasts in the enterprise (Warner, 2004). It must be made clear however that this contract is not fully equivalent to Western-style collective bargaining as there are no independent unions. In addition, there is increasing autonomy of management, issues such as the rights to hire and fire, performance evaluation, managerial decision on performance standards and the way of conducting evaluation, performance related matters, such as pay and promotion.

Since China joined the WTO, it has added an international dimension to the complicated domestic employment relations systems (Zhu and Warner, 2004b). There was increasing pressure from international governing bodies, such as the ILO and WTO and other international trade unions like the International Confederation of Free Trade Unions (ICFTU), with regard to the issues of labour rights, the role of unions and labour standards, as well as broader concerns about human rights, social protection and political reform in China (*ibid.*). The empirical study of Zhu and Warner (2004b) regarding firms' response towards WTO accession identifies that an increasing number of firms have an active response through innovative strategies and new HR practices. Enterprises with foreign ownership, those that have transformed from SOEs to joint stock enterprises (JSEs), those that are located in the coastal region, those have weaker links with the traditional State planning system, those have experienced modern management systems and internationalization, and those in high-value-added sectors and the new economy are more likely to have proactive HRM responses (*ibid.*).

Clearly, at this time, there is no a homogeneous model of HRM in Chinese enterprises. Individual enterprises are reforming their HRM systems differently on the basis of their existing conditions and the impact of the economic reforms.

As another socialist market economy, Vietnam has experienced many changes, from the early years of Chinese political and cultural influence (111 BC–939 AD), French colonization, Japanese invasion, and American occupation, to later communist rule and independence, and more recently economic reforms and entering the global economy. Therefore, there are significant marks left in Vietnamese society from all those historical events.

Fundamentally, traditional thinking in Vietnam has been influenced by ancient Chinese philosophies, predominantly by Confucianism. For many years, Vietnam had been the focal point of the struggle for and against colonialism, of the ideological war between capitalism and socialism and, more recently, of the conflict between different approaches of reform (Beresford, 1989). Vietnam started taking its first steps towards economic reform in 1986, marked by the party-state resolution of '*doi moi*', namely economic renovation (Ljunggren, 1993; Perkins, 1993).

Before the economic reforms started, SOEs were the major economic sector and they were integrated into a system of mandatory state planning (as in China). Enterprise inputs, including labour, were assigned by a five-year government plan. Enterprises did not necessarily acquire labour with the right set of skills and were invariably overstaffed because the labour administration arranged employees for individual firms (Doanh and Tran, 1998). In addition, enterprises had few ways to motivate or discipline employees. The reward-system had only an indirect relation to enterprise efficiency and individual labour effort. It was based on a narrowly defined egalitarianism as well as the tendency to reward labour on the grounds of seniority and contribution to the Party as well as to the war-effort in the past.

In order to create a more flexible people-management system as part of the reform agenda, the government relinquished its control over the recruitment and employment of workers. Therefore, individual firms gained the autonomy to decide on the number of workers hired, the terms of employment and the discharge of employees. Even so, there has been a relatively slow pace of transforming lifetime employment into a new contract-employment system, with predominantly fixed-term contract employment, since the new system was initially introduced in 1987.

Another major change has been the transformation of wage-system. The central task was transforming the old egalitarian system in which levels of wage were based on length of service, to the new system in which levels of wages link more closely with company and individual performance in terms of profit, productivity, responsibility and skills. The employee, however, now receives a basic wage and additional benefits that accrue from several forms of bonuses (Zhu and Fahey, 1999).

The third issue of reforming people-management system is changing the old welfare system into a new social insurance system (Norlund, 1993). The old 'from cradle to grave' type of welfare system (even it only covered a minority of labour force who were working at public sector) is considered a financial burden on enterprises. Thus, individual firms seek ways to minimize welfare costs. In order to speed up the reform process and reduce the burden of SOEs, the government issued a new policy on introducing social insurance system to replace the old welfare system.

The fourth issue of reforming the people-management system has been in the area of management-labour relations. Certainly, the central aim of economic reform is increasing the autonomy of enterprise management. The results are varied, but it seems that managers have enjoyed an increase in power. In addition, informal bargaining remains important to the success of the enterprise and this proceeds most smoothly through personal connections. Although economic reform is premised on a reduction of Party influence in the enterprise, political networks form a readily accessible structure for informal bargaining and personal connections, generating problems ranging from unpredictability to corruption (Zhu and Fahey, 2000).

A survey undertaken by one of the authors shows that the realization of flexibility and competitiveness of enterprises depends on the type of people-management system established and practiced by the management (Zhu, 2002). There is a mixture of control and nurturing in management practices. Most senior management have taken on a more transformational leadership, and the middle management and the HR manager show a more transactional approach. In addition, more firms emphasized personnel procedures and rules as the basis of good managerial practice. This indicates that compliance with rules was more important, although the aim is how to encourage greater employee commitment (Zhu, 2002, 2005). In addition, the variation concerns the strategic role for the HR manager is also problematic. Generally speaking, the position of the HR manager was not a specialized one and in most of the firms was filled by line-managers (Zhu, 2002). The HR managers had little involvement in their firm's strategic planning. In fact, the HR task was more operational (wage, social welfare calculations and so on) than strategic. This was clearly the traditional role of the so-called 'personnel manager'.

In addition, a paternalist management pattern still has certain residual influence (Warner *et al.*, 2005). However, in the post-reform era, this attitude has gradually changed, especially among younger employees. The new fixed-term contract employment system has largely contributed to this change. The philosophy of collectivism is also found in the Vietnamese organization in terms of their group-oriented approach. Group-based activities including teamwork and decision-making, quality control and incentives are common managerial practices. In Vietnamese organization, leadership and decisions are team-centred (Zhu, 2002). Another group-based matter is a collective-oriented bonus (Zhu, 2002). Information-sharing schemes have been widely adopted as well. In fact, not only was general information on production plans and schedules provided, but also this information was accompanied with strategies to improve production and employee performance. Individual grievance mechanisms also existed in a majority of the firms. In most of the cases, parallel grievance channels through both HR and the trade unions also do exist.

Based on these findings, Zhu's (2005) recent empirical research adds *numerically flexible strategies* and *functional flexibility strategies* into consideration in order to illustrate the changes of people-management in recent years, in particular since the Asian Crisis. The findings suggest that labour flexibility strategies were not fully adopted by the sample companies. The results indicate that political, cultural, legal and economic factors make labour flexibility in Vietnam are different from that in other countries (Zhu, 2005). For instance, companies are not able to adjust the size of regular employees due to the constraints of legislation. In addition, Vietnamese cultural traditions that place great emphasis on organizational and personal commitment, and harmonious working environments prevent the full deployment of functional flexibility (Zhu, 2005).

Discussion

One of the central themes of this article is to illustrate the similarity and difference of HRM systems among the key players in East Asia. Table 2 identifies the key characteristics of people-management in East Asia by summarizing the major comments on the seven East Asian economies reviewed in the previous section. This table presents these cases by dividing the issues into three sub-categories, namely existing dimensions, the US influence and the European influence.

By examining the existing dimensions horizontally, we can see that under the group orientation section, almost all the cases have very high of those four key dimensions, namely common goal and value, group-based performance evaluation, group-based incentives and teamwork. There are three items with a high rather than a very high level, namely group-based incentives in Malaysia and Thailand where individual incentives also influence the incentive schemes to a certain degree compared with other cases, while teamwork is high in China, but not very high due to the disruption of the 'Cultural Revolution' with some internal 'fighting' elements at workplace that planted the roots of suspicion among co-workers.

Among the other dimensions, harmony is very high in most of the cases except China with high level due to the same reason under the influence of the 'Cultural Revolution'. Communist egalitarian principle also influences China and Vietnam having less hieratical power relationships and less paternalist management system than other Asian counterparts. Japan has the most advanced information sharing system than other cases. Multi-skilling is better developed in Japan, Korea and Malaysia than other cases. All the cases have the strong role of State and China and Vietnam have the most influential State comparatively due to their Communist single Party-state status. Training and

Table 2 *The characteristics of people-management in East Asia: existing dimensions and influenced by the US and Europe*

Items	Japan	Korea	Taiwan	Malaysia	Thailand	China	Vietnam	Total
Existing dimensions								
Group orientation								
Common goal and value	5	5	5	5	5	5	5	35
Group-based performance evaluation	5	5	5	5	5	5	5	35
Group-based incentives	5	5	5	4	4	5	5	33
Teamwork	5	5	5	5	5	4	5	34
Others								
Harmony	5	5	5	5	5	4	5	34
Hierarchy	5	5	5	5	5	4	4	33
Information sharing	5	4	4	4	4	4	4	29
Multi-skilling	4	4	3	4	3	3	3	24
Paternalism	5	5	5	5	5	3	3	31
The strong role of state	4	4	4	4	4	5	5	30
Training and development	5	5	4	4	4	4	4	30
Unions' influence	3	4	3	2	2	3	3	20
Sub-total	**36**	**36**	**33**	**33**	**32**	**30**	**31**	
The US influence								
Individual orientation								
Individual contract	4	4	4	4	4	4	4	28
Individual goal and value	3	2	4	3	2	3	3	20
Individual performance evaluation	3	3	4	3	3	3	3	22
Individual pay and incentives	3	3	4	3	3	2	2	20
Individual career development	3	3	4	3	3	3	3	22
Others								
Downsizing and retrenchment	4	4	4	4	4	4	4	28
Fixed-term contract	4	4	3	4	4	5	5	29
Freedom to hire and fire	3	4	3	4	4	3	3	24
Strategic role of HRM	3	3	4	4	4	3	3	24
Unitary labour-management approach*	1	1	2	2	2	1	1	11

Table 2 (*Continued*)

Items	Japan	Korea	Taiwan	Malaysia	Thailand	China	Vietnam	Total
Sub-total	**31**	**31**	**36**	**34**	**33**	**31**	**31**	
The European influence								
Co-determination/partnership								
Collective negotiation and agreement	4	4	3	2	2	3	3	21
Workers' participation (i.e. Supervisory Board) 3	3	3	3	2	2	3	3	19
Work council/congress at firm level	4	4	2	2	2	3	3	20
Others								
Institutional building	4	4	2	2	2	3	3	20
Legalistic environment	4	4	4	3	3	3	3	24
Regional/international labour standardization	3	3	3	3	3	3	3	21
Sub-total	**22**	**19**	**19**	**15**	**14**	**17**	**17**	

Notes: 5 = very high; 4 = high; 3 = medium; 2 = low; 1 = very low.*We are aware that pluralistic approach does exist among unionized organizations in the US, but they are a minority. *Source:* Bae and Rowley, 2001; Benson and Debroux, 2004; Ding *et al*, 2002; Lawler and Atmiyanandana, 2004; Smith and Abdullah, 2004; Warner *et al.*, 2005a; Zhu, 2002, 2003, 2004, 2005.

development are important HR policies in all cases; in particular, Japan and Korea have developed the most advanced systems compared with other counterparts. Union influence is very hard to judge on the surface. In fact, majority cases have firm-based union activities except in Malaysia and Thailand. There are certain forms of negotiations between management and unions in developed economies such as Japan, Korea and Taiwan, and socialist market economies such as China and Vietnam. Labour laws defined the role of unions in those societies clearly but a key matter is the lack of implementation and enforcement of those laws in reality. Unions in Korea have made strong protests from time to time but the real impact on key decision-making process has declined in recent years.

The next sub-category is US influence among these East Asian cases. The most profound influences are individual contracts, fixed-term contracts, and downsizing and retrenchment. Other influences such as freedom to hire and fire, strategic role of HRM, individual performance evaluation, and individual career development are 'moderate', with majority of medium-level adoption. The last group of dimensions such as individual goal and value, individual pay and incentives, and unitary labour-management approach have relatively lower levels of adoption due to their underpinning values contradict the fundamental belief-systems in East Asian philosophy, as well as the basic human relationship norms and management practices in the workplace.

The third sub-category is the European influence. Generally speaking, the European influence among the East Asian economies is less than the US influence. However, some key aspects of European-oriented people-management system such as co-determination and social partnership as well as institutional building and legalistic environment do help East Asian economies to transform the society towards the 'rule of law' and embracing the institutionalization process at the macro-level and workers' participation and industrial democracy at firm-level. The general trend is that the developed economies such as Japan, Korea and Taiwan adopt more European dimensions than the developing economies. This maybe reflects that the development of institutionalization need accompany of advanced economic system. The danger is that most East Asian economies have not fully developed institutional frameworks and if they suddenly follow the trend of de-institutionalization, it may damage the long-term sustainable capacity to be a mature political, economic and social entity.

Table 3 provides more complementary information on the people-management changes, factors causing the changes and time. The common phenomenon is that when there is a crisis, that leads to some opportunities for drastic changes as the meaning of the Chinese character of 'crisis' – '*weiji*' literally means 'danger and opportunity'. The major changes in Japan started in 1992 when its economy went into the recession. Other economies mainly started to reform in the late 1997 when the Asian Crisis occurred. China and Vietnam launched reforms of its management system as part of overall economic renewal agenda in the late 1980s and further changes later as a response towards WTO entry for China and the Asian Crisis for Vietnam. The major changes are predominately introducing some 'hard' HRM elements as well as responding to the crisis. In other words, short-term oriented drastic measures being adopted with the conceptual notion of improving flexibility under the economic restructuring or economic reform process.

Conclusion

The people-management system in East Asia has, we would argue, some distinctive even unique characteristics. First, the process of the formation and transformation has been

Table 3 The changes of people-management system in East Asia: factors and time

Cases	Changes	Factors	Time
Japan	1) introducing flexible HR systems 2) more 'merit-based' approach 3) emphasizing new HRD strategies	1) economic recession & changing State policy 2) mismatching HRM & business needs 3) changing attitudes of young employees	since 1992
Korea	1) recruiting competencies 2) reinforcing competencies 3) retaining competencies 4) replacing competencies	1) the Asian Crisis 2) strategic choice 3) state policy & institutional influence	since 1997
Taiwan	1) adopting international standardized HRM 2) more flexible HR systems	1) industrial restructuring, relocation & MNCs' influence late 1990s 2) low economic growth & relatively high unemployment	late 1990s
Malaysia	1) more 'hard' HRM with remaining 'soft' element 2) more flexible HR systems	1) the Asian Crisis 2) economic restructuring & foreign capital influence 3) changing State policy & institutional environment	since 1997
Thailand	1) introducing 'HPWS' 2) more performance-based pay 3) adopting 'core-peripheral' workforce	1) the Asian Crisis 2) reforming law and management systems 1) foreign capital influence	since 1997
China	1) introducing HRM system but mixed with PM 2) more firms adopt proactive HRM responses	1) economic reform 2) WTO accession & international pressure	late 1980s since 2002
Vietnam	1) more flexible people-management system 2) mixed PM & HRM systems with more HRM orientation	1) economic reform 2) the Asian Crisis	late 1980s since 1997

Source: Benson and Debroux, 2004; Bae and Rowley, 2001; Smith and Abdullah, 2004; Ding *et al*, 2001; Lawler and Atmiyanandana, 2004; Warner *et al*, 2005a; Zhu, 2002, 2003, 2004, 2005.

marked by some self-determined factors related to the traditional cultural/value systems and historical evolution. Represented with group-orientation, key people-management dimensions such as common goal and value, teamwork, harmony, information sharing, training and development, and so on are part of the so-called 'new' HRM paradigm. However, with increasing global competition and influence of MNCs' management practices, the US-oriented individualistic HRM dimensions have also been gradually adopted among majority East Asian economies. Key aspects such as individual fixed-term contracts, individual performance evaluation, individual career development, downsizing and retrenchment, freedom to hire and fire, strategic role of HRM and so on have become increasingly important in the East Asian people-management system. In addition, the European influences of social partnership, institutional building and legalistic environment play a positive role on the society transformation towards the 'rule of law' and institutionalization. The next challenge for East Asian economies is not embracing the trend of de-institutionalization but building strong social and institutional framework that enables them to achieve sustainable development. In addition, individual country's effort could be weak and a regional-based approach towards 'labour market regulation' and 'labour-right standardization' (like the EU's approach) may be the eventual outcome for the entire regional development.

Figure 1 demonstrates the current triangle-influence of people-management system between East Asia, the US and Europe. It is very clear that the US is the dominant power in both 'hard' and 'soft' approaches towards people-management system with the emphasis on individualist and unitary approaches. Through their FDI activities in Asia and Europe, as well as developing new paradigm for management education, the US

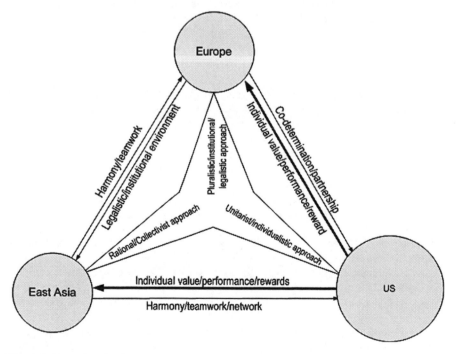

Figure 1 *Triangle influence*

plays the so-called leadership role on influencing and forming management philosophies, policies, programmes, practices and processes (5-P). On the other hand, both East Asia and Europe have some influence on each other as well as on the US with their unique characteristics. For example, the East Asian model emphasizes collective approach, harmony and relational based business operation (i.e. social network approach). The European model then pays attention to pluralistic labour-management relations and legalistic environment. International collaboration on labour standards is also useful for other countries, especially among East Asian countries, to follow.

The last but not least key point is that the factors shaping the development of people-management systems in East Asia can be summarized now as the following. First, there is a strong foreign influence, in particular the US influence on the process of globalization. The more dependent on foreign capital and MNCs' activities, e.g. Taiwan, Malaysia and Thailand, the more the so-called 'HPWS' oriented HRM practices are adopted.

Second, there is a strong State-influence. All the cases in our study show that the influence from the State is strong or very strong. The development model in East Asia used to be labelled as 'the state-led development'. In fact, the people-management system is also strongly linked with the state policy on industrial relations (IRs) and labour market regulations. Certainly, the state policy shifts from time to time. Generally speaking, the state policy on IRs among the East Asian capitalist economies has transformed from initial pro-capital between the 1960s and the mid of 1980s as part of the overall industrialization policy, to 'pro-labour' between the late 1980s and 1997 as part of democratization movement, and then converted to pro-capital again after the 1997 Asian Crisis when the economy went into a downturn and unemployment grew, accompanied by intensified regional and global competition. On the other hand, the two socialist market economies, namely China and Vietnam, have been undergone a period of State-led economic reform and people-management system has been part of the reform agenda, transforming from the traditional PM model into the concurrent one of hybrid model with the combination of PM and HRM. Therefore, the people-management system has been undergone a period of reform and retrenchment over the past three decades.

Third, the over-all social and economic development stage influences the people-management system related to functional social and institutional framework in East Asia. The evidence shows that more developed economies have more advanced social and institutional framework and better-established legalistic environment. However, the less developed economies, no matter how many pieces of legislations they passed, the implementation and enforcement of law and regulation have always been problematic. Therefore, the social and institutional development relies on the level of education, income and income distribution, awareness of citizenship and legal rights. Without adequate social and economic development, the established social and institutional framework could not function effectively.

Fourth, the history is an important factor determining both individual and organizational behaviour. Adopting and implementing certain HRM policies and practices are related to a 'fit' with the historical path and norm in a particular organization. The historical path could be related to national history, e.g. the 'Cultural Revolution' in China with internal fighting and suspicious behaviour, and individuals' joining the army in Korea, Taiwan and Vietnam (war experiences in Vietnam in particular) and bringing military-oriented management style into workplace, or organizational history such as family traditions among a number of private businesses in Korea, Taiwan, Malaysia and Thailand, and SOEs' traditions in China and Vietnam, while particular type of management practices remains as core practices and they are very hard to be replaced.

Given all of the evidence and argument in this article, we can see that it would be foolish to define an 'Asian HRM Model' as such. However, the implications of this study are manifold. We tried to identify some commonalities as well as differences within the current HRM policies and practices among the seven key East Asian economies in order to illustrate the key questions being asked in the beginning of this article. The purpose of this study is not about showing who has a more superior people-management system than others, but identifying what elements do exist in East Asian people-management system, what other new elements have been adopted into the existing system and then what factors determining such changes. We have demonstrated in this article that HRM is in a reforming process in East Asia towards a hybrid people-management system by combining many the US and European people-management aspects. However, this reforming process is not one-way only. In fact, many elements of East Asian people-management system also influence the US and Europe as we indicated in Figure 1. In addition, multi-factor are shaping the outcome of reforming people-management system in East Asia, identified as foreign influence, the State's influence, the stage of social and economic development, and national and organizational historical path. Therefore, the future changes may go ahead along the lines of shaping factors and influences presented in this article. Other economies – no matter whether in East Asia or other parts of the world – may draw some lessons from this study, as we hoped as part of our initial planning in writing up this article.

References

ADB Annual Report (2005) *Annual Report 2005*. Manila: Asian Development Bank.

ADB Key Indicators (2005) *Key Indicators 2005: Labor Market in Asia: Promoting Full, Productive, and Decent Employment*. Manila: Asian Development Bank.

Asma, A. (2001) 'Influence of Ethnic Values at the Malaysian Workplace'. In Abdullah, A. and Low, A. (eds) *Understanding the Malaysian Workforce: Guidelines for Managers*. Kuala Lumpur: MIM, pp. 1–24.

Aycan, Z. (2005) 'The Interplay between Cultural and Institutional/Structural Contingencies in Human Resource Management Practices', *International Journal of Human Resource Management*, 16(7): 1083–119.

Bae, J. and Rowley, C. (2001) 'The Impact of Globalisation on HRM: The Case of South Korea', *Journal of World Business*, 36(4): 402–28.

Bae, J. and Rowley, C. (2004) 'Changes and Continuities in South Korean HRM'. In Rowley, C. and Benson, J. (eds) *The Management of Human Resources in the Asia Pacific Region: Convergence Reconsidered*. London: Frank Cass, pp. 76–105.

Benson, J. and Debroux, P. (2004) 'Flexible Labour Markets and Individualized Employment: The Beginnings of a New Japanese HRM System?'. In Rowley, C. and Benson, J. (eds) *The Management of Human Resources in the Asia Pacific Region: Convergence Reconsidered*. London: Frank Cass, pp. 55–75.

Benson, J. and Zhu, Y. (1999) 'Market, Firms and Workers: The Transformation of Human Resource Management in Chinese Manufacturing Enterprises', *Human Resource Management Journal*, 9(4): 58–74.

Beresford, M. (1989) *National Unification and Economic Development in Vietnam*. London: Macmillan.

Bhopal, M. and Rowley, C. (2002) 'The State in Employment: The Case of Malaysian Electronics', *International Journal of Human Resource Management*, 13(8): 1166–85.

Boxall, P.F. (1992) 'Strategic Human Resource Management: Beginning of a New Theoretical Sophistication?', *Human Resource Management Journal*, 2: 60–79.

Brewster, C. (1995) 'Towards a European Model of Human Resource Management', *Journal of International Business*, 26: 1–22.

Budhwar, P.S. and Debrah, Y. (2001) 'Rethinking Comparative and Cross-national Human Resource Management Research', *International Journal of Human Resource Management*,, 12(3): 497–515.

Chen, M. (1995) *Asian Management Systems*. London: Routledge.

Chen, S.J., Lawler, J. and Bae, J. (2005) 'Convergence in Human Resource systems: A Comparison of Locally Owned and MNC Subsidiaries in Taiwan', *Human Resource Management*, 44(3): 237–56.

Child, J. (1994) *Management in China during the Era of Reform*. Cambridge: Cambridge University Press.

Ding, D.Z., Lan, G. and Warner, M. (2001) 'A New Form of Chinese Human Resource Management? Personnel and Labour-Management Relations in Chinese TVEs', *Industrial Relations Journal*, 32: 328–43.

Doanh, L.D. and Tran, T.C. (1998) 'The SOE Reform Policies in Vietnam and Their Implementation Performance'. In Ministry of Planning and Investment: *Study on Economic Development Policy in the Transition Toward a Market-oriented Economy in Vietnam, Phase 2*. Hanoi: Ministry of Planning and Investment and Japan International Cooperation Agency, 4, pp. 19–49.

Fombrun, C.J., Tichy, N.M. and Devanna, M.A. (1984) *Strategic Human Resource Management*. New York: Wiley.

Galbraith, J. and Nathanson, D. (1978) *Strategic Implementation: The Role of Structure and Process*. St Paul, MI: West Publishing.

Guest, D.E. (1991) 'Personnel Management: The End of Orthodoxy?', *British Journal of Industrial Relations*, 29: 147–75.

Hendry, C. and Pettigrew, A.M. (1992) 'Pattern of Strategic Change in the Development of Human Resource Management', *British Journal of Management*, 3: 137–56.

Hendry, C., Pettigrew, A.M. and Sparrow, P.R. (1988) 'Changing Patterns of Human Resource Management', *Personnel Management*, 20: 37–47.

Hyman, R. (2001) *Understanding European Trade Unionism: Between Market, Class and Society*. London: Sage.

Kim, S. and Briscoe, D. (1997) 'Globalization and a New Human Resource Policy in Korea: Transformation to a Performance-Based HRM', *Employee Relations*, 19(5): 298–308.

Koizumi, T. (1989) 'Management of Innovation and Change in Japanese Organizations', *Advances in International Management*, 4: 245–54.

Lawler, J. and Atmiyanandana, V. (2004) 'HRM in Thailand: A Post-1997 Update'. In Rowley, C. and Benson, J. (eds) *The Management of Human Resources in the Asia Pacific Region: Convergence Reconsidered*. London: Frank Cass, pp. 165–85.

Ljunggren, B. (1993) 'Concluding Remarks: Key Issues in the Reform Process'. In Ljunggren, B. (ed.) *The Challenge of Reform in Indochina*. Cambridge, MA: Harvard University Press, pp. 349–83.

Moore, J. (1987) 'Japanese Industrial Relations', *Labour and Industry*, 1(1): 140–55.

National Statistics of China (2006) *National Statistics of China 2006*. Beijing: Chinese National Statistic Bureau.

National Statistics of Japan (2006) *Japanese Working Life Profile 2005/2006 – Labour Statistics*. Tokyo: The Japan Institute for Labour Policy and Training.

National Statistics of Korea (2006) *Labour Force Survey 2006*. Seoul: National Statistical Office.

National Statistics of Malaysia (2006) *Labour Force Survey Report, 2006*. Kuala Lumpur: Department of Statistics.

National Statistics of Taiwan (2006) *Key Economic and Social Indicators 2006*. Taipei: Executive Yuan.

National Statistics of Vietnam (2006) *National Statistics Data 2006*. Hanoi: National Statistical Office.

Norlund, I. (1993) 'The Creation of a Labour Market in Vietnam: Legal Framework and Practices'. In Thayer, C.A. and Marr, D.G. (eds) *Vietnam and Rule of Law*. Canberra: Australian National University Press, pp. 173–89.

Perkins, D.H. (1993) 'Reforming the Economic Systems of Vietnam and Laos'. In Ljunggren, B. (ed.) *The Challenge of Reform in Indochina*. Cambridge, MA: Harvard University Press, pp. 1–19.

Poole, M. (1997) 'Industrial and Labour Relations'. In Warner, M. (ed.) *IEBM Concise Encyclopaedia of Business and Management*. London: International Thomson Business Press, pp. 264–82.

Porter, M.E. (1990) *The Competitive Advantage of Nations*. London: Macmillan.

Rowley, C. and Bae, J. (2003) 'Management and Culture in South Korea'. *Management and Culture in Asia*. London: Curzon, pp. 187–209.

Sano, Y. (1995) *Human Resource Management in Japan*. Tokyo: Keio University Press.

Schuler, R.S. (1992) 'Linking the People with the Strategic Needs of the Business', *Organizational Dynamics*, Summer: 18–32.

Schuler, R.S. and Jackson, S.E. (1987) 'Organizational Strategy and Organizational Level as Determinants of Human Resource management Practices', *Human Resource Planning*, 10: 125–41.

Smith, W. and Abdullah, A. (2004) 'The Impact of Asian Financial Crisis on Human Resource Management in Malaysia', *Asia Pacific Business Review*, 10(3/4): 402–21.

Sparrow, P.R. and Hiltrop, J.M. (1994) *European Human Resource Management in Transition*. London: Prentice Hall.

Suzuki, Y. (2001) 'Switch to Merit-Based Pay Takes Some Time Getting Used to', *Nikkei Weekly*, 4 June. p. 1.

Warner, M. (1992) 'How Japanese Managers Learn', *Journal of General Management*, 17(3): 56–71.

Warner, M. (1995) *The Management of Human Resources in Chinese Industry*. London: Macmillan and New York: St Martin's Press.

Warner, M. (1997) 'China's HRM in Transition: Towards Relative Convergence?', *Asia Pacific Business Review*, 3(4): 19–33.

Warner, M. (2004) 'China's HRM Revisited: A Step-wise Path to Convergence?'. In Rowley, C. and Benson, J. (eds) *The Management of Human Resources in the Asia Pacific Region: Convergence Reconsidered*. London: Frank Cass, pp. 15–31.

Warner, M. (ed.) (1999) *China's Managerial Revolution*. London: and Portland, OR: Frank Cass.

Warner, M. (ed.) (2000) *Changing Workplace Relations in the Chinese Economy*. London: Macmillan and New York: St Martin's Press.

Warner, M. (ed.) (2005) *Human Resource Management in China Revisited*. London: Routledge.

Warner, M. and Ng, S.H. (1999) 'Collective Contracts in Chinese Enterprises: A New Brand of Collective Bargaining under "Market Socialism"', *British Journal of Industrial Relations*, 37(2): 295–314.

Warner, M., Edwards, V., Polansky, G., Pucko, D. and Zhu, Y. (2005) *Management in Transitional Economies: From the Berlin Wall to the Great Wall of China*. London and New York: Routledge-Curzon.

Zhu, Y. (2002) 'Economic Reform and Human Resource Management in Vietnamese Enterprises', *Asia Pacific Business Review*, 8(3): 115–34.

Zhu, Y. (2003) 'The Post Asian Financial Crisis: Changes in HRM in Taiwanese Enterprises', *Asia Pacific Business Review*, 9(4): 147–64.

Zhu, Y. (2004) 'Responding to the Challenges of Globalization: Human Resource Development in Japan', *Journal of World Business*, 39(4): 337–48.

Zhu, Y. (2005) 'The Asian Crisis and the Implications for Human Resource Management in Vietnam', *International Journal of Human Resource Management*, 16(7): 1262–77.

Zhu, Y. and Fahey, S. (1999) 'The Impact of Economic Reform on Industrial Labour Relations in China and Vietnam', *Post-Communist Economies*, 11(2): 173–92.

Zhu, Y. and Fahey, S. (2000) 'The Challenges and Opportunities for the Trade Union Movement in the Transition Era: Two Socialist Market Economies – China and Vietnam', *Asia Pacific Business Review*, 6(3&4): 282–99.

Zhu, Y. and Warner, M. (2001) 'Taiwanese Business Strategies vis-à-vis the Asian Financial Crisis', *Asia Pacific Business Review*, 7(3): 139–56.

Zhu, Y. and Warner, M. (2004a) 'HRM in East Asia'. In Harzing, A.W. and Ruysseveldt, J.V. (eds) *International Human Resource Management*, 2nd edn. London: Sage, pp. 195–220.

Zhu, Y. and Warner, M. (2004b) 'Changing Patterns of Human Resource Management in Contemporary China', *Industrial Relations Journal*, 35(4): 311–28.

Comparative HRM: European views and perspectives

Chris Brewster

Introduction

Human Resource Management (HRM) is an American concept: it came, and new ideas about it tend still to come, to researchers and practitioners in Europe from the United States of America. How relevant is it to the European context? What is distinctive about the European notion of HRM? Is there evidence of one model of HRM in Europe, or of many? And are approaches to HRM in Europe coalescing around a US model, or a distinctly European model, or are they staying embedded in their own national contexts so that there are as many models as there are countries?

This paper argues that HRM is seen differently in Europe and different approaches are often taken to research. The first part of the article, reprises, briefly, the US origin of the concept, explores some of the conceptual differences that can be found in the European context, and argues that these differences have led to a different research paradigm and a more critical approach to the subject of HRM in Europe. The second part of the article with, inevitably, considerable generalization describes some of the key things that are happening in HRM in Europe.

The US origins of theories of HRM

In its modern conception, our understanding of management in general, and human resource management in particular, has been heavily influenced by thinking in the United States of America. This is perhaps not surprising for a country that has been for decades the largest and most powerful economy in the world. The spread of American culture and American business practices has been widely heralded and, in HRM as elsewhere, there are signs of the hegemony of the US model. *Prima facie* evidence of the power of the US exemplar in HRM can be seen in the spread across continents of downsizing, contingent (flexible) working practices, and employer antagonism to trade unions.

Two seminal texts in 1984 launched a new approach to what had until then been the study of personnel management, 'partly a file clerk's job, partly a housekeeping job, partly a social worker's job and partly fire-fighting to head off union trouble . . . ' (Drucker, 1989: 269). These texts, it was true, were based on previous teaching by the respective authors and built on extensive antecedents, but they popularized a whole new way of looking at the people within an organization – as 'human resources'. Fombrun *et al.*'s (1984) 'Michigan' model emphasized the link between human resource strategy and the business strategy of the firm: the business strategy should define and determine the types of employee, employee deployment and employee performance. Employees are a resource like any other: they 'are to be obtained cheaply, used sparingly and developed and exploited as fully as possible' (Sparrow and Hiltrop, 1994). The other text offered the 'Harvard' model (Beer *et al.*, 1984). This argued that employees are not a resource like any other – their understanding and commitment are crucial – whatever the corporate strategy is. Hence, the business strategy is bound in with, rather than leading, the HR strategy.

An undeclared assumption in these texts was that HRM was scientific (Brewster, 1999); the theories were universalistic in the same way that the laws of natural science were: 'relationships between the structural characteristics of work organizations and variables or organization context will be stable across societies' (Hickson *et al.*, 1974: 63). Kidger (1991) argued that businesses that grew in isolation from the (US dominated) world economy will find their approaches superseded by universally applicable techniques. The impact of globalization (incorporating cultures, institutions and organizational level practices) has also been called into evidence as a force for convergence (Geppert *et al.*, 2003). The argument is that US MNCs, and perhaps other mechanisms such as consultants and business schools, will disseminate 'best practice' across the globe (DiMaggio and Powell, 1983).

HRM in the US: core assumptions

There are, perhaps, two core assumptions underlying the classic models of HRM that have come to us from the USA (Brewster, 1995). The first assumption is that the employing organization has considerable latitude in regard to the management of personnel, including (*inter alia*) freedom to operate contingent pay policies and an absence of, or at least a minimal influence from, trade unions. In the context of the weakness of the trade union movement in the USA (where membership is currently probably less than one tenth of the working population, and its activities are predominantly site based), and the comparatively low levels of state subsidy, support and legislative control, this makes sense. It also fits comfortably with the notion that the state should not interfere in business, or do so as little as possible, and that it is the right of every individual to do the best for themselves without external interference (Guest, 1990). Such notions may be less common in Europe.

The second, closely connected, core assumption is that the subject of study is the way that employing organizations manage the human beings (human resources) they deploy. Attempts have been made to distinguish 'strategic HRM (SHRM)' from HRM generally, but it seems increasingly that definitions of HRM include, intrinsically or explicitly, the notion of a strategic approach to the subject. The assumption that underlies HRM is that its purpose is to improve the operation of the organization. The purpose of the study of HRM and, in particular SHRM (Fombrun *et al.*, 1984; Wright and Snell, 1991; Wright and McMahan, 1992), is seen as being about generating understanding in order to improve the way that human resources are managed strategically within organizations, with the ultimate aim of improving organizational performance, as judged by its impact on the organization's declared corporate strategy (Huselid, 1995), the customer (Ulrich, 1989) or shareholders (Becker *et al.*, 1997; Huselid, 1995). Further, it is implicit that this objective will apply in all cases. Thus, the widely cited definition by Wright and McMahan states that SHRM is 'the pattern of planned human resource deployments and activities intended to enable a firm to achieve its goals' (1992: 298).

It has been argued elsewhere (Beaumont, 1991) that much of the US literature is prescriptive – discussing what should happen even though, perhaps, it doesn't happen that way in practice. The research that is done in the States, and the papers that the US or international journals are prepared to accept, come from a *universalist* paradigm (Brewster, 1999). The term paradigm is used here in Kuhn's (1970) sense as an 'accepted' model or theory, with the implication that other paradigms are often seen as not just different but wrong.

The universalist paradigm dominates much (although not, of course, all) of the research in the United States of America and, given the hegemony of US research, teaching and journals, is widely used in many other countries. It is essentially a nomothetic social science approach: evidence is gathered specifically to test generalizations of an abstract and law-like character. For people operating with this paradigm, social science, like natural sciences, should proceed deductively. Hypotheses should be formulated that can be answered 'yes' or 'no' (and hence can be used for prediction); collecting data to test those hypotheses and using recognized statistical tests to check for validity. Research is not deemed to be 'rigorous' unless it is drawn from existing literature and theory, focused around a tightly designed question and contains a structure of testing that can lead on to prediction. The research base is centred mostly on a small number of private sector 'leading edge' exemplars of 'good practice', often large, multinationals, and often from the manufacturing or even specifically the high-tech sector.

The value of this paradigm lies in the simplicity of focus, the coalescing of research around this shared objective and the clear relationship with the demands of industry. Good research based upon it tends to have a clear potential for theoretical development, it can lead to carefully drawn research questions, the research tends to be easily replicable and research methodologies are sophisticated, and there is a coherence of criteria for judging the research. Of course, in any particular case, inappropriate techniques or dubious lines of causality can negate much of the value of this form of research (see Gerhart, 1999, 2005). Even where the data and analysis are sound, however, a disadvantage of this paradigm, perhaps of the US research tradition in particular, is that the pressure to publish and the restricted nature of what is acceptable has led to much careful statistical analysis of small-scale, often narrow, questions whose relevance to wider theoretical and practical debates is sometimes hard to see. There are inevitably problems created by ignoring other potential focuses, the resultant narrowness of the research objectives, and the ignoring of other levels and other stakeholders in the outcomes of HRM (Brewster, 1995; Guest, 1990; Kochan, 1999; Legge, 2005; Pieper, 1990; Poole, 1990). This has been summed up, by an American commentator, in the notion of the 'drunkard's search' – looking for the missing key where visibility is good, rather than where the key was lost.

HRM in the European context

Whether the US-derived visions of HRM apply everywhere in the world is an important question for both theory and practice, since following US prescriptions in either area may be detrimental if the theories are not transferable. Forster and Whipp (1995), for example, talk about the need for a contingent approach encompassing cultural, sectoral and regional differences. Similarly, other theorists have also argued for the need to cover both national differences and organizational contingencies, though they have used different terminologies: macroeconomic, micro-economic (Farmer and Richman, 1965; Gronhaug and Nordhaug, 1992); exogenous, endogenous (Schuler *et al.*, 1993); external, internal (Jackson and Schuler, 1995).

How the theory applies, in particular, to the European setting remains a conceptual and empirical challenge.

An initial problem is to define 'Europe'. The geographical boundaries of Europe have always been a little uncertain: how far east does the boundary lie? Although the focus here will be on the European Union states, plus Norway and Switzerland, the advent of the new central and eastern European states has meant that they have to be included as part of Europe.

Of course, 'Europe' is only one possible level of analysis. Within Europe, there are familiar regional cultural clusters: Ronen and Shenkar's (1985) Nordic, Germanic, Anglo and Latin European clusters for example (see also, e.g., Hofstede, 2001; House *et al.*, 2004). Regional clusters may be institutionally as much as culturally based (Hall and Soskice, 2001; Hollingsworth and Boyer, 1997; Maurice *et al.*, 1986; Whitley, 1999). These sorts of clusters of countries have also been found in studies of HRM in Europe (see, e.g., Due *et al.*, 1991; Ignjatovic and Sveltic, 2003; Sparrow *et al.*, 1994; Tregaskis and Brewster, 2006) – see Table 1. Beyond the regional clusters, the individual countries in Europe remain clearly distinctive in how they manage their HRM (see, e.g., Brookes *et al.*, 2005; Lane, 1989; Luthans *et al.*, 1997; Ramirez, 2004; Thomson *et al.*, 2001; Tregaskis and Brewster, 2006).

Finally, of course, taking our focus down one more notch, we should also note, for completeness, that within any one of these countries there will be a diverse range of HRM models and practices in operation – differences between sectors, between organizations within a sector and even differences between the sites of one organization and, at the most micro level, even between the way that individual managers deal with their subordinates.

Discussing European approaches to HRM, therefore, involves substantial generalization. And, if we can see clear differences between the approaches at the European level to approaches in the USA, we must, nevertheless, remain aware of the substantial differences within North America, even within individual states in the USA; and the differences within Europe.

Despite the complexities, and the problems of generalization, it is clear that HRM operates in a different context in the USA from that in Europe (Brewster, 1999) – government support, the legal constraints, trade union influence, for example are all different – and the way HRM is conceptualized, researched and understood is also different. The effort to understand these differences is important.

HRM in Europe: different antecedents

What, then, might make one wary of the assumption that a subject area and theoretical approaches develop in the United States of America would apply in Europe and that the European conception of HRM would, at most, be the same, even if slightly adapted to different circumstances? Four antecedents might make us treat that assumption with caution (Brewster, 1999).

Table 1 *HR clusters in Europe*

Due et al. (1991)	Filella (1991)	Sparrow et al. (1994)	Tregaskis and Brewster (2000)	Ignjatovic and Sveltic (2003)	Stavrou and Brewster (2005)
Sweden	Sweden		Sweden	Sweden	Sweden
Denmark	Denmark		Denmark	Denmark	Finland
Norway	Norway		Belgium	Norway	
Finland			UK	Finland	
Ireland					
UK			Finland	Switzerland	
				Belgium	
				Netherlands	
				France	
				Switzerland	
	UK	UK		Belgium	UK
Germany	Germany	Germany	Germany(W)	Netherlands	Germany(W)
Belgium	Denmark	Italy	Netherlands	France	
Netherlands	Switzerland		Switzerland	UK	
France			Norway		
Italy	France	France	France	Spain	France
Greece	Italy		Ireland	Czech	Belgium
Spain	Spain			Slovenia	Italy
	Portugal			Italy	
		Spain		Portugal	Spain
				Bulgaria	Portugal
				Estonia	Ireland
				Greece	
				Cyprus	
				Turkey	
				Ireland	

Source: Brewster (2005)

Less focus on individualism

Even if the subject is much discussed, there is a dearth of serious empirical data on national cultural differences (Hofstede, 2001; House, 2004; Schwartz, 1992, 1994; Schwartz and Sagiv, 1995; Spony, 2003; Trompenaars, 1993), but what we have indicates the unusual nature of the United States. It is, as one of the most popular commentators in this field wrote, 'quite untypical of the world as a whole' (Trompenaars, 1985). US culture is significantly more individualistic and achievement-oriented than most other countries (Hofstede, 2001; House, 2004). Indeed, it has been argued (Guest, 1990) that the assumption of business freedom and autonomy is peculiarly American (US) and is related to the American view of their country as a land of opportunity that rewards success. In HRM, this translates into a view that business owners should be as free as possible to run their businesses the way that they want and that individuals have to take individual responsibility for their situation. This culture of individualism is clearly discernible in the thinking that underpins North American notions of reward systems, with their emphasis on individual performance-based rewards and the US 'hire-and-fire' mentality. In Europe, the situation is different, with a widespread feeling that businesses need to be controlled and to treat their employees in a socially responsible way.

The role of the state

Legislation has been seen as a significant reflector of national values (Hofstede, 2001) and it is no surprise therefore to find that the USA, which is characterized by high levels of individualism and comparatively low levels of uncertainty avoidance, has overall comparatively less legislative control over (or interference from, or support for) the employment relationship than is found in most of Europe. Pieper (1990), making this point, included the greater regulation of recruitment and dismissal, the formalization of educational certification, and the quasi-legal characteristics of the industrial relations framework in comparison to the United States. One could also include legislative requirements on pay, on hours of work, on forms of employment contract, rights to trade union representation, requirements to establish and operate consultation or co-determination arrangements - and a plethora of other legal requirements. These are all additional to those few areas, such as the legislation on equality or health and safety, which intrude on the employment relationship on both sides of the Atlantic. While some European states are committed to reducing legislative restrictions in this area, and countries remain very different (OECD, 2006), European employment is heavily regulated by legislation.

Moreover, Europe is unique in the world in having 27 of its countries at present (and perhaps more soon) committed to a supra-national level of legislation on a considerable range of aspects of the employer–employee relationship. The European Union, particularly through the Social Charter and its associated Social Action Programme is having an increasing legislative influence on HRM. While the rhetoric of governments reflects a clear intention to reduce the restrictions imposed by legislation at the national level, there is an equally clear trend to extend the influence of the supranational regulations. Recent developments include restrictions on the hours that individuals can work and a requirement for larger firms to set up Works Councils where employee representatives meet with senior managers on a regular basis to debate a series of subjects laid down in the legislation.

Pieper, a German authority, pointed out that 'the major difference between HRM in the US and in Western Europe is the degree to which [HRM] is influenced and determined by state regulations. Companies have a narrower scope of choice in regard to personnel management than in the US' (Pieper, 1990: 82). This remains an accurate assessment. Blanchard (1999) argued that employment protection has three main dimensions: the length of the notice period to be given to workers; the amount of severance pay to be paid according to the nature of the separation; and the nature and complexity of the legal process involved in laying off workers. Blanchard finds that the US is significantly different from Europe in general and Italy, Spain and Portugal in particular. There is, simply, less protection for workers in the USA.

A wider view of the legislative requirements on pay and conditions of work also shows marked differences. For example, the International Labour Organization reports that whereas in Europe legislative developments have ensured that average hours worked have fallen over the last two decades, in the USA they have risen. Thus, in the United States, almost 80 per cent of male workers and 65 per cent of working women now work more than 40 hours in a typical week. By contrast, in France the working week is by law limited to thirty-five hours with overtime limited to 130 hours a year (Boulin *et al.*, 2006). This policy even extends to making unpaid overtime by senior employees a penal offence: in June 1999, a director of a defence company, Thompson Radars and Countermeasures, was fined after the government's jobs inspectorate had monitored executives, researchers and engineers and uncovered substantial unrecorded overtime. In the USA, such a case would be inconceivable.

Underpinning these legislative dimensions is a wider, normative, concept of what role the state should play in the economic arena (Albert, 1991). State involvement in HRM in Europe is not restricted to legislation. In broad terms, in Europe as compared to the USA, the State has a higher involvement in underlying social security provision, a more directly interventionist role in the economy, provides far more personnel and industrial relations services and is a more substantial employer in its own right by virtue of a more extensive government-owned sector. For example, most European countries have a substantial share of the 18–24 age group in higher education and in addition provide substantial support to employers through state-aided vocational training programmes. And in most European countries, much higher proportions of GDP are spent by the state on labour market programmes. This includes training, retraining and job transition support, job creation schemes and programmes to help younger people and the long-term unemployed get into the labour market. Substantial proportions of employment (up to 50 per cent in some countries) are in the public sector (OECD, 1995; Brewster, 1995).

Overall, governments in Europe, and the European Union itself, tend to have more of a controlling (through legislation) and supporting (through finance and institutions) role in HRM than is the case in the United States of America. The corollary is that employers are less autonomous *vis-à-vis* the State.

The role of trade unions and consultation

A third core feature of European states is the legislative status and influence accorded to trade unions. The definition, meaning and reliability of union membership figures vary between countries (Blanchflower and Freeman, 1990; Walsh, 1985). However, it is quite clear that, in general, the European countries are more heavily unionized than most other areas of the world. Trade union membership and influence varies considerably by country, of course, but it is always significant. Sweden has union membership of 85 per cent of the working population and the other Nordic countries also have union density figures of over two thirds, Belgium and Ireland have almost half the working population as trade union members, the UK and the Netherlands around one quarter.

A more important issue is trade union recognition, that is whether the employer deals with a trade union in a collective bargaining relationship that sets terms and conditions for all or most of the employees (Morley *et al.*, 1996). In this respect, Europe differs to a considerable degree from most other countries. In most European countries, there is legislation requiring employers over a certain size to recognize unions for consultative purposes. Morley *et al.* note that 'Europe has a tradition of collectivism and consensus building and trade unions have a social legitimacy in Europe on a much grander scale than in the US' (1996: 646). Collective bargaining coverage is considerably more widespread than union membership (see Table 2).

Closely related to the issue of trade union recognition is the European practice of employee involvement. Legislation in countries such as the Netherlands, Denmark and, most famously, Germany has for a long time required organizations to have two-tier management boards, with employees having the right to be represented on the more senior Supervisory Board. In all European Union countries, the law requires the establishment of employee representation committees in all organizations except

Table 2 *Union density and bargaining coverage, 2001*

Country	2001 union density (%)	2001 bargaining coverage (%)
Austria	39.8	98
France	9.1	90–5
Finland	79.0	90
Sweden	79.0	90
Belgium	69.2	90
Italy	35.4	90
Portugal	30.0	87
Netherlands	27.0	88
Denmark	87.5	83
Spain	15.0	81
Germany	29.7	67
UK	29.0	36
USA	13.5	15

Source: EIRO (2002)

the smallest. These arrangements give considerable (legally backed) power to the employee representatives and, unlike consultation in the USA, for example, they tend to supplement rather than supplant the union position (Brewster *et al.*, 2007). In relatively highly unionized countries, it is unsurprising that many of the representatives of the workforce are, in practice, trade union officials. In Germany, for instance, four-fifths of them are union representatives.

A central theme of HRM is the requirement to generate significant workforce commitment through developing channels of communication. However, in the Rhineland countries of Germany, the Netherlands, etc., it is noticeable that the provision of information to the workforce involves the use of the formal employee representation or trade union channels as well as the widespread use of individualized communication. And when upward communication is examined, the two most common means in Europe, by a considerable margin, are through immediate line management and through the trade union or works council channel (Morley *et al.*, 2000)

Patterns of ownership

Patterns of ownership also vary from one side of the Atlantic to the other. Public ownership has decreased to some extent in many European countries in recent years – although it has grown considerably in Norway, for example; but it is still far more widespread in European countries than it is in the United States. And private sector ownership may not mean the same thing. In many of the southern European countries particularly, ownership of even large companies remains in the hands of single families rather than of stock-market trading shareholders. On the other hand, in Germany, a tight network of a small number of substantial banks owns a substantial proportion of companies. Their interlocking shareholdings and close involvement in the management of these corporations mean less pressure to produce short-term profits and a positive disincentive to drive competitors out of the market place. The effect of these variations is that there is less pressure for management teams to take short-term views of investments and results.

HRM in Europe: a different concept

Given these contextual differences it is worth testing the assumption that HRM in Europe covers the same ground as the concept developed in the USA. There are four subsets of issues that need to be addressed in thinking about conceptualizing the study of HRM. It is argued below that these issues are seen differently in Europe from the way they are seen elsewhere. The issues are:

- the contested nature of the concept (what we are studying);
- the levels at which it can be applied (the range of our studies);
- the focus (what it aims to do); and hence
- the research paradigm.

The nature of HRM

HRM is a subject without an agreed definition. The confusion in the appropriate subject matter for HRM has been noted by many (Boxall, 1993; Dyer and Kochan, 1994; Legge, 2005). Despite the fact that identification of specific activities and policies is central to theoretical approaches to HRM (Weber and Kabst, 2004), there is no agreed list of what HRM covers. Some subjects seem to be included in most lists of the topics covered by HRM – resourcing, development, reward – but other topics may or may not be included. Thus, subjects like employee participation, trade union relationships, health and safety, equal opportunities, flexible working, career progression, work design and the countless combinations of HR practices, are included in some conceptions of HRM and ignored in others.

There is, perhaps, greater consistency in the US around what is included in the study of HRM and even around the notion of what constitutes 'good' HRM: a coalescing of views around the concept of 'high performance work systems'. These have been characterized by the US Department of Labor (1993) as having certain clear characteristics: careful and extensive systems for recruitment, selection and training; formal systems for sharing information with the individuals who work in the organization; clear job design; local level participation procedures; monitoring of attitudes; performance appraisals; properly functioning grievance procedures; and promotion and compensation schemes that provide for the recognition and financial rewarding of high-performing members of the workforce. Alongside similar lists, which all differ to some degree, the Department of Labor list can be taken as an exemplar of the universalist paradigm: most US writers would be broadly in agreement with such a list.

In Europe, however, almost every item on the list is the source of debate. Thus, in much of southern Europe, recruitment and selection schemes rely heavily on the network of family and friends (the *cunha* in Portugal, for example). HRM experts in these countries would argue that this is a cheap and effective method of recruitment, and gives the organization an extra means of motivating and controlling employees. Interestingly, such systems are now increasingly being recognized by larger organizations in northern Europe as legitimate. Formal systems for sharing information with individuals at their workplaces are significantly different from sharing information at the strategic level with trade union representatives skilled in debating the organizational strategy – a common requirement across Europe. Clear job design (which can presumably be linked with the performance appraisal and incentive schemes for the individual job holder) can be inimical to the need for flexibility, teamwork and responsiveness to the pace of change seen as important by most European organizations. And so on through the list ...

Common to this debate is the assumption that HRM, and particularly SHRM, is concerned with the aims and actions of management within the organization. Perhaps in a country like the USA which has as an avowed aim of most politicians the objective of 'freeing business from outside interference', it makes sense to develop a vision of human resource management that takes as its scope the policies and practices of management. Europeans, however, find that the universalist paradigm ironically excludes much of the work of HR specialists and many of the issues which are vital for the organization – areas such as compliance, equal opportunities, trade union relationships and dealing with government, for example. They are often critical of the universalist model of HRM common in the USA (see, e.g., Brewster, 1999; Guest, 1990; Legge, 2005; Pieper, 1990). European authors have argued that 'rather than copy solutions which result from other cultural traditions, we should consider the state of mind that presided in the search for responses adapted to the culture' (Albert, 1989: 75, translation in Brewster and Bournois, 1991).

HRM in the US typically focuses on the firm. In Europe, the nature of HRM is broader, providing better explanation of the potential differences in views about the topic and a better fit with the concerns of the specialists, by including national institutional and cultural issues such as the trade union movement, national legislation and labour markets as not just external influences but as part of the topic (Brewster and Bournois, 1991; Brewster, 1995).

The level of HRM

A second key question concerns the levels of HRM. As Kochan *et al.* (1992) and Locke *et al.* (1995) have pointed out, cross-national comparisons can be made at various levels. We can use the analogy of a telescope (Brewster, 1995): with each turn of the screw, things that seemed similar are brought into sharper focus so that we can distinguish between, say, the forest and the fields, then with another turn between one tree and another, and then between one leaf and another. Each view is accurate; each blurs some objects and clarifies others; each helps us to see some similarities and some differences.

The universalist paradigm works with the organizational or, in some cases, the sub-organizational (e.g. business unit), level of analysis. Europeans are more likely to assume that HRM can apply at a variety of levels, i.e. that the scope is not restricted to the organizational or sub-organizational level. Thus, in Europe there are discussions of the strategic human resource management policies of the European Union or of particular governments or sectors. Debates about HRM policies between groups of EU member states are often lively. National governments have HRM policies (for example, reducing unemployment, encouraging flexible working practices) and indeed, some of the strategy literature has located the economic success of organizations, and economies, at the national level (see, for example, Porter, 1990; Sorge, 1991). Within a country, specific areas may have HRM policies and practices (raising training standards to attract inward investment, establishing local employment opportunities, etc.). All these levels, which might be seen as exogenous factors impinging upon HRM in the universalist paradigm, are seen in Europe as within the scope of HRM (Brewster, 1995).

It is difficult to discuss more than one level of analysis at a time. It is even more difficult to research more than one. Researchers and commentators often resolve this problem by simply ignoring it. Thus many of the seminal texts in our field draw their data from one level but are written as if the analysis applies at all levels: what Rose (1991) has called 'false universalism'. Many of these texts are produced in one country and base their work on a small number of by now well-known cases. For analysts and practitioners elsewhere, and with interests in different sectors, countries and so on, many of these descriptions and prescriptions fail to meet their reality. Our task, therefore, is not necessarily to change what we write or believe, but to specify the level at which we can show it to be true.

The relevant level of analysis will depend upon the question being asked. The important point is not that any level is necessarily correct or more instructive than the others but that the level needs to be specified to make the analysis meaningful.

The focus of HRM

What is the focus of academic work in HRM? To put it bluntly, are we analysing the management of people as a contributor to finding more cost-effective ways it can be done in order to ensure that the top management's organizational objectives are met or are we critically analysing the way human resources are managed? How important is the 'so what' question? A strong stream of neo-Marxist theorizing (e.g. Friedman, 1997) has focused on managerial approaches to controlling potential dissidence. Thus, questions of 'fit' between the organization's corporate strategy and its HRM are open to challenge at both ends. While not always within the influence of this stream of writing, the willingness to challenge managerial objectives and actions remains relevant. In general terms, European researchers and writers have been more critical of the concept of HRM than the US experts.

The HRM/performance linked literature is a good example. Most of the critique of that literature from those writing in the universalist paradigm has been concerned with weaknesses in the empirical or statistical data (Cappelli and Newmark, 2001; Gerhart, 1999, 2005; Huselid and Becker, 1996). The critiques of the concept within Europe have tended to be more wide-ranging, examining the assumptions of universalism, of the inevitable 'goodness' of the link and the effects on those other than managers in the system (Guest, 1997; Guest *et al.*, 2003; Marchington and Grugulis, 2000; Paauwe and Boselie, 2005; Wood, 1999).

The research paradigm

The effect of the differences in the three issues noted so far is that, by contrast with the universalistic paradigm, many researchers in Europe operate within a *contextual paradigm*. The contextual paradigm is idiographic, searching for an overall understanding of what is contextually unique and why. It is focused on understanding what is different between and within HRM in various contexts and what the antecedents of those differences are. Among most researchers working in this paradigm, it is the explanations that matter - any link to firm performance, for example, is secondary. It is assumed that societies, governments or regions can have HRM policies and practices as well as firms. At the level of the organization (not firm − public sector and not-for-profit organizations are also included), the organization's objectives (and therefore its strategy) are not necessarily assumed to be 'good' either for the organization or for society. There are plenty of examples where this is clearly not the case. Nor, in this paradigm, is there any assumption that the interests of everyone in the organization will be the same or any expectation that an organization will have a strategy that people within the organization will support. Employees and the unions have a different perspective to the management team (Kochan *et al.*, 1986; Purcell and Ahlstrand, 1994; Storey, 1992). Even within the management team, there may be different interests and views (Hyman, 1987; Kochan *et al.*, 1986). These, and their impact on HRM, are issues for empirical study. As a contributor to explanation, this paradigm emphasizes external factors such as ownership structures, labour markets, the role of the state and trade union organization as well as the actions of the management within an organization.

Methodologically, the research mechanisms used in Europe are more likely to be inductive. Theory is drawn from an accumulation of data collected or gathered in a less directed (or constrained) manner than would be the case under the universalist paradigm. Research traditions are different: focused less upon testing and prediction and more upon the collection of evidence. There is an assumption that if things are important they should be studied, even if testable prediction is not possible or the resultant data are complex and unclear. The policies and practices of the 'leading edge' companies (something of a value-laden term in itself) which are the focus of much HRM research and literature in the USA are of less interest to many European researchers than identifying the way labour markets work and what the more typical organizations are doing. Much more work in Europe, therefore, is based on finding out and understanding what is happening: hence there is a stronger tradition of detailed idiographic case studies and, conversely, of large-scale survey work, both of which lend themselves to analyses of the different stakeholders and the environmental complexity of organizations. Similarly, HRM research in Europe is more often focused on the services sector or the public or not for profit sectors of employment than is the case for the US.

Those in Europe operating in the contextual paradigm seem more likely to challenge the declared corporate strategy and approach to HRM laid down by senior management by asking whether these have deleterious consequences for individuals within the organization, for the long-term health of the organization and for the community and country within which the organization operates.

The practice of HRM in Europe

Clearly, the practice of HRM cannot be divorced from its institutional context or the way that the subject is conceived. The North American model may be a viable possibility for US organizations because of the context within which they operate. Whether it can – or should – be replicated in the European context is a matter of empirical evidence and opinion. Looking at Europe, we have to be more aware of the cultural, regional and sectoral differences and adopt a contingent (Forster and Whipp, 1995) or contextual (Brewster, 1999) approach.

Different models of HRM have been offered by European researchers (Thurley and Wirdenius, 1990; Brewster and Bournois, 1991; Sparrow and Hiltrop, 1994). What they have in common is the need to adopt a multi-level view of the actors in the system and to see business strategy, HR strategy and HR practice located within an environment of national culture, national legislation, state involvement and trade union representation. These factors are seen as part of HRM and not merely as antecedents to it.

How does this play out in practice? It is not possible to cover all aspects of HRM within the scope of an article, but a few examples are given below.

The nature of work

One issue that is attracting increasing attention throughout the world is the issue of flexibility in labour patterns. This is an area bedevilled with terminological problems. This paper uses the term 'flexibility', adopting the terminology most commonly used in Europe. The European Commission prefers the term 'atypical working' and some trade unionists talk about 'vulnerable work'. Certain aspects of this subject are referred to as 'contingent working' in the United States of America. Arguably, all of these terms are to a degree inaccurate and certainly all the terms come with their own metaphorical baggage. Whatever the terminology, the assumption has been made that, with the amount of employment legislation and the embeddedness of the trade unions in the EU, the European workforce is highly inflexible and that this is linked to high levels of unemployment in some European states (see European Commission, 1995).

The evidence shows that this is wrong. Our research, comparing organizations at national level across Europe (Brewster and Tregaskis, 2003; Tregaskis and Brewster, 2006) is consistent with the national labour market statistics (European Commission, various) in showing extensive and growing use of flexible working across Europe. Furthermore, some of these forms of flexibility (temporary employment and self-employment) are more widespread in Europe than in the US, and in others (part-time work) the US has about a median position on a ranking with the European countries (Standing, 1997).

Overall, organizations in Europe have tended to increase their use of contingent employment contracts over the last decade or so, although the pattern of use remains distinctive in each country (Tregaskis and Brewster, 2006).

Temporary and fixed-term contracts are underpinned by different legal and industrial relations frameworks across Europe. During the 1990s, temporary contracts were not highly regulated except in Germany, where there was a lower use of these contracts. The more liberal legislation elsewhere enabled a greater degree of commonality in organizational practice in terms of the adoption of temporary contracts. Equally, fixed-term contracts in, for example, the UK and Sweden are less favourable to the employer and as a result are used less by organizations in those countries. New common EU level requirements may change these country level differences.

Training and development

Education and training provision is to a considerable degree influenced by the educational and training infrastructure and the concomitant social and technical relationships that go with them and will have a significant effect on an organization's RHM and SHRM (Boxall, 1995; Mabey, 2004). Although human resource development practices vary considerably by country in Europe (Mabey, 2004; Tregaskis 1997), in world comparative terms the provision is extensive and of good quality. State support for post-education training is also high and gives these countries an advantage in country level competitive terms (Porter, 1990; Wever, 1995). Furthermore, while decentralization and devolvement mean that (as in the USA) many specialists are unable to say how much their organizations spent on training, employer expenditure is considerable and provides significant numbers of days training for all levels of employees (Brewster *et al.*, 2004). Furthermore, this training is evaluated systematically by most organizations. In terms of subject matter, people management and supervisory training was the highest priority in most of Europe.

The managerial role

Key to the concept of HRM is the notion of a strategic role for HR specialists and the responsibility of line managers for HRM.

On the first issue, it was pointed out some time ago that the rhetoric of the integration of the HR specialist function at the board level has outpaced the reality (Legge, 2005). That has not changed (Brewster *et al.*, 2004), although there have been some small increases in such integration in some countries, notably Germany. Of course, in a number of European countries – most clearly, but not exclusively, Germany and the Netherlands – HRM issues are bought into the strategic level discussions by the presence of employee representatives on the board. In other cases, the presence of works councils with legal power, or pervasive unionism, means that in practice the interests of the employees feature in all major operational decisions.

The debate about the growing role of line managers in strategic (and indeed in operational) HRM is widespread in Europe. The notion of line management accepting greater responsibility for human resource management (HRM) within employing organizations is now received wisdom, but it is not unproblematic (Brewster and Larsen, 2000; Renwick, 2000). Line managers may not want this responsibility; they may not have the time to deal with it properly; they may not have the ability to handle HR issues effectively; nor the training for it; they are often ignorant about recent developments in thinking about HRM; they may not take a comprehensive organizational or longer term view of the topic; and they are poor at making policy in this area.

Overall, the trends are complex: there seems to be evidence of increased line management responsibility, but it is patchy and the situation appears not to have changed that much over the last decade and a half. Those countries that always had a lot of line manager involvement in HRM (such as Denmark) tend to stay at that end of the scale; those that have much less (such as the UK) tend to stay at the opposite end of the scale. European countries stay distinctive in the way that they manage their HRM.

Communication and consultation with employees

Some of the key questions in SHRM are about communication and consultation with the workforce. Employee representation, or 'voice', may take individual or collective forms. The collective forms include both union-centred and non-union mechanisms. The range and type of employee representation and involvement is a defining feature of different national business systems, as demonstrated in the extensive literature on the varieties of capitalism (Amable, 2003; Hall and Soskice, 2000; Whitley, 1999). Individually, effective communication, it could be argued, is at the heart of effective human resource management. Therefore, it might be expected to be increasingly common everywhere. There are, however, good reasons to suppose that cultural differences, in particular the influence of hierarchy (Hofstede, 2001; House *et al.*, 2004), will have an impact on the way that managers communicate to their workforce, so that the drive for greater efficiency, which might lead to convergence, will be counteracted to some degree by the national cultures. It is certainly going to be influenced by the institutional and legislative issues noted above.

There is now clear evidence that organizations across Europe are increasing the amount of communication and consultation in which they involve those employees (Brewster *et al.*, 2004). If there has been a tendency to associate the concept of HRM developed in the USA with the individualization of communication and a move away from, or even antagonism towards, the concept of communication and consultation which is collective, and particularly that which is trade union based, that is not occurring in Europe. The EU's Works Council Directive and the desire of organizations to use as many communications channels as possible has ensured that although there has been a growth in the use of individual channels of communication, the collective channels are still widely used amongst larger employers at least. In Europe, both individual and representational communication are growing (Morley *et al.*, 1996). There has been an increase in the use of direct verbal and direct written mechanisms, potentially reflecting the necessity to increase employee commitment in order to achieve organizational success. This increase, however, runs in parallel with the collective channels, thus supporting the argument that the two are not incompatible (Brewster *et al.*, 2007).

Conclusions

The evidence suggests that in Europe there is a tendency towards labour market deregulation; more extensive training and development of staff; increased flexibility; ever-greater line management influence; increasing individual communication and reducing trade union membership. As such, this is reflective of the findings of researchers on HRM in the USA. Comparison of policies and practices is made difficult by the fact that there is little large-scale evidence of HRM practices in the United States. There is a danger therefore of comparing what is happening in most organizations in Europe with more limited examples from the US.

It seems fairly clear, however, that many aspects of HRM practice are different. For example, those adopting a universalist viewpoint would see the increasing institutional and legislative influence of the European Union on employment contracts as an outside influence rather than part of HRM. The fact that employers in Europe are increasing communication through trade union influenced consultation structures and that it is employee representation that ensures that HR issues are included in strategic decision-making are difficult to explain without reference to the contextual paradigm. The European evidence suggests that managements, particularly perhaps in the Nordic countries, can see the unions, for example, as social partners with a positive role to play in human resource management. The successful integration of HRM with collective bargaining and more traditional approaches to industrial relations, dependent on employers co-operating with union representatives, and unions adopting a less adversarial approach, which has been called for by American critiques of the HRM concept (Kochan, 1999; Strauss, 1992), already exists in parts of Europe.

These empirical differences have important implications for practitioners. Even for those accepting that the focus of HRM should be on improving the performance of the firm, Gerhart has argued that 'it seems unlikely that one set of HRM practices will work equally well no matter what the context' (Gerhart, 2005; 178). Bloom and Milkovich (1999) point to the twin needs of understanding both the contextual differences surrounding an organization (at local, national and continental levels) and the strategic portfolios of the organization.

More generally, the representative data supports theoretical (Smith and Meiksins, 1995) and case study evidence (Ferner and Quintanilla, 2002), which indicated the complexity of these issues, the national embeddedness of HRM practices and the dynamic nature of evolving national business systems. Beyond the empirical evidence of difference, this paper has argued that, compared to the USA, the country of origin of HRM, there are conceptual differences in the way that HRM is viewed in Europe. The more critical approach to HRM found in much of the European literature adds an extra dimension to our knowledge of HRM. The study of HRM in general will only be enhanced by further debate between these researchers and those working from a universalist paradigm.

References

Albert, M. (1991) *Capitalisme contre Capitalisme*. Paris: Seuil.

Amable, B. (2003) *The Diversity of Modern Capitalism*. Oxford: Oxford University Press.

Beaumont, P.B. (1991) 'The US Human Resource Management Literature: A Review'. In Salaman, G. (ed.) *Human Resource Strategies*. Milton Keynes, The Open University.

Becker, B., Huselid, M., Pickus, P. and Spratt, M. (1997) 'HR as a Source of Shareholder Value: Research and Recommendations', *Human Resource Management*, 36(1): 39–47.

Beer, M., Spector, B., Lawrence, P., Quinn-Mills, D. and Walton, R. (1984) *Managing Human Assets: The Groundbreaking Harvard Business School Program.* New York: The Free Press.

Blanchard, O. (1999) 'European Unemployment: The Role of Shocks and Institutions', unpublished working paper, Massachusetts Institute of Technology.

Blanchflower, D. and Freeman, R. (1990) 'Going Different Ways: Unionism in the US and Other Advanced OECD countries', Centre for Economic Performance Discussion Paper 5, London, LSE.

Bloom, M. and Milkovich, G. (1999) 'An SHRM Perspective on International Compensation and Reward Systems'. In Wright, P. M., Dyer, L. D., Boudreau, J. W. and Milkovich, G. T. (eds) *Strategic Human Resources Management in the Twenty-First Century. Research in Personnel and Human Resource Management*, Supplement 4: 283–303.

Boulin, J.-Y., Lallement, M., Messenger, J.C. and Michon, F. (eds) (2006) *Decent Working Time: New Trends, New Issues.* Geneva: ILO.

Boxall, P. (1995) 'Building the Theory of Comparative HRM', *Human Resource Management Journal*, 5(5): 5–17.

Brewster, C. (1995) 'Towards a European Model of Human Resource Management', *Journal of International Business Studies*, 26(1): 1–21.

Brewster, C. (1999) 'Strategic Human Resource Management: The Value of Different Paradigms', *Management International Review*, 39: 45–64.

Brewster, C. (2005) 'European Perspectives on Human Resource Management', *Human Resource Management Review*, 14(4): 365–82.

Brewster, C. and Bournois, F. (1991) 'A European Perspective on Human Resource Management', *Personnel Review*, 20(6): 4–13.

Brewster, C. and Larsen, H.H. (2000) 'Responsibility in Human Resource Management: The Role of the Line'. In Brewster, C. and Larsen, H.H. (eds) *Human Resource Management in Northern Europe.* Oxford: Blackwell.

Brewster, C. and Tregaskis, O. (2003) 'Convergence or Divergence of Contingent Employment Practices? Evidence of The Role of MNCs in Europe'. In Cooke, W. (ed.) *Multinational Companies and Global Human Resource Strategies.* Greenwood, IL: Quorum Books, pp. 143–66.

Brewster, C., Mayrhofer, W. and Morley, M. (eds) (2004) *Human Resource Management in Europe: Evidence of Convergence?* London: Butterworth Heinemann.

Brewster, C., Wood, G., Croucher, C. and Brookes, M. (2007) 'Are Works Councils and Joint Consultative Committees a Threat to Trade Unions? A Comparative Analysis', *Economic and Industrial Democracy*, 1, forthcoming.

Brookes, M., Brewster, C. and Wood, G. (2005) 'Social Relations, Firms and Societies: A Study of Institutional Embeddedness', *International Sociology*, 20(4): 403–26.

Cappelli, P. and Newmark, D. (2001) 'Do "High-performance" Work Practices Improve Establishment Level Outcomes?', *Industrial and Labour Relations Review*, 54(4): 737–75.

DiMaggio, P.J. and Powell, W.W. (1983) 'The Iron Cage Revisited: Institutional Isomorphism and Collective Rationality in Organizational Fields', *American Sociological Review*, 48: 147–60.

Drucker, P.F. (1989) *The New Realities: in Government and Politics, in Economics and Business, in Society and World View.* New York: Harper & Row.

Due, J., Madsen, J.S. and Jensen, C.S. (1991) 'The Social Dimension: Convergence or Diversification of IR in the Single European Market?', *Industrial Relations Journal*, 22(2): 85–102.

Dyer, L. and Kochan, T. (1995) 'Is There a New HRM? Contemporary Evidence and Future Directions'. In Downie, B., Kumar, P. and Coates, M.L. (eds) *Managing Human Resources in the 1990s and Beyond: Is the Workplace Being Transformed?* Kingston, Ontario: Industrial Relations Centre Press, Queen's University.

EIRO (2002) *Collective Bargaining Coverage and Extensions Procedures.* Dublin: European Foundation for the Improvement of Living and Working Conditions.

European Commission (1995) *Employment in Europe.* Luxembourg: DG for Employment, Industrial Relations and Social Affairs, Office for Official Publications of the European Communities.

Farmer, R.N. and Richman, B.M. (1965) *Comparative Management and Economic Progress.* Homewood, IL: Irwin.

Ferner, A. and Quintanilla, J. (2002) 'Between Globalization and Capitalist Variety: Multinationals and the International Diffusion of Employment Relations', *European Journal of Industrial Relations*, 8(3): 243–51.

Filella, J. (1991) 'Is There a Latin Model in the Management of Human Resources?', *Personnel Review*, 20(6): 14–23.

Fombrun, C., Tichy, N. and Devanna, M. (1984) *Strategic Human Resource Management.* John Wiley and Sons.

Forster, N. and Whipp, R. (1995) 'Future of European Human Resource Management: A Contingent Approach', *European Management Journal*, 13: 434–42.

Geppert, M., Matten, J. and Williams, K. (2003) 'Global, National and local Practices in Multinational Corporations – Towards a Socio-political Framework'. Paper for seminar on the diffusion of HRM to Europe and the role of US multinationals, 5 December, Cranfield School of Management.

Gerhart, B. (1999) 'Human Resource Management and Firm Performance: Measurement Issues and Their Effect on Causal and Policy Inferences'. In Wright, P., Dyer, L., Boudreau, J. and Milkovich, G. (eds) *Research in Personnel and HRM.* Greenwich, CT: JAI Press Inc.

Gerhart, B. (2005) 'Human Resources and Business Performance: Findings, Unanswered Questions and an Alternative Approach', *Management Revue*, 16: 174–85.

Gronhaug, K. and Nordhaug, O. (1992) 'Strategy and Competence in Firms', *European Management Journal*, 10(4): 438–45.

Guest, D.E. (1990) 'Human Resource Management and the American Dream', *Journal of Management Studies*, 27(4): 377–97.

Guest, D.E. (1997) 'Human Resource Management and Performance: a Review and a Research Agenda', *International Journal of Human Resource Management*, 8. 263–76.

Guest, D.E., Michie, J., Conway, N. and Sheehan, M. (2003) 'Human Resource Management and Corporate Performance in the UK', *British Journal of Industrial Relations*, 41: 291–314.

Hall, P.A. and Soskice, D. (2001) *Varieties of Capitalism: The Institutional Foundations of Comparative Advantage.* Oxford: Oxford University Press.

Hickson, D., Hinings, C.R., McMillan, C.J. and Schwitter, J.P. (1974) 'The Culture-free Context of Organization Structure: A Tri-National Comparison', *Sociology*, 8: 59–80.

Hofstede, G. (2001) *Culture's Consequences: Comparing Values, Behaviours, Institutions, and Organizations Across Nations*, 2nd edn. Thousand Oaks: Sage.

Hollingsworth, J.R. and Boyer, R. (1997) 'Coordination of Economic Actors and Social Systems of Production'. In Hollingsworth, J.R. and Boyer, R. (eds) *Contemporary Capitalism.* Cambridge: Cambridge University Press.

House, R.J., Hanges, P.J., Javidan, M., Dorfman, P.W. and Gupta, V. (2004) *Culture, Leadership and Organizations: the GLOBE Study of 62 Societies.* New York: Sage.

Huselid, M. (1995) 'The Impact of Human Resource Management Practices on Turnover, Productivity and Corporate Financial Performance', *Academy of Management Journal*, 38: 635–72.

Huselid, M.A. and Becker, B.E. (1996) 'Methodological Issues in Cross-sectional and Panel Estimates of the Human Resource-Firm Performance Link', *Industrial Relations*, 35: 400–22.

Ignjatovic, M. and Sveltic, I. (2003) 'European HRM clusters', *ESB Review*, 17: 25–39.

Jackson, S. and Schuler, R. (1995) 'Understanding Human Resource Management in the Context of Organizations and Their Environments', *Annual Review of Psychology*, 46: 237–64.

Kidger, P.J. (1991) 'The Emergence of International Human Resource Management', *International Journal of Human Resource Management*, 2(2): 149–63.

Kochan, T. (1999) 'Beyond Myopia: Human Resources and the Changing Social Contract'. In Wright, P., Dyer, L., Boudreau, J. and Milkovich, G. (eds) *Research in Personnel and HRM.* Greenwich, CT: JAI Press Inc., pp. 199–212.

Kochan, T., Batt, R. and Dyer, R. (1992) 'International Human Resource Studies: A Framework for Future Research'. In Lewin, D., Mitchell, O.S. and Sherer, P.D. (eds) *Research Frontiers in*

Industrial Relations and Human Resources. Madison, WI: Industrial Relations Research Association.

Kochan, T., Katz, H. and McKersie, R. (1986) *The Transformation of American Industrial Relations.* New York: Basic Books.

Kuhn, T. (1970) *The Structure of Scientific Revolutions.* Chicago: University of Chicago Press.

Lane, C. (1989) *Management and Labour in Europe.* London: Edward Elgar.

Legge, K. (2005) *Human Resource Management: Rhetorics and Realities.* Basingstoke: Macmillan.

Locke, R., Piore, M. and Kochan, T. (1995) 'Introduction'. In Locke, R., Kochan, T. and Piore, M. (eds) *Employment Relations in a Changing World Economy.* Cambridge, MA: MIT Press, pp. 359–84.

Luthans, F., Marsnik, P. and Luthans, K. (1997) 'A Contingency Matrix Approach to IHRM', *Human Resource Management*, 36(2): 183–99.

Mabey, C. (2004) 'Developing Managers in Europe: Policies, Practices and Impact', *Advances in Developing Human Resources*, 6(4): 404–27.

Marchington, M. and Grugulis, I. (2000) '"Best Practice" Human Resource Management: Perfect Opportunity or Dangerous Illusion?', *International Journal of Human Resource Management*, 11(6): 1104–24.

Maurice, M., Sellier, F. and Silvestre, J. (1986) *The Social Foundations of Industrial Power.* Cambridge, MA: MIT Press.

Morley, M., Brewster, C., Gunnigle, P. and Mayrhofer, W. (1996) 'Evaluating Change in European Industrial Relations: Research Evidence on Trends at Organizational Level', *International Journal of Human Resource Management*, 7(3): 640–56.

Morley, M., Mayrhofer, W. and Brewster, C. (2000) 'Communication in Organizations: Dialogue and Impact'. In Brewster, C. and Holt-Larsen, H. (eds) *Human Resource Management in Northern Europe: Trends, Dilemmas and Strategy.* Oxford: Blackwell.

OECD (2006) *OECD Annual Employment Outlook.* Paris: OECD.

Paauwe, J. and Boselie, P. (2005) 'Best Practices . . . . in Spite of Performance: Just a Matter of Imitation?', *International Journal of Human Resource Management*, 16: 987–1003.

Pieper, R. (ed.) (1990) *Human Resource Management: An International Comparison.* Berlin: Walter de Gruyter.

Poole, M. (1990) 'Human Resource Management in an International Perspective', *International Journal of Human Resource Management*, 1(1): 1–15.

Purcell, J. and Ahlstrand, B. (1994) *Human Resource Management in the Multi-Divisional Company.* New York: Oxford University Press.

Ramirez, M. (2004) 'Comparing European Approaches to Management Education, Training and Development', *Advances in Developing Human Resources*, 6(4): 428–50.

Renwick, D. (2000) 'HR-Line Work Relations: A Review, Pilot Case and Research Agenda', *Employee Relations*, 22(1/2): 179–201.

Ronen, S. and Shenkar, O. (1985) 'Clustering Countries on Attitudinal Dimensions: A Review and Synthesis', *Academy of Management Journal*, September: 435–54.

Rose, M. (1991) 'Comparing Forms of Comparative Analysis', *Political Studies*, 39: 446–62.

Schuler, R.S., Dowling, P.J. and De Cieri, H. (1993) 'An Integrative Framework of Strategic International Human Resource Management', *International Journal of Human Resource Management*, 4(4): 717–64.

Schwartz, S.H. (1992) 'Universals in the Content and Structure of Values: Theoretical Advances and Empirical Tests in 20 Countries'. In Zanna, M.P. (ed.) *Advances in Experimental Social Psychology*, Vol. XXV. San Diego, CA: Academic Press.

Schwartz, S.H. (1994) 'Beyond Individualism/collectivism, New Cultural Dimensions of Values'. Cross-Cultural Research and Methodology Series In Kim, U., Triandis, H., Kâgitçibasi, Ç., Choi, S.-C. and Yoon, G. (eds) *Individualism and Collectivism, Theory, Method and Applications*, Vol. XVIII. London: Sage.

Schwartz, S.H. and Sagiv, L. (1995) 'Identifying Culture-specifics in the Content and Structure of Values', *Journal of Cross-Cultural Psychology*, 26(1): 92–116.

Smith, C. and Meiskins, P. (1995) 'System, Society and Dominance Effects in Cross-national Organisational Analysis', *Work, Employment and Society*, 4(3): 451–70.

Sorge, A. (1991) 'Strategic Fit and the Social Effect: Interpreting Cross-national Comparisons of Technology, Organization and Human Resources', *Organization Studies*, 12: 161–90.

Sparrow, P. and Hiltrop, J.M. (1994) *European Human Resource Management in Transition*. Hemel Hempstead: Prentice Hall.

Sparrow, P., Schuler, R.S. and Jackson, S. (1994) 'Convergence or Divergence: Human Resource Policies and Practices for Competitive Advantage Worldwide', *International Journal of Human Resource Management*, 5(2): 267–99.

Spony, G. (2003) 'The Development of a Work-value Model assessing the Cumulative Impact of Individual and Cultural Differences on Managers' Work-value Systems: Empirical Evidence form French and British Managers', *International Journal of Human Resource Management*, 14(4): 658–79.

Standing, G. (1997) 'Globalisation, Labour Flexibility and Insecurity: The Era of Market Regulation', *European Journal of Industrial Relations*, 3(1): 7–37.

Stavrou, E.T. and Brewster, C. (2005) 'The Configurational Approach to Linking Strategic Human Resource Management Bundles With Business Performance: Myth or Reality?', *Management Revue*, 16(2): 186–201.

Strauss, G. (1992) 'Human Resource Management in the USA'. In Towers, B. (ed.) *Handbook of Human Resource Mangement*. Oxford: Blackwell.

Thomson, A., Mabey, C., Storey, J., Gray, C. and Iles, P. (eds) (2001) *Changing Patterns of Management Development*. Oxford: Blackwell.

Thurley, K. and Wirdenius, H. (1990) *Towards European Management*. London: Pitman.

Tregaskis, O. (1997) 'The Role of National Context and HR Strategy in Shaping Training and Development Practice in French and UK Organisations', *Organization Studies*, 18(5): 857–75.

Tregaskis, O. and Brewster, C. (2006) 'Converging or Diverging? A Comparative Analysis of Trends in Contingent Employment Practice in Europe over a Decade', *Journal of International Business Studies*, 37(1): 111–26.

Trompenaars, A. (1985) 'Organisation of Meaning and the Meaning of Organisation: A Comparative Study on the Conception of Organisational Structure in Different Cultures'. unpublished PhD thesis, University of Pennsylvania (DA 8515460).

Trompenaars, F. (1993) *Riding the Waves of Culture: Understanding Cultural Diversity in Business*. London: Economist Books.

Ulrich, D. (1989) 'Assessing Human Resource Effectiveness: Stakeholder, Utility, and Relationship Approaches', *Human Resource Planning*, 12(4): 301–15.

US Department of Labor (1993) *High Performance Work Practices and Firm Performance*. Washington, DC: US Government Printing Office.

Walsh, K. (1985) *Trade Union Membership, Method and Measurement in the European Community*. Luxembourg: Eurostat.

Weber, W. and Kabst, R. (2004) 'Human Resource Management: The Need for Theory and Diversity', *Management Revue*, 15: 171–7.

Wever, K. (1995) *Negotiating Competitiveness: Employment Relations and Industrial Adjustment in the USA and Germany*. Boston: Harvard Business School Press.

Whitley, R. (1999) *Divergent Capitalisms: The Social Structuring and Change of Business Systems*. Oxford: Oxford University Press.

Wood, S. (1999) 'Human Resource Management and Performance', *International Journal of Human Resource Management*, 1: 367–413.

Wright, P.M. and McMahan, G.C. (1992) 'Theoretical Perspectives for Strategic Human Resource Management', *Journal of Management*, 18(2): 295–320.

Wright, P.M. and Snell, S.A. (1991) 'Toward an Integrative View of Strategic Human Resource Management', *Human Resource Management Review*, 1: 203–25.

Vertical integration of corporate management in international firms: implementation of HRM and the asset specificities of firms in China

Yanni Yan, John Child and Chan Yan Chong

Introduction

Scholars of corporate management have highlighted how business success is dependent upon a combination of vertical integration decisions that define whether a firm's goods or services should be transferred in-house or sold to outsiders (Birkinshaw *et al.*, 1998). The study of vertical firm-specific asset boundaries has received considerable attention due to the issues of asset heterogeneity, the imperfect mobility of resources and the effective utilization of organizational capabilities (Barney and Arikan, 2001). In service industries, corporate management is increasingly driven by rapid changes in the business environment, such as technology transformation, economic upheaval and heightened market competition, and many service firms are actively searching for new ways in which to improve their organizational structure to gain increased levels of organizational collaboration, enhanced operational excellence and improved quality of information exchange (Bhandarker, 2003). Previous studies highlight the notion that the vertical integration of corporate management implies a rationalization of long-term business development, as the level of a firm's structural efficiency is mainly dependent upon the degree of management coherence in cross-functional collaboration (Edwards and Kuruvilla, 2005). Other studies have demonstrated that the co-ordination between the various management levels of a firm is associated with the organizational alignment of one function to other related functions in making joint decisions on business development (Grewal and Tansuhai, 2001). Furthermore, the vertical integration of a firm's management is related to the synergistic benefits that result from the introduction of human resource management (HRM) as an institutionally supported package (Yan, 2003). It follows that studies on corporate management have become critically important in the process of strategic management, especially when the vertical integration of human assets specificities involves significant organizational changes (Meilich, 2005).

Scholars assert that an efficient HRM function can exert a positive influence on people-related competencies and management endowments (Maxwell *et al.*, 2004). Heffernan and Flood (2000) argue that the advantage of the vertical integration of a firm's asset specificities rests in its managing principles and its ability to organize the relationships that exist between top and line management within the organization. Specifically, they argue that the role of vertical integration in corporate management, such as the promotion of a firm's top management mandate, is often perceived to be key to the integration of the business strategies of an organization. The study of the vertical integration of corporate management has recently been extended to incentive structures (Coase, 1937), ownership (Grossman and Hart, 1986), competitive factors (Birkinshaw *et al.*, 1995), manager initiatives (Roth and Morrison, 1992), human resource development (Wright *et al.*, 2001) and transaction costs economics (Williamson, 1999). Harrigan (1986: 535) states that firms face a host of structural decisions about whether to adopt full integration, tapered integration or quasi-integration. She investigates 192 firms that operate in diverse strategic environments to ascertain how the successful deployment of vertical integration differs from less successful deployments, and concludes that the vertical integration of corporate management is influenced by factors such as industry structure and evolution, competitive posture and the strategic position of the firm. Previous studies have examined whether the definition of vertical firm-specific resource boundaries is intimately associated with the development structure in which a firm's asset specificities are embedded and the means through which the firm accesses and influences managers who are controlled by the local organizational infrastructures (Marchington and Vincent, 2004; Mota and De Castro, 2004).

Studies of the effects of vertical integration on corporate management concentrate on one of three areas. The first is strategic orientation, which is increasingly employed to guide businesses, as it provides a method for planning the coordination of a firm's business development activities. The drive to achieve a strategic orientation can act as trigger for an organization to accomplish its missions and goals (Grewal and Tansuhai, 2001). More specifically, a firm's strategic orientation for the achievement of long-term business development is closely related to the assessment of the business environment, the recognition of corporate culture and an emphasis on performance evaluation (Maxwell *et al.*, 2004). The second area is contractual control, which is seen as pivotal to ensuring that service qualities are well managed. Contractual power over a firm's asset specificities mainly serves to mobilize, allocate and leverage resources and capabilities. Studies of transactional cost economics have provided rich insights into how a firm's underlying transactional efficiencies vary through contractual control to safeguard its asset specificities. The final area of vertical integration is organization formalization, which establishes the specific rules, regulations, procedures and authority relations that characterize the operations of an organization (Meilich, 2005). Studies on the notion of organization formalization systematically examine the extent to which a firm's rules and regulations are appropriately employed and upgraded.

The empirical analysis of the vertical integration of corporate management has increasingly captured the interest of many academics and practitioners (Ding *et al.*, 1997; Luo, 2002; Schroeder *et al.*, 2002). There has been an increasing interest in the effective use of vertical firm-specific assets and HRM in national or global business surroundings when a firm is predominantly constrained by its heritage of administrative traditions. Scholars have identified that the vertical integration of corporate management within actual organizational settings provides little effective control over the assets of firms, and that their HRM policies remain vague (Edwards and Kuruvilla, 2005). Nevertheless, there is conflicting evidence as to whether a firm's administrative heritage directly affects its asset advantages in a volatile and dynamic environment (Cannon *et al.*, 2000). Although previous studies have mainly concentrated on the economic use of a firm's assets within the context of choices about how a firm's integration arrangements should be directed toward generating products and services (Birkinshaw *et al.*, 1998; Harrigan, 1986: 536), there is an important gap in the empirical research on vertical integration requirements as a basis of institutional development for a firm's business expansion. Studies of structural efficiencies are important for firms that place an emphasis on the vertical integration of corporate management, because a firm may gain significant benefit from the lessons that are learned across its operations as a result of the diffusion of effective HRM practices, which enhance efficiencies in other parts of the firm's operations (Edwards and Kuruvilla, 2005: 2).

We attempt to uncover whether corporate managements differ in their vertical integration processes. The IJV hotels in China are included in the sample exhibit contrasting asset specificities and distinct HRM practices that provide a broad organizational setting for our investigation. Drawing data from an extensive exploration of IJV hotels highlights how the method of vertical integration of corporate management that is employed influences the nature of a firm's management properties, such as strategic orientation, contractual control and organization formalization. More specifically, the hotel sector contains demonstrated vertically integrated organizations that can be easily contrasted with firms that are not vertically integrated. We analyse vertical integration using three identified integration variables to explore the differences that are exhibited when these variables are implemented individually or in combination to ensure a full exploration of the vertical firm-specific assets and HRM practices of each firm.

The paper is organized as follows. It begins with a brief literature review and a discussion of the hypotheses. The research methods are then described and the findings elaborated. Finally, management insights are drawn in the conclusion.

Vertical HRM and the asset specificities of firms

Harrigan (1986: 538) identifies that the most commonly used measures of vertical integration are the degree, stage, breadth and form of a firm's value chain activities. The degree of internal integration can be measured by the proportion of a particular output that is transferred to integrated units. The number of integrated stages in which a firm engages can be estimated by taking account of the number of steps that are undertaken by a firm in the transformation process. The third measure, breadth of integration, refers to the number of activities at each integrated stage of the process. Finally, the ownership form of integration refers to the percentage of equity that a firm intends to place in an organization.

If one undertakes a transactional costs economics analysis, then the method hinges on the assumption that vertical human asset specificity is associated with higher levels of tacit knowledge and adaptability. Previous studies emphasize that the role of a firm's vertical integration activities is important in terms of its environment transformation, especially if integrated HRM practices are devised to focus on long-term business development (Bhandarker, 2003; Farley *et al.*, 2004). HRM practices are important for firms because they are inherently valuable, scarce and inimitable, and a successful firm invariably takes into account the interactive effects of HRM activities on its performance when corporate management makes vertical integration decisions (Gamble, 2003; Mishra *et al.*, 2001). These studies stressed the importance of HRM practices that take into account a firm's multinational experience, market potential and corporate culture (Dubois, 1998; Law *et al.*, 2004; Talyor *et al.*, 1996).

Edwards and Kuruvilla (2005) believe that strategic orientation should be employed to guide the development of a comprehensive and future-oriented business plan, as it provides an institutional framework within which to orient corporate management. Creating a strategic orientation means delivering a firm's products and services through the ongoing monitoring of market conditions. Scholars assert that studies on strategic orientation should examine the interaction effects of various facets of the environment and a firm's organizational changes. A firm that has achieved a relatively greater market potential is expected to have a strongly established strategic orientation, and if there is a fit between a firm's development priorities and the organizational structures that are put in place for the achievement of long-term business goals, then the firm will be able to exploit its assets effectively. The vertical integration of a firm's strategic orientation is usually accomplished through ongoing monitoring of market conditions and continued organizational adaptation (Slater and Narver, 1994). Given the significance of strategic orientation to service firms, the attainment of a consistently superior performance is largely contingent upon the ability of a firm's business to create a sustainable competitive edge. The development of a strategic orientation should make it possible for a firm to implement business development processes effectively, and although the establishment of long-term business policies has a significant impact on the achievement of new market deployment, such as the establishment of business presence among competitors, the setting of strategic priorities and the appointment of appropriate senior managers are the crucial parts of vertical integration that most influence the effective use of corporate management resources (Guest *et al.*, 2003). Accordingly, it should be no surprise that strategic orientation is generally employed as a useful set of vertical integration guidelines by which managers can effectively coordinate, build and reconfigure their development plans within their organizations.

A strategic orientation that includes vertical integration concepts has become increasingly critical to performance, because a firm must have the ability to integrate its various business, functional and personal expertise to make the major strategic moves to redefine its organization (Eisenhardt and Martin, 2000; Guthrie *et al.*, 2002). Within the constraints of a strategic orientation approach, effective integration decisions may confer benefit to a firm's business networking. Eisenhardt and Galunic (2000) suggest business that networking benefits are the result of 'resource and capability complementarities' within an organization that generate new and synergistic resources. In this context, long-term business decisions are more likely to alter corporate management activities through the vertical integration of human asset specificities (Hoque, 1999). The assessment of a firm's business development in relation to its strategic orientation is perceived to be a method of establishing competitive, economic and efficient rationales that a firm can use to make vertical integration decisions. Although some scholars believe that the establishment of a strategic orientation benefits the development of a firm's asset specificities, others question whether strategic orientation really does provide a platform for the integration of different developments in ways that leverage a firm's asset specificity advantages (Luo *et al.*, 2001). An answer to this question is that if a firm implements a consistent set of development platforms, then there may be a reduction in the cost of information sharing, which is imperative to organizations with fuzzy bounded divisions. However, strategic orientation is also important in guiding the vertical integration decisions that define whether a firm should maintain corporate management control throughout its organizational systems and information reporting and communication networks to achieve superior performance.

> *Hypothesis 1*: The greater the level of vertical integration within corporate management, the better the performance that will be generated through the establishment of a strategic orientation.

Contractual control can be employed to examine how the benefits from the vertical integration of a firm's capital equipment, marketing, information systems, cost structures and innovation can be maximized (Yasai-Ardekani, 1997). The best-known contractual agreements in the service industry are management contracts. Contractual control of a firm's products and services offers a relatively high degree of organizational control, because the in-built explicit control standards and methods can enforce unit conformance. Academics use contractual control to classify the extent to which a binding business contract is used to specify a suitable price for a firm's asset specificities and to define role and obligation of management in using the firm's assets. As one of the primary economic considerations of a firm's business transactions, contractual control over firm-specific assets is seen as a way to create imperfect replication through provisional control, which can protect a firm's assets and mitigate its market transaction costs, even in a high-risk environment (Ghoshal, 1987). Although little is known about the actual influence of contractual control over vertical firm-specific assets, scholars believe that the implementation of contractual control may create various safeguards that regulate a firm's transactional roles when circumstances are ambiguous, especially when the asset value of the ability of a firm to replicate standards and services in multiple locations is high. It is quite clear that the adoption of contractual control in an organization aids resource and knowledge transfers at low costs (Luo *et al.*, 2001), and when a firm employs contractual control over its asset specificities, it should ensure that asset complementarities, such as qualified managerial employees and firm-specific assets, are readily available. The employment of specific contractual control over a firm's proprietary services helps it to increase its productivity and bargaining positions among its competitors. Managers may also minimize difficulties by exercising contractual control over marketing and supplier procedures, which is justified by the understanding that standard transaction costs ensure a consistent corporate management basis for the formulation of suitable pricing policies (Harrigan, 1986). The employment of contractual control by default incorporates the expectations and obligations of a firm's management needs. Scholars who study contractual control suggest that a firm should refrain from entering a market if the perceived risks, knowledge dissipation, deterioration of service quality and cost of enforcing contracts are high. Contractual control enables roles, promises, expectations or obligations to be defined in the execution of business transactions.

The establishment of contractual control over a firm's resources, knowledge and capabilities is believed to provide a necessary condition for the successfully deployment of its assets. According to transaction costs economics, the identification of vertical firm-specific resources and capabilities is also associated with the assessment of the minimal transaction costs of a firm to deliver the desired quantity, price and quality of a supplier's services. If a firm has implemented provisional control over its assets, then it may be able to share its assets at an acceptable long-term risk under certain corporate management considerations. The use of contractual control limits the cost of responding to future contingencies for a firm. Knight (1921) suggests that the provisional use of firm-specific assets should involve the establishment of a firm's development priorities if its asset specificities are to be successfully transferred, assimilated and employed within its organization. Consequently, managers find that the employment of contractual control over assets may contribute positively to the development of the firm's brand name, corporate image and business reputation. However, a firm's ability to redefine the possession and re-composition of its assets on a relatively broad scale is the main reason for the adoption of contractual control (Winter, 1993: 191). It has been suggested that the adoption of contractual control protects a firm's service know-how through legal means that include intellectual property law, copyright, trademarks, patents and licences (Hakansson and Snehota, 1995). Equally, the establishment of contractual control may improve a firm's economic certainty when dealing with the contextual hazards that are caused by its institutional and task environments. As the adoption of contractual control defines a firm's relational properties and reduces its financial risks, scholars have suggested there would be significant benefits to the identification of the key factors that affect a firm's vertical integration decisions in adapting to dynamic markets (Langlois, 1998: 195).

Hypothesis 2: The greater the vertical integration that is employed in corporate management, the better the performance that will be generated through the establishment of contractual control.

Formalization is the most commonly discussed dimension of organizational studies and is often used to diagnose the fuzzy boundaries and structural indeterminacy that determine a firm's integration decisions, particularly when the objective is to achieve organizational efficiency (Meilich, 2005). Studies of formalization are mainly devoted to tracking the degree to which integration decisions are made and whether activities are carried out in accordance with explicit operational routines, lines of authority and working relationships (Hedlund, 1994). The most important explanations of formalization concentrate on the communication quality, management participation, coordination and information exchange of a firm, but other studies have provided theoretical support for the contribution to performance of organizational formalization decisions through the manipulation of the resources and capabilities that are available within a firm (Hewett and Bearden, 2001). The assessment of formalization is imperative, as its consequent procedures, rules and regulations are employed to regulate a firm's behaviour in information sharing, decision reporting and corporate culture, and such organizational routines may determine what, where and how a firm should respond to corporate management decisions (Meyer and Scott, 1992). Recent research has emphasized that formalization is a primary rationale for the vertical integration of corporate management activities, and scholars have tested this notion by studying how officially established rules, regulations and procedures are employed to regulate the behaviour of corporate management activities. The effect of the complementary relationship between corporate management activities and formalized control over a firm's performance can help in the systematic searches for information that are occur within an organization (Becker and Huselid, 1998).

The vertical integration of the units in a firm's business development portfolio has been identified as a critical channel of corporate management (Araujo *et al.*, 2003). Formalization is aimed at the continuation of current capital, product and knowledge flows within an organization, which is critical to the survival of a firm's operations (Thompson, 1967). A primary function of formalization is to help a firm to engage in a more systematic scanning of organizational information. Formalization provides not only an operating platform for the making of decisions about how existing stocks of firm-specific resources and capabilities are mobilized, but also allows a firm to benefit from the scale economies of the marketplace while avoiding the bureaucratic disadvantages that accompany its integration decisions (Grossman and Hart, 1986). Equally, formalization can be employed to aid the creation of architectural resources and new capabilities (Loasby, 1998). As formalization can also increase efficiency, provide greater flexibility and increase organizational learning, a firm needs to ensure that its managers have concrete and mutual experiences of working together in a way that increases their commitment to operations. When formalization is well established, it may positively influence both the process and outcome of the vertical integration decisions of corporate management. There is evidence of the positive impact of formalization on a firm's performance, and it might be expected to exert a great influence on corporate management activities in areas such as the processes of acquiring supplies, producing services and delivering services to customers, and the provision of after sales service (Porter, 1985). In this study, formalization refers to the way in which organizational efficiencies are achieved, and includes the establishment of hierarchical decentralization and lateral communication (Moorman and Miner, 1998). As a complement to formalization, the regulation of a firm's network may reduce its vulnerability to the market hazards to which it is exposed.

Hypothesis 3: The greater the vertical integration of corporate management activities, the better the performance that will be generated through the establishment of formalization.

The asset specificities of vertical firms are widely regarded to be key to the attainment and sustenance of competitive advantage. The more specific the assets employed by a firm, the greater are their potential as a source of competitive advantage. Although the asset specificities that relate to vertical integration may be viewed as heterogeneous in their distribution, conventional studies highlight that the effective use of these asset specificities is primarily determined by environmental forces (Chekitan *et al.*, 2002). Studies on the identification of the idiosyncratic resources, knowledge and capabilities of a firm have been extended to the structure of management properties that involve strategic orientation, contractual control and formalization. Normative decision theory suggests that vertical firm-specific assets should be based upon trade-offs between risk and return (Leiblein and Miller, 2003), and given the various choices that are available in most integration decisions, the effects of the vertical integration of a firm's asset specificities may be felt in a firm's business transactions, which is where such decisions are implemented through the integration of value chain activities. A firm is expected to choose the vertical integration decision that offers the highest risk-adjusted return on its asset specificities. From the viewpoint of the resource-based advantages that are appropriated within and between organizations, a vertically integrated firm will display a set of idiosyncratic resources and capabilities that are embedded in its economic needs, and will use its available network of relationships to influence the distribution of its asset specificities (Araujo *et al.*, 2003; Mota and Castro, 2004). However, behavioural evidence indicates that vertical integration decisions can be determined by the availability of assets and the control needs of corporate management. A firm that expects to possess additional superior resources, knowledge and skills may find that making vertical integration decisions can help its organization to achieve economic gains that are sufficient to counter the higher cost of servicing in the host market.

The theory of vertical integration has been studied through the examination of the differences between a firm's asset specificities and its development structure to measure transaction costs (Coase, 1937). Vertically integrated firm-specific assets are generally classified into the three categories: physical resources, which encompass buildings, equipment, facilities and locations; tacit resources, which comprise skills, knowledge, expertise, brands, patents and trademarks; and organizational resources, which include management reporting, organizational relationships and corporate culture. The vertical integration of firm's asset specificities helps the entire organization to achieve the benefits of an extensive use of the firm's physical, tacit and organizational resource bases (Leiblein and Miller, 2003). Furthermore, decisions that are made on the vertical integration of firm-specific assets can be used to explain how a firm's economic requirements may have influenced its systems, methods and performance. In the past firms may have made different integration decisions about the best use of their assets, but Gold *et al.* (2001) state that an effective way for firms to reinforce their business reputation is the use of branding. The effective use of organizational resources includes the establishment of corporate culture, empowerment and organizational and management principles. In addition, Srivastava *et al.* (2001) suggest that a firm's asset specificity is reflected by its ability to develop differentiated products or services. Although the vertical integration of firm-specific assets is expected to place an emphasis on acquisition, conversion, application and protection, it is more likely that the competitive ability of a firm's management will be derived from the provision of a wide range of amenities, quality service, low prices and superior promotion (Hewett and Bearden, 2001).

> *Hypothesis 4*: The greater the vertical integration of corporate management, the better the performance will be that is generated through the establishment of a strategic orientation, contractual control and formalization.

Research methods

Sample

The primary objective of this study is to examine the impact of vertical integration on corporate management activities that involve strategic orientation, contractual control and formalization. The data were collected from interviews with managers of IJV hotels in China by an independent management research project team. The National Tourist Bureau of China provided the requisite contact information for the hotels, and all of hotels in this study are located in Beijing, Shanghai or Guangdong province. The sample consists of IJV hotels that are jointly owned by local and foreign firms, with foreign equity shares ranging from 30 to 90 per cent. Where there are multiple local or foreign partners, the majority parent firm normally takes the most active part in the management. The completed sample was limited to 136 IJV hotels by the constraints of funding, timescale and the location of the research team. The final sample represents a positive response rate of approximately 20 per cent of all of the hotels that were contacted. The IJV hotels in this study are mostly large employers with more than 400 employees. On-site visits were made to all of the hotels and records were consulted to obtain financial information where permission was granted. Background firm documentation was also collected. The IJV hotels that were approached were able to provide high-quality data that allow us to generate useful insights into the multiple aspects of the vertical integration of corporate management activities.

A checklist was developed in both English and Chinese and verified by a process of translation and back-translation to ensure the conceptual equivalence of the alternative renditions. The developed checklist used IJV hotels as the unit of analysis. Our research team used the closed-end checklist to conduct interviews with IJV hotel managers, including the general manager, deputy general manager, financial controller, front office manager, marketing director and human resources manager. We decided that the respondents would need to hold a managerial position in the IJV hotel firm to have a sufficient understanding of its corporate management activities. We sent each IJV hotel two questionnaires that included a section on company background, the purpose of which was to identify any major contradictory factors that might arise from the response of two or more IJV hotel managers from the same establishment. We discussed the checklist with the hotel managers to confirm the clarity of the instructions and to determine the scaling of the items. The validity of each question in the checklist was assessed according to the suggestions of the hotel managers that were interviewed, together with comments from the research project team. We checked for the threat of common method variance by conducting a factor analysis, in which all of the variables were revealed in the checklist. Table 1 shows that a single factor did not emerge and that there was no general factor that could account for the majority of the covariance in these variables, which suggests that there is no noticeable threat of common method variance.

Measurement of the variables

The depth of the checklist combined with the good quality of information provided a sound basis for analysis and allowed useful conclusions to be drawn. The reason for choosing the hotel sector for this study is that the firms in this sector have many common organizational characteristics in terms of the vertical integration of corporate management activities. An IJV hotel must involve its managers in the handling of 'service complexities' given the rapid changes in international service standards and in the local business environment (Cai *et al.*, 2000), and the theoretical development of firm-specific assets and HRM is significantly influenced by the needs of corporate management to continuously upgrade its international service standards (Dunning and Kundu, 1995; Gamble, 2003). The vertical integration of corporate management activities in the hotel service sector is relevant because the upstream value chain activities of such firms are primarily dominated by service expertise and service knowledge, whereas the downstream activities are affected by service offerings and sale promotions (Yu, 1999). The influence of hotel management activities in this study is measured by the specific service packages of the IJV hotels, including the rapidity of the acceptance of new products by customers, economies of scale in marketing-support expenditure and the level of risk that is associated with the introduction of a new manual (Hoque, 1999).

IJV hotels that operate in China are reported to emphasize strategic orientation, including the establishment of business presence in new markets, the use of profits, the setting of strategic priorities and the allocation of senior managerial positions. These four items were thus used to construct sub-scales of strategic orientation by aggregating the scores for the four items into an internal consistency indicator with a listed alpha of .782. The most difficult challenges that face the international service sector are concentrated in areas such as competition on the basis of the provision of a wide range of amenities,

Table 1 *Means, standard deviations and correlations (N = 136 IJV hotels)*

Variables	Mean	Std	2	3	4	5	6	7	8	9	10	11	12
1 Strategic orientation	5.262	1.51											
2 Contractual control	5.029	1.99	.472**										
3 Formalization	3.181	1.09	-.088	.146*									
4 Firm-specific assets[1]	4.232	1.54	.251**	.421**	.030								
5 Number of employees	514	308	.275**	.379**	.061	.353**							
6 Business duration	15.43	21.60	-.241*	.107	.236*	-.255*	-.099						
7 Location	2.40	1.17	-.169*	-.052	.324**	.142*	-.118	.455**					
8 Star	3.79	0.89	.340**	.400**	.147*	.315**	.641**	-.084	-.012				
9 Profitability	5.40	1.15	.347**	.417**	-.010	.176*	.332**	-.176	-.287**	.355**			
10 Growth of sales	5.39	1.19	.342**	.383**	-.032	.152*	.306**	-.307**	-.382**	.413**	.701**		
11 Market share	5.550	1.31	.361**	.416**	-.116	.062	.344**	.006	-.495**	.407**	.731**	.772**	
12 Overall performance	5.450	3.32	.386**	.466**	-.060	.140	.361**	-.245*	-.433**	.432**	.887**	.908**	.926**

Notes: One-tailed probabilities: *p < 0.05; **p < 0.01.
[a 1] Firm-specific assets refer to an array of resources, including physical, tacit and organizational resources.

service quality, low prices and superior promotion. Thus, our understanding of strategic orientation encompasses all of the efficiencies that are available in the utilization of assets and the overall management of development processes.

Four items were used to measure the perceived importance of contractual control: brand names, marketing procedures, supplier procedures and professional service procedures. Contractual control is primarily exercised through the responsibilities that an IJV hotel firm exerts over its tacit resources, including its intellectual properties, patents, trademarks, copyrights, proprietary reservations and logistics systems. The brand name and marketing reservations system of IJV hotels are believed to be important indicators of the level of contractual control that is employed, as these factors are more likely to place limits on business actions. Sub-scales of contractual control were constructed by aggregating the scores of the four items into an internal consistency indicator with a listed alpha of .702. Thus, the contractual control variable includes all of the structural aspects of asset management.

Four items were used to measure the perceived importance of organizational formalization, including the perceived reliance on detailed financial reporting, the establishment of formal systems, the setting of performance targets and the use of performance-related rewards and appraisals, all of which were assessed using seven-point scales. We also asked questions regarding the extent to which the hotel managers agreed with the use of regulations, rules and operating procedures that spell out their detailed tasks and activities, and the standard operating procedures, rules and policies that are employed to support corporate management needs. Formalization was measured by the analysis of established formal documents that set the standard operating procedures and measure the improved service efficiencies. Sub-scales of the formalization constructs were then aggregated into a group score with a listed alpha of .753 so as to include all of the soft aspects of HRM development in the measure of formalization.

Firm size was assessed using the number of full-time employees as the primary measure. The business duration of each IJV hotel was measured by the number of years that the hotel had been in operation, and the age of the hotel was estimated by subtracting the year of formation from the year of the survey. International experience was measured by asking the respondents to indicate the number of years of experience that their hotels had had in operating in China. A number of predictors of performance, such as profitability, growth of sales and market share, was also used. The combination of all three performance indicators has an alpha of .834, which is deemed to be statistically acceptable.

Results

Table 1 presents the descriptive statistics and zero-order correlations for all of the variables in the study. The results show that the asset specificities of the IJV hotel firms influence the selection of corporate management priorities. Positive correlations are found between the key variables of strategic orientations, contractual control and performance. Our results suggest that the enhancement of an IJV hotel's asset specificities gives the hotel the flexibility to achieve the type of strategic orientation and contractual control that it needs to improve its performance. However, the correlation between strategic orientation and formalization is negative and not statistically significant.

Table 2 presents the ANOVA results that examine the level of importance and the actual performance as perceived by the hotel managers. The ratings show that most of

Table 2 *ANOVA of the strategy needs of the hotel firms (N = 136 IJV Hotels)*

	Mean scores		Paired sample t-test	
Variables	Importance	Performance	Value of t	Value of p
Strategic orientation				
Establishing business presence in new markets	5.7941	5.3346	4.442	.000
The use of profit	4.0809	4.4265	−2.412	.017
The setting of strategic priorities	5.6612	5.6691	.217	.828
The allocation of senior managerial positions	5.4853	4.9265	5.958	.000
Contractual control				
Brand names	4.7574	4.3676	3.641	.000
Marketing procedures	5.3088	3.9412	9.156	.000
Supplier procedures	4.7022	4.3601	3.641	.000
Professional service procedures	5.2206	4.8676	3.700	.000
Formalization				
Detailed financial reporting	6.1985	5.9853	1.990	.049
Laying down formal systems, procedures, and rules	5.9265	5.4265	6.084	.000
Setting performance targets, rewards, and appraisals	5.6838	4.9265	8.038	.000

Notes: One-tailed probabilities.

the items of corporate management across the areas of strategic orientation, contractual control and formalization are significantly emphasized.

Table 3 presents an ordinary least-square multiple regression analysis of the performance of the IJV hotels. We have regressed dimensions of IJV hotels' performance predictors for the sample. The first model presents the results for strategic orientation. The standard coefficients between overall performance and strategic orientation (.188*) and firm-specific assets (.428**) are positive and statistically significant, and therefore the strategic orientation model is significant (F = 6.879, p < 0.00, adjusted R^2 = 0.378). The second model deals with contractual control. The standard coefficients between overall performance and contractual control (.314**) and firm-specific assets (.433**) are positive and statistically significant (F = 9.113, p < 0.00, adjusted R^2 = 0.456). The regression analysis of contractual control predicts 45.6 per cent of the variance in performance, and Hypothesis 2 is consequently supported. The third model reveals that the indictors of formalization predict 38.2 per cent of the variance in performance, but Hypothesis 3 is not supported, as the results show that formalization has a negative influence on business performance (β = . − 139, p < .245). Model IV in Table 3 has regresses strategic orientation, contractual control and formalization together with the performance indicator. The measurement of the main effects of performance shows that the vertical firm-specific assets of IJV hotels are subject to their customer service and service technicalities, and thus Hypothesis 4 is partially accepted. This full model is significant (F = 6.397, p < 0.00, adjusted R^2 = 0.506) and the regression analysis of the full model predicts of 50.6 per cent of the variance in performance.

Table 3 *Logistic-regression results of the performance of the IJV Hotels (N = 136 Hotels)*

Variable	Model I standardized coefficients (β)	Model II standardized coefficients (β)	Model III standardized coefficients (β)	Model IV standardized coefficients (β)
Main effects				
Strategic orientation	.188*			− 1.114
Contractual control		.314**		.3110**
Formalization			− .139	− 1.431
Firm-specific resources	.428**	.433**	.422**	.366**
Size	.133	.094	.138	.030
Business duration	− .256**	− .342**	− .242*	− .264*
Location	.409**	.446**	.384**	.380**
Star indicator	.248**	232*	.278*	.233*
Interaction effects				
SO x CC				− 2.446
CC x F				− 1.274
F x SO				− 2.777
Model statistics				
Model chi-square	6.879	9.113	6.979	6.397
Sig. of F change	.000	.000	.000	.000
Adjusted R^2	.378	.456	.382	.506
Change in R^2	.443	.513	.446	.600

Notes: One-tailed probabilities: *$p < 0.05$; **$p < 0.01$.

Analysis

This study empirically investigates the extent to which the vertical integration of corporate management influences the implementation of a strategic orientation, contractual control and formalization in a firm. The classification of the vertical integration activities of corporate management is used to ascribe success values to a firm's HRM activities and the criticalities of its asset bundles from a theoretical viewpoint. As regards strategic orientation, our results suggest that the more intense the use of a firm's customer-oriented services, the better the performance that can be expected from the firm's business. Many of the IJV hotel managers of this study gave a high ranking to strategic orientation for the establishment of business presence in new markets and the setting of strategic priorities, and confirmed that their hotels have fully deployed complex logistics, marketing and inventory control systems. The vertical integration of the management of an IJV hotel is not only reflected in a good marketing mix that targets various client groups in China, but also in the availability of various options to deal with heterogeneity in the customer portfolio through the employment of distinct HRM policies. In this study, most of the IJV hotels demonstrated superior marketing ability in terms of meeting the requirements of their international cliental through the use of advanced service systems that have mostly been developed by their foreign parent firms.

Our findings also suggest that the establishment of strategic orientation often focuses on the allocation of senior managerial positions. Most IJV hotels in China prefer to contract hotel management out to their foreign parents, as local managers are not entirely familiar with standard HRM practices and international service criteria. Due to the obstacles of human resources and market accessibility, local managers are still weak in some key areas, such as reservation systems, financial control, marketing, international service standards and branding, which lead to a heavy reliance on expatriate managers in many of the IJV hotels. The competitive advantages that these hotels compared to local Chinese hotels are derived from the inputs of their foreign parents in the areas of management expertise, service knowledge, financing, business networking, distribution channels and centralized reservation systems. Our respondents stated that many IJV hotel firms in China have the privilege of direct access to knowledge about international service expertise from their parent firms, and these hotels have also benefited from having an excellent knowledge of the international working environment that they can combine with an understanding of the Chinese political, regulatory, financial and social systems.

Our study indicates that most IJV hotels achieve better performance when their parent firms have confidence in the management of their subsidiaries, and when the service support that is provided by the foreign parent in terms of branding, service expertise, trademark, business reputation and corporate image has brought the benefits that were predicted at the formation of the IJV. Although some believe that the mobility of IJV hotel managers enhances the skills, adaptability and career potential of individual managers, there is clearly a trade-off for top management at head office between the need to replace local knowledge and the allocation of senior managerial positions that results in the best quality HRM. Most IJV hotel managements are distinct in that a larger number of the key managerial positions are held by foreign personnel. IJV hotels tend to recruit expatriates for the important posts, such as general manager and chief financial officer, and place a significant emphasis on service and international training, marketing capabilities and local networking. Our respondents confirm that service qualities are more likely to be appropriately integrated when expatriates are seconded to key positions in IJV hotels, as it appears that the development policies that such personnel implement are better guided. Expatriate managers are inclined to emphasize rigid job descriptions, corporate norms and information sharing structures.

Contractual control is seen as being central to vertical integration, as it provides the appropriate obligations, promises and safeguards from the top management of the parent firm to the management of the IJV hotels. Our findings suggest that most IJV hotels heavily emphasize the use of contracts to manage their business, as their managers believe that the establishment of marketing contracts can effectively govern their network relationships with local suppliers. Thus, the exercise of contractual control over suppliers, marketing, professional services and customer networking is expected to have a positive influence over the brand name, copyrights, company logos and business image of IJV hotels. Our results suggest that most IJV hotels are willing to promote the maximum number of interactions possible with their customers through marketing activities and utilize contractual control to manage their local service networks with the aim of crafting new procedures for setting up marketing, supplier and professional services. In addition, the effective use of international brand names has also encouraged many IJV hotels to use contractual control with their customers to safeguard their asset specificities. With regard to the establishment of effective employment service policies, our findings suggest that offering new services must be significantly associated with service credibility, company logo and brand name, and it should be noted that service image and reputation normally take many years to build. The establishment of contractual control also requires IJV hotel managers to know when and how to draw on their resources, and when and how to contribute their asset specificities.

The employment of contractual control allows IJV hotel firms to exert a substantial power over the use of their intellectual properties, service patents, trademarks, copyrights and logistic service systems. The asset specificities of IJV hotel firms comprise physical resources, superior tacit service capabilities and organizational resources, because it is believed that these generate certain monopolistic advantages. The process of asset transfer from parent firms to IJV hotels usually starts with attention to the contractual control that is needed to match the offerings of other international hotels. IJV hotel managers emphasize that the establishment of contractual control in their corporate management is usually based on service prices, service quality and promptness in responding to service queries. Our findings indicate that most IJV hotels in China heavily invested in service facilities at the time of their formation, and that their subsequent investment compared to many local hotels has also been quite high. However, IJV hotels seldom share service facilities with other hotels in the same chain, as managers believe that investment in physical hotel buildings and facilities should focus on the distinct corporate management needs of the individual hotel and the compatibility between the hotel's own property development requirements and its international clients. Of the recent rapid changes that have taken place in the hotel service market, many IJV hotel managers indicated that contractual control over hotel services has intensified the market competition, which has led to the need to manage the change, co-ordination and performance of asset specificities. Along with other market indicators, most IJV hotels in China face great strategic and economic challenges in implementing contractual control in terms of updating services such as room service, food and beverage offerings and recreation facilities.

Formalization is used to measure the co-ordination, standardization, communication and information reporting within an organization. Our results state that the deployment of formalization has not had a significant influence in enhancing the asset specificities of IJV hotel firms. The IJV hotel managers confirmed that the establishment of rules and regulations to improve service standards has generated significant value, but our findings suggest that the development of better service practices and thus the capabilities of IJV hotel firms and formalization are not strongly related. In establishing strategic development plans, most expatriate managers are encouraged to share financial information with local managers, and some IJV hotels have elaborate procedures for dealing with contingencies within their financial plan. Budgetary control tends to focus on formal recruitment and selection procedures, business expansion, job descriptions and management development programmes, and the retention of strong corporate control through formalization is regarded by IJV managers as helpful in the effective use of a hotel's services. The management of IJV hotels believes that the creation of effective management structures using hierarchical principles encourages teamwork and cross-functional communication.

Theoretical and managerial implications

Our findings offer three significant implications for IJV hotels. The first implication relates to the finding that a firm's strategic orientation has a direct impact on performance. It appears that strategic orientation is more appropriate in dynamic business conditions, and although most international clients are very demanding in terms of delivery quality, prices and service practices, IJV hotels in China have risen to the challenge and have effectively employed international service procedures. By highlighting the need for strategic orientation to be compatible with long-term business developments, most IJV hotels have greatly increased their opportunities to penetrate new markets in China. Second, although the economic transition has meant that IJV hotels have had to adopt a proactive response to the rapidly changing market, our findings suggest that the Western management and marketing techniques that derive from the foreign parent firm are regarded as effective tools by local management. More specifically, the competitive environment in the service sector appears to have had a positive influence on performance. The establishment of effective contractual control has helped IJV hotels to protect the distinctiveness of their service specialties, and when IJV hotel firms in China commit their tacit resources, a well-specified contract can be effectively employed to encourage corporate management activity and promote greater information exchange with other local hotels. Finally, IJV hotels that operate in transition economies should be aware of the investment conditions and, in fact, any firm's formalization should be consistent with its strategic objectives and business environment. Our findings suggest that most IJV hotels have already built up a high quality of formalization compared to local hotel firms, and the achievement of formalization has helped to integrate the resources, knowledge and capabilities of these hotels within their organizations, especially when transferring or combining the assets that are held by foreign parent firms that are expected to enhance their marketing development portfolios.

Conclusion

Most of the IJV hotels in this study place significant emphasis on the vertical integration of corporate management, including key manager transfers, training programmes, visits by experts and the employment of expatriates. When these findings are considered jointly, we can draw certain conclusions regarding the appropriateness of strategic orientation, contractual control and formalization based on the performance that these hotels have achieved. Our study lends weight to the argument that complex IJV hotel management should be guided by a corporate strategic orientation, as this promotes a greater long-term trust-based customized service approach for the management. The key strategic orientation that enables the vertical integration in an IJV hotel firm is a focus on service knowledge, expertise and client relationships. The adoption of contractual control over the vertical integration of corporate management is significantly benefited by the employment of tacit service expertise, as this enables hotel managers to craft more complex contracts that are able to cope with unforeseeable outcomes. The competitive circumstances that are faced by IJV hotels in China have ensured that the benefits of adopting greater vertical integration through contractual control have increased. In this study, organizational formalization and the normative behaviour that underlies it are regarded to be self-enforcing safeguards that maximize the benefit of corporate management activities overall. Although most IJV hotels pay great attention to the creation of service value, our results indicate that the establishment of formalization in a firm does not contribute directly to performance. Furthermore, our findings suggest that the further successful development of IJV hotels in China can only be ensured by a policy of the continuous upgrade of international service practices in line with corporate management activities and the constant development of new service capabilities to cope with evolving market demand.

Acknowledgements

Grateful acknowledgment is made of funding provided by the Direct Allocation Grant (7100227) and the Hong Kong Research Grant Council in support of the research on which this paper draws.

References

Araujo, L., Dubois, A. and Gadde, L. (2003) 'The Multiple Boundaries of the Firm', *Journal of Management Studies*, 40(5): 1255–77.

Barney, J.B. and Arikan, A.M. (2001) 'The Resource-based View: Origins and Implications'. In Hitt, M.A., Freeman, R.E. and Harrison, J.S. (eds) *Handbook of Strategic Management*. Oxford: Blackwell, pp. 124–88.

Becker, B. and Huselid, M. (1998) 'High Performance Work Systems and Firm Performance: A Synthesis of Research and Managerial Implications', *Research in Personnel and Human Resources Management*, 16: 53–101.

Bhandarker, A. (2003) 'Building a Corporate Transformation, New HRAgand', *Vision*, July–December: 1–23.

Birkinshaw, J., Hood, N. and Jonsson, S. (1998) 'Building Firm-specific Advantages in Multinational Corporations: The Role of Subsidiary Initiative', *Strategic Management Journal*, 19(3): 221–41.

Birkinshaw, J.M., Morrison, A.J. and Hulland, J. (1995) 'Structural and Competitive Determinants of A Global Integration Strategy', *Strategic Management Journal*, 16(8): 637–55.

Cai, L., Zhang, L., Pearson, T. and Bai, X. (2000) 'Challenges for China's State-run Hotels: A Marketing Perspective', *Journal of Hospitality and Leisure Marketing*, 7(1): 29–46.

Cannon, J.P., Achrol, R.S. and Gundlach, G.T. (2000) 'Contracts, Norms, and Plural Form Governance', *Academy of Marketing Science*, 28(2): 180–95.

Chekitan, S.D., Erramilli, M.K. and Agarwal, S. (2002) 'Brands Across Borders: Determining Factors in Choosing Franchising or Management Contracts for Entering International Markets', *Cornell Hotel and Restaurant Administration Quarterly*, 43(6): 91–104.

Coase, R. (1937) 'The Nature of the Firm', *Economica*, 4: 386–425.

Ding, D., Fields, D. and Akhtar, S. (1997) 'An Empirical Study of HRM Policies and Practices in Foreign-invested Enterprises in China: The Case of Shenzen Special Economic Zone', *International Journal of Human Resource Management*, 8(5): 595–613.

Dubois, A. (1998) *Organizing Industrial Activities Across Firm Boundaries*. London: Routledge.

Dunning, J. and Kundu, S.K. (1995) 'The Internationalization of the Hotel Industry: Some Findings From a Field Study', *Management International Review*, 35(2): 101–34.

Edwards, T. and Kuruvilla, S. (2005) 'International HRM: National Business Systems, Organizational Politics and the International Division of Labour in MNCs', *International Journal of Human Resource Management*, 16(1): 1–21.

Eisenhardt, K.M. and Galunic, D.C. (2000) 'Coevolving: At Last, A Way to Make Synergies Work', *Harvard Business Review*, 78(1): 91–101.

Eisenhardt, K.M. and Martin, J. (2000) 'Dynamic Capabilities: What Are They?', *Strategic Management Journal*, 21(10–11): 1105–21.

Farley, J., Hoenig, S. and Yang, J. (2004) 'Key Factors Influencing HRM Practices of Overseas Subsidiaries in China's Transition Economy', *International Journal of Human Resource Management*, 15(4/5): 688–704.

Gamble, J. (2003) 'Transferring Human Resource Practices from the United Kingdom to China: The Limits and Potential for Convergence', *International Journal of Human Resource Management*, 14(3): 369–87.

Ghoshal, S. (1987) 'Global Strategy: An Organizing Framework', *Strategic Management Journal*, 8: 425–40.

Gold, A.H., Malhotra, A. and Segars, A.H. (2001) 'Knowledge Management: An Organizational Capabilities Perspective', *Journal of Management Information System*, 18: 185–214.

Grewal, R. and Tansuhai, P. (2001) 'Building Organizational Capabilities for Managing Economic Crisis: The Role of Market Orientation and Strategic Flexibility', *Journal of Marketing*, 65: 67–80.

Grossman, S. and Hart, O. (1986) 'The Costs and Benefits of Integration: A Theory of Vertical and Lateral integration', *Journal of Political Economy*, 94(4): 691–719.

Guest, D., Michie, J., Conway, N. and Sheehan, M. (2003) 'Human Resource Management and Corporate Performance in the UK', *British Journal of Industrial Relations*, 41(2): 291–314.

Guthrie, J., Spell, C. and Nyamori, O. (2002) 'Correlates and Consequences of High Involvement Work Practices: The Role of Competitive Strategy', *International Journal of Human Resource Management*, 13(1): 183–97.

Hakansson, H. and Snehota, I. (1995) *Developing Relationships in Business Networks*. London: Routledge.

Harrigan, R.K. (1986) 'Matching Vertical Integration Strategies to Competitive Conditions', *Strategic Management Journal*, 7(6): 535–55.

Hedlund, G. (1994) 'A Model of Knowledge Management and the N-Form Corporation', *Strategic Management Journal*, 15: 73–91.

Heffernan, F. and Flood, P. (2000) 'An Exploration of the Relationships between the Adoption of Managerial Competencies, Organizational Characteristics, Human Resource Sophistication and Performance in Irish Organizations', *Journal of European Industrial Training*, 24(2/3/4): 128–36.

Hewett, K. and Bearden, O.W. (2001) 'Dependence, Trust, and Relational Behavior on the Part of Foreign Subsidiary Marketing Operations: Implications for Managing Global Marketing Operations', *Journal of Marketing*, 65: 51–66.

Hoque, K. (1999) 'Human Resource Management and Performance in the UK Hotel Industry', *British Journal of Industrial Relations*, 37(3): 419–43.

Knight, F. (1921) *Risk, Uncertainty and Profit*. Boston, MA: Houghton Mifflin.

Langlois, R. (1998) 'Capabilities and the Theory of the Firm'. In Foss, N. and Loasby, B. (eds) *Economic Organization, Capabilities and Co-ordination – Essays in Honour of G.B. Richardson*. London: Routledge, pp. 183–202.

Law, K., Wong, C. and Wang, K. (2004) 'An empirical Test of the Model on Managing the Localization of Human Resources in the People's Republic of China', *International Journal of Human Resource Management*, 15(4-5): 635–48.

Leiblein, M.J. and Miller, D.J. (2003) 'An Empirical Examination of Transaction- and Firm-level Influences on the Vertical Boundaries of the Firm', *Strategic Management Journal*, 24(9): 839–59.

Loasby, B.J. (1998) 'The Concept of Capabilities'. In Foss, N. and Loasby, B. (eds) *Economic Organization, Capabilities and Co-ordination – Essays in Honour of G.B. Richardson*. London: Routledge, pp. 163–82.

Luo, Y. (2002) 'Organizational Dynamics and Global Integration: A Perspective From Subsidiary Managers', *Journal of International Management*, 8(2): 189–215.

Luo, Y., Shenkar, O. and Nyaw, M.K. (2001) 'A Dual Parent Perspective on Control and Performance in International Joint Ventures: Lessons from a Developing Economy', *Journal of International Business Studies*, 32(1): 41–58.

Marchington, M. and Vincent, S. (2004) 'Analyzing the Influence of Institutional, Organizational and Interpersonal Forces in Shaping inter-organizational Relations', *Journal of Management Studies*, 41(6): 1029–56.

Maxwell, G., Watson, S. and Quail, S. (2004) 'Quality Service in the International Hotel Sector: A Catalyst for Strategic Human Resource Development?', *Journal of European Industrial Training*, 28(2-4): 159–82.

Meilich, O. (2005) 'Are Formalization and Human Asset Specificity Mutually Exclusive? A Learning Bureaucracy Perspective', *The Journal of American Academy of Business*, March: 161–9.

Meyer, J.W. and Scott, W.R. (1992) *Organizational Environments*. London, Newbury Park, New Delhi: Sage.

Mishra, B., Mahalakshmi, R. and Mohan, M. (2001) 'Captialising on Human Capital-seeking Alignment with Business'. In Varkkey, B., Parasher, P. and Brahma, G. (eds) *Human Resource Management: Changing Roles, Changing Goals*. New Delhi: Excel Books.

Moorman, C. and Miner, A.S. (1998) 'Organizational Improvisation and Organizational Memory', *Academy of Management Review*, 23: 698–723.

Mota, J. and De Castro, L.M. (2004) 'A Capabilities Perspective on the Evolution of Firm Boundaries: A Comparative Case Example from the Portuguese Moulds Industry', *Journal of Management Studies*, 41(2): 295–316.

Porter, M.E. (1985) *Competitive Advantage: Creating and Sustaining Superior Performance.* New York: Free Press.

Roth, K. and Morrison, A.J. (1992) 'Implementing Global Strategies: Characteristics of Global Subsidiary Mandates', *Journal of International Business Studies*, 23: 715–35.

Schroeder, R.G., Bates, K.A. and Junttila, M.A. (2002) 'A Resource-based View of Manufacturing Strategy and the Relationship to Manufacturing Performance', *Strategic Management Journal*, 23: 105–17.

Slater, S.F. and Narver, J.C. (1994) 'Does Competitive Environment Moderate the Market Orientation-Performance Relationship', *Journal of Marketing*, 58(1): 46–55.

Srivastava, R.K., Fahey, L. and Christensen, H.K. (2001) 'The Resource-based View and Marketing: The Role of Market-based Assets in Gaining Competitive Advantage', *Journal of Management*, 27: 777–802.

Talyor, S., Beechler, S. and Napier, N. (1996) 'Towards an Integrative Model of Strategic International Human Resource Management', *Academy of Management Review*, 21(4): 959–85.

Thompson, J.D. (1967) *Organizational in Action.* New York: McGraw-Hill.

Williamson, O.E. (1999) 'Strategy Research: Governance and Competence Perspectives', *Strategic Management Journal*, 20(12): 1087–108.

Winter, S. (1993) 'On Coase, Competence and the Corporation'. In Williamson, O. and Winter, S. (eds) *The Nature of the Firm. Origins, Evolution and Development.* New York: Oxford University Press, pp. 179–95.

Wright, P.M., Dunford, B.B. and Snell, S.A. (2001) 'Human Resources and the Resource Based View of the Firm', *Journal of Management*, 27: 701–21.

Yan, Y. (2003) 'A Comparative Study of Human Resource Management Practices in International Joint Ventures: The Impact of National Origin', *International Journal of Human Resource Management*, 14(4): 487–510.

Yasai-Ardekani, M. (1997) 'Contextual Determinants of Strategic Planning Processes', *Journal of Management Studies*, 34(5): 729–67.

Yu, L. (1999) *The International Hospitality Business: Management and Operations.* New York: Haworth Press.

Appendix A: selected items from the checklist

(a) **Firm-specific assets** (Cronbach's alpha $= .734$; seven-point Likert scale: $1 =$ *not very satisfied to* $7 =$ *extremely satisfied*).

1   Quicker acceptance of new products by customers.
2   Achievement of economics of scale in marketing-support expenditure.
3   Lowering the risk that is associated with the introduction of a new manual.

(b) **Strategic orientation:** (Cronbach's alpha $= .782$; the respondents were asked to indicate the importance of the following questions using a scale of $1–7$: $1 =$ *not important to* $7 =$ *very important*). Please indicate the degree to which your company has established a strategic orientation in the following areas.

1   Establishing business presence in new markets.
2   The use of profit.
3   The setting of strategic priorities.
4   The allocation of senior managerial positions.

(c) **Contractual control** (Cronbach's alpha = .702; seven-point Likert scale: *1 = not very important to 7 = very important*). Please indicate the degree to which your company has established contractual control in the following areas.

1 Brand names.
2 Marketing procedures.
3 Supplier procedures.
4 Professional service procedures.

(d) **Formalization** (Cronbach's alpha = .753; the respondents were asked to indicate the importance of the following questions using a scale of 1–7: *1 = not important to 7 = very important*).

1 Detailed financial reporting.
2 Laying down formal systems, procedures and rules.
3 Setting performance targets.
4 Using performance-related rewards and appraisals.

(e) **Performance** (Cronbach's alpha = .834; the respondents were asked to indicate the achievement of the following using a scale of 1–7: *1 = not achieved at all to 7 = fully achieved*).

Profitability.
Growth of sales.
Market share.

(f) **Organization profile**

Turnover.
Registered capital.
Number of employees.
Date of establishment.
Ownership.

What drives adoption of innovative SHRM practices in Indian organizations?

Ashok Som

Introduction

The topic of adoption of innovative practices has come into existence as an outcome of progressive developments in management science and practice. Theoretical research argues that it is important to analyse organizations' work practices as a coherent system. This systems perspective is based on the notion that human resource management (HRM) practices often complement each other, so that the adoption of one HRM practice is only effective when it is adopted in combination with one or more supporting work practices (Ichniowski and Shaw, 1999). Continuing with this line of thought, Colbert (2004) argued that 'this system is a coherent whole, and that this system is of critical strategic importance – it includes the skills, behaviours, and interactions of employees that have the potential to provide both the foundation for strategy formulation and the means of strategy implementation. The firm's HRM practices are strategic and are instrumental in developing the strategic capability of its pool of human resources'. The innovative strategic human resource (SHRM) practices are defined within the system of strategic human resource management. Ichniowski and Shaw (1999) had observed that more research is required on the limited adoption of innovative HRM practices. This article tries to understand and explore the adoption of strategic human resource management practices in the Indian context. Adoption of innovative SHRM practices within the framework of SHRM systems occur in highly complex social, political and economic environments (Kossek, 1987). Liberalization, growing competition and changing environments make adoption of innovative practices inevitable prerequisites for growth, success and survival of an organization (Kossek, 1987; Som, 2006b). Analysis of the adoption of innovative SHRM practices in organizations, therefore, requires a better understanding of the environment in which the skills, behaviours and interactions among employees within an organization function. For this article, innovative SHRM practices are defined as:

> Any intentional introduction of HRM programme, policy, practice or system designed to influence or adapt employee the skills, behaviors, and interactions of employees and have the potential to provide both the foundation for strategy formulation and the means of strategy implementation that is perceived to be new and creates current capabilities and competencies. (Som, 2006b)

This definition implies that not all changes involve innovation, since whatever an organization adopts is not perceived to be new. It also reflects the wide scope of innovative practices, from functional activities to wide ranging strategic initiatives aimed at building capabilities and competencies that organizations need in a competitive environment. The definition also implies that adoption of such practices that are *perceived* to be new in the current context and that are in the domain of HR systems which creates current capabilities and competencies would be considered as innovative.

Indian context

Fifteen years have elapsed since the Indian government enacted economic reforms, effectively bringing one-sixth of the world's population into the global economy. After decades of protectionism, India experienced a revolutionary change when it shifted from a regulated to a 'free market' economy. The liberalization of the foreign investment climate in India especially facilitated the integration of Indian economy with the global economy (Khandwalla, 2002; Som, 2002). This liberalization resulted in sudden and increased levels of competition for Indian organizations. Among other things, liberalization brought globalization and internationalization of domestic businesses, unbridled imports, concerns for total quality management, incentives to export, demographic changes in the employee profile, retraining and redeployment of workforce, focus on performance appraisal and performance based incentive systems and rightsizing (Budhwar and Sparrow, 1997; Sparrow and Budhwar, 1997; Som, 2006b). Som (2002), in his study of 54 Indian corporations, revealed that out of eight items of rated change in the business environment over the past five years, the four largest perceived changes were greater turbulence in the product market environment characterized by many unexpected changes; more intense competition; greater buoyancy and growth potential; and greater requirement for technological sophistication. Liberalization created opportunities for technology upgrading and sophistication, resource mobilization from new sources, highly competitive input/output market, high growth and buoyant environment and HRM issues associated with strategic initiatives of diversification, mergers and acquisitions, restructuring, joint ventures, strategic alliances and for overall internationalization of the economy. With liberalization, there had been an increasing pressure on organizations in India to change from indigenous, costly, sub-optimal technology to performance-based, competitive and higher technology provisions.

The changing business environment within India that started with the liberalization process needs better understanding to comprehend the functioning of organizations and the factors that lead to adopting innovative SHRM practices in the Indian context.

India was chosen as a context of analysis because of the following reasons. First, India (in 2006) is the second largest and the second fastest growing economy in the world. India has grown at an average rate of 8 per cent for the past three years. Its savings rate is now over 29 per cent of GDP and the investment rate is about 31 per cent of GDP. Together with this a growing young population and a vibrant marketplace, the Indian economy has become more hospitable to foreign direct investment. Continuing with liberalization, in 2005, policies relating to investment, taxation, foreign trade, FDI, banking, finance and capital markets have evolved to make Indian industry and enterprise more competitive globally. Sector-specific mega-investment regions with investments of up to US$10 billion in each location are being promoted, beginning with telecommunications, chemicals, petrochemicals and the entire energy sector including petroleum, natural gas, power and captive coal mining offer exciting opportunities.

Second, due to this change in environment, organizations are adopting innovative practices either to gain market share or to save their businesses. This phased liberalization created intensive competition through easier entry and greater foreign participation. For example, multi-national companies (MNCs), like Hyundai Motors, Ford, Renault, Toyota, Honda, Volvo, Cummins, Daimler Chrysler, Wal-Mart, GAP, Hilfiger, Asian Paints, Delphi, Eli Lilly, General Electric, Hewlett Packard, Heinz and Daimler Chrysler, GE Plastics, Monsanto, Whirlpool, HP Labs, Microsoft, Oracle are in India. India has slowly become a competitive battleground for more than 15,000 MNCs. This entry of MNCs into the Indian market has changed the dynamics of doing business in India. Liberalization enabled these organizations to expand, diversify, integrate and globalize more freely.

As a result, several Indian firms undertook significant organizational changes along with adoption of SHRM practices during the late 1990s. Firms like Hero Honda, Tata Motors, Bharat Forge, Hindustan Inks, Sundaram Clayton, Essel Propack, BPCL, Maruti, Tata Iron and Steel, TVS Steel, Ranbaxy, Infosys, Wipro and Satyam were able to successfully adapt to the dynamic corporate scenario. The reasons that helped these organizations adapt were their foresightedness, expertise and abilities to adopt innovative SHRM practices.

Third, factors adopting innovative SHRM practices have not been studied at depth in an emerging country scenario, especially India, where liberalization has initiated a competitive environment that was not the case before. Researchers to date have mainly confined themselves to the USA, Japan (Ichniowski and Shaw, 1999; Kossek, 1997) and some countries in Europe (Gooderham *et al.*, 1999; Som and Cerdin, 2004). The extensiveness of the typology of managerial innovation has been confined mainly to the west and has not penetrated many developing countries and their organizations. It is no surprise then that even less research has been conducted in the field of SHRM and its innovative practices in India. There has been very little empirical research to understand how organizations adopt managerial innovation and inculcate strategic human resource practices to make organizations more competitive. Even though there has been accumulating evidence of the economic impact of strategic HRM (e.g. Harel and Tzafrir, 1999; Huselid, 1995; Schuler and Jackson, 1999), cross-cultural equivalence is paramount in order to meaningfully apply the implications for management practices and the concepts of SHRM.

This article attempts to understand the drivers of adoption of innovative SHRM practices in the context of economic liberalization. The research questions that the article focuses on are: what are the drivers of adoption of innovative SHRM practices in the Indian context? How universal are the adoptions i.e. how relevant are they to most sectors and industries in the world wherever there is a competitive market economy or a movement towards it? The research tries to develop five propositions of adoption of innovative SHRM practices in Indian organizations.

Literature survey

Insights offered by organizational theories reveal that innovative practices are adopted by organizations mainly to improve organizational performance. Walston *et al.* (2001) argue that innovative practices promise to enhance efficiency, are particularly attractive to organizations facing intense competition and/or performance deficiencies and can be thought of as either driven by economic efficiency or by non-economic factors. Adoption and diffusion occur as they encompass generation, development and implementation of new ideas or behaviours (Damanpour, 1991) and are influenced by characteristics of individual people, of the organization itself and of the context in which it operates and out of which it emerges (Kimberly, 1981; Kimberly and Evanisko, 1981).

Management researchers like DiMaggio and Powell, (1983) and Scott (1995) have emphasized that organizations tend to adopt innovative practices due to institutional factors such as normative and regulatory pressures. Within these organizational pressures, the capacity to adopt innovative practices is determined by the HRM practices (Gooderham *et al.*, 1999; Kossek, 1987; Wolfe, 1995). These strategic HRM like other organizational functions contribute to new organizational demands, requirements and organizational performance. Researchers (Ulrich, 1999) have been increasingly studying how HRM can be used to plan activities strategically and how to effectively manage HRM. Research (Schuler and Jackson, 1999, Schuler *et al.*, 1993) suggests that not only innovative SHRM practices result in tangible organizational results (Huselid, 1995; Inchinowski *et al.*, 1996) but also assist organizations in developing innovative solutions as the need arises.

To attend to the question why organizations adapt SHRM practices, the SHRM literature has debated and discussed a variety of perspectives drawn from organizational theory, including institutional theory (Wright and McMahan, 1992), contingency theory (Lengnick-Hall and Lengnick-Hall, 1988), universalistic, contingency and configurational perspectives (Delery and Doty, 1996), behavioural perspectives (Schuler and Jackson, 1999) and complex systematic perspective (Colbert, 2004). The basic premise of the institutional approach is that many structures, programmes and practices in organizations attain legitimacy through the social construction of reality. The contingency theory argues that the adoption of SHRM practices are dependent on both the internal and external environment that the organization operates in it allows for interaction effect on the presence of a contingent variable such as strategy. Universalistic or 'best-practice' approach assert that certain HR practices are found to consistently lead to higher organizational performance, independent of an organization's stated strategy. Configurational perspective on the other hand tries to focus on patterns of HR practices that are holistic and mutually reinforcing and have a correlation with organizational performance. The behavioural perspective has its roots in contingency theory and focuses on employee behaviour as the mediator between strategy and firm performance. The complexity perspective assumes that system-level, path-dependent resources and capabilities only emerge out of the dynamic interplay within a given system and allows for the creation of creative and adaptive SHRM capabilities of the organization. Some of these approaches are central to this research in understanding the adoption of SHRM practices in Indian organizations.

A wide array of SHRM practices such as recruitment, selection, training, appraisal and reward systems (Fornbrum, 1984) can be construed as an innovation, when practiced for the first time in an organization. Wolfe (1995) interviewed and surveyed a sample of 60 US HR professionals and over 40 different innovations were named. Participants were asked to name an HR innovation and then to identify an innovation they had actually implemented or helped implement. Examples provided included human resource information systems; 360-degree appraisals; internet recruiting; online access to employee information; telecommuting; Six Sigma; People Soft; realistic job previews; training, re-training and redeployment, outsourcing; and competency-based compensation.

Gooderham *et al.* (1999) reported in their study of adoption of SHRM innovations in six European countries that it might be determined to a considerable extent by the imperative of maintaining external legitimacy through adherence to institutional structures, rules, and norms at the national level-and may vary as a result of dissimilar national contexts. Geary and Roche (2001) in their study of Irish SHRM practices argue that foreign owned firms are distinctive in their practices in comparison with indigenous firms. The compliance with local laws and regulations lead to differentiated and innovative practices. In other instances, foreign firms may seek to resemble local firms to compete more effectively in the local market to 'fit in' by imitating local practices.

SHRM literature individually have identified the linkage of adoption process and institutional environment (Wright and McMahan, 1992); however, detailed discussion regarding the adoption of innovative SHRM practices and the institutional variables has not been addressed adequately for liberalized economies. Gooderham *et al.* (1999) in their findings highlight the need to incorporate country-specific, institutional factors in studies of patterns of organizational practices in general and SHRM practices in particular. Their analysis indicates that the national institutional embeddedness of firms plays a far more important role in shaping SHRM practices than their industrial embeddedness. In this context, it is believed that a study of the adoption of innovative SHRM practices by Indian companies will add to the nascent body of knowledge in the context of liberalizing economies.

Evolution of SHRM practices in India

Formalized personnel functions have been common in Indian organizations for decades (for a detailed history of development of personnel and human resource development (HRD) in India, see Budhwar, 2001; Rao, 1999; Sen Gupta 2004). HRD, in the Indian context, had two meanings. One necessarily meant training, where training was defined in terms of learning experience, building employee competence, commitment in building a strong organizational culture and organizational development (OD). The second essentially meant a normative model of man-management or personnel management. HRD differed from HRM in that in HRM the line managers take primary responsibility for HRM while the responsibility for HRD in the organization seems to lie primarily with the HRD department (Sen Gupta, 2004). Rao (1999: 9–10) had argued,

> The emphasis during the pre-liberalization period was more on HRD as a philosophy and as a value and culture of corporation. Profits were taken for granted and the argument was that since the employees contribute so much to the corporation the corporation should take care of them. When the corporation took care of its people, they, in turn will also took care of the corporation. Thus people were put first in HRD and business goals were taken for granted. However, in the post-liberalization period, the focus of HRD has shifted to establishing direct links with business improvement. If the corporation did not survive, there is little it can do to take care of its employees. Hence business survival has become a significant and a non-negotiable goal and all HRD efforts have to be redirected towards business goals.

The last 20 years have seen radical changes take place in the HRM function in India (Rao, 1999). Rao *et al.* (2001), in their in-depth HRD audit study of Indian organizations, reported that HRD function in India is not well structured, inadequately differentiated and poorly staffed. In the last 10 years, HRM specialists and departments were under severe pressure to bring about large-scale professionalized changes in organizations in order to cope with the challenges brought about by the challenges thrown by the new economic environment (Som, 2002, 2006b). Indian organizations needed to cope with the need to develop a highly diverse workforce into well-trained, motivated and efficient employees with the subsequent de-skilling, re-retraining and multi-skilling problems, workforce reduction policies, retention and career development issues (Venkata Ratnam, 1995). A study of 54 organizations (Som, 2002) reported that more and more Indian organizations are creating a separate HRM/HRD department and adopting innovative SHRM practices. The HR department has been more open to changes, suggestions, more flexible, fair and focused on building employee–employer relationship while playing a definitive role in the success of the organization. The HR department utilized modern technologies and HR personnel were well trained in those technologies. The HR departments were no longer being labelled as 'a cost centre and a place for maintenance, administration, salary processing, paper pushing and sending personnel to training programmes'. Line managers were delegated HR functions and HR department is concerned about business needs and reduction of costs. The study also noted a significant increase in recruiting specialists and professionally trained personnel. Recruitment strategies included fair, open systems with discussion, orientation and induction programmes built into the overall programme. Promotion policies were attuned with recruitment policies and favoured personnel with needed competencies. Promotions were no longer time bound and reflected emphasis on the capabilities. Competent people were promoted faster. Organizations were practicing job rotation, re-training and re-deployment to develop the necessary competencies and skills of their personnel. Retraining was being provided to both managerial and non-managerial staff. Selection to special teams and training personnel for special teams were seen to be a motivator. Career paths involving retraining and redeployment options were seen as reward mechanisms. There were indications of a movement towards performance related pay and compensation policies. Organizations were designing innovative performance appraisal systems that were linked to compensation. HR departments were reported to be explaining and communicating to personnel about the new performance appraisal system. Roles were being clarified, which made workers more accountable. Compensation policies and reward mechanisms were being linked directly to performance and contribution to work. Remuneration policies and its implementation were being clarified and acted as a motivator for enhanced organizational performance. Organizations were getting more and more cost conscious and tended to outsource non-essential functions.

In another recent survey of the trends and emerging practices in SHRM, Belout *et al.* (2001) point to the importance of the adoption of SHRM practices. They point out that organizations are asking their HRM departments for innovative approaches and solutions to improve productivity and the quality of work life, while complying with the law in an environment of high uncertainty, energy conservation and intense international competition. The structural change from a regulated environment to a free market environment had direct implications for SHRM practices in India (Budhwar, 2001; Krishna and Monappa, 1994; Rao, 1999; Som, 2006).

Status of labour regulations and unionization

At present, there are over 150 state and central laws in India that govern various aspects of HRM at the enterprise level (Budwar, 2001; Venkata Ratnam, 1995). The legislation still dictates most HRM policies and practices. Some of the prominent labour laws are: (a) The Factories Act, 1948; (b) The Industrial Employment (Standing Orders) Act, 1946; (c) Industrial Disputes Act, 1948; (d) Trade Unions Act, 1926; (e) Minimum Wages Act, 1948; (f) Payment of Wages Act, 1936; (g) Payment of Bonus Act, 1965; (h) Employee State Insurance Act, 1948; (i) Compensation Act, 1923; (j) Apprenticeship Act, 1961; and (k) Maternity Benefit Act, 1961.

In mid-2001, the India government changed labour legislation to promote workplace flexibility – and this announcement was accompanied by a policy of increasing separation benefits, in line with employment-income protection logic. At least three states – Maharashtra, Kerala and Uttar Pradesh – had changed their labour laws to make it easier for employers to deal with unions, an important issue in attracting foreign investment (Frenkel and Kuruvilla, 2002). With increasing competition and continuous restructuring to remain competitive, Indian organizations were restructuring, reducing their workforce through voluntary retirement schemes (VRS) and increasing subcontracting. The existing labour laws in India prevent employers from terminating the services of the employees easily. According to Section 25(O) of Industrial Disputes Act, 1947, employers are required to take prior permission of the appropriate government for retrenchment of workers where the number of employees is 100 or more. Such permission is rarely granted in India due to socio-political considerations. Socially, the implementation of VRS in India carries many concerns. In a country characterized by one of the highest unemployment rates in the world, employment is also a status symbol in the society. Domestic business groups have for decades taken a generous paternalistic view towards labour, providing housing and other welfare benefits. For example, in 2001, State Bank of India (SBI), the largest public sector bank of India, offered voluntary retirement scheme (VRS) to trim its workforce as recommended in a report by FICCI (Federation of Indian Chamber of Commerce and Industry) that the banking industry in India was overstaffed by 35 per cent. In 2002, TISCO, one of largest steel makers, laid-off about 30,000 workers and it emerged as one of the lowest-cost producers in the world. The unions protested and organizations were forced to question a culture as old as their existence.

The influences of trade unions on HRM practices are still significant. With liberalization, Indian unions are now playing a more co-operative and less militant role (Venkata Ratnam, 1995). Nevertheless, they still greatly influence HR policies and practices in Indian companies, for example, in the recruitment of new employees, payment of bonuses and internal transfers. The unions are strong due to the political support they enjoy and the existence of pro-labour laws in India (Budhwar, 2001; Frenkel and Kuruvilla, 2002; Venkata Ratnam, 1995).

Cultural values and institutional environment

Hofstede (1991) scores indicate that India has a low to moderate uncertainty avoidance, high power distance, low masculinity, and low individualism. Although it is only indicative, yet it reveals that Indians are probably risk-averse, reluctant to make important decisions in work-related matters, probably lacks initiative, probably not inclined to accept responsibility for job-related tasks and an indifference to job feedback. It also reflects that the hierarchical nature of Hinduism (Budwar, 2001), the early socialization process that highlights the importance of the family structure, respect for age and seniority which might have a direct bearing on decisions about promotion and pay. Low masculinity might indicate that most Indian organizations follow a paternalistic management style and preference for personalized relationships rather than a more divorced performance orientation. Low individualism probably implies that family and group attainments take precedence over work outcomes.

In early 2000, many organizations across a variety of industries were beginning to introduce new forms of work organization, including teams and performance-related or skill-based pay, and to apply those pay criteria in appraisal systems that were borrowed from the West. Worker training was receiving increased attention, particularly in the software industry, which had been experiencing chronic labour shortages. In most sectors, firms had recently reduced their headcount. This was accomplished through negotiated voluntary retirement programmes (VRS), for which it was difficult to lay off or retrench workers in India. While labour–management relations remained conflictual, employers were successfully avoiding strikes by pursuing aggressive anti-union strategies, including, as indicated above, an increase in the number of non-union workplaces. This was a significant departure from the pre-liberalization period (Frenkel and Kuruvilla, 2002).

In this changing scenario, together with this diverse cultural workforce, managing organizations efficiently and competing globally, organizations had started institutionalizing systems and processed and adopting and institutionalizing innovative SHRM practices. The Indian organizations were geared to develop a constant awareness of their vision, mission, goals, ensure continuous appraisal of internal strengths, enhance innovation, improve compensation schemes, introduce more informal communication and develop better employee relations (Budhwar, 2001; Som, 2006). For example, during the late 1990s, many Indian organizations, such as State Bank of India, Mahindra & Mahindra, Wipro, ICICI Bank, Infosys, Modi Xerox, TCS, BPCL, Clariant India, Tata Group of companies and Aditya Birla Group, implemented 360-degree performance appraisal systems, merit-based recruitment and promotion systems, incentive-based pay systems, team building, re-training and redeployment within the group companies, web-based training and integrated knowledge management systems, career and succession planning, voluntary retirement schemes etc. in their organizations to enhance productivity and performance. Most of these practices, which were not practiced before, though created an awareness of strategic HRM in Indian organizations but most organizations failed to implement them due to lack of commitment from the top management and an un-integrated approach towards adopting these practices. Post 2000, these SHRM practices were more adopted by Indian organizations due to benchmarking exercises and interventions of foreign consultants to make Indian organization competitive in the face of liberalization.

In the light of the above-mentioned discussion, the need for adoption of innovative SHRM practices in Indian organizations had become a necessity.

Hypotheses and discussion

The differences in the adoption of SHRM innovation can be attributed to external environmental conditions that often distinguish organizations from one industry to another (Kossek, 1987). Most of the innovation scholars (Kimberly, 1981; Gooderham *et al.*, 1999) have studied external environmental and institutional forces in developed nations but very few have studied the context of transition nations. In the post-liberalization India, these conditions are national environment, organizational restructuring, legitimizing, ownership structure, and culture and role of HRM department. Figure 1 summarizes the propositions of this study.

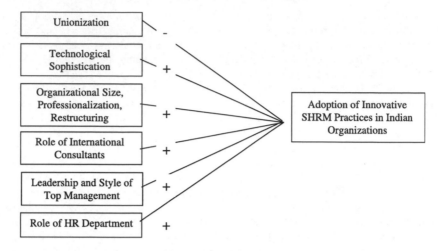

Figure 1 *Propositions for adoption of innovative SHRM practices in Indian organizations*

National environment for innovative SHRM adoption

'National environment' refers to the influence possessed by aspects such as the institutional framework, culture and incentive structures for innovative practices. Recent research has suggested that national factors can have an impact on the type of innovative SHRM practices adopted (Gooderham *et al.*, 1999). In addition to SHRMs' vulnerability to legislative changes, the function is also susceptible to changes in the socio-political landscape. Economic liberalization on the one hand intensifies competition by lowering barriers to entry and on the other opens up many opportunities for growth through removal of regulations and artificial barriers on pricing and output decisions, investments, scale economies, M&As, technology imports, joint ventures, etc. (Khandwalla, 2002). The multi-faceted competition from diverse sources (Khandwalla, 2002; Som, 2002) has to cope with the changes of developing a diverse work force with competitive skill sets. The development of competitive skill-set is challenging in the face of hyper-competition. This is so because the Indian work force has a very diverse socio-economic background and the antagonistic nature of trade unions makes it very difficult to make them work as a team (Budhwar and Sparrow, 1997; Venkat Raman, 1995). Kossek (1987) postulates that external environmental forces such as unions, technological change and labour market conditions distinguish HRM innovation across industries.

Extent of unionization and sector characteristics

In general, the literature examining the impact of trade union activity suggests a positive effect on the adoption of innovative SHRM practices (Ng and Maki, 1994). In fact, a considerable research contradicts the popular perception that trade unions hinder or resist the implementation of innovative practice (e.g. Wagar, 1997). Rather unionized workplaces tend to demonstrate greater degree SHRM practice sophistication and are more likely to possess a more formalized model of HRM (Jackson *et al.*, 1989; Ng and Maki, 1994).

On the other hand, Ramaswamy and Schiphorst (2000) suggest that the presence of an active labour union in companies restricts HR managers to innovate their processes.

The high degree of resistance that comes through the legitimate labour institutions in India act as a hindrance for managers (to innovate) and new processes such as SHRM.

Even though managers might innovate such processes, their adoption remains indeterminate as it depends upon the collective bargaining of labour unions. Each process, which reflects changes in the workforce management, needs an approval from the union leaders before it can be implemented. Long negotiation processes often tend to weaken the innovative process because of the time lag between the conception of innovative measure and approval by the management in conjunction with the union leaders. The rate of diffusion of such processes is also affected by approval or non-approval of new HR strategies by unions. For example, during the liberalization process, SBI implemented a VRS or the 'Golden Handshake' system. The vast work force that was once regarded as one of SBI's strongest assets became a liability following the computerization of the bank. The introduction of this scheme led to strong protests from officers and staff unions that claimed that the bank had taken a hasty decision without undertaking correct manpower planning measures. The ensuing struggle and media debate took a year to solve the issue amicably between the management and the unions. After prolonged discussion, the eligibility criterion of the VRS scheme was modified to personnel above the age of 55. During this time in 2002, a large number of competent employees accepted the offer and joined competitor banks. SBI was faced with a prospect of losing its talented employees and be left with less efficient employees. Hence, in the Indian context:

Proposition 1A: The higher the extent of unionization in an organization, the lower is the adoption of innovative SHRM practices.

The differences among sectors are also often cited as possible determinants of adoption of innovative practices (Kimberly and Rottman, 1987). Sector or industry characteristics influence adoption decisions by providing the context within which 'meanings are construed, effectiveness is defined, and behaviours are evaluated' (Jackson and Schuler, 1995: 252). The desire of organizations to be seen as 'good corporate citizens', socially responsive, or 'employers of choice' is also a powerful driver of innovation adoption (Kossek, 1987, 1989; Tannenbaum and Dupuree-Bruno, 1994). In the Indian context, labour unions are more prominent in the manufacturing sector than in the services sector. For example, Mahindra and Mahindra Ltd, the flagship company of the Mahindra Group, was suffering from manufacturing inefficiencies, low productivity, an over-stretched production cycle and poor output. The primary reason behind this inefficiency was the under productive and excessively unionized labour force. In 1995, the company introduced Business Process Reengineering (BPR), focusing on a total overhaul of the style in which the company was organized. The unions were made a party to the decision- making process and some specific innovative SHRM practices, like working in cross-departmental and cross-functional teams, regular meetings amongst workers and HR personnel, and hiring training, re-training and redeploying the workforce were adopted. The unions understood the urgency and the BPR programme achieved success after five years. On the other hand, adoption of innovative SHRM practices in the software services sector in companies like Infosys, Wipro, Tata Consulting Services, Mindtree Consulting, etc., started right from their inception. Hence in the Indian context:

Proposition 1B: The extent of adoption of innovative SHRM practices is lesser in the manufacturing sector than in the service sector.

Technological sophistication

Like unionization, technology affects SHRM innovation in a number of ways (Kossek, 1987). The impact of rapid structural changes in India saw evolution and development of technological sophistication. Som (2002), in his study of 54 Indian organizations, reported that there was a sharp rise in the establishing of comprehensive, computer-based information systems, technical vendor development and use of sophisticated technology for business. Tasks had been subdivided, job contents had enlarged and access to information had increased. Increased access enabled employees to be privy to information that was once only a managerial prerogative, which has ramifications for power relations and task environments that encourage additional SHRM innovations (Kossek, 1987). Increased technological sophistication in the job redefined work environments where employees had more time and information for experimentation and innovation. Regular personnel functions such as administration, paper work, salary processing needed less time due to the sophisticated use of technology. The adoption of innovative SHRM practices had long-term implications in the Indian scenario. The administrative expert role of HR (Ulrich, 1997; Som, 2006) were getting reduced or often outsourced while the strategic partner and change agent role were being redefined. For example, in organizations like BPCL (Som, 2003), an Indian Government owned company, the HRM function was redefined, became strategic and embedded in 'shared services' at the corporate HQ whereas the administrative functions were more delegated at the SBU level. With implementation of SAP, BPCL faced surplus manpower in areas of dispatch, logistics, projects and HRM. To tackle this situation, BPCL adapted innovative re-training and redeployment practices to absorb the excess workforce giving a chance for the workforce to build new competencies. It was practically impossible for BPCL, being a Government owned company, to take the route of retrenchment. Another example to note is the private banking industry that had witnessed a sea change in technological sophistication. With the advent of ATMs and Internet banking, new-age organizations like ICICI Bank have begun gaining competitive advantage compared to the nationalized banks. Hence in the Indian context:

Proposition 1C: The higher the extent of technological sophistication in organizations the higher the chance of adoption of innovative SHRM practices.

Organizational restructuring and ownership structure as drivers of innovative SHRM practices

In the post-liberalization scenario, organizational structures seem to be changing to cope with greater competition and to avail of growth opportunities afforded by globalization (Som, 2002, 2006b). Corporate restructuring – by involving the services of international management consultants – had become more frequent (Khandwalla, 2002). The main reason for restructuring is usually unsatisfactory corporate structure and business processes. Intensive scanning of the national and the international environment for growth opportunities has been on the rise, and so has been comprehensive strategy making that is integrated with human resource management strategy (Som, 2002). Economic and market pressures influenced the adoption of strategic HRM during the organizational restructuring process. Large, diversified, family-owned business houses, such as the Duncan Goenka Group, regrouped their varied product lines spread over diverse companies into synergistic product clusters for sharper focus; while Godrej graduated its product divisions into 'strategic business units' with more freedom given to make financial and investment decisions and to enter into alliances; Modi Xerox converted its functional departments into profit centres via the transfer pricing mechanism for greater bottom line consciousness; Tata Consultancy Services and Wipro Infotech, in the business of executing projects, resorted to a matrix structure in which staff members were grouped both by areas of core competencies, principal markets or industries served. Most of the large organizations, like the TATA Group of companies (TISCO, TELCO), Aditya Birla Group, undertook restructuring programmes with the help of foreign consultants. The objective was to achieve an increase in organizational differentiation through decentralization through setting up of self-contained, autonomous units with bottom line responsibility, increasing integration through a system of apex co-ordination, use of co-ordinating committees and cross-functional teams, internal communication, participative decision making, and institutionalization of core values (Som, 2002). The SHRM systems were characterized by an increasing emphasis on professionalism, skills development, incentives, accountability, flexibility, openness and rightsizing (Som, 2002). For example, the Aditya Birla Group, the third largest business group in India, grew from a US$1.5bn diversified conglomerate in 1995 to a US$7.59bn in 2006. With this growth came the necessity to restructure its businesses. The Group started restructuring its businesses to compete in the liberalized environment focusing on larger investments in fewer businesses. To manage the increasing size of the Group, it built systems and processes and institutionalized the Corporate Centre. The HR was a key player in this change process. The top-management and the HR department understood that to manage growth and size focus would have to be in building competencies and meritocracy. The growth necessitated push on the people front. The HR department institutionalized innovative HRM practices like created a management talent pool that identified over 200 managers as performers and put them on a fast track. With a view to provide for systematic and structured processes for career growth, the HR department trained more than 100 managers as job analysts and another 100 as job evaluators. With this evaluation, 5,000 jobs had been evaluated, resulting in the formation of 11 distinct job bands. These now embrace the entire life cycle of the employees' engagement with the organization. New initiatives were taken towards the well-being of the employees, particularly in the area of healthcare, education of their children and other critical aspects that could have a significant bearing on the employees' performance. For this, the Group started practising bigger challenges and providing incentives to achieve them, which were thought to be the key in preparing the organization for growth. Consistently, the Aditya Birla Group contemporized a talent pool through lateral inductions across all levels. The HR department had established a Group Management Trainee Scheme that helped recruit entry level managers from reputed business schools and academic institutions. To track employee satisfaction, the Group has institutionalized the process of an Organizational Health Survey, which is a well-regarded tool globally. The process that linked rewards to performance and encourage excellence had been institutionalized both at the individual and at the team level (Som, 2006a).

These were some of the SHRM practices that were thought to be innovative within the Indian context, as they were never practised before in business groups, like Aditya Birla Group in a formal manner. Hence,

Proposition 2A: The greater the size of the organization, the greater is the likelihood of adoption of innovative SHRM practices

Sparrow and Budhwar (1997) in their study of 137 fully-owned Indian organizations with more than 200 employees, located in north, central and western states in six manufacturing sectors, like food processing, plastics, steel, textiles, pharmaceuticals and footwear, suggest that they are still not geared to adopt innovative SHRM practices. Their findings state that 48% of the Indian HRM professionals see little or no value in adopting 360-degree performance appraisal systems, 48 per cent see no role of using new technology to promote corporate-wide communication and 45 per cent see no role in providing employees with more access to information systems. The National Management Forum of All India Management Association conducted a survey in 1995 to study the responses of Indian organizations to the change *vis-à-vis* corporate restructuring. The study surveyed 32 public sector organizations and 60 private sector organizations. It observed that in order to cope with uncertain and competitive environment, 65 per cent of the public sector organizations were undergoing restructuring and another 25 per cent were planning to restructure compared to 75 per cent and 10 per cent in the private sector respectively. Public sector organizations deemed abolition of license regime, end of monopoly, reduction of import duties and the need for upgrading and technological sophistication as causes for restructuring. The reasons for restructuring cited by the private sector organizations ranged from new economic policies, opportunities in the local as well as international markets, shrinking of domestic markets for existing products and scarce resources. Private sector organizations, mostly family owned, wanted to concentrate on core competencies and focus on capacity enhancement while the main aim for public sector was to gear themselves to face competition. Participants such as Mahindra and Mahindra, during their restructuring process adopted innovative HRM practices, such as group work, flat structure and formation of inter-departmental teams that used the 'churning effect' to change the traditional mind-set of the employees. The participants also cited improving customer focus, reducing hierarchies in organizations to obtain a 'flat' structure for faster response in decision-making and communication, as reasons for restructuring. Aditya Birla Group initiated a well-orchestrated internal and external communication process along with intense training, re-training and re-deployment programmes. It started with 300 Senior Managers at Management Development Institute, Gurgaon for Strategic Leadership programme, building '*Ganyodaya*' which is the Aditya Birla Institute of Management Learning akin to Corporate University that offered a variety of programmes like multi-tier programmes, functional programmes, role-specific programmes, competency-based programmes, and business focus programmes to the Group's employees.

The reasons for restructuring differed between the public and private sector. For public sector organizations, the chances of adoption of innovative SHRM practices will be lower and time consuming and these will hamper their adoption process – as the degree of bureaucracy and red tape is high, in addition to large power distance between the management and employees, low level of empowerment (Ramaswamy and Schiphorst, 2000) and the presence of unions. In the case of private sector organizations, mainly family owned organizations, the process of adoption of innovative SHRM practices will also be slow and tedious, as the adoption process will depend on the motivation, style of leadership and management of the business head, financial resources, cost of adoption and implementation of innovative SHRM practices and pressures originating from institutional forces (Abrahamson, 1991; Abrahamson and Rosenkopf, 1993; Walston *et al.*, 2001). For example, the adaptation of innovative practices in the Aditya Birla Group took about five–six years. It was a slow process and the innovative practices were adopted in a phased manner.

The reasons for restructuring of Indian corporations as suggested by the two studies (National Management Forum, 1995; Sparrow and Budhwar, 1997) include adopting of innovative, professional management practices and policies. Restructuring of Indian companies was necessitated to build partnerships with foreign firms – looking for growth by way of new products, new market development, M&A, JV and strategic alliances. Foreign investors usually recruit a consulting firm in their home country that assesses potential partners in India. Such firms offer additional services to ensure a smooth integration of the two partners, conduct training to transfer innovative practices in general and SHRM in particular to partner firms in India. Through such transfer of managerial innovation techniques, adoption of processes occurred. Indian organizations that have foreign partnerships exhibit a greater extent of managerial innovation techniques and offer conducive environments for an early adoption and a relatively faster speed of diffusion of innovative practices. Hence:

Proposition 2B: The greater the need to professionalize and to be competitive, the greater the need for restructuring of public sector, private sector and organizations with foreign participation, the greater the chances of adoption of innovative SHRM practices.

Proposition 2C: Family owned organizations will likely be late and slow adopters of innovative SHRM practices while organizations with foreign participation will have a higher likelihood of faster adoption of innovative SHRM practices.

Legitimizing drivers of innovative SHRM adoption

Use of international consultants by Indian organizations

According to institutional theorists, executives tend to follow social norms and try to mimic (DiMaggio and Powell, 1983) each other to secure their firm's legitimacy. The rapid spread of SHRM innovations, particularly among Fortune 500 companies, can be explained partially as a phenomenon to legitimize their existence and changes in their environments. DiMaggio and Powell (1983) view institutional isomorphism as 'a constraining process that forces one unit in a population to resemble other units that face the same set of environmental conditions'.

In India, organizations have been trying to be competitive by involving the services of international management consultants (Som, 2002). A study by Mukherjea *et al.* (1999) indicated that a significant proportion of the largest 200 companies in India have been restructured or were being restructured by the same group of international consultants. International consultants deem SHRM strategies, i.e. job rotation, training, redeployment, performance appraisal, compensation, reward mechanisms and succession planning as key indicators for improvement. International consultants reinforce a higher level of adoption of innovative SHRM practices as they are perceived to offer better services and global benchmarks, as a result management approach and reaction to such consultants change automatically. The consultants recommend cost optimization, recruitment of specialists, retraining, redeployment, performance-based management systems and rightsizing to name a few from the bundle of SHRM recommendations, in order to improve management skills. Most of the family owned conglomerates, like Tatas, Birlas, Ambanis, Modis, Mahindras, Chabrias, Godrej, Bajaj, Mehtas, etc. had recruited the services of international consultants and had other companies, such as State Bank of India, Arvind Mills, BPCL, Maruti Udyog Limited, etc. Hence:

Proposition 3: Greater the extent of use of international management consultants, the greater the chances of adoption of innovative SHRM practices.

Organizational culture for innovative SHRM adoption

Liberalized India had been inducing significant cultural and management systems related changes in the corporate sector. The main challenges before the chief executives are in the creation of flexible systems in order to develop a culture of excellence, facilitate teamwork, empower employees, and speed up and decentralize data flow (Mukherjea *et al.*, 1999). There may still be a gap between rhetoric and reality. But the change in corporate culture and management had been increasingly compatible with a competitive market environment (Khandwalla, 2002). A common feature of strong culture organizations such as TATA Group, Infosys, BPCL, Clariant India, had influential role of top management in HRM issues and the organizational impact that the leaders in these organizations have on their adoption process. Peters and Waterman (1982) in their *Search for Excellence* demonstrated how philosophies of leaders, especially the founders, regarding the way employees should be treated have become institutionalized. Organization leaders determine the role of the HR function of an organization (Kane and Palmer, 1994). Organizational leadership had a significant impact on the development of 'innovation friendly' cultures, in order to provide a clear vision, sense of direction (Peters and Waterman, 1982) and a focus for innovative activity (Arad *et al.*, 1997). Organizational cultures demonstrating high levels of internal communication, promoting interactive behaviours and an ability to deal with change encourages innovative behaviour (Hauser, 1998). Research had also shown that the presence of existing SHRM practices increase the adoption rate of additional 'high performance' HR practices (Huselid, 1995; Huselid *et al.*, 1997). High performance HR practices foster innovation through the development of innovation values, encouraging of information sharing, goal setting and appropriate training and development (Arad *et al.*, 1997). Major innovations in HRM practices occured when senior line managers take the lead (Kossek, 1987) and their adoption depends on the attitude of top management and their relationship with the HR department. For example at the Aditya Birla Group, Mr Kumara Mangalam Birla, Chairman, with the help of the HR department changed the cultural heritage of his group. There were three prevalent HR policies that were practised through decades of this 150-year-old company. These were the 'Babu culture', Womb-to-tomb' and 'Kith-and-Kin' policies. The 'Babu' culture symbolized always looking up to the head of the company for direction and decisions. 'Womb-to-tomb' policy meant that there were no fixed retirement age and loyalists of the family stayed on with the company as many years they could work and be of help to the company (similar to the age-old Japanese system). When they could not work anymore, they would request the 'babu' to guarantee their children a job in the company which led to the 'Kith-and-Kin' policy. It was a means of guaranteed jobs for family members in the Group. What used to happen was that if one son was very bright, he went to work for a multinational. The other son, if he wasn't good enough for anywhere else, was sent off to work for the Group. In the words of Mr Kumar Mangalm Birla:

> I felt that if people never retired, then there was no place for younger people to rise. So it was important to institute a retirement policy. We introduced a path-breaking retirement policy that saw 325 senior executives, mostly at the Vice-President step down between 62 to 65 after years of service. Together with this he started building a team by hiring senior people from outside, a marked departure from the past. They have been replaced with 190 young executives I also felt that the company should instil meritocracy rather than compliance, the so called Kith-and-Kin policy. So I instituted a policy that vetted all applications from family members of existing employees. (Som, 2006a)

Thus:

Proposition 4: The more influential is the organizational leadership, the stronger is the
likelihood of creating an organizational culture of innovation and
the more the likelihood of adoption of 'high performance' innovative
SHRM practices.

Role of HRM department as a facilitator in adoption of SHRM practices

Kimberly (1981) postulated how managerial adoption was imbibed in an organization
and also how this innovation spreads in the population, i.e. diffusion of innovation.
Kossek (1987, 1989) argued that major HRM innovations occurred when senior
management takes the lead and adoption of innovative SHRM practices is dependent on
the nature of relationship of the HR Department with the CEO and the line managers.
Legge (1978) had commented on the actions of personnel practitioners in the innovation
process suggested that adoption innovative practices by an organization depends largely
on HR practitioners' credibility with information and resource providers. HR department
and managers played a strategic role (Ulrich, 1997) linking the HR strategy with the
business strategy of the organization. Hence, the characteristic of the role of HR
department and managers cannot be ignored in the process. The knowledge possessed by
an HR practitioner depended on the extent to which he/she undertook activities
associated with professionalism. Activities undertaken by members of a profession
should include, among others, maintenance and development of an individual knowledge
base, ensuring continued competence levels (Hatcher and Aragon, 2000). Possession of a
current knowledge base and the ability to research new developments via methods such
as benchmarking and networking are widely acknowledged as key determinants in the
adoption of innovation (Sanchez *et al.*, 1999). The same is true for the HR department.
Considering that knowledge is the prime source of innovation or the motivation for
innovation, one can argue that companies that have the cognitive knowledge of
employees accumulated through academics act as a stimulus for innovation.

Awamleh (1994), in his study on the civil services of Jordan, tested the
relationship between education and managerial innovation. The results from
the regression reveal that there is a positive relationship between innovation and
education of the staff and the management. However, the degree of this interdependence
is not clear, as it depends on the cultural and vocational conditioning of the staff. Som
(2002) reported from his study of Indian organizations that the role of the HR department
was positively related to organizational performance and the HR department played a
significant role in the adoption of 'best practices'. For example, in the knowledge
intensive industry, such as Information Technology and IT related services, the Software
Engineering Institute (SEI) at the Carnegie Mellon University (CMU) developed the
People Capability Maturity Model (PCMM) to integrate technology and people
processes in 1995. This was a SHRM exercise for HR development specifically targeted
towards personnel involved in software and information systems development. The
adoption of PCMM in organizations entailed to help organizations integrate workforce
practices into a system to facilitate management involvement in their development.
PCMM involved five levels, each level consisting of 3–7 KPAs (key process areas) that
aimed at achieving workforce capability enhancing goals. At each level, process areas
created an inter-linked system of processes, which would transform the capability of the
workforce and result in attaining organizing capability. The emergence of PCMM in
India was attributed to high attrition rates in the software industry, which was booming

in the late 1990s. Companies such as Wipro were doubling its workforce every two years and employee retention became a major concern for many IT companies. Starting the process of implementing PCMM in 1999, Wipro, at the end of 2001 could attain PCMM Level 5 certification. This adoption of PCMM helped Wipro not only in implementing change management effectively throughout the organization, but it also achieved its organizational goal of integrating its HR with its business development and strategic objectives. It also helped Wipro achieve increased productivity and current skill sets. With the new capability development, Wipro was in a position to adapt better to rapid changes in the Indian information technology environment.

However, it is worth mentioning that employees if not taken care of, will utilize the industry cluster through networking in order to gain access to other companies where their innovative ideas would be adopted quickly for better rewards. It becomes imperative for companies to recognize such employees and retain them to gain competitive advantage. For example, the International Technology Park in Bangalore, Hyderabad, had self-contained power facilities, modern gymnasiums, food courts and other amenities. Narayan Murthy, Chief Mentor of Infosys, understood the adoption of SHRM practices from the very beginning. He said,

> My employees seek challenging opportunities, respect, dignity and the opportunity to learn new things. I keep telling them that my assets are not this building, the business or foreign contact. My assets, in 2001 – all 8000 of them – walk out the gate every evening and I wait for them to come back to me the next morning.

To retain talent, Infosys issue stock option as early as 1997. By 2001, Infosys had about 2000 rupee-millionaires and more than 213 dollar-millionaires. In 2006, Infosys has about 52,715 employees, predicted to grow to over 75,000 by 2007. Thus, in the Indian context:

> *Proposition 5*: The more professionally managed is the HR Department, the greater is the strategic role of the HR Department in terms of its ability to identify, develop and manage support resources and greater is the likelihood of adoption of SHRM practices.

Conclusion

This study provided valuable insights into the adoption of innovative SHRM practices in Indian organizations. Consistent with prior research, the study finds that institutional pressures have influenced the adoption of SHRM practices in the post liberalization scenario in India. It demonstrated that organizations adopt SHRM practices for a variety of reasons. The antecedents of innovative SHRM practices include national environment (extent of unionization and sector characteristics, technological sophistication), organizational restructuring and ownership structure, legitimizing driver (use of international consultants), organizational culture and the role of HR department.

The theoretical contribution of this article is that it analyses drivers of adoption of innovative SHRM practices within Indian firms due to changes occurring in the macro-environment through a contingency-based framework. Adoption of SHRM practices, represent a strategic choice. The adoptions are contingent upon the strategic and systemic organizational responses of Indian firms. Strategic responses related to the changes in business strategy of the organization. It became evident that as the country liberalized the rules of the game changed as well. Systemic responses are those related to organizational structures, functions, cultures and processes. This study focused and adds to the literature on drivers of systemic responses and how they translate to the adoption of SHRM practices in Indian organizations in the context of economic liberalization.

The article pointed out that though the institutional environment is specific to the Indian context the propositions are not. With respect to HRM practices, the question for researchers and practitioners is two fold: how generalizable are these propositions, and what is the value of them?

The propositions of this study are close to those found in the literature meant for developed economies (Kimberly, 1981; Kossek, 1987, 1989; Gooderham *et al.*, 1999; Walston *et al.*, 2001; Wolfe, 1995) and therefore may be relevant to most sectors and industries anywhere in the world wherever there is a competitive market or a movement towards it. The propositions are grounded in managerial innovation and SHRM literature. Due to paucity of studies in innovative SHRM practices, more research is needed to test for generalizability of the hypothesis. It seems that there are fairly strong logical reasons why these practices may have wide relevance in liberalizing economies.

In the post-liberalized India, a hyper-competitive business environment presented a number of challenges and opportunities, both external and internal. External challenges and uncertainties included barriers that were difficult to control. Internal challenges like dramatic advances in technology, changing of organizational forms necessitated redesigning of SHRM practices like recruitment and selection, promotion, retraining and redeployment, performance appraisal and rightsizing. The globalization of business brought with it a global workforce and practiced that needed to be adopted and diffused to create a global work place. It is true that adoption of innovative SHRM practices in organizations take place at a slow pace and some innovations are particularly slower than others are. Potential payoffs, cost of adoption, power relations and social factors hinder adoption process in organizations and more so in a liberalizing economy. Successful adoption, diffusion and implementation of SHRM practices can be critical determinants for organizational success and effectiveness. When innovative SHRM practices are adopted, they provide a sustainable competitive advantage depending on how creatively and effectively they are interpreted and executed.

Acknowledgement

The author acknowledges the research grant from ESSEC Research Centre for this Project.

Note

1 According to Section 25(O) of Industrial Disputes Act, 1947, employers are required to take prior permission of the appropriate government for retrenchment of workers where the number of employees was 100 or more.

References

Abrahamson, E. (1991) 'Managerial Fads and Fashions: the Diffusion and Rejection of Innovations', *Academy of Management Review*, 16(3): 586–612.

Abrahamson, E. and Rosenkopf, L. (1993) 'Institutional and Competitive Bandwagons: Using Mathematical Modelling as a Tool to Explore Innovation Diffusion', *Academy of Management Review*, 18: 487–517.

Arad, S., Hanson, M. and Schneider, R. (1997) 'A Framework for the Study of Relationships Between Organizational Characteristics and Organizational Innovation', *Journal of Creative Behaviour*, 31(1): 42–58.

Awamleh, N.A.H.K. (1994) 'Managerial Innovation in the Civil Service in Jordan', *Journal of Management Development*, 13(9): 52–60.

Belout, A., Dolan, S.L. and Saba, T. (2001) 'Trends and Emerging Practices in Human Resource Management', *International Journal of Manpower*, 22(3): 207–15.

Budhwar, P.S. and Sparrow, P.R. (1997) 'Evaluating Levels of Strategic Integration and Development of Human Resource Management in India', *The International Journal of Human Resource Management*, 8(4): 476–94.

Budhwar, P.S. (2001) 'Human Resource Management In India'. In Budhwar, P.S., Pawan, S. and Debrah, Y.A. (eds) Part I: Human Resource Management In Asia, *Human Resource Management in Developing Countries*. London: Routledge, pp. 75–90.

Colbert, B. (2004) 'The Complex Resource-Based View: Implications for Theory and Practice in Strategic Human Resource Management', *Academy of Management Review*, 29(3): 341–58.

Damanpour, F. (1991) 'Organizational Innovation: A Meta-analysis of Effects of Determinants and Moderators', *Academy of Management Journal*, 34(3): 555–90.

Delery, J.E. and Doty, D.H. (1996) 'Modes of Theorizing in Strategic Human Resource Management: Tests of Universalistic, Contingency, and Configurational Performance Predictions', *Academy of Management Journal*, 39: 802–35.

DiMaggio, P.J. and Powell, W.W. (1983) 'The Iron Cage Revisited: Institutional Isomorphism and Collective Rationality in Organizational Fields', *American Sociological Review*, 48: 147–60.

Fombrun, C.J., Tichy, N.M. and DeVanna, M.A. (1984) *Strategic Human Resource Management*, vol. 23. New York: Wiley.

Frenkel, F. and Kuruvilla, S. (2002) 'Logics of Action, Globalization and Changing Employment Relations in China, India, Malaysia, and the Philippines', *Industrial and Labor Relations Review*, 55(3): 387–412.

Geary, J.F. and Roche, W.K. (2001) 'Multinationals and Human Resource Practices in Ireland: A Rejection of the 'New Conformance Thesis', *International Journal of Human Resource Management*, 12(1): 109–27.

Gooderham, P.N., Nordhaug, O. and Ringdal, K. (1999) 'Institutional and Rational Determinants of Organizational Practices: Human Resource Management in European Firms', *Administrative Science Quarterly*, 44(3): 507–32.

Harel, G.H. and Tzafrir, S.S. (1999) 'The Effect of Human Resource Management Practices on the Perceptions of Organizational and Market', *Human Resource Management*, 38(3): 185–99.

Hatcher, T. and Aragon, S. (2000) 'A Code of Ethics and Integrity for HRD Research and Practice', *Human Resource Development Quarterly*, Summer: 179–85.

Hauser, M. (1998) 'Organizational Culture and Innovativeness of Firms – An Integrative View', *International Journal of Technology Management*, 16(1–3): 239–55.

Hofstede, G. (1991) *Culture's Consequences: Software of the Mind*. London: McGraw-Hill Book Company.

Huselid, M. (1995) 'The Impact of Human Resource Management Practices on Turnover, Productivity, and Corporate Financial Performance', *Academy of Management Journal*, 38(3): 635–70.

Huselid, M., Jackson, S.E. and Schuler, R.S. (1997) 'Technical and Strategic Human Resource management Effectiveness as Determinants of Firm Performance', *Academy of Management Journal*, 40(1): 171–88.

Ichniowski, C. and Shaw, K. (1999) 'The Effects of Human Resource Management Systems on Economic Performance: An International Comparison of US and Japanese Plants', *Management Science*, 45(5): 704–21.

Jackson, S. and Schuler, R. (1995) 'Understanding Human Resource Management in the Context of Organizations and Their Environments', *Annual Review of Psychology*, 45: 237–64.

Jackson, S.E., Schuler, R.S. and Rivero, J.C. (1989) 'Organizational Characteristics of Personnel Practices', *Personnel Psychology*, 42: 727–86.

Kane, R. and Palmer, I. (1994) 'Strategic HRM or Managing the Employment Relationship?', *International Journal of Manpower*, 16(5–6): 6–21.

Khandwalla, P.N. (2002) 'Effective Organisational Response by Corporates to India's Liberalisation and Globalisation', *Asia Pacific Journal of Management*, 19(2/3): 423–48.

Kimberly, J.R. (1981) 'Managerial Innovation'. In Nystorm, P.C. and Starbuck, W.H. (eds) *Handbook of Organizational Design*. Amsterdam: Elsevier, pp. 84–104.

Kimberly, J.R. and Evanisko, M.J. (1981) 'Organizational Innovation: The Influence of Individual, Organizational and Contextual Factors on Hospital Adoption of Technological and Administrative Innovations', *Academy of Management Journal*, 24(4): 689–713.

Kimberly, J.R. and Rottman, D.B. (1987) 'Environment, Organization and Effectiveness: A Biographical Approach', *Journal of Management Studies*, 24(6): 595–620.

Kossek, E. (1987) 'Human Resources Management Innovation', *Human Resource Management*, 26(1): 71–92.

Kossek, E. (1989) 'The Acceptance of Human Resource Innovation by Multiple Constituencies', *Personnel Psychology*, 42: 263–81.

Krishna, A. and Monappa, A. (1994) 'Economic Restructuring and Human Resource Management in India?', *Indian Journal of Industrial Relations*, 29: 490–501.

Legge, G.E. (1978) 'Sustained and Transient Mechanisms in Human Vision: Temporal and Spatial Properties', *Vision*, 18: 69–81.

Lengnick-Hall, C.A. and Lengnick-Hall, M.L. (1988) 'Strategic Human Resource Management: A Review of the Literature and a Proposed Typology', *Academy of Management Review*, 13: 454–70.

Mukherjea, D.N., Narayan, S. and Dhawan, R. (1999) 'Companies on the Couch', *Business World*, 7–12 February: 24–31.

National Management Forum (1995) *Corporate Restructuring – A Survey of Indian Experience*, All India Management Association. India: Excel Books.

Ng, I. and Maki, D. (1994) 'Trade Union Influence on Human Resource Management Practices', *Industrial Relations*, 33(1): 121–35.

Peters, T. and Waterman, R. (1982) *In Search of Excellence*. New York: Harper and Row.

Ramaswamy, E.A. and Schiphorst, F.B. (2000) 'Human Resource Management, Trade Unions and Empowerment: Two cases from India', *International Journal of Human Resource Management*, 11(4). 664–80.

Rao, T.V., Rao, R. and Yadav, T. (2001) 'A Study of HRD Concepts, Structure of HRD Departments, and HRD Practices in India', *Vikalpa*, 26(1): 49–63.

Rao, T.V. (1999) *HRD Audit*. New Delhi: Response Books.

Sanchez, J., Kraus, E., White, S. and Williams, M. (1999) 'Adopting High Involvement Human Resources Practices: The Mediating Role of Benchmarking', *Group and Organisation Management*, 24(4): 461–78.

Schuler, R.S. and Jackson, S.E. (eds) (1999) *Strategic Human Resource Management: A Reader*. London: Blackwell.

Schuler, R.S., Dowling, P.J. and De Cieri, H. (1993) 'An Integrative Framework of Strategic International Human Resource Management', *International Journal of Human Resource Management*, 4: 717–64.

Scott, R.W. (1995) *Institutions and Organizations*. London: Sage.

Sengupta, A.K. (2004) 'HRD in India: What Is It?', *Decision*, 31(1): 145–76.

Som, A. (2002) "Role of Human Resource Management in Organizational Design", Unpublished doctoral dissertation, Ahmedabad: Indian Institute of Management.

Som, A. (2003) 'Building Sustainable Organizations through Restructuring: Role of Organizational Character in France and India', *International Journal of Human Resource Development and Management*, 3(1): 2–16.

Som, A. (2006) 'Bracing MNC Competition through Innovative HRM practices: The Way Forward for Indian Firms', *Thunderbird International Business Review*, 48(2): 207–37.

Som, A. (2006a) 'Aditya Birla Group: Redesigning to become a Fortune 500 Company', *European Case Clearing House*.

Som, A. and Cerdin, J.-L. (2005) 'Vers Quelles Innovations RH dans les Entreprises Françaises?: Une Etude Exploratoire', *Gestion 2000*, 2(5): 143–9.

Sparrow, P.R. and Budhwar, P.S. (1997) 'Competition and Change: Mapping the Indian HRM Recipe against World-Wide Patterns', *Journal of World Business*, 32(3): 224–42.

Tannenbaum, S.I. and Dupuree-Bruno, L.M. (1994) 'The Relationship between Organizational and Environmental Factors and the Use of Innovative Human Resource Practices', *Group and Organization Management*, 19(2): 171–203.

Ulrich, D. (1997) *Human Resource Champions: The Next Agenda for Adding Value and Delivering Results*. Boston, MA: Harvard University School Press.

Venkata Ratnam, C.S. (1998) 'Multinational Companies in India', *The International Journal of Human Resource Management*, 9(4): 567–89.

Walston, S.L. and Kimberly, J.R. (2001) 'Institutional and Economic Influences on the Adoption and Extensiveness of Managerial Innovation in Hospitals: The Case of Reengineering', *Medical Care and Research Review*, 58(2): 194–228.

Wolfe, R. (1995) 'Human Resource Management Innovations: Determinants of their Adoption and Implementation', *Human Resource Management*, 34(2): 313–27.

Wright, P.M. and McMahan, G.C. (1992) 'Theoretical Perspectives for Strategic Human Resource Management', *Journal of Management*, 18(2): 295–320.

Building flexibility into multi-national human resource strategy: a study of four South African multi-national enterprises

Albert Wöcke, Mike Bendixen and Rasoava Rijamampianina

With global expansion, multi-national enterprises (MNEs) are under pressure to find the appropriate balance between global and local practices. The standardization of global practices across the MNE help to smooth the transfer of MNE competencies across the organization while local conditions may require that the affiliate in a host country adopt different practices, for example, to comply with local regulations or accommodate a culture diverse from that of the MNEs original country (Aycan, 2005). The primary issue in the co-ordination of an MNE's global operations is the co-ordination of management practices to enable the transfer of firm-specific advantages (FSAs) between the parent and affiliates, whether they are location based or not (Rugman and Verbeke, 2003). Key in this regard is the degree of influence that the parent exercises over its affiliates, and many studies have used similarity between the HRM practices of parent and affiliate as an indicator of this relationship (Hannon *et al.*, 1995; Martinez and Ricks, 1989; Rosenzweig and Nohria, 1994), and leads to a search for HRM practices that are flexible enough to co-ordinate and integrate multiple affiliates but still enable the transfer of FSAs (Braun and Warner, 2002). This is particularly pertinent to MNEs from emerging markets in general and Africa in particular. African MNEs differ from Asian MNEs in that their competencies are developed in countries that have distinct disadvantages due to the erosion of natural resources and a lack of investment in infrastructure, both physical and human capital (Wells, 2003). Despite these location problems, the four South African MNEs managed to develop the necessary strategic capabilities to compete in the global arena, *viz.* national responsiveness, global integration (efficiency) and worldwide learning (Bartlett and Ghoshal, 1987; Malnight, 2001). Additionally the South African social and regulatory environment would have played a role in the development of these capabilities. According to Gomez and Sanchez (2005), a country's institutional environment and, in particular, its regulatory framework has a very powerful influence on the way a firm is managed. In the case of South Africa, the four firms have had to contend with the management and advancement of diversity as driven by regulations such as The Employment Equity Act (55 of 1998; Republic of South Africa, 1998) and an emergent black middle class with diverse demands and tastes and rapidly expanding economic power. These developments have meant that for South African firms to be successful, they would have to have developed the competencies to manage high degrees of complexity and ambiguity, capabilities that would provide an advantage when operating in different national cultures. Additionally Hannon *et al.* (1995) found that when a subsidiary (or affiliate) is highly dependent on the parent to provide crucial resources that the parent was likely to exert influence through formal coordination mechanisms. The exercise of influence is done mainly through the use of integrated international human resource (IHR) strategies, which are intended primarily to balance the tensions between local responsiveness and global integration (e.g. Taylor and Beechler, 1996).

Substantial and important previous work on strategic international human resource management deals with the content of an MNEs corporate, or parent level, strategy and compares differences in approaches based on country (e.g. Aycan, 2005; Luthans *et al.*, 1997), while others deal with the issues arising from the management of an MNE across a variety of countries (e.g. Ghoshal and Nohria, 1993; Taylor and Beechler, 1996) but do not deal with the design problem of building the appropriate level of flexibility into an MNE corporate HR strategy. This is consistent with the observations of Brewster *et al.* (2005), who point out that HR functions at a variety of levels in an MNE, including philosophy, policy, practice and process. This in turn requires an understanding of deeper complexity than the traditional IHRM focus on comparative studies of cultural relativity in the implementation of core HR functional processes, such as high performance work systems (HPWS) (e.g. Huselid, 1995).

Configuration of HR strategies

Very little work has been done on the configuration or the methods for implementing and controlling the translation of HR strategy by affiliates of an MNE. The configuration of the MNE's corporate strategy has to take into account the balance between those activities that need to be centralized or standardized and the degree of flexibility required by the affiliate to operate in the host country.

The configuration of HR strategies is distinguishable by variance in terms of level of abstraction and scope. The level of abstraction refers to the level at which the HR strategy is focused. According to Schuler *et al.* (1993), there are different levels of abstraction in the design of a global HR system. Levels vary from recommendations, or policy-, to operational-level procedures. With a policy-level of abstraction, affiliates are given the freedom to implement their own HR strategies within the broad parameters of the standardized policies. However, with an operational level of abstraction, affiliates are

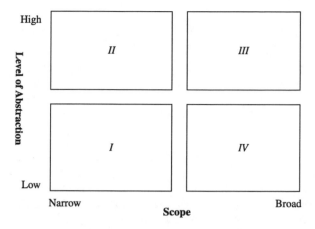

Figure 1 *Types of corporate HR strategy*

expected to implement a more detailed HR management practice. Scope refers to the extent of HR management practices dealt with in the HR strategy. For example, the HR strategy may have a narrow scope and focus on two or three key areas, or it may have a wide scope and deal with the more comprehensive list of practices such as those described in the HPWS movement (e.g. Huselid, 1995; Ulrich, 1997). The four possible configurations are shown in Figure 1 above.

In the four MNEs examined, we found that the determination of the appropriate configuration model is largely dependent on the business model, the impact of national culture on the business model, and the role of an MNE's organizational culture in directing and controlling affiliates, which has an impact on the degree of convergence, or isomorphism present in the organization. This is demonstrated in Figure 2.

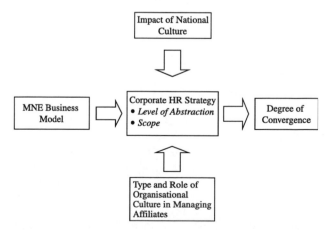

Figure 2 *Variables impacting on the configuration of corporate HR strategy*

Business model

The business model largely drives corporate HR strategy and there is a need for congruence and alignment of HR management practices and business strategy (Briggs and Keogh, 1999; Mabey *et al.*, 1998; Schuler, 1992). The increased complexity of MNEs is the result of MNEs pursuing value-creating opportunities that become available when firms have a global presence (e.g. Gupta and Govindarajan, 2001), but the increased complexity requires the appropriate organizational architecture, of which HR is a critical component.

A most useful way of explaining MNE business models is the eclectic paradigm (Dunning, 1988). In terms of the paradigm firms invest across national borders because of an interplay between a firm's ownership-specific advantages (Firm Specific Advantages), the location attractiveness of countries or regions, and advantages gained from internalizing cross-border operations within the MNE; the so-called OLI approach. The first factor, Ownership, refers to a firm's specific competencies and an understanding of how they develop, the second, Location, relates to an appreciation of the transferability of a firm's competencies between markets, while the third factor, Internalization, deals with the alternative modes of market entry in a competitive context. The choice of location is influenced by a combination of FSAs and country-specific factors, such as the availability of natural resources, access to markets, or assets that complement the FSA. These respective approaches are referred to as Resource Seeking Foreign Direct Investment (FDI), Market Seeking FDI and Strategic Asset Seeking FDI (Dunning, 2003). Resource and market seeking activities were the primary drivers of FDI since the 1970s but this trend has reversed as the value of services and intangible assets increase. This has led to MNEs seeking more knowledge-based assets in the form of intellectual capital or low-cost skilled labour, which in turn favours destinations with knowledge intensive assets or learning advantages away from those with purely natural resources. In all four cases, the firms are primarily exporting knowledge intensive FSAs that will either give them access to new markets (Nando's) or support their existing FSAs (SABMiller, MTN and Sasol).

By implication, it can be expected that the role of social capital, and consequently HR, plays a more significant role in strategic asset seeking MNE business models than resource seeking or purely market seeking business models (Gomez and Sanchez, 2005). This is consistent with the findings of Malnight (2001), who found that MNE business models are evolving into differentiated businesses that are characterized by a global dispersion of operations, interdependence and tight coupling of subunits, and an emphasis on cross-subsidiary learning and structural flexibility. Malnight (2001), in his study of two pharmaceutical firms, found varying evidence of this trend towards a common model and a greater complexity was developing within firms which was characterized by a growing internal differentiation in internal structures of MNEs. This is also discussed by Rugman and Verbeke (2003) who refer to firms with a high level of internal differentiation as differentiated network MNEs and these firms are characterized by a high level of transfer of knowledge, both location and non-location based, in multiple directions. Rugman and Verbeke (2003) show that different approaches to managing subsidiaries arise from the varying needs of subsidiaries for access to different bundles of knowledge, these may be location bound (e.g. local market responsiveness) or non-location bound (LB and NLB knowledge bundles). In addition, the movement of the bundles may be unidirectional – from parent to affiliate, or multi-directional – affiliate to parent or from networks of subsidiaries.

The impact of national culture on the MNE

The impact of national culture on the operations of an MNE is experienced most strongly in its HR management practices. National culture impacts on the implementation of corporate HR strategy as personal motivations, the way that information is synthesized, and economic utilities are culture bound (Grossman and Schoenfeld, 2001; Hofstede, 1993; Schwartz and Sagiv, 1995; Trompenaars, 1993). Rowley and Benson (2002) show that national culture provides an important role in limiting the depth and acceptance of universal management practices across an MNE. The significance of national culture on moderating HRM practices was explored by Ferner *et al.* (2001), who examined the differences between management practices in MNEs and their operations in host countries and found in their study of German MNEs operating in Britain and Spain. They discovered that although there are pressures on MNEs to adopt US-style business practices such as standardized international policies on appraisal, performance management and so on, that the influence of the German business system persists.

This view was a challenge to a study by Child *et al.* (2000), who examined what types of changes would be introduced to British companies when taken over by foreign companies. In particular, the study tried to identify whether there were nationally distinct approaches to management following the acquisitions. The study found that the process of acquisition was rapidly followed by significant changes in management practice but that some practices were common to all companies while others conformed to accepted characterizations of national management practice. The national conformation was clear in the case of Japanese and US acquirers, but less so for French and German firms.

Organizational culture in management of corporate HRS

Countering the role of national culture and local conditions is organizational culture; a strong organizational culture unites employees in their actions which, in turn, influences performance (Ghobadian and O'Regan, 2002; Levin, 2000). Organizational culture is often seen as an instrument to maintain unity and control between parent and affiliate, and can play a role in moderating the freedom of the affiliate to change and adapt its HR strategy from the corporate HR strategy. Yaconi (2001) found that substantial differences in management role expectations exist both across and inside MNEs, which suggests that differences result from more than national cultures and may indicate the role of organizational culture.

Ghobadian and O'Regan (2002) explore the relationship between organizational culture, strategy and performance. They find that there is a positive relationship between culture and performance and that strategy is influenced by culture, which in turn, influences and develops the corporate culture. It then follows that it is in the interest of organizations to establish and build an organizational culture that provides both a competitive advantage and a distinctive identity. Aycan *et al.* (2000) distinguish between internal work culture and external culture. Internal work culture is similar to organizational culture and is construed as a pattern of shared managerial beliefs and assumptions that directly influence HR practices. These beliefs and assumptions in turn relate to both the task and employees. Managerial assumptions about the task relate to the nature of the task and how it should be performed, while those assumptions relating to employees relate to the nature and behaviour of employees. Managerial assumptions of task and employees are influenced, in turn, by institutional level culture and societal-level culture. The transfer of organizational culture is often done through the use of expatriates. Expatriates from the MNEs parent country are used in managing the interests of the organization and transferring its competencies, systems and even aspects of its organizational culture to its subsidiaries in foreign locations. This is referred to as an ethnocentric approach, as opposed to a polycentric approach where affiliates are staffed by host country nationals, or a geocentric approach which staffs affiliates and subsidiaries with staff from a third country (Perlmutter, 1969).

For MNEs, organizational culture fulfils an additional role in that it determines the method of exercising control or influence over the affiliates and the cross-MNE implementation of corporate HR strategy. In an organization with an organic culture (Reigle, 2001), formal control systems are likely to cause dissonance while the same is true for an organization with a mechanistic culture not utilizing formal processes.

Convergence

Convergence, also known as isomorphism, is the process whereby MNEs will gravitate towards a series of universal management practices that provide competitive benefits for themselves (Childs and Yanni, 2001; Pauly and Reich, 1997). The drivers of convergence at organizational level are efficiency, growth, and the development and utilization of technology. Convergence can be regarded as continuous organizational learning and the development and application of practices that lead to organizational efficiency, but are still flexible enough to be applied generally (Hickson and Pugh, 2001). It follows that convergence is also occurring in the adoption of international HR practices; with increased complexity facing MNEs, there has been less emphasis on formal structure and a greater focus on HR management policies and practices, which form an integral part of the process-input control systems of modern MNEs. This has led to an upsurge in the search for global best practices or HR strategies that can be applied across all cultures (Braun and Warner, 2002).

The contingent view of HR strategy in MNEs emphasizes that there is one best method, even within contingent variables such as stage of internal corporate evolution (Rowley and Benson, 2002). Typical of the contingent view is that of Bjorkman and Lu (1999) who investigated the standardization of Western practices in Chinese-Western joint ventures. The study showed that overall HRM practices had become similar to those in Western MNEs, especially when compared with data gathered in 1992. This was seen as due to the spread of Western ideals in the Chinese business network, the greater emphasis that Western MNEs were placing on HR management, and the limited liberalization of Chinese employment legislation. It was noted that few Western companies had made the total transfer of HRM policies to China; this was not due to national cultural differences but local conditions.

Gooderham *et al.* (1999) came to a similar general view, although in a different context when they compared HRM practices in European firms in six divergent countries. Gooderham *et al.* (1999) found that although there were differences in management practices across these firms, that this was more likely due to the role of legal and political structures in the various countries than cognitive orientation. Most firms wanted to adopt the latest management practices prescribed in American literature and supported by business consulting firms across Europe, but could not because of varying regulative and political conditions.

Some evidence is emerging that there exists a hybrid between divergence and convergence (Horwitz *et al.*, 2002). This is defined as cross-vergence, which refers to cross-cultural diffusion of high performance work practices (HPWPs). The motivation for adopting HPWPs includes the need for efficiency, productivity, and high quality goods and services but these are tempered by contextual factors present in the host country. Cross-vergence provides an integrative alternative to the convergence/divergence debate and accommodates diversity, at both country level and within-country level. Cross-vergence also implies reverse diffusion.

Additional factors influencing the configuration of HR strategies

Additional factors that would influence the configuration of MNE HR strategies are institutional and cognitive factors. Institutional factors include regulatory factors in the home country that would impact on the translation of corporate HR strategy by an affiliate in a host country. Gomez and Sanchez (2005) point out that a country's institutional framework and its cognitive sets impede or enhance the application of HR practices such as performance appraisals. Rosenzweig and Nohria (1994) in a study of 249 US affiliates of foreign-based MNEs found that in general, affiliate HRM practices closely resemble practices of local (US) firms. Where differences do exist, these are influenced by method of founding, dependence on local inputs, the presence of expatriates and the extent of communication with the parent. These findings were further elaborated by Martinez and Ricks (1989) and Hannon *et al.* (1995) who found that the affiliate's dependence on host institutions would be reduced when a subsidiary (or affiliate) is highly dependent on the parent to provide crucial resources and when the parent was likely to exert influence through formal coordination mechanisms.

Methods

The methodology used for the study was a qualitative type using a multiple-case study approach. This approach is appropriate for this type of study, as qualitative studies produce a description to reveal the nature of situations, settings and relationships and allow for the verification of assumptions, claims, theories or generalizations within real-world contexts, and can provide a means through which a researcher is able to judge the effectiveness of particular policies, practices or innovations (Holliday, 2002; Leedy and Ormrod, 2001).

Multiple-case sampling is a method of deductive reasoning where a range of similar and contrasting cases are studied to enable a high degree of generalization. The choice of cases is made based on conceptual grounds rather than representation. Additionally the multiple-case sampling method is essentially a replication strategy where one is able to generalize from one case to another based on agreement with underlying theory. In other words, a finding is more robust if it is shown that it holds true in one setting, and then holds true in a comparable setting, but it does not hold true in a contrasting setting (Miles and Huberman, 1994).

Sampling in qualitative research generally consists of small samples of people nested within their context and studied in-depth, unlike quantitative research, which aims for larger numbers of context-stripped cases and seeks statistical significance (Miles and Huberman, 1994). For this reason, qualitative samples are generally of the non-probability type. The use of case-study techniques requires information-rich data, which is more important for analysis than the ability to make statistical inferences about the characteristics of the population. Generalizations about a population may still be made from the samples but not on statistical grounds. The research conducted used purposive, or judgemental, sampling to determine the cases and populations that would best answer the research questions (Saunders *et al.*, 2003).

This study was limited to four South African MNEs, selected for the profundity that they may provide as stand-alone cases. The MNEs chosen are prominent in South African society and have been successful examples of MNEs from emerging markets. The MNEs are from the petro-chemical (commodity) industry, the Fast Moving

Consumer Goods (FMCG) industry and manufacturing industry, the telecommunications industry and the fast-food retail industry. This particular selection of MNEs permitted both comparisons and contrasts in business models and corporate HR strategies. Key employees who were interviewed had to be at the appropriate levels within the MNEs to provide detail and richness to the cases. The respondents were the senior executives responsible for the company wide HR strategy at parent level and the HR executives at affiliate level. Specifically the persons interviewed per organization were: the Group HR director, or equivalent; the HR director, or equivalent, of an identified affiliate; and selected support staff at parent and affiliate responsible for planning and implementation of the HR strategy across the group. In total, 24 persons were interviewed for the study. Triangulation was achieved by additional sources of data, including company documentation, published research and newspaper or journal reports, and personal interviews at various levels in the respective firms.

Data were analysed by means of content analysis, and in particular, according to the method suggested by Leedy and Ormrod (2001) in which the data is first analysed in a coherent form together with a brief description of each firm and its context. The data is then categorized into meaningful groups, which were derived from prior theory and additional themes that occurred through the process. Following this process, interpretation of specific instances was performed to explore specific meanings related to the theory. Finally, the syntheses and generalizations of each case were compared by means of a cross-case analysis.

The four South African MNEs

The four South African MNEs selected as cases to compare were Nando's International, Sasol, MTN International and SABMiller.

Nando's International

Nando's International is an international food franchise organization that was started in 1987 from the successful Nando's brand in South Africa to take advantage of the opportunities offered by taking the brand international. In 1995, the company had grown to 45 outlets in South Africa with an additional 17 in other southern African countries (Namibia, Botswana, Zimbabwe and Swaziland). By 2003, Nando's International was operational in 22 countries and had revenues of about US$300 million.

Nando's International does not yet have a formal HR strategy although key elements of such a strategy are present. The lack of HR strategy is a product of the recent history of Nando's International's global expansion, the nature of the industry and the franchise relationship. Nando's International's first forays into international markets were largely unstructured and based on trial and error, with mixed success. Lessons learnt were applied to the operating systems and financial reporting systems. As Nando's International moved up the learning curve and understood its product better, it began to adopt global practices, most notably in the form of standardized operating systems and financial reporting systems. HR systems lagged and guidelines were offered from the South African context to guide franchisees but country operations are free to interpret these for local conditions.

Because of the franchise arrangements, Nando's International's role is that of a facilitator of group-wide HR management practices. Nando's International identifies best practice and policies and encourages the dissemination of information and management practice between affiliates in various countries. For example, the group has identified the UK operation as the best practice in recruitment while the South African operation is best from a technical point of view. The process of searching for best practice across the group is not yet deeply entrenched and is limited to direct interventions from Nando's International and annual conferences.

SABMiller

SABMiller is a South African based brewing company with operations in eastern Europe, Africa, Central America, Asia and North America. At the end of the 2003 financial year, SABMiller had achieved total beverage volumes of 151.4 million hectolitres, of which 115.8 million hectolitres were lager. Revenue was US$9.1 billion with earnings of US$1.2 billion.

The SABMiller growth model is people-dependent, not brand-dependent as brands are largely regionally based, with very few international brands being successful in the industry. The business strategy with newly acquired businesses is to send a core of expatriate managers, usually numbering between four and six, into the operation to begin transferring the SABMiller organizational culture and to evolve the operations to ideal efficiencies and quality at which time SABMiller's global brands are introduced to that market. The enormity of the challenge can be understood when one considers that the South African operation's workforce is only approximately 5,000, yet it has managed to create about 160 senior executives to expand the business globally.

MTN International

MTN is a mobile telecommunications supplier and offers cellular network access and associated services through subsidiaries and joint ventures in Nigeria, Cameroon, Uganda, Rwanda and Swaziland. In 2003, MTN had a subscriber base of about 2 million outside of South Africa and revenues of US$ 1 billion in 2003.

The Human Resources function is an integral part of the MTN Group's operations and it plays a key role in leveraging business areas through performance management, talent management, human capital development and allocation. The key components of the MTN HR strategy are an ongoing policy and procedure development across the group, which are implemented from start-up of operations in all affiliates and subsidiaries. The provision of robust quality practices and policies by the head office would support developing countries to achieve their business plans. This is supported by the use of expatriate managers and technicians seconded from South Africa into new operations. This, in itself, has led to certain obstacles created by a largely Western-oriented leadership while lower level employees and customers have a local orientation.

By the end of 2003, 80 per cent of HR policies were standardized across all subsidiaries with the objective of achieving 100 per cent standardization. Policies that were standardized include recruitment policies, job grading systems, remuneration policies and Human Resource Information Systems.

Sasol

Sasol is a South African petro-chemical corporation built on the application and commercialization of unique technologies. Sasol has a global value chain with upstream and downstream operations, from coal and gas upstream, through to synthetic fuels, and chemicals and waxes downstream. By 2003, Sasol was operational in 23 countries, exporting to more than 100, and was one of the top five publicly listed companies in South Africa, with listings on the JSE Securities Exchange and NYSE. Revenue was about US$ 11 billion. Exports from South African operations and revenue from operations outside South Africa accounted for 52 per cent of group revenue.

The impact of Sasol's global business strategy is to centralize the content of its HR strategy and the drive towards global best practice is becoming stronger with the transfer of knowledge across the global value chain and the vertical integration of businesses across national boundaries. This drive is increasing as Sasol rolls-out its business strategy and global HR standards are dictated from the centre. To achieve its HR strategy, Group HR has created six Centres of Expertise: talent management (retention); talent attraction; development of people; remuneration; productivity improvement and diversity management. These Centres of Expertise guide the development of policy across the group in their respective areas. They continuously research for best practice and update HR policy in addition to enabling line managers to be effective channels for people management.

Analysis and findings

When one applies Figure 1 to the four case studies, Nando's fits into quadrant one, SABMiller into quadrant two, MTN International into quadrant three and Sasol into quadrant four, as shown in Figure 3.

Nando's has the narrowest scope in its HR strategy of the four cases, and it has a low level of abstraction because of the detail in identified-best practice. There is no formalized corporate HR strategy, although elements are present in terms of values and recruitment guidelines. Affiliates are able to implement their own HR strategies, as long as these do not contradict the overall Nando's product and experience. Components of a corporate HR strategy are emerging with the adoption of best practice amongst affiliates. This is developing as Nando's country operations are assisted to compare best practice with other national operations and to adopt best suitable practice for their respective operations. On the other hand, Sasol's corporate HR strategy is the most comprehensive, yet it has the lowest level of abstraction. Affiliates are required to implement a comprehensive set of practices at operational level, developed by centres of expertise and which are coordinated from the centre.

MTN International has a comprehensive HR strategy that has a high level of abstraction. At MTN International, corporate HR strategy is developed by the centre and

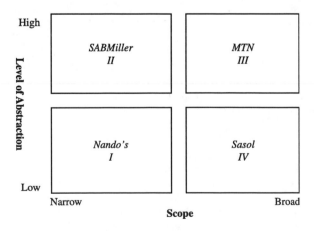

Figure 3 *South African MNEs and corporate HR strategy configuration*

is at policy level to allow flexibility at operational level. In MTN International, the drive is for conformance by affiliates to operational, marketing and HR policies in line with its vision of a single continent-wide network. SABMiller's Africa-Asia hub HR strategy is less comprehensive than that of MTN and Sasol and deals with three core areas: performance management, strategic people resourcing and capacity to manage organizational change. Yet, like MTN International, the level of abstraction is high, as affiliates are free to develop their own HR strategies, as long as they incorporate the three core areas. This is carefully monitored from the centre, with assistance being offered and given where and when required by the affiliate.

In all of the cases, the HR strategy, whether implied or formalized, is an integral part of the business strategy. This supports the view of Ulrich (1997), who argues that, in addition to HR strategy being an important component of the business strategy, alignment and congruence with the business model are essential.

A comparison of the four MNEs by business model, impact and accommodation of national culture on host country activities, type of organizational culture, and degree of convergence is represented in Table 1.

The choice of business model is driven by the degree of emphasis on either global integration of operations to gain efficiencies, or local market responsiveness. The business model will determine the degree of global integration or localization of business practices and this is reflected in the comparison of Sasol and Nando's where Sasol's need is for efficiency when selling industrial commodities to other MNEs, while Nando's requires a high degree of localization for the successful interpretation of its core values. A higher level of global integration requires the HR strategy to be more comprehensive as more operations need to be standardized to gain efficiencies across the group. A higher degree of standardization of operations and standards are generally aided by the rollout of enterprise resource planning systems and the development of a core group of critical human resources that are able to operate in any of the enterprise's diverse locations.

National culture and local regulations will have varying degrees of influence on the practicality of the corporate HR strategy for the affiliate and this is reflected by the degree of adaptation of the corporate HR strategy by the affiliate. In all four cases, the impact of national culture on the implementation of the respective HR strategies is clear, consistent with the views of Murray *et al.* (1976) and Schuler and Rogovsky (1998). National culture is regarded as an independent variable as it affects the implementation of a MNEs corporate HR strategy, as it did in all four cases. However, the impact and the degree of accommodation of national culture varied between the cases where the HR strategy was adapted more in the case of those firms that needed a higher degree of local responsiveness than those that had a more integrated value chain. The level of responsiveness is offset somewhat against the resource dependency of the affiliate on the parent (Taylor and Beechler, 1996) and the flow of location and non-location bound information (Rugman and Verbeke, 2003). This is illustrated in a comparison between SABMiller and Sasol, in the case of SABMiller the local operation's high level of local responsiveness to national culture declines as the operation modernizes and global brands are successfully introduced. Global brands are introduced as the operation matures and the local operation develops the capacity to replicate the SABMiller FSAs with limited assistance from the parent. In the case of Sasol, the local operation is closely integrated into the global value chain, which requires a high level of certainty and consistency as its fortunes are closely tied to that of the other operations and the emphasis is on co-ordination of the global value chain.

Organizational culture, an important component of social capital, is another variable in building flexibility in MNE HR strategy. The role of organizational culture is most

Table 1 *Comparison of four South African MNEs*

	Type I: Nando's	*Type II: SABMiller*	*Type III: MTN International*	*Type IV: Sasol*
(a) Corporate HR strategy: level of abstraction and scope	Low level of abstraction, narrow scope	High level of abstraction and narrow scope	High level of abstraction and wide scope	Low level of abstraction and wide scope
(b) MNE business model – emphasis on global integration or local market responsiveness	Local responsiveness	Maintain the balance between global integration and local responsiveness	Focus on global integration with degree of local responsiveness	Global integration of value chain and focus on efficiency
(c) Accommodation of national culture	High level of adaptation	Medium to high level of adaptation	Low to medium level of adaptation	Very limited adaptation
(d) Organizational culture and primary method of managing affiliates	Organic culture; personal relationships and coaching used to influence affiliates	Organic culture; relationships and development primary method of influence over affiliates	Mechanistic-organic culture; mixture of formal processes and relationships to influence affiliates	Mechanistic culture; formal systems and processes primarily used to influence affiliates
(e) Convergence of IHRM practices	Lowest degree of convergence – evidence of cross-vergence	Medium convergence	Medium convergence	High convergence

strongly experienced as a control mechanism in HR strategy. In all four organizations there was evidence that organizational cultures were important enablers of HR strategy, in line with the views of Gomez and Sanchez (2005), but that the role of the culture varied according to mechanistic or organic cultural orientation (Reigle, 2001). Organizations with a more mechanistic culture, Sasol and to a lesser degree MTN, preferred to use more formal mechanisms to control the manner in which local operations implemented the corporate HR strategy, while those with a more organic culture, Nando's and SABMiller, relied on relationships and coaching to implement and control the direction of the corporate HR strategy.

The design and implementation of corporate HR strategy and the evolution of the modern MNE into a differentiated enterprise is likely to lead to higher levels of convergence in HR management practices (Braun and Warner, 2002; Malnight, 2001). This view is consistent with all respondents who expressed a wish for universal, or standardized, HR management practices across all operations. Advantages of universal practices identified by respondents included the ability to allocate scarce skills across the global organization, consistency in the measurement and reward of high performers across the group, succession planning and management, and building a strong organizational culture. By implication then, a stable HR strategy that is sufficiently flexible to accommodate the complexities of foreign conditions is likely to lead to HR management practices that are universally applied in all of an MNEs operations.

Contributions of the research

The four dimensions of the model show that flexibility is an important component of the design of a MNE-wide HR system. The model addresses both main streams of thought in IHRM, the degree of similarity between parent and affiliate HR management practices (e.g. Aycan *et al.*, 2000; Budhwar and Sparrow, 2002; Taylor and Beechler, 1996), and country comparisons (e.g. Hickson and Pugh, 2001; Hofstede, 1993).

The model further demonstrates that IHRM researchers need to consider IHRM in at least two dimensions, the level of abstraction and scope. These are important when designing systems to manage the transferability of FSAs across the organization and add greatly to the dilemma about centralization vs. decentralization in MNEs. Additionally, the model builds on the work in the field of international human resource management by integrating the concepts of MNE business models (e.g. Bartlett and Ghoshal, 1987; Gupta and Govindarajan, 2001; Rugman and Verbeke, 2003), organizational culture (e.g. Reigle, 2001), national culture (e.g. Hofstede, 1993), human resource strategy (e.g. Ulrich, 1997) and convergence (e.g. Braun and Warner, 2002). The HRS configuration model also highlights the role of corporate HR strategy and organizational culture in the culture free-culture rich (or convergence-national culture) debate, an area not adequately researched to date and shows how business models impact on the design of HR strategy in MNEs.

The limitations of the study relate to the sample and the methodology used. The size of the sample was limited to four and included a wide scope of business model, industry and nationality, which highlighted inter-case differences. However, the limited size of the sample does preclude conclusions drawn from differences between cases in the same industry, nationality or using the similar business models. The sample used South African-based MNEs that, while reducing confounding variables, such as the nationality of the MNE, may also limit the ability of the study to generalize for other MNEs that are from countries with a large cultural distance from South Africa. In addition, the complex nature of international business means that there are additional variables and factors that could impact on the development and implementation of corporate HR strategies in multi-nationals. Additional variables could include the role of expatriates (although this is implied in the choice and implementation of the corporate HR strategy), the maturity of the industry or business cycles.

Finally, with a caveat, the four MNEs all originate from South Africa and are recent MNEs. Their experience and competencies have been formed against the backdrop of a rapidly changing society that values and embraces diversity. This has meant that these four MNEs learnt lessons about managing and serving diverse customers while pursuing efficiency and standardization within one country. MNEs from more stable and homogenous home countries would likely follow a slightly different route to developing the ability to balance stability with flexibility and the translation of their FSAs in their HR strategies.

Acknowledgement

The authors would like to acknowledge the contribution of the reviewers to this paper.

References

Aycan, Z. (2005) 'The Interplay Between Cultural and Institutional/structural Contingencies in Human Resource Management Practices', *International Journal of Human Resource Management*, 16(7): 1083–119.

Aycan, Z., Rabinda, N.K., Mendonca, M., Yu, K., Deller, J., Stahl, J. and Kurshid, A. (2000) 'Impact of Culture on Human Resource Practices: A 10-Country Comparison', *Applied Psychology: An International Review*, 49(1): 192–221.

Bartlett, C.A. and Ghoshal, S. (1987) 'Managing Across Borders: New Strategic Requirements', *Sloan Management Review*, Summer: 7–17.

Bjorkman, I. and Lu, Y. (1999) 'The Management of Human Resources in Chinese–Western Joint Ventures', *Journal of World Business*, 34(3): 306–24.

Braun, W. and Warner, M. (2002) 'The "Culture-free" Versus the "Culture-specific" Management Debate'. In Warner, M. and Joynt, P. (eds) *Managing Across Cultures, Issues and Perspectives*, 2nd ed. London: Thomson Learning.

Brewster, C., Sparrow, P. and Harris, H. (2005) 'Towards a New Model of Globalizing HRM', *International Journal of Human Resource Management*, 16(6): 949–70.

Briggs, S. and Keogh, W. (1999) 'Integrating Human Resource Strategy and Strategic Planning to Achieve Business Excellence', *Total Quality Management*, 10(4/5): 447–53.

Child, J. and Yanni, Y. (2001) 'National and Transnational Effects in International Business: Indications from Sino–Foreign Ventures', *Management International Review*, First Quarter: 53–75.

Child, J., Faulkner, D. and Pitkethly, R. (2000) 'Foreign Direct Investment in the UK 1985–1994: The Impact on Domestic Management Practice', *Journal of Management Studies*, 37(1): 141–67.

Doz, Y. and Prahalad, P.K. (1986) 'Controlled Variety: A Challenge for Human Resource Management in the MNC', *Human Resource Management*, 25(1): 55–71.

Dunning, J.H. (1988) 'The Eclectic Paradigm of International Production: A Restatement and Some Possible Extensions', *Journal of International Business Studies*, 19(Spring): 1–31.

Dunning, J.H. (2003b) 'Some Antecedents of Internalization Theory', *Journal of International Business Studies*, 34 (March): 108–17.

Ferner, A., Quintanilla, J. and Varul, M.Z. (2001) 'Country-of-origin Effects, Host-country Effects, and the Management of HR in Multinationals: German Companies in Britain and Spain', *Journal of World Business*, 36(2): 107–28.

Ghobadian, A. and O'Regan, N. (2002) 'The Link Between Culture, Strategy and Performance in Manufacturing SMEs', *Journal of General Management*, 28(1): 16–35.

Ghoshal, S. and Nohria, N. (1993) 'Horses for Courses: Organizational Forms for Multinational Corporations', *Sloan Management Review*, Winter: 23–35.

Gomez, C. and Sanchez, J.I. (2005) 'HR's Strategic Role within MNCs: Helping Build Social Capital in Latin America', *International Journal of Human Resource Management*, 16(12): 2189–200.

Gooderham, P.N., Nordhaug, O. and Ringdal, K. (1999) 'Institutional and Rational Determinants of Organisational Practices: Human Resource Management in European Firms', *Administrative Science Quarterly*, 44(1999): 507–31.

Grossman, W. and Schoenfeld, L.F. (2001) 'Resolving Ethical Dilemmas Through International Human Resource Management: A Transaction Cost Economics Perspective', *Human Resource Management Review*, 11: 55–72.

Gupta, A.K. and Govindarajan, V. (2001) 'Converting Global Presence into Global Competitive Advantage', *Academy of Management Executive*, 15(2): 45–56.

Hannon, J.M., Ing-Chung, H. and Bih-Shiaw, J. (1995) 'International Human Resources Strategy and its Determinants: The Case of Subsidiaries in Taiwan', *Journal of International Business Studies*, 26(4): 531–55.

Hickson, D.J. and Pugh, D.S. (2001) *Management Worldwide, Distinctive Styles Amid Globalization*. London: Penguin.

Hofstede, G. (1993) 'Cultural Constraints in Management Theories', *Academy of Management Executive*, 7(1): 81–94.

Holliday, A. (2002) *Doing and Writing Qualitative Research*. London: Sage Publications.

Horwitz, F.M., Kamoche, K. and Chew, I.K.H. (2002) 'Looking East: Diffusing High Performance Work Practices in Southern Afro-Asian Context', *International Journal of Human Resource Management*, 13(7): 1019–41.

Huselid, M. (1995) 'The Impact of Human Resource Managment Practices on Turnover, Productivity and Corporate Financial Performance', *Academy of Management Journal*, 38: 635–72.

Leedy, P.D. and Ormrod, J.E. (2001) *Practical Research: Planning and Design*, 7th edn. Upper-Saddle River, NJ: Prentice-Hall Inc.

Levin, I.M. (2000) 'Five Windows into Organization Culture: An Assessment Framework and Approach', *Organization Development Journal*, 18(1): 83–94.

Luthans, F., Marsnik, P.A. and Luthans, K.W. (1997) 'A Contingency Matrix Approach to HRM', *Human Resource Management*, 36(2): 183–200.

Mabey, C., Salaman, G. and Storey, J. (1998) 'Strategic Human Resource Management: The Theory of Practice and the Practice of Theory'. In Mabey, C., Salaman, G. and Storey, J. (eds) *Strategic Human Resource Management*. London: Sage Publications Ltd, pp. 1–13.

Malnight, T.W. (2001) 'Emerging Structural Patterns within Multinational Corporations: Toward Process-based Structures', *Academy of Management Journal*, 44(6): 1187–210.

Martinez, Z. and Ricks, D. (1989) 'Multinational Parent Companies' Influence Over Human Resource Decisions of Affiliates: US Firms in Mexico', *Journal of International Business Studies*, 20: 465–88.

Miles, M.B. and Huberman, A.M. (1994) *An Expanded Sourcebook; Qualitative Data Analysis*, 2nd edn. Thousand Oaks, CA: Sage Publications.

Murray, V.V., Jain, H.C. and Adams, R.J. (1976) 'A Framework for the Comparative Analysis of Personnel Administration', *Academy of Management Review*, 1: 47–57.

Pauly, L.W. and Reich, S. (1997) 'National Structures and Multinational Corporate Behavior: Enduring Differences in Age of Globalization', *International Organization*, 51: 1–30.

Perlmutter, H.V. (1969) 'The Tortuous Evolution of the Multinational Corporation', *Columbia Journal of World Business*, 4(1): 9–18.

Reigle, R.F. (2001) 'Measuring Organic and Mechanistic Cultures', *Engineering Management Journal*, 13(4): 3–8.

Republic of South Africa (1998) The Employment Equity Act 55.

Rosenzweig, P.M. and Nohria, N. (1994) 'Influences on Human Resource Management Practices in Multinational Corporations', *Journal of International Business Studies*, 25: 229–51.

Rowley, C. and Benson, J. (2002) 'Convergence and Divergence in Asian Human Resource Management', *Californian Management Review*, 44(2): 90–105.

Rugman, A.M. and Verbeke, A. (2003) 'Extending the Theory of the Multinational Enterprise: Internalization and Strategic Management Perspectives', *Journal of International Business Studies*, 34: 125–37.

Saunders, M., Lewis, P. and Thornhill, A. (2003) *Research Methods for Business Students*, 3rd edn. Harlow: Pearson Education Limited.

Schuler, R.S. (1992) 'Strategic Human Resources Management: Linking the People with the Strategic Needs of the Business', *Organizational Dynamics*, 21(1): 18–30.

Schuler, R.S. and Rogovsky, N. (1998) 'Understanding Compensation Practice Variations Across Firms: The Impact of National Culture', *Journal of International Business Studies*, 29: 159–77.

Schuler, R.S., Dowling, P.J. and De Cieri, H. (1993) 'An Integrative Framework of Strategic International Human Resource Management', *International Journal of Human Resource Management*, 4: 717–64.

Schwartz, S.H. and Sagiv, L. (1995) 'Identifying Culture-specifics in the Content and Structure of Values', *Journal of Cross-Cultural Psychology*, 26(1): 92–116.

Taylor, S. and Beechler, S. (1996) 'Toward an Integrative Model of Strategic International Human Resource Management', *Academy of Management Review*, 12(4): 959–85.

Trompenaars, F. (1993) *Riding the Waves of Culture*. London: Economist Books.

Ulrich, D. (1997) *Human Resource Champions: The Next Agenda for Adding Value and Delivering Results*. Boston, MA: Harvard Business School Press.

Wells, L.T. Jr (2003) 'Multinationals and the Developing Countries'. In Brewer, T.L., Young, S. and Guisinger, S.E. (eds) *The New Economic Analysis of Multinationals: An Agenda for Management, Policy and Research*. Cheltenham: Edward Elgar Publishing Limited, pp. 106–21.

Yaconi, L.L. (2001) 'Cross-Cultural Role Expectations in Nine European Country-Units of a Multinational Enterprise', *Journal of Management Studies*, 38(8): 1187–215.

Globalization of HR at function level: four UK-based case studies of the international recruitment and selection process

Paul R. Sparrow

Introduction: literature review

Most academics still subscribe to the view that globalization is more a work in progress, the boundaries of which are still hard to fathom. Only a few firms are considered to have developed an effective capability to locate, source and manage human resources anywhere in the world (Lewin and Volberda, 2003) and multinational enterprises (MNEs) continue to have assets, sales, ownership of workforces and control concentrated in home countries or regions (Rugman and Verbeke, 2004). The observation that stateless organizations operating independently of national borders under global rules of economic competition are few and far between (Ferner and Quintanilla, 1998) would still seem to hold true. Yet, considerable globalization is in progress, with 63,000 transnational corporations (TNCs) shaping trade patterns account for about two-thirds of all world trade but the top 100 of these corporations accounting for 12 per cent of foreign assets, 18 per cent of sales and 14 per cent of employment of all TNCs in the world (UNCTAD, 2005). We need to understand better how this process operates in relation to the human resource management inside organizations.

Globalization is examined at different levels of analysis, each tending to produce different perceptions of how advanced or pervasive the process is and the extent of its influence over IHRM policies and practices. The main models and frameworks that have been used in the field concentrate on five levels of analysis:

1   Comparative analysis of national business and management systems (Brewster *et al.*, 1996; Pieper, 1990; Whitley, 1992, 2000) which itself can have different embedded levels of analysis from business system down to specific HR practices (Brewster, 2007).
2   The globalization of industries (Bartlett and Ghoshal, 1989; Makhija *et al.*, 1997; Morrison and Roth, 1992).
3   Relative levels of internationalization of the firm (Ramaswamy *et al.*, 1996; Sullivan, 1994, 1996).
4   The progressive building of international capabilities within organizations (Ashkenas *et al.*, 1995; Caves, 1996; De Saá-Pérez and García-Falcón, 2002; Dunning, 1993; Hamel and Prahalad, 1985; Prahalad and Doz, 1987; Stonehouse *et al.*, 2000; Yip, 1992).
5   Processes of functional realignment taking place in response to globalization (Brewster *et al.*, 2005; Kim *et al.*, 2003; Malbright, 1995; Sparrow *et al.*, 2004).

Each of these produces valuable insights. Most of the theoretical developments within the field of IHRM (as opposed to comparative HRM) are driven by attention to the third and fourth levels of analysis (Schuler and Tarique, 2007). However, globalization at functional level revolves around complexity evidenced in two ways. First, through the range of theory that we have to draw upon, and the competing theoretical issues that surface depending on the level of analysis that is adopted; and second, through the different assumptions about the level and scope of globalization that might emerge depending upon the level of analysis that is adopted.

Staffing policies are often used as broader indicators of overall IHRM strategy on the assumption that analysis of company use of staff provides insight into and 'may tell about strategies, policies or practices' (Torbiörn, 2005: 47). At a policy level, much of the literature on global staffing focuses on the recruitment of senior lead positions in headquarters or subsidiaries (i.e. the resourcing of senior international managers such as directors or expatriates) with attention being directed at whether the pattern of such appointments is ethnocentric, polycentic, regiocentric or geocentric. It concentrates on the international transfer of expatriates or inpatriates. Harzing (2004: 252) notes that '. . . although the term expatriate could literally be taken to mean any employee that is working outside his or her home country, it is normally reserved for parent country nationals and sometimes third-country nationals working in foreign subsidiaries of the MNC for a pre-defined period'. The advantages and disadvantages of such policies draw upon conceptual literature from the 1980s or early 1990s (for example, Harzing (2004) cites Negandhi (1987), Phatak (1989) and Dowling and Schuler (1990)) and a handful of empirical studies (for example, Harzing, 2001; Kopp, 1994; Tung, 1982). The factors given attention by international staffing theory include cultural distance or levels of uncertainty avoidance between HQ and subsidiaries, educational levels, living costs and political risks of host country; industry sector; or age, size and performance of subsidiary (Harzing, 2004).

There has also been methodological critique of the global staffing field. The use of 'manager counts' as a face-level criterion of IHRM or of some assumed policy provides limited insight into issues of control, co-ordination or competence and ignores many of the realities of options open to organizations (Torbiörn, 2005). This literature also often uses either single-source respondents or archival data such as ratios of appointments between PCN, HCN and TCNs to assess policy focus, perhaps accounting for the previous set of revealed conceptual factors. Where there is analysis of motivations for international staffing, it tends to concentrate on motivations for expatriate assignments such as co-ordination and control, management development or knowledge transfer.

Wright and Boswell (2002) note that such methods do not capture different perceptions of policy and practice nor do they help reveal the causal influences between these two levels of analysis. Strategic issues of competitiveness, external fit to goals and internal fit in terms of coherence '... may not be verified through inspection of staffing patterns' (Torbiörn, 2005: 51). The existing literature and the conceptual factors it discusses are mainly descriptive of structural factors and may have limited linkage to the decision logics that guide internal strategy in practice, either within the central HR function or in devolved business partners. The strategic content and organizational processes of MNCs have mainly been examined through study of the conflicting demands surrounding the adaptation of practice. The constructs of integration (central co-ordination by headquarters, sometimes also called unification) towards common goals through control mechanisms based on personal decision-making, bureaucratic, output or socialization and responsiveness (either subsidiary influence over strategic and operational issues or local differences in customer preferences and need for adaptation to local marketing, also called differentiation or fragmentation) result in typologies of action labelled as global, international, multi-domestic and transnational (Bartlett and Ghoshal, 2000).

When examining parent-subsidiary relationships, different organizational needs for control and integration affects the strategic use of recruitment and selection (Taylor *et al.*, 1996). Understanding the impact of globalization on IHRM helps solve the 'Differentiation-Integration' puzzle and the adoption of 'best fit' approaches based on the standardization or optimization of HR practices. This conceptual distinction remains central to the field of IHRM, but has been criticized on the grounds of understating the role of worldwide learning and knowledge transfer (Harzing, 2004) so theory is based on the study of recruitment and selection of expatriates and international managers, talent management policies at HQ or local level, and some attention to more flexible forms of international business travellers, virtual teams and inpatriates (Scullion and Collings, 2006).

Yet, as Briscoe and Schuler (2004: 223) note, the definition of international employee inside organizations continues to expand: 'the tradition of referring to all international employees as expatriates – or even international assignees – falls short of the need for international HR practitioners to understand the options available ... and fit them to evolving international business strategies'. In the context of international resourcing, this now includes a fragmentary group of individuals, ranging from: contract expatriates (Baruch and Altman, 2002); assignees on short-term or intermediate term foreign postings (Mayerhofer *et al.*, 2004a; Morley and Heraty, 2004); permanent cadres of global managers (Suutari, 2003); international commuters (*The Economist*, 2006); employees utilized on long-term business trips (Mayerhofer *et al*, 2004b); international transferees (moving from one subsidiary to another) (Harvey *et al.*, 1999; Salt and Millar, 2006); virtual international employees active in cross-border project teams (Janssens and Brett, 2006); skilled individuals working in geographically remote centres of excellence serving global operations (Sparrow, 2006); self-initiated movers who live in a third country but are willing to work for a multinational (Tharenou, 2003); immigrants actively and passively attracted to a national labour market (Salt and Millar, 2006; Briggs, 2003); and domestically based employees in a service centre but dealing with overseas customers, suppliers and partners on a regular basis.

Not only has international recruitment and resourcing moved away from its traditional focus on managing pools of expatriates, but the changing structure and role of international HR functions means that these functions and their HR business partners now have to help their organizations manage a very wide range of options associated with global resourcing (Hustad and Munkvold, 2005). Salt and Millar (2006) draw attention to a number of factors that have increased demand for new forms of international mobility: the need for skilled expatriates to help build new international markets (Findlay *et al.*, 2000); temporary and short-term access to specialized talent in sending countries to assist the execution of overseas projects (Hocking *et al.*, 2004; Minbaeva and Michailova, 2004); and the need for highly mobile elites of management to perform boundary-spanning roles to help build social networks and facilitate the exchange of knowledge (Tushman and Scanlan, 2005). In addition to the process of fragmentation, the opportunity for broader resourcing strategies has increased markedly in certain labour markets that have themselves become globalized (Ward, 2004). Considerable attention has been given for example to the globalization of healthcare markets (Aiken *et al.*, 2004; Clark *et al.*, 2006; Kingma, 2006; Oberoi and Lin, 2006).

Research questions

Kim *et al.* (2003) argue that we need to study processes of functional realignment within globalizing organizations if we are to understand the driving forces within business functions as they seek to co-ordinate (develop linkages between geographically dispersed units of a function) and control (regulate functional activities to align them with the expectations set in targets) their activities across borders. Malbright (1995: 119) similarly argues that true 'Globalisation occurs at the level of the function, rather than the firm'. We therefore need to understand how organizations enhance the ability of specific functions to perform globally. This paper examines the process of functional realignment due to globalization within one of the core IHRM functions, that of resourcing (international recruitment and selection). Recent empirical analysis of these pressures conducted at the level of the HR function in its totality has revealed five factors driving the organizational strategy of globalizing firms, each associated with different combinations of the above issues: efficiency; information exchange/organizational learning; global provision; core business process convergence; and localization (Brewster *et al.*, 2005). The requirement for efficiency has witnessed the pursuit of three key delivery mechanisms for global HRM: a focus on shared service structures, the e-enablement of many HR processes on a regional or global scale, and the pursuit of global centres of excellence. This global reconfiguration of activity has extensive ramifications for the field of IHRM. Historically, it was the preserve of those HR actors dealing with managers working on overseas postings, with attention given to the need to identify the particular skills and competencies that were important to be an effective international manager. Attention has now shifted to the need not just to have a separate IHRM function for a dedicated group of managers, but also to internationalize all of the fundamental HR processes of an organization.

> *RQ1*: Does the study of globalization processes at functional level (staffing) provide useful insights for the IHRM literature?

A second issue concerns the need to understand how the impact of global markets becomes internalized inside organizations. Harvey *et al.* (2000: 382) argue that many firms have not yet internalized the influence of global markets and 'what is needed is a global management staffing strategy that enables global consistency among various managerial pools and the foreign subsidiaries'. They concluded that the proper integration of a transcultural emphasis in global staffing systems would be an intriguing future research topic. In order to understand such transcultural influences, we need to explore staffing policies and practice as they apply to both domestic and overseas markets. Wright and Boswell (2002) noted that the field of HRM has traditionally separated out analysis of strategic (macro) issues from treatment of specific HR function or practice (micro) issues. They developed a typology of HR research with two dimensions (level of analysis and number of practices) and argued that we need to better understand the intersections between these dimensions. However, micro-level research examining functions (such as recruitment, selection or training) has typically analysed individual-level impacts. The research here is an example of research that examines a macro-level phenomenon (globalization) as applied to micro-level issues (stated policy and individual HR actor perceptions of recruitment policy and practice). Specifically, it examines the interplay between HR policies, defined as 'the firm or business unit's stated intention about the kinds of HR programs, processes' and actual HR practices, defined as 'techniques that actually get operationalized in the unit', as suggested by Wright and Boswell (2002: 263). In order to ensure that the correct balance of standardization versus differentiation is reached, rhetoric would have it that geographical partners have to be treated as equal partners in the ensuing debate. Often the local in-country or functional HR business partners have to manage the tensions between policy and practice. Consequently, research needs to give attention to the role of local HR business partners in this process of interpretation and negotiation. By identifying the issues *within* each case study that lead to there being either alignment or divergence between policy and actual practice, it is argued here that we may identify a more appropriate set of indicators.

RQ2: What sort of indicators evidence globalization of recruitment at the functional level and might these form the basis of future research?

The literature review showed that a distinction is made between integration and differentiation of practice which in turn involves either centralized or decentralized co-ordination and control of policy. However, tensions between central policy and in-country HR actors clearly vary depending on the relative levels of dependency on home or overseas labour markets. In an environment of globalizing labour markets, central policy makers might be responsible for and have control over dealing with skills shortages in domestic labour markets that now require novel recruitment and resourcing strategies directed at overseas labour markets. In this instance, integration pressures and issues would be felt within the HQ but would be experienced mainly by home labour-market HR actors. However, there may be central policy control over the need to deal with resourcing issues, but with activity directed at overseas markets, where operations require the injection of specialized skills or higher volumes of specific skills in order to resource market growth. Integration pressures would still be experienced within the HQ, but be experienced mainly in the overseas markets. Conversely, the dependency might operate the other direction. There may be more localized or devolved control over resourcing issues, but with activity still directed towards home-market priorities or to overseas-market priorities. A second issue concerns the need to understand how the impact of global markets becomes internalized inside organizations. As noted earlier,

Harvey *et al.* (2000) argued that firms need to internalize the influence of global markets. In order to understand such transcultural influences, we need to explore staffing strategies that enable global consistency among various managerial pools and foreign operations. They concluded that the proper integration of a transcultural emphasis in global staffing systems would be an intriguing future research topic. In order to understand such transcultural influences, we need to explore staffing policies and practice as they apply to both domestic and overseas markets. Such macro-level questions about global resourcing strategy are addressed by analysis across case studies conducted where the focus is on domestic or overseas labour markets.

> *RQ3*: Can we detect patterns or strategies within the global HR recruitment activity of organizations across domestic and overseas labour markets and can these patterns be explained by existing theory?

Methodology

The case studies were selected to fit into the following theoretical sampling frame. The first dimension is that of integration, based on Kim *et al.*'s (2003) call for examination of processes of functional realignment through the proxies of control (regulation of functional activities and alignment with corporate expectations) and co-ordination (linkages developed between geographically dispersed units of a function) within globalizing organizations if we are to understand the driving forces within business functions as they seek to co-ordinate and control their activities across borders. The cases are selected for either centralized and decentralized control and co-ordination. In order to examine Harvey *et al.*'s (2000) call for study of transcultural influences, the cases examine the conduct of these activities in destination labour markets that are either primarily domestic or overseas. The four UK-based case studies are:

1   BBC World Service (centralized control and international recruitment primarily for domestic labour market). The case looks at the process of resourcing specialist skills for use primarily in home markets in the context of an ongoing process of outsourcing (although the services were broadcast for overseas markets). Many organizations now have to resource very specialist technical skills whose location is flexible and whose services may be deployed in both home and overseas markets and, at the same time, manage a strong employer brand.

2   Barclaycard International (centralized control and recruitment primarily for overseas labour markets). The case examines recruitment in the context of an internationalization strategy. It focuses on the activities necessary to set up operations in a series of new countries as part of a strategy to massively expand the scale of international business activity. It centres around issues of expatriate mobility, a smooth process of new country start ups, and changes in the role of in-country HR partners.

3   South East London Strategic Health Authority (de-centralized control and international recruitment primarily for domestic labour market). Within the National Health Service, international recruitment is from overseas countries for employment into the home (UK) market. The case looks at the experiences of as it operated a number of programmes to attract overseas candidates into the UK.

4   Save the Children (decentralized control and recruitment primarily for overseas labour markets). The case examines experiences of and learning from the not-for-profit sector as the need to combine diversity priorities with central needs for talent

management is tackled through a decentralized responsibility for international recruitment activity.

The BBC, Save the Children and the National Health Service are not typical MNCs and do not need to employ long-term expatriates. Barclaycard International does need such staff as part of a general mix of resourcing necessary to support an internationalization strategy. The BBC is also different from Save the Children in that it cannot rely on local resources to report news; it has to send short-term assignees (flexpatriates) overseas or outsource to local news agencies. However, Save the Children has to rely on local resource and may maintain only a 'loose connection' with local branches. The National Health Service is a domestic organization, but one that operates in an increasingly globalized labour market and domestic skills shortages, necessitating considerable overseas recruitment.

Data were gathered from February 2005 through to March 2006. Semi-structured interviews were conducted in English with 15 HR actors. Within each of the four case studies, the question asked to select interviewees was 'who is responsible for international recruitment?'. At a policy level, interviews were held with five HR actors who had this responsibility (an HR Director International, Director of Workforce Development, Head of Resourcing, International HR Manager, and Talent Director). The initiatives that these actors saw as being central to their function were then examined and key HR actors associated with the implementation identified. To examine the issues at an HR practice level interviews were held with 10 HR actors. These were eight country-level HR business partners in the UK, Spain, Germany and Ireland, and two functional HR business partners, a country-level recruitment consultant and a resourcing business partner. Interviews lasted from 30 minutes to two hours and were transcribed with field notes taken about emerging issues after each round of interviewing. HR actors in central/director roles were expected to provide most insight into policy issues; while HR actors in devolved (country or business partner) level roles were expected to provide most insight into the realities of actual practice, though both sets of actors were asked questions about both policy and practice under the themes noted below.

The interviews focused on the main issues for international HR actors when operating in each of the four contexts. The case studies were used to explore policy, practice and variance between the two (Wright and Boswell, 2002). With regard to policy, questions focused on the following themes: strategic nature and motivations behind the HR interventions; political/process skills brought to bear during design and delivery of the intervention; perceived links to organizational effectiveness and contribution to strategy (mission, objectives, structure, systems, culture); and the perceived risks/cost of failure. With regard to practice, question themes focused on: contrasting expectations of the intervention role between central and business partner roles; factors that facilitated or impeded consistency of execution; and technical knowledge needed by HR community.

To help contextualize each case, organization websites and intranets were accessed to gather data on employment policy and an external search of professional and press coverage conducted. As part of a reliability process, in each instance, the case study was sent to all interviewees from the organization for interpretation and further comment and insight on events. Finally, as part of a validity check and in order to provide peer interpretation of the findings, each of the emerging case studies was disseminated and interpreted at three workshops involving HR professionals and service providers not involved in the case organizations. The workshops were hosted by the European Association of Personnel Management and the Chartered Institute of Personnel and Development (CIPD) in May and July 2005 and March 2006. In most instances, the case studies were co-presented by the policy-level HR actor and the researcher, and workshops and practitioner questions were used to generate writing themes for the final case studies.

Global HR strategies often emerge in the context of rapid contextual change (Sparrow *et al.*, 2004). In each case study, the opportunity afforded by the year of study enabled some secondary analysis of the changing context for study over the period through reference to publicly released information. For example, BBC World Service continued to clarify and develop its strategy around outsourcing and within the NHS changes in national immigration rules in the UK resulted in a public discussion about the ethics of overseas recruitment. Similarly, decisions about the nature of central co-ordination roles were made at Barclaycard International.

Case study findings

Sufficient case detail is provided here to enable an understanding of how the complexity of the initiatives patterns. This is outlined by examining the range and sequence of activity surrounding the development of the international resourcing function and concentrating on the policies. The findings show the complexity of functional-level developments at this level of analysis, especially once attention is turned away from the traditional focus on MNCs. The disparities between policy and practice, and patterns across the cases are interpreted in the context of IHRM literature in the discussion section.

South East London Strategic Health Authority (de-centralized control and international recruitment primarily for domestic labour market)

The situation in the British National Health Service (NHS) shows the complex issues faced by HR professionals in coping with overseas recruitment into domestic markets. The NHS is the largest single employer within the UK, employing over a million people: 5 per cent of the working population. There are numerous careers in over 70 professions. International recruitment is an option mainly used by to fill vacancies in particular geographical areas or medical specialties with recognized shortages. These have grown markedly. However, by 2003, just 4 per cent of nurses had qualified overseas and the flow of new and young nurses had become highly internationalized. In 2002–3, 43 per cent of new nurse registrants were from abroad. The number of work permits issued to foreign nurses nearly doubled from 2000 to 2003. The vast majority of nurses arriving in London in the last ten years came from just six countries: the Philippines, South Africa, Australia, New Zealand, Nigeria and Ghana. The flow of skilled professionals had also become more internationalized. In each year from 1993 to 2002, nearly half of all new registrants to the General Medical Council were from abroad, increasing to nearly two-thirds by 2003 (King's Fund, 2004; National Primary Care Research and Development Centre, 2003). The case study reviewed the experience of the NHS in general and the South East London Strategic Health Authority in particular in dealing with international recruitment. The need for international recruitment was inextricably linked to demand for skills and HR professionals with time dedicated to managing international recruitment found that the nature of their role changed both in line with the level of demand for candidates, but also in line with a set of evolving needs. At a national level, the Department of Health established codes of practice and ethical policies in order to promote the best possible standards in international recruitment, discourage inappropriate practices which could harm other countries' healthcare systems or the interests of those who apply for posts. The use of external service providers carried both reputational and technical risk for the purchasers of these services if the conduct was not appropriate and the content of the

Code of Practice evolved through three iterations to tighter specification of recruitment practice relating to specific country practice, financial arrangements with applicants and recruitment processes, as more was learned about the management of international recruitment. Government to government agreements were set up with some countries to ensure that UK recruitment drives did not strip other national health systems of talent; global advertising campaigns were run and web gateways established; and schemes designed to attract specialists in short supply. A value proposition for international recruits was communicated on websites. Selection and assessment procedures differed for each group depending on vocational and professional bodies. Across all occupational groups, however, the assessment of English language competence was a crucial issue. Two basic aspects of English language competence needed to be established: levels of language proficiency that ensured safe and skilled communication with all stakeholders; and levels of knowledge and effectiveness comparable with UK vocational and educational standards. Prior to arrival, a range of issues had to be managed, including: occupational health clearance; Criminal Records Bureau clearance; references; registration with professional bodies; work permit applications; and assistance with finding accommodation and schools for children. The key issues that arose from international migration of talented labour were:

- Establishing where professional expertise and technical insight lay (which sector bodies, HR networks, agencies and service providers could help).
- Deciding whether the initiative required a targeted campaign or a longer-term strategic move to sourcing from specific countries or regions.
- Understanding and establishing base technical competence of recruitees and setting up assessment processes where necessary.
- Considering the ethical and reputational issues associated with campaigns.
- Ensuring a local infrastructure in receiving units to handle the increasing workforce diversity that resulted from successful campaigns.
- Building the reputation of receiving units' operations so that they could be seen as internationally competitive and attractive (thereby aiding subsequent retention and the success of future campaigns).

Sourcing employees internationally also needed three strategies:

- Active recruitment policies: where specific skill groups and countries were targeted; arrangements with service providers established; different media and channels to labour market known and tested; overseas recruitment trips normalized and codes of practice reflected in internal practice.
- Passive recruitment policies: where the applicants took the initiative that needed to be capitalized on, and where candidates could be captured simply because there had been an increase in both the 'flow' and 'stock' of international employees or qualified refugees.
- Longer-term strategies to ensure the continued ability to compete in international labour markets.

The activity of the HR function shifted as it worked its way through the initial challenges of attracting and recruiting overseas professionals, on to the longer-term issues associated with then managing this cadre of overseas recruits through the organization's career systems.

BBC World Service (centralized control and international recruitment primarily for domestic labour market)

The BBC World Service case study shows how the agenda for those involved in international recruitment and selection is determined by the use of technology and the attractions of shared service models applied on a global basis. International recruitment activity initially moved from World Service Broadcasting to BBC People in April 2004 but was subsequently substantially outsourced. Around 500 people are employed worldwide in the BBC World Service, which broadcasts in 43 languages to 148 million people, competing for audience figures with Voice of America, Radio Monte Carlo and Al Jazeera. The bulk of international recruitment activity concerned recruiting journalists (producers) for language services of World Service in the UK and also some staff to work at home and overseas in the World Trust Service. The latter candidates needed very specialized skills (media skills but also experience of global news issues such as HIV/AIDS, dysentery) in order to make media programmes for developing countries. In many international organizations, there is a challenge to understand what the local issues are and adapt service provision accordingly. The World Service Trust has the challenge of managing projects that are driven by local conditions, with programmes made for particular countries and cultures, but managed from London in line with overall brand values. In all instances, the BBC's employment brand was a key differentiating factor for recruitment in local countries. Programming needed an independent and impartial approach, but also had to effect local behaviour change. Work was carried out centrally to identify brand values, reflected in brochures, with adjectives such as: international; trustworthy; award winning; accessible; impartial; educational; and online. Although London-based producers in the World Service worked within their own culture in terms of language used, BBC values covered their conduct with the people with whom they worked and audiences broadcast to. Campaigns were run by a central team of eight HR professionals for different areas of the world, offering advice and expertise on the best recruitment media in local labour markets, interviewing, applying for work permits, assisting new recruits with visa applications, and providing training. A recent Arabic campaign received applications from 34 countries. Assessments (written journalistic and language skills and voice tests) were held across countries at a similar time. Candidates were tested on technical and language skills, suitability of voice for radio and ability to write and work for radio and online. Judgements were made about the cross-cultural validity of tests (overseas applicants might achieve lower consistency and lower scores) to counter risks that test performance favoured candidates from specific countries, which could limit the diversity of the candidate base and lead to claims of unlawful discrimination. Judgements about how best to organize international recruitment activity were bound up in general changes in HR delivery that had been taking place over a three-year period, culminating in a ten-year outsourcing deal worth £100 million and producing savings of £50 million (Griffiths, 2005; *International Herald Tribune*, 2005; People Management, 2005; Pickard, 2006). The BBC underwent two waves of downsizing, eliminating 3,780 jobs (19 per cent of its UK workforce, or nearly 14 per cent of its worldwide staff of 27,000). HR was centralized and a business-partner model introduced. Professional services, including parts of HR, were outsourced. Employment within BBC People fell from 1,000 to 450. Eleven areas for possible outsourcing were drawn up (resourcing, remuneration, contracting, relocation, disability access services, HR advice and occupational health) including the conduct of international recruitment. The functions finally outsourced included recruitment, pay and benefits (excluding pensions), assessment, outplacement and some training, HR administration, relocation, occupational health and disability access services. Service delivery to line managers, driven by service level agreements, was split from strategic HR, the latter focusing on building capability within divisions.

Barclaycard International (centralized control and recruitment primarily for overseas labour markets)

The Barclaycard International case study demonstrated how firms can use the development of a multicultural workforce to the advantage of an internationalization strategy. Barclaycard was the UK's first credit card and as one of the largest global credit card businesses now has a rapid growth strategy. Outside the UK, it operates in the United States, Germany, Spain, Greece, Italy, Portugal, Ireland, Sweden, Norway, France, Asia-Pacific and across Africa. A strategy to become as meaningful a contributor to the Group, as Barclaycard UK currently is, by 2013 has witnessed alliances with Standard Bank of South Africa, acquisition of Juniper Financial Corporation (rebranded as Barclays USA) and a series of in-country launches. It employed 3,000 staff, with 15 per cent based in the UK. To enable expansion, Barclaycard International built a platform of people management processes (processes, structures and frameworks) to bring stability, governance and control. Challenges varied across countries but always included ensuring rigour and consistency across operations in very different cultures, business markets and labour markets. Primary agenda items for the HR team in 2006 were international resourcing, international mobility, talent acquisition and development of global policies and frameworks. Resourcing, then transferring, capability globally – either within an existing business or during start up and building of a local business – necessitated a range of preferred recruitment suppliers and the building of networks across them to transfer learning about the management of different types of supplier and agency; assessment of their true global capability; and availability of skills available in each labour market. Intranets exchanged vacancy information between Hamburg, Zaragoza and Dublin. A new International Resourcing Business Partner role acted as a support mechanism for HR business partners and business leaders to facilitate the acquisition of top talent through negotiation of global preferred supplier arrangements for head-hunters and research institutions; development of an employee value proposition and employment brand across countries; advice on global vs. local process; sources of best practice; and appropriate geographical diversity in the use of international talent.

Barclaycard's call centre in Dublin acted as a central platform and nursery for future international expansion. It grew from 10 to 360 people in 1997–2006. Initially intended to support non-UK operations, it grew to serve eight countries including Ireland, Italy, Spain, France, Germany, Portugal, Greece, and Botswana. Dublin was chosen because of the nature of the role, the employee base and the City's labour market. The recruitment population was well qualified, with intentions to stay in country for around 12 to 18 months. Employees spoke (and were hired for) their mother tongue in the markets they served, requiring principles of cross-cultural management to be applied to a single internal labour market. The acquisition of Banco Zaragozano enabled a new contact centre in Spain. Thirty-five employees moved from Dublin to Spain to help transfer practices. HR business partners dealt with setting up legal entities to transfer employees; deciding the best mix of local recruitment; use of local job centres; assessing funding support; and understanding the implications and ramifications of local employment law and sector agreements. New country operations oversaw other start-up operations (Portugal and Italy were initially resourced under the guidance of the Spanish HR partner). Considerable insight into country capability resided at HR partner level. A 'framework for growth' was established to replicate in-country moves and transfer learning. Many aspects of recruitment and selection could be 'cut and pasted' across operations (procedures, training plans, interview and induction processes, job standards) while others had to be dealt with flexibly (for example, criteria-based interviewing and diversity practices). Dublin acted as a nursery (providing people to facilitate international expansion).

Rapid global expansion required the deployment of skills and experience in a multitude of countries at short notice, not always achievable at pace through local recruitment. A new international mobility framework reduced the cost and complexity of expatriating individuals by securing talented employees on global contracts with a premium for global mobility but only 'light' expatriation benefits. Assignments were designed by HR business partners and International Assignments Services (IAS) teams located within key global regions. Two initiatives supported a global mindset: awareness building among the senior leadership community through workshops on the cultures of current and potential labour markets; and cross cultural training interventions linked to a global induction programme. Talent management tools and techniques supported international resourcing through successive application to: top leadership roles, senior cross-Barclays role potential, top 450 leadership potential and, finally, a broad business talent population. Succession planning and talent identification processes were integrated with long-term incentives tied to identified capabilities. The top 10 per cent within internal expertise fields were identified on a global basis. Rather than wait until Barclaycard International was in or near-market, people were recruited for target markets ('resourcing ahead of the curve') with investments made in forward market mapping (using research agencies and head-hunters to map a wider range of geographical labour markets, and researching people working in target roles). Global policies and frameworks operated on an exception basis (even if culturally uncomfortable, explicit guidance and global protocols governed activity unless it was illegal to do so) to ensure consistency, rigour, global governance and risk management. Finally, control-monitoring processes were aligned with institutional requirements such as Sarbanes Oxley in areas like pre-employment screening policy. The case revealed a clear sequence of HR issues regarding choice of HR processes to be managed globally or in country and the role of local HR business partners developed in relation to recruitment and selection activity, and emerging sophistication of insights into the behavioural implications of central HR policies within local cultures.

Save the Children (decentralized control and recruitment primarily for overseas labour markets)

Not-for-profit organizations have had to learn quickly how to combine diversity priorities with globalized talent management processes (Czerny, 2006). The final case study analyses developments at Save the Children. It has a mission to 'fight for children in the UK and around the world who suffer from poverty, disease, injustice and violence and to work with them to find lifelong answers to the problems they face'. Emergency relief activity runs alongside long-term development and prevention work. At the time of the case it operated across six geographical regions and recruited to opportunities in three different categories: long-term development posts based overseas, emergency posts based overseas and locally appointed posts based in the UK and countries where it worked. Candidates were subject to host country requirements, with large responses to vacancies and three-quarters of applicants usually screened out. It was working on a number of measures to attract and recruit talent to worldwide roles, repositioning the HR function and looking at long-term strategy. It launched a new brand positioning statement and confirmed a new strategic direction focusing on national level advocacy, decentralizing operations and devolving accountability to line managers, passing the entire recruitment process down to 40 country directors. Recruitment was impacted in a number of ways: a smaller, more strategic global head office HR function; changes in the skill specification for international appointments; developments to improve the sophistication of the selection processes; more attention to the employer brand; focusing of talent management processes on creating a cadre of internationally mobile staff on permanent contracts; and building the capacity and careers of national staff. The HR team at headquarters was reduced in size, becoming less operational and providing central expertise, including: a specialist international resourcing team to develop more creative and co-ordinated recruitment support and initiatives; and toolkits and training for country operations on strategies and key steps in recruiting international staff. The Global HR team was tasked with understanding the labour markets that sourced candidates and competitors for talent, and developing the organization's resourcing capability. Induction was costly. Speed was everything, particularly when an emergency hit, as NGOs competed for the same high calibre candidates. Many staff in the sector moved out of an organization to return later on another programme and charities competed with each other for staff needing to be mobilized at short notice. Sourcing capability was developed in four ways:

1   Regional HR manager roles, spotting internal talent at local level, understanding local media, expanding candidate networks, building databases of potential employees and re-evaluating retention strategies.
2   Global protocols were established, such as a 'recruitment planner' for developing new assignments, setting resourcing strategies, identifying likely whereabouts of suitable candidates and ways to market roles.
3   Talented employees and people for specialist functions tracked both whilst they worked for the organization and when engaged elsewhere, through use of networking skills.
4   Agencies and charities recognized the need to grow more talent for the sector through collaborative arrangements, with Save the Children contributing a Child Protection trainee scheme to assist resourcing in this difficult specialist area.

Selection criteria were broadened to include experience in a developing country (two years), understanding of development issues, and a range of cultural skills, with staff resourced from broader backgrounds and better links forged with the corporate sector. A more flexible candidate risk management approach attracted candidates from different sectors (military, finance, sales and marketing) counterbalanced by greater attention to induction, learning, development and evaluation. Recruitment relied on the overall brand and image of the organization and all advertising was fitted with the brand. On-line recruitment was adapted for international resourcing. Appointments were marketed strongly and attention given to key selling points of working in a particular programme, country or region. Advertising became more customized and e-resourcing capability reviewed to ensure fast and effective access at local as well as global level. Selection techniques became more formalized with psychometrics used more often, requiring understanding of issues associated with using tests across cultures to be understood. Talent management processes were developed. An International Core Team was launched in 2006 to establish long-term relationships with international staff, building expertise and global perspectives. Permanent contracts were offered for moving to a new country posting every three to five years, supported by more attention to skills development and career planning. The forward strategy included more work around the employer brand, incorporation of this into resourcing strategies, and a redefinition of volunteer and secondment work to use skills on a global basis.

Discussion

The first research question asked if the study of globalization processes at functional level (staffing) provides useful insights for the IHRM literature. There are two important implications for the field of IHRM from the developments tracked in relation to this question.

The first concerns the role of complexity (Schuler and Tarique, 2007) and its confounding impact on traditional theoretical constructs of integration and differentiation. These changing dynamics between integration and differentiation appear to be due to two factors. The issue of complexity also shows that the theoretical sampling frame used to select cases in this study is hard to maintain in practice. For example, in BBC World Service, the move towards shared service structures brought activities for previously discrete overseas and domestic labour market recruitment under a single umbrella, and the fact that international employees could be used flexibly to produce services for domestic or overseas markets makes the geographic labour market less of an issue. The distinction between integration and differentiation based on assumed central (HQ) and (operations) does not neatly fit real practice. In the National Health Service, even within the single function of international recruitment, some activities were subjected to centralized co-ordination whilst others were within the control of separate Trusts.

The power of central functions to insist on integration or differentiation is changing as the IHRM function moves from its historical focus on the management of internationally-mobile employees and expatriates, to more globalized contexts. As functions forge new relationships with contiguous functions new activity streams are developing, and the shifts in expertise at firm-level lead to changing professional groupings/alliances, which may influence the strategic thought process inside organizations in novel ways. This research has indicated that HR-marketing-corporate communications and HR-IS functions are pursuing increasingly common agendas and sharing tools and techniques. The HR function is realigning itself in response to a process of cross-function globalization (building new alliances with these functions) creating new activity streams and new roles and skills required of the HR function (Sparrow *et al.*, 2004). The case studies suggest that a number of new tools and techniques have become part of the mainstream armoury of HR functions, bringing the language of employee value propositions and employment branding (for example to assist passive recruitment in the NHS or address skills shortages in the Francophone aid worker market in Save the Children), corporate social responsibility (for example, as part of the branding at BBC World Service), market mapping and recruiting ahead of the curve (for example to plan for new market entry in Barclaycard International or to exploit local networks among aid workers in Save the Children) into the mix of international HR resourcing activity. Parallel developments in topics of academic interest are occurring, with new dialogues between researchers studying these topics.

The second implication concerns the issue of risk in international recruitment. There is a complex combination of value creation and value protection logics at function level. HR theory emphasizes the HR function's role in value creation but the case studies also revealed the need for IHRM to protect the value of the organizations. In both the NHS and BBC World Service, there was a need to possess a higher contextual understanding of language given the potentially high risks involved if misunderstandings occur. The literature has always focused on the (hidden) costs of poor expatriate selection, but the risks associated with broader patterns of international resourcing produce more immediate performance effects.

However, a basic assumption of examining HR globalization at the functional level is the belief that distinct HR functions can be discussed without pointing out their relationship with other functions. For example, does international recruitment relate to the implementation of compensation or other functions? Can the assumption of analysis of HR functions be justified? The answer is a qualified yes, but only when the interaction between both practice and policy is analysed. Schuler and Tarique (2007) draw attention to the work of Higgs *et al.* (2000) on the adoption of a systems approach to strategic HRM, in terms of both horizontal alignment (to other HR functions) and vertical alignment (to internal contextual factors such as vision, values and culture), noting that this has led to the inclusion of a much wider range of activity under the umbrella of selection inside organizations. Clearly, staffing strategies have implications for other HR functions but the combinations or configurations that need to be understood depend on the policy context. Employment branding strategies are an example of this. Adopting a systems' view revealed that a large number of HR practices previously considered as distinct activities required a process of entire global system consistency and internal integrity. For example, in Barclaycard International, globalization of international resourcing activity required aligned developments in expatriate management, the process of creating new in-country operations, talent management and the HR business partner role. The boundaries between many sub-functions such as international recruitment, development and rewards became opaque in the pursuit of globalized strategies. The pay strategy and associated benchmarks defined the calibre of applicants in geographical labour markets. The link between the consequent calibre of attracted local applicants and consistency in the local employee experience (influenced by the competencies and leadership capability of candidates and their adherence to brand values) had to be understood through judgement and learning at HR business partner level.

However, managing the employment brand for international recruitment purposes also required judgements about the capability of the international operations. Alignment of rewards to the realities of the local labour market was also a source of tension in internationalizing organizations. By examining the interplay between policy and practice (Wright and Boswell, 2002), it was evident that much knowledge about rewards and competency markets resides in-country, whilst development and design of global standards for recruitment and rewards exists at HQ. Such globalized strategies can only be executed effectively where there is considerable reverse diffusion of HR knowledge (Edwards and Ferner, 2004).

Examining processes of globalization at the functional level also showed that the new corporate architectures being adopted are often more advanced than the ability of either central or local HR functions to make this architecture work effectively. There is also considerable potential for a lack of alignment between the global HR strategies pursued at functional level and the prerogatives created as a consequence of the mode of internationalization. Global expansion may be delivered through mergers and acquisitions or joint ventures (absorbing operations to whom the host employment brand is meaningless) or the creation of 'young' operations in new countries. Naïve labour markets may make it difficult to bed down perceptions of an employment brand. Outsourcing and global redistribution of work can mean that in addition to operations sited in a country because of local market need, other operations might be sited in-country (from call centres through to advanced centres of excellence) creating a range of operations based on very different business cost models, again making it difficult to develop a common brand and employee experience within a single country, let alone across countries.

The second research question asked if globalization is evidenced at the functional level, what sort of indicators evidence this and should they form the basis of new future research? In the methodology section, it was noted that there is often variance between macro-level policy (in this case employment branding strategies) and what happens when these processes are translated into actual employee (or HR manager's) perceptions and behaviour (Wright and Boswell, 2002) and that by identifying the issues that lead to there being divergence between policy and actual practice, it would be possible to identify a more appropriate (i.e. realistic) set of indicators of true progress. When is this alignment best achieved or not achieved? If one were to ask what evidence should be used to assess the presence of globalized HR at the level of sub-function (as opposed to the more traditional focus on commonality of HR practice associated with comparative HR traditions), questions could be asked about the extent to which processes of functional realignment against global strategic agendas and new hybrid professional groups and sources of expertise existed inside organizations.

How should researchers judge how global a recruitment function is? Taking one key example, that of talent management, researchers should measure those activities or attributes that lead to there being less variance between policy and practice. These were: the extent to which firms research consumer insights into the employment brand across international operations; the ability to specify business models that enabled prediction and recruitment 'ahead of the curve' in different international labour markets; consistency of global communications; frameworks for global risk management; the existence of centres of excellence to gain control over the skill formation process; and use of global suppliers that altered the tools, techniques and services offered. Measurement against such indicators, and an articulation of the gap between policy and practice, may provide a different view of how rapidly resourcing functions have globalized.

The third research question asked whether we can detect patterns or strategies within the global recruitment activity of organizations across domestic and overseas labour markets? Organizations face the challenge of on the one hand providing some degree of consistency and integration (through either standardization or optimization) of HR practices around the world so that their operations use the same tools and techniques to obtain candidates who increasingly act as part of a more global community, and on the other hand maintaining locally responsive and differentiated approaches (Wiechmann *et al.*, 2003). Are we seeing a new wave of global co-ordination of resourcing activity? The answer varies depending on the phenomenon being looked at. In line with other research, a picture of more localized and culturally-dependent processes still exists from this research when one observes factors such as models of global labour supply and immigration rules; the legislative context (Posthuma *et al.*, 2006); variation in qualifications, language skills and implicit capabilities (Suutari, 2004); retention/career advancement behaviour; preferences for use of specific recruitment tools (Huo *et al.*, 2002; Ryan *et al.*, 1999); competency specification at behavioural indicator level (Ryan *et al.*, 2003); test behaviour and desirability (Van de Vijver, 2002); and employee engagement behaviour or buy-in to corporate values (Universum, 2005). It would still be fair to say that while resourcing philosophies may be generalizing, convergence of selection process/detail and employee behaviour around these philosophies lags behind.

Significant issues of local cultural sensitivity aside, the cases also evidenced renewed attempts at global co-ordination and control in the interests of consistency. In practice, global HRM revolves around the ability of organizations to use concepts that have 'relevance' to managers across several countries. Corporate strategy is expressed through performance management systems applied globally to measure and manage a balanced series of outcomes. There were three *super-ordinate themes* used to socialize employee behaviour and action and provide consistency in worldwide people management. First, core strategic competences considered to differentiate the firm and lead to its competitive advantage, being reflected in a series of organizational capabilities or competencies that once specified were integrated into career development and/or performance management systems. Second, talent management initiatives were pursued at global level. Third, corporate and global brands were pursued, whereby organizations think about their external brand image and corporate reputation, and the ways in which their employees identify with and actively support the brand. This strategy has received some attention of late (Davies *et al.*, 2003; Harris and de Chernatony, 2001; Martin and Hetrick, 2006) and the case studies showed organizations have learned important lessons. For example, despite operating in very different labour market contexts, BBC World Service, Save the Children and Barclaycard International all attempted to differentiate their employment brand.

Can these patterns be explained by existing IHRM theory? Under the second research question, a series of indicators of globalization at the functional level were identified. By applying social capital theory to the conduct of IHRM (Lengnick-Hall and Lengnick-Hall, 2006), we may well better understand how progress along these indicators could be managed. The more sophisticated the skills and networks that exist around these indicators, the more successful and strategic the work. However, the less capability there is in the HR function to manage these indicators, the higher the chance of failure and the more research will continue to demonstrate convergence in HR at high levels of policy but local re-establishment of cultural control.

From a resource-based view of the firm, the pursuit of a global employment brand is an example of the development of an inimitable source of labour market advantage (Morris *et al.*, 2005). From an institutional theory perspective, this advantage ultimately depends on how strong the level of identification with the brand was across geographical labour markets (Kostova and Roth, 2002). Institutional theory (Björkman, 2006) reminds us that organizations imitate each other in situations of uncertainty (the pursuit of global employment branding could be seen in this context). It can explain the various pulls and blocks behind employment branding strategies. In practice, the global themes were still operationalized with local adaptation (Kostova and Roth, 2002). For Kostova (1999), successful transfer of practice is dependent on implementation (diffusion of sets of rules to subsidiary employees, rules being implied by practices, and reflected in objective behaviours and actions in the actions of employees) and internalization (ability of subsidiary employees to make sense of and attribute meaning to rules in the same way as host country or headquarters employees). Organizations used scores on key 'tracker' opinion survey items to assess this level of internalization (Martin and Hetrick, 2006). There was a clear sequence of implementation, developed over time, through which institutional blocks to global co-ordination were reduced by 'stabilizing' key people management processes across different geographical operations. Early and basic considerations were: creating the same physical brand (e.g. logo and literature); sharing a common mission, vision and set of stated values; setting minimum HR standards and conditions to shape a generic (cross-country) process of employee engagement; examining how the pay strategy and associated benchmarks defined the calibre of applicants; and then understanding how this helped bring consistency to the employee experience in each geographical labour market in terms of competencies and leadership capability.

However, once the full range of resourcing options open to IHRM functions are considered, there is still a need for more micro theory to explain the behaviour of the different international employee groups, and the processes used to manage them. Better micro theory is needed for example to explain the link between value orientations (at national, corporate, product division, and service brand levels of analysis) and employee engagement behaviours, and an examination of the relevance of the service-profit chain work across cultures. The growth of networks and teams as part of international resourcing strategies also draws attention to the need to understand *mutual adjustment* processes from an interactionalist view of culture (Erez and Gati, 2004; Sackmann and Phillips, 2004; Zimmermann and Sparrow, 2007). We need to refine our understanding of the skills that are needed to effectively navigate, work and manage in cross-cultural contexts that demand the maintenance of partial and multiple identities. This is moving attention back into understanding the role of power and political capital theories (Harvey and Novicevic, 2004). Finally, cultural distances inside organizations are likely increasing as a result of globalization strategies. The strategy seen at Barclaycard International is not exceptional. The development of multicultural workforces in global city labour markets has raised the importance of skills and competencies important for successful 'within-culture functioning' (Bandura, 2001, 2002; Matveev and Nelson, 2004; Pires *et al.*, 2006). Such study is clearly relevant to the study of adaptation across expatriate and other expertise networks but also has practical benefits for selection systems that are now being designed for a much broader range of international employees, especially in the context of HR functions recruiting more culturally diverse workforces, even in their domestic markets, because of new forms of international working.

Conclusions

The first research question asked if the study of globalization processes at functional level (staffing) provides useful insights for the IHRM literature. The answer is yes, but only when analysis concentrates on the interaction between practice and policy and the alignment between the two. It was clear that the power of central IHRM functions to insist on integration or differentiation is changing as they move from their historical focus on the management of internationally-mobile employees and expatriates, to more globalized staffing contexts. The IHRM function is forging new relationships with contiguous functions and as new activity streams develop, shifts in expertise at firm-level are changing the professional groupings and alliances that influence the strategic thought process. This thought process suggests a complex combination of value creation and value protection logics at the function level. The second research question asked what sort of indicators should be used as evidence of globalization at the function level. It is argued that the variance between macro-level policy and what happens when these processes are translated into actual employee (or HR manager) perceptions and behaviour can help identify a more appropriate (i.e. realistic) set of indicators of true progress, rather than relying on rather generic assumptions about policies and the messages that they suggest about integration and differentiation. The third research question asked whether we can detect patterns or strategies within the global recruitment activity of organizations across domestic and overseas labour markets. Three co-ordinating themes could be detected: the use of core strategic competences considered to differentiate the firm and lead to its competitive advantage, talent management initiatives pursued at global level, and the adaptation of corporate and global brands into employment strategies aimed at developing pan-national patterns of employee identification. Social capital theory, the resource-based view of the firm and institutional theory can all be used to help position these themes. However, there is a need for more and better micro theory to explain the gaps between policy and practice in these areas and in this regard there is potential in the use of power and political capital theories, interactionalist views of culture and theories of within-culture functioning. In conclusion, the research has shown that the HR function in internationalizing organizations has to meet a series of challenges, but three key observations about the role of HR professionals working in the field of international recruitment and selection can be made. The added value of the HR function in an international firm lies in its ability to manage the delicate balance between globally co-ordinated systems and sensitivity to local needs, including cultural differences, in a way that aligns with both business needs and senior management philosophy. There now appears to be a distinction between international HRM (HR policies and practices directed at the management of cadres of international employees) and global HRM (the development of more globalized people management processes at all levels of the organization in the context of competing demands for optimization and localization). In navigating this transition, the old functional divides between international recruitment, international management development, and international reward management have become increasingly weak and a more nuanced and systemic perspective is needed.

Acknowledgements

This research was funded by the UK's Chartered Institute of Personnel and Development. The author is grateful for comments on earlier versions of the paper by the four reviewers; Randall Schuler, Marta Elvira, Ingmar Björkman and Anne-Wil Harzing.

References

Aiken, L.H., Buchan, J., Sochalski, J., Nichols, B. and Powell, M. (2004) 'Trends in International Nurse Migration', *Health Affairs*, 23(3): 69–78.

Ashkenas, R., Ulrich, D., Jick, T. and Kerr, S. (1995) *The Boundaryless Organization*. San Francisco, CA: Jossey-Bass.

Bandura, A. (2001) Social Cognitive Theory: An Agentic Perspective *Annual Review of Psychology, Volume 52*. Palo Alto, CA: Annual Reviews Inc.

Bandura, A. (2002) 'Social Cognitive Theory in Cultural Context', *Applied Psychology: An International Review*, 51(2): 269–290.

Bartlett, C.A. and Ghoshal, S. (1989) *Managing Across Borders: The Transnational Solution*. Boston, MA: Harvard Business School Press.

Bartlett, C.A. and Ghoshal, S. (2000) *Transnational Management*, 3rd edn. Boston, MA: Irwin McGraw-Hill.

Baruch, Y. and Altman, Y. (2002) 'Expatriation and Repatriation in MNCs: A Taxonomy', *Human Resource Management*, 41(2): 239–59.

Björkman, I. (2005) International Human Resource Management Research and Institutional Theory. In Bjorkman, I. and Stahl, G. (eds) *Handbook of Research into International HRM*. London: Edward Elgar.

Brewster, C. (2007) 'Comparative HRM: European Views and Perspectives', *International Journal of HRM*, 18(5): 769–87.

Brewster, C., Sparrow, P. and Harris, H. (2005) 'Towards a New Model of Globalizing HRM', *International Journal of Human Resource Management*, 16(6): 953–74.

Brewster, C., Tregaskis, O., Hegewisch, A. and Mayne, L. (1996) 'Comparative Research in Human Resource Management: A Review and an Example', *International Journal of Human Resource Management*, 7(3): 585–604.

Briggs, V.M. (2003) *Mass Immigration and the National Interest: Policy Directions for the New Century*, 3rd edn. New York: M.E. Sharpe.

Briscoe, D. and Schuler, R.S. (2004) *International Human Resource Management*, 2nd edn. New York: Routledge.

Caves, R.E. (1996) *Multinational Enterprise and Economic Analysis*. Cambridge: Cambridge University Press.

Clark, P.F., Stewart, J.B. and Clark, D.A. (2006) 'The Globalisation of the Labour Market for Health-care Professionals', *International Labour Review*, 145(1/2): 37–64.

Czerny, A. (2006) 'Save the Children Hands over Recruitment to Line Managers', *People Management*, 12(6): 12.

Davies, G., Chun, R., Da Silva, R.V. and Roper, S. (2003) *Corporate Reputation and Competitiveness*. London: Routledge.

De Saá-Pérez, P. and García-Falcón, J.M. (2002) 'A Resource-based View of Human Resource Management and Organizational Capabilities Development', *International Journal of Human Resource Management*, 13(1): 123–40.

Dowling, P.J. and Schuler, R.S. (1990) *International Dimensions of Human Resource Management*. Boston, MA: PWS-Kent.

Dunning, J.H. (1993) *Multinational Enterprises and the Global Economy*. Reading, MA: Addison-Wesley.

Economist, The (2006) 'Travelling More Lightly', *The Economist*, 379(8483): 99–101.

Edwards, T. and Ferner, A. (2004) 'Multinationals, Reverse Diffusion and National Business Systems', *Management International Review*, 1/2004: 49–79.

Erez, M. and Gati, E. (2004) 'A Dynamic, Multi-level Model of Culture: From the Micro Level of the Individual to the Macro Level of a Global Culture', *Applied Psychology: An International Review*, 53(4): 583–98.

Ferner, A. and Quintanilla, J. (1998) 'Multinational, National Business Systems and HRM: The Enduring Influence of National Identity or a Process of "Anglo Saxonization"?', *International Journal of Human Resource Management*, 9(4): 710–31.

Findlay, A.M., Li, F.L.N., Jowett, A.J. and Skeldon, R. (2000) 'Skilled International Migration and the Global City: A Study of Expatriates in Hong Kong', *Applied Geography*, 20(3): 277–304.

Griffiths, J. (2005) 'BBC Gets Creative as HR Jobs Are Cut', *People Management*, 11(9): 9.

Hamel, G. and Prahalad, C.K. (1985) 'Do You Really Have a Global Strategy?', *Harvard Business Review*, July/August: 139–48.

Harris, F. and de Chernatony, L. (2001) 'Corporate Branding and Corporate Brand Performance', *European Marketing Journal*, 35(3/4): 441–56.

Harvey, M. and Novicevic, M.M. (2004) 'The Development of Political Skill and Political Capital by Global Leaders Through Global Assignments', *International Journal of Human Resource Management*, 15(7): 1173–88.

Harvey, M.G., Novicevic, H.M. and Speier, C. (2000) 'An Innovative Global Management Staffing System: A Competency-based Perspective', *Human Resource Management*, 39(4): 381–94.

Harvey, M.G., Price, M.F., Speier, C. and Novicevic, M.M. (1999) 'The Role of Inpatriates in a Globalization Strategy and Challenges Associated with the Inpatriation Process', *Human Resource Planning*, 22(1): 38–60.

Harzing, A.W.K. (2001) 'Who's in Charge? An Empirical Study of Executive Staffing Practices in Foreign Subsidiaries', *Human Resource Management*, 40(2): 139–58.

Harzing, A.W.K. (2004) 'Composing and International Staff'. In Harzing, A.W.K. and van Ruysseveldt, J. (eds) *International Human Resource Management*, 2nd edn. London: Sage.

Higgs, A., Papper, E. and Carr, L. (2000) 'Integrating Selection With Other Organizational Processes and Systems'. In Kehoe, J.F. (ed.) *Managing Selection in Changing Organizations*. San Francisco, CA: Jossey-Bass, pp. 73–122.

Hocking, J.B., Brown, M. and Harzing, A.-W. (2004) 'A Knowledge Transfer Perspective of Strategic Assignment Purposes and Their Path-dependent Outcomes', *International Journal of Human Resource Management*, 15(3): 565–86.

Huo, Y.P., Huang, H.J. and Napier, N.K. (2002) 'Divergence or Convergence: A Cross-national Comparison of Personnel Selection Practices', *Human Resource Management*, 41(1): 31–44.

Hustad, E. and Munkvold, B.E. (2005) 'IT-supported Competence Management: A Case Study at Ericsson', *Information Systems Management*, 22(2): 78–88.

International Herald Tribune (2005) 'BBC Announces 2050 More Job Cuts', *International Herald Tribune*, 22 March: 14.

Janssens, M. and Brett, J.M. (2006) 'Cultural Intelligence in Global Teams: A Fusion Model of Collaboration', *Group and Organization Management*, 31(1): 124–53.

Kim, K., Park, J.-H. and Prescott, J.E. (2003) 'The Global Integration of Business Functions: A Study of Multinational Businesses in Integrated Global Industries', *Journal of International Business Studies*, 34: 327–44.

King's Fund (2004) *London Calling: The International Recruitment of Health Workers to the Capital*. London: King's Fund Publications.

Kingma, M. (2006) *Nurses on the Move: Migration and the Global Health Care Economy*. Ithaca, NY: Cornell University Press.

Kopp, R. (1994) 'International Human Resource Policies and Practices in Japanese, European and United States Multinationals', *Human Resource Management*, 33(4): 581–99.

Kostova, T. (1999) 'Transnational Transfer of Strategic Organizational Practices: A Contextual Perspective', *Academy of Management Review*, 24(2): 308–24.

Kostova, T. and Roth, K. (2002) 'Adoption of an Organizational Practice by Subsidiaries of Multinational Corporations: Institutional and Relational Effects', *Academy of Management Journal*, 45(1): 215–33.

Lengnick-Hall, M.L. and Lengnick-Hall, C. (2005) 'International Human Resource Management Research and Social Network/social Capital Theory'. In Bjorkman, I. and Stahl, G. (eds) *Handbook of Research into International HRM*. London: Edward Elgar.

Lewin, A.Y. and Volberda, H.W. (2003) 'Beyond Adaptation-Selection Research: Organizing Self-Renewal in Co-Evolving Environments', *Journal of Management Studies*, 40(8): 2109–10.

Makhija, M.V., Kim, K. and Williamson, S.D. (1997) 'Measuring Globalization of Industries Using a National Industry Approach: Empirical Evidence Across Five Countries and Over Time', *Journal of International Business Studies*, 28(4): 679–710.

Malbright, T. (1995) 'Globalisation of an Ethnographic Firm', *Strategic Management Journal*, 16: 119–41.

Martin, G. and Hetrick, S. (2006) *Corporate Reputations, Branding and People Management*. Oxford: Butterworth-Heinemann.

Matveev, A.V. and Nelson, P.E. (2004) 'Cross Cultural Communication Competence and Multicultural Team Performance: Perceptions of American and Russian Managers', *International Journal of Cross Cultural Management*, 4(2): 253–70.

Mayerhofer, H., Hartmann, L.C. and Herbert, A. (2004) 'Career Management Issues for Flexpatriate International Staff', *Thunderbird International Business Review*, 46(6): 647–66.

Mayerhofer, H., Hartmann, L.C., Michelitsch-Riedl, G. and Kollinger, I. (2004) 'Flexpatriate Assignments: A Neglected Issue in Global Staffing', *International Journal of Human Resource Management*, 15(8): 1371–89.

Minbaeva, D.B. and Michailova, S. (2004) 'Knowledge Transfer and Expatriation in Multinational Corporations: The Role of Disseminative Capacity', *Employee Relations*, 26(6): 663–79.

Morley, M. and Heraty, N. (2004) 'International Assignments and Global Careers', *Thunderbird International Business Review*, 46(6): 633–46.

Morris, S.S., Snell, S.A. and Wright, P.M. (2005) 'A Resource-based View of International Human Resources: Towards a Framework of Integrative and Creative Capabilities'. In Bjorkman, I. and Stahl, G. (eds) *Handbook of Research into International HRM*. London: Edward Elgar.

Morrison, A.J. and Roth, K. (1992) 'A Taxonomy of Business-led Strategies in Global Industries', *Strategic Management Journal*, 13(6): 399–418.

National Primary Care Research and Development Centre (2003) 'The International Market for Medical Doctors: Perspectives on the Positioning of the UK', *Executive Summary No. 28*. University of Manchester: Manchester Centre for Healthcare Management.

Negandhi, A.R. (1987) *International Management*. Newton, MA: Allyn and Bacon.

Oberoi, S.S. and Lin, V. (2006) 'Brain Drain of Doctors from Southern Africa: Brain Gain for Australia', *Australian Health Review*, 30(1): 25–33.

People Management (2005) 'Three Firms in Running for BBC Outsourcing Contracts', *People Management*, 11(24): 9.

Phatak, A.V. (1989) *International Management*. Boston, MA: PWS-Kent.

Pickard, J. (2006) 'Conflicting Schedule', *People Management*, 12(5): 14–15.

Pieper, R. (ed.) (1990) *Human Resource Management: An International Comparison*. Berlin: Walter de Gruyter.

Pires, G., Stanton, J. and Ostenfeld, S. (2006) 'Improving Expatriate Adjustment and Effectiveness in Ethnically Diverse Countries: Marketing Insights', *Cross Cultural Management*, 13(2): 156–70.

Posthuma, R.A., Roehling, M.V. and Campion, M.A. (2006) 'Applying US Employment Discrimination Laws to International Employers: Advice for Scientists and Practitioners', *Personnel Psychology*, 59(3): 705–39.

Prahalad, C.K. and Doz, Y. (1987) *The Multinational Mission: Balancing Local Demands and Global Vision*. New York: The Free Press.

Ramaswamy, K., Kroeck, K.G. and Renforth, W. (1996) 'Measuring the Degree of Internationalization of a Firm: A Comment', *Journal of International Business Studies*, 27(1): 167–77.

Rugman, A. and Verbeke, A. (2004) 'A Perspective on Regional and Global Strategies of Multinational Enterprises', *Journal of International Business Studies*, 35: 3–18.

Ryan, A.M., McFarland, L., Baron, H. and Page, R. (1999) 'An International Look at Selection Practices: Nation and Culture as Explanations for Variability in Practice', *Personnel Psychology*, 52: 359–91.

Ryan, A.M., Wiechmann, D. and Hemingway, M. (2003) 'Designing and Implementing Global Staffing Systems: Part II: Best Practices', *Human Resource Management*, 42(1): 71–82.

Sackmann, S.A. and Phillips, M.E. (2004) 'Contextual Influences on Culture Research: Shifting Assumptions for New Workplace Realities', *International Journal of Cross Cultural Management*, 4(3): 370–90.

Salt, J. and Millar, J. (2006) 'International Migration in Interesting Times: The Case of the UK', *People and Place*, 14(2): 14–25.

Schuler, R.S. and Tarique, I. (2007) 'International Human Resource Management: A North American Perspective. A Thematic Update and Suggestions for Future Research', *International Journal of Human Resource Management*, 18(5): 717–44.

Scullion, H. and Collings, D.G. (eds) (2006) *Global Staffing*. London: Routledge.

Sparrow, P.R. (2006) 'Knowledge Management in Global Organisations'. In Stahl, G. and Björkman, I. (eds) *Handbook of Research into International HRM*. London: Edward Elgar, pp. 113–38.

Sparrow, P.R., Brewster, C. and Harris, H. (2004) *Globalizing Human Resource Management*. London: Routledge.

Stonehouse, G., Hamill, J., Campbell, D. and Purdie, T. (2000) *Global and Transnational Business: Strategy and Management*. Chichester: Wiley.

Sullivan, D. (1994) 'Measuring the Degree of Internationalization of a Firm', *Journal of International Business Studies*, 25(2): 325–42.

Sullivan, D. (1996) 'Measuring the Degree of Internationalization of a Firm: A Reply', *Journal of International Business Studies*, 27(1): 179–92.

Suutari, V. (2003) 'Global Managers: Career Orientations, Career Tracks, Life-style Implications and Career Commitment', *Journal of Managerial Psychology*, 18(3): 185–233.

Suutari, V. (2004) 'Global Leader Development: An Emerging Research Agenda', *Career Development International*, 7(4): 218–33.

Taylor, S., Beechler, S. and Napier, N. (1996) 'Towards an Integrative Model of Strategic International Human Resource Management', *Academy of Management Review*, 21(4): 959–85.

Tharenou, P. (2003) 'The Initial Development of Receptivity to Working Abroad: Self-initiated International Work Opportunities in Young Graduate Employees', *Journal of Occupational and Organizational Psychology*, 76: 489–515.

Torbiörn, I. (2005) 'Staffing Policies and Practices in European MNCs: Strategic Sophistication, Culture-bound Policies or Ad-hoc Reactivity?'. In Scullion, H. and Linehan, M. (eds) *International Human Resource Management: A Critical Text*. Basingstoke: Palgrave Macmillan.

Tung, R.L. (1982) 'Selection and Training Procedures of US, European, and Japanese Multinationals', *California Management Review*, 25(1): 57–71.

Tushman, M.I. and Scanlan, T.J. (2005) 'Boundary Spanning Individuals: Their Role in Information Transfer and Their Antecedents', *Academy of Management Journal*, 24(2): 289–305.

UNCTAD (2005) *World Investment Report 2005: Transnational Organizations and the Internationalization of R&D*. Geneva: United Nations.

Universum (2005) *Employer Branding: Global Best Practices 2005*. Stockholm: Universum.

Van de Vijver, F.J.R. (2002) 'Cross-Cultural Assessment: Value for Money?', *Applied Psychologist: An International Review*, 51(4): 545–66.

Ward, K. (2004) 'Going Global? Internationalization and Diversification in the Temporary Staffing Industry', *Journal of Economic Geography*, 4: 251–73.

Whitley, R.D. (ed.) (1992) *European Business Systems: Firms and Markets in Their National Contexts*. London: Sage Publications.

Whitley, R.D. (2000) *Divergent Capitalisms: The Social Structuring and Change of Business Systems*. Oxford: Oxford University Press.

Wiechmann, D., Ryan, A.M. and Hemingway, M. (2003) 'Designing and Implementing Global Staffing Systems: Part I: Leaders in Global Staffing', *Human Resource Management*, 42(1): 85–96.

Wright, P.M. and Boswell, W.R. (2002) 'Desegregating HRM: A Review and Synthesis of Micro and Macro Human Resource Management Research', *Journal of Management*, 28(3): 247–76.

Yip, G.S. (1992) *Total Global Strategy*. Englewood Cliffs, NJ: Prentice Hall.

Zimmermann, A. and Sparrow, P.R. (2007, in press) 'Mutual Adjustment Processes in International Teams: Lessons for the Study of Expatriation'. *International Studies in Management and Organisation*.

The human resource challenge to outward foreign direct investment aspirations from emerging economies: the case of China

Rosalie L. Tung

While the majority of foreign direct investment (FDI) stock in the world is still held by multinational companies (MNCs) from the advanced, industrialized countries, in recent years, outward FDI (OFDI) from developing countries has become a 'major factor in the world economy' (Schifferes, 2006). As recipients of FDI, some developing countries have benefited from the massive infusion of foreign capital, technology and technological know-how that accompanied these investments. This inflow, coupled with endogenous factors, has enabled some of these recipient countries to develop into emerging economies (EEs). EEs are also known as emerging markets, developing or transitional economies. Over time, many of these EEs have become foreign investors themselves (Luo and Tung, in press).

Take the case of China, for example. In the past two decades, China has been an attractive destination for foreign investment. In 2003, China overtook the US to become the largest recipient of FDI in the world (http://www.nyconsulate.prchina.org). Despite persistent perceptions of lack of transparency, China continues to be ranked as the top destination of FDI. Every year since 2002, based on surveys of CEOs and CFOs from around the world, China has received the highest ranking on A.T. Kearney's Foreign Direct Investor Confidence Index (http://www.atkearney.com). These rankings are based on CEO and CFO perceptions of the attractiveness of certain countries as FDI destinations and do not reflect the actual amount of investment received by these economies. Besides China, five other EEs have also taken the top ten spots on the Investor Confidence Index in 2006. These include India (#2), Poland (#5), Russia (#6), Brazil (#7) and Hong Kong (#10).

The continued influx of foreign investment into China coupled with the intention by indigenous Chinese companies to invest abroad (Accenture, 2005) have contributed to a high demand for people whom Kanter (1995) has labelled as 'cosmopolitans', i.e. those who are globally-minded, managerially and technologically savvy and who meet world-class standards. This relentless demand for cosmopolitans has generated a situation that Farrell and Grant (2005) have characterized as 'the shortage among plenty' – that is, despite the fact that China is the most populous nation in the world, there is a critical shortage of human talent to meet China's dual objective of pursuing continued economic prosperity at home and success abroad. This situation is not unique to China, however. According to the 2006 White Paper by Manpower Inc. entitled 'Confronting the Coming Talent Crunch: What's Next?', there will be an 'acute' and 'widespread' global labour shortage in the next decade, culminating in a fierce 'war for talent' among nations to attract and retain the best and most qualified people wherever they could be found.

This competition for brainpower (*The Economist*, 2006), on a global basis, is possible because of the general lowering of immigration and emigration barriers in most countries, thus resulting in the relative freedom of movement of people across international boundaries; and also because people worldwide are more willing to relocate outside of their home countries. Together, these two developments have facilitated the emergence of 'boundaryless careers' (DeFilippi and Arthur, 1996; Stahl *et al.*, 2002; Tung, 1998) and a 'boundaryless workforce' (Towers Perrin, 2006).

This shortage of talent could be particularly acute in the case of EEs, such as China and India where, on the one hand, growing affluence at home has enabled more and more of their people to pursue advanced education abroad. Upon graduation in disciplines that are in high demand, such as information technology (IT) and computer science, many of these foreign-born students are lured to remain in their adoptive countries through higher salaries and living standards. On the other hand, however, because of rapid economic development at home, the native countries of these students are also anxious to attract them to return.

This paper seeks to shed light on how China will fare in the human resource challenge in relation to its OFDI aspirations. Through two inter-related studies, this paper attempts to explore the important question of whether China will be able to attract and retain much needed human talent to facilitate its OFDI aspirations. The first study investigates the intention of Chinese university students in a major city in western Canada to return to work in China upon graduation. The second study explores the willingness of non-Chinese students at the same university to work for Chinese firms in North America or in China. These two surveys are supplemented by in-depth interviews with Chinese who remained overseas and those who have returned home. Together, these studies can provide a more comprehensive picture of how China will most likely fare in the decades ahead as it seeks to pursue its dual objectives of sustaining economic growth at home and 'spreading its wings' overseas.

Before presenting the methodology and findings of these studies, the paper will first present the theoretical underpinnings of this study, namely: (a) the role of human capital in dominant theories of FDI; and (b) the deployment of people in international assignments, particularly as they pertain to self-initiated assignments (SIAs). The paper will then review some factors that have contributed to the 'shortage among plenty' paradox, and how the growing 'boundaryless' nature of the Chinese workforce can affect China's ability to meet this human resource challenge in the decades ahead. Where relevant, comparisons will be made with other EEs.

The role of human capital in FDI theories

While numerous theories have been advanced to explain for FDI across countries, the ones that highlight the role that human capital can play in facilitating FDI and hence performance include the theories of monopolistic advantage and internalization. In addition, the international technology gap theory and Michael Porter's competitive diamond, while not strictly theories of FDI, also focus on the importance of human capital in explaining for a country's development and/or international competitiveness. Since the focus of this paper is not on FDI theories, each of these relevant theories is discussed only very succinctly.

Monopolistic advantage theory

Proponents of this theory (Dunning, 1988; Kindleberger and Andretch, 1983; Root, 2001) argued that investor firms typically possess monopolistic advantages that enable them to succeed over indigenous firms in their operations abroad. These monopolistic advantages stem from superior knowledge and/or oligopoly. Superior knowledge pertains to the investor company's intangible assets, such as 'technology, management and organization skills, marketing skills, and the like' (Root, 2001: 376). These intangible assets reside within the human talent in the firm. Thus, in order to gain a competitive advantage firms seek to acquire and retain such human talent – this explains why much of the January 2006 World Economic Forum at Davos, Switzerland focused on the looming 'war for talent' (http://www.weforum.org). It also serves to explain why talent poaching is common. The recent lawsuit filed by Microsoft against Google for hiring the former's speech recognition expert, Dr Kai-fu Lee, highlights the intensity of competition among companies for brainpower (Lohr, 2006).

Internalization theory

Internalization theory, also known as transaction-cost theory, asserts that firms seek to lower transaction costs by replacing external markets with internal flows (Casson, 1987; Root, 2001). In the context of new knowledge generation, 'the most direct way to prevent disclosure and thereby earn monopoly rent is for the firm to internalize its knowledge. Instead of selling (licensing) its knowledge to outsiders, the firm applies that knowledge only to production under its control' (Root, 2001: 378). The creation and transfer of new knowledge are made possible by and through human talent in the organization. Thus, in order to attain and maintain a firm's competitive advantage and excel abroad, it is imperative that the company succeeds in attracting and retaining human talent.

International technology gap theory

This theory is also known as the product life-cycle theory of international trade (IPLC) (Vernon, 1966). As noted earlier, while this is not specifically a theory of FDI, the IPLC explains how imitator countries (as in the case of EEs) close the technology gap by acquiring and learning the technology of the innovator country, so much so that over time, the innovator country becomes the net importer of the product that they developed. Witness, for example, the case of Galanz, a Chinese company, which entered into a limited licensing agreement on microwave technology with Toshiba in 1993 and rapidly became the world's largest producer of microwave ovens (http://en.wikipedia.org/wiki/Galanz). In order to close the technological gap, the imitator country has to possess the human power who can acquire and absorb the advanced technology.

Porter's competitive diamond

As noted earlier, Porter's competitive diamond is not strictly a FDI theory. Rather it seeks to account for a country's international competitiveness through an analysis of its factor conditions; demand conditions; related and supporting industries; firm strategy, structure and rivalry; government; and chance (Porter, 1990). The 'factor conditions' refer to a country's factors of production, labour (or more specifically, human capital) being one of them.

In summary, all the aforementioned theories point to the pivotal role that highly trained and developed human resources – human capital or talent, in short – can play in affecting a country's ability to expand abroad through FDI and/or gain international competitiveness.

Deployment of people in international assignments

Since the publication of Tung's (1981) seminal work on selection and training of expatriates for international assignments, there has been a plethora of research on the subject. A review of the literature on expatriate assignments reveals that while a litany of criteria has been advanced to assist firms to select people who are most likely to succeed abroad, researchers (e.g. Harris and Brewster, 1999; Selmer, 2001; Tung and Varma, in press) have found that the selection decisions typically come down to finding those who are willing to go on such assignments, provided they possess the technical competencies to perform the job. This finding is not surprising in light of Tung's (1981) contingency paradigm of international assignments, where she argued that a first step in the selection process is to gauge the candidate's willingness to undertake an international assignment, otherwise no amount of training could prepare effectively the person for the challenges of living and working abroad.

While the focus of this study is on the attitudes of Chinese and non-Chinese students towards working for Chinese companies, and not specifically in the context of their being selected to work for a multinational's operations in China, the literature on expatriate selection, particularly as they pertain to SIAs, is relevant. Thus, it is important to understand whether students, who are prospective cosmopolitans, are willing to work for Chinese companies. In addition, even though willingness is a pivotal first step in the selection process, in order to enhance the chances of success, international firms should be aware of the challenges these cosmopolitans would most likely encounter in such relocations. In the case of Chinese students returning to China, they could experience many of the challenges encountered by repatriates, including reverse culture shock and family issues (Harvey, 1989). In the case of non-Chinese students, their plight would be similar to that of expatriates, particularly where assignments to culturally distant and developing countries are concerned (Tung, 1998).

Paradox of scarcity among plenty

As China has become the 'workshop of the world' by virtue of its cheap and abundant labour, over time, this asset has turned into somewhat of a liability – there is a growing shortage of employees at all levels in China (Barboza, 2006). According to Fuller (2005), there are 88 and 16 job vacancies for every blue-collar worker and factory technician, respectively, in Guangdong and Fujian – two southern provinces that have experienced the most rapid growth rates in the past two decades. The focus of this paper is not on assembly line workers, however. Rather, the attention is on the human resource challenge in terms of managerial and professional talent. In this paper, following Towers Perrin's definition, talent is 'not a euphemism for workforce ... (rather, the term refers to) leadership and key professional and technical contributors (that typically account for) 15 per cent of total workforce' in a given country (*Talent Management: State of the Art*, 2005: 3). Human talent has variously been referred to as 'brainpower' (*The Economist*, 2006) and 'knowledge workers' (Drucker, 1994).

According to Farrell and Grant (2005), China's current management talent pool numbers 5,000 when it needs 75,000 executives. Hewitt Associates pointed to the high turnover at the managerial level as a result of this shortfall in talent: in 2004, the national average was 11.3 per cent, up from 8.3 per cent in 2001. The situation was worse for certain functions, such as marketing where the national average was 14 per cent turnover; and in some major cities such as Beijing and Shanghai where the turnover rates across all functional areas were 14.9 and 14.5 per cent, respectively. In the words of Steve Gilman, B&Q's CEO for Asia, 'talent is among our biggest challenge. In any of the mature markets, it's a lot easier to nick people from a competitor than it is in an immature market' (Desvaux and Ramsay, 2006: 90). This challenge is even more acute in smaller companies. Jurgen Viethen, general manager for F&G China Electric, a Spanish-owned small electrical manufacturer in China, lamented that despite his offer of a 50 per cent wage increase to his key employees, he still has problems attracting and retaining people: 'I spend most of my time on human resources, not sales' (*The Economist*, 2005).

Several factors have contributed to this talent shortfall and concomitant high turnover rates. These are: (a) demand from foreign-invested enterprises (FIEs); (b) the Chinese government's 'go global' policy and objective to become a 'technology powerhouse'; (c) the rise of Chinese multinationals; and (d) institutional baggage and imperfections. Each of these factors is briefly examined below:

Demand from FIEs

As noted earlier, since 2002, China has become the most popular destination of FDI. According to UNCTAD, an estimated $1 billion in new investments enter China every week. In addition, many multinational enterprises (MNEs) have chosen to establish their R&D facilities in China. In fact, according to the 2005 World Investment Report (WIR) entitled *Transnational Corporations and the Internationalization of R&D*, leading multinationals from around the world in different industries and sectors have ranked China as the top choice for R&D expansion, ahead of the US and India. In 2005, there were 750 foreign-invested R&D facilities in that country, a three-fold increase from 2001.

Chinese government's 'go global' policy and objective to become a 'technology powerhouse'

Buoyed by rapid economic development at home, in 2002, then Chinese Premier Zhu Rongji announced China's 'go global' policy. Under this initiative, the Chinese government encourages indigenous companies to expand internationally. The objective is to create 30 to 50 'national champions' from the most promising Chinese state-owned but not government-run enterprises (SOEs). Through generous incentives by the Chinese government, China hopes that these national champions could compete successfully on a global basis by 2010 (Zhang, 2005). In 2005, China's total stock of OFDI reached

$46 billion and ranked seventh among outward investment from EEs; Hong Kong and Taiwan ranked numbers 1 and 5, respectively, at $470 billion and $97 billion (Schifferes, 2006). The People's Republic of China (or China, in short), Hong Kong and Taiwan are collectively referred to as 'Greater China'. The focus of this paper is on China, however.

In 2005, according to the Chinese Ministry of Commerce, there were 1,067 Chinese invested enterprises abroad (Ministry of Commerce of the People's Republic of China, 2006). With a few notable exceptions – such as Lenovo's purchase of IBM's PC division for US$1.75 billion, Nanjing Automotive's acquisition of MG Rover, Haier's aborted attempt to buy Maytag, and China's National Offshore Oil Corporation (CNOOC)'s $18.5 billion failed bid to acquire Unocal – most Chinese investments abroad are relatively small and in developing countries, i.e. south-south investments.

Based on a survey conducted jointly by the Asia Pacific Foundation of Canada and the China Council for the Promotion of International Trade of 296 small and medium-sized Chinese enterprises in 2005 about their intentions to invest abroad in the future, over 40 per cent indicated that they planned to increase their activities 'moderately' or 'substantially' (Asia Pacific Canada Foundation and China Council for the Promotion of International Trade, 2005: 3). Thus, it appears that a growing number of Chinese small and medium-sized enterprises, besides the large SOEs, will seek to venture abroad in the years ahead. In February 2006, China overtook Japan to become the country with the largest foreign reserves in the world. This huge accumulation of foreign reserves has made China cash rich, thus facilitating its attempts to invest overseas.

Alongside its 'go global' policy, the Chinese government seeks to become a 'technology powerhouse' in the not too distant future. This was one of the stated objectives in China's eleventh five-year plan (2006–10). To attain this goal, in 2005, the Chinese State Council allocated $29.4 billion for R&D purposes. In comparison, the R&D budget in India for the same year was $4.9 billion. By 2020, China hopes to boost its R&D expenditures to 2.5 per cent of that country's GDP as compared to 2.7 per cent for the US (Lemon, 2006). The European Union Commission has predicted that China's R&D expenditure will most likely surpass Europe's by 2010 (Minder, 2005).

Rise of Chinese multinationals

Even though the total stock of China's OFDI is currently small, it has grown very rapidly in the recent past. According to the World Bank, about one-third of Chinese enterprises abroad have lost money, 65 per cent of them have failed, and 85 per cent of these CEOs have acknowledged that 'differences in managerial styles and corporate cultures are the main reason for the failure' (Tan, 2005: 1). While these figures may appear to very high, it is important to note that, except for a few sizable investments abroad, most OFDI from China is on a very small scale. Viewed in this context, the high incidence of failure is not significantly different from the rate of demise of small business start-ups in the US.

In a 2005 survey of 25 Chinese international firms where respondents were asked to identify barriers, both internal and external, to OFDI, 'suitable human resources' (mean of 3.9 out of 5) emerged as the most significant challenge, out-ranking other *external* factors such as 'poor brand perception' (3.3), 'foreign regulations' (3.1), 'trade barriers' (2.6), and 'financing difficulties' (2.1); and *internal* considerations such as 'cultural integration' (3.1), 'global organization management' (3.0), 'technology competitiveness' (3.0), 'access to market channels' (3.0), 'global process integration' (2.7) and 'financial risks' (2.2) (Beebe *et al.*, 2006: 10). Similarly, in a study of 150 Chinese companies operating abroad, Battat and Aykut (2005: 4) found that over one-half of the respondents 'have faced important or very important challenges in understanding the host country's culture'.

To illustrate the magnitude of this challenge, consider the case of the international joint venture formed between Chinese TCL and French MNC, Alcatel. In April 2004, the venture was announced with much fanfare and 'euphoria'. A short nine months later, the venture was dissolved. While the reasons for the rapid deterioration in relations between the two parties were multiple, most analysts agreed that the fatal blow to this short-lived alliance was cultural incompatibility – all the senior executives and marketing personnel from Alcatel left shortly after the conclusion of the joint venture: 'The biggest difference is that ... (Alcatel) emphasizes human-oriented management while ... (TCL) is more like a militarized management' (Tan, 2005: 3).

While failure to bridge the cultural gap between two corporate and cross-national cultures is not synonymous with shortage of human talent, the former stems from deficiencies in the latter. Perhaps it was recognition of this critical challenge that led Lenovo to embark on the fairly unconventional path of relocating the head office of the acquirer to the country of the acquired company – i.e. moving Lenovo's head office from China to the US in order to absorb the managerial know-how and expertise in running a MNC (Liu, in press).

Institutional baggage and imperfections

Institutional baggage and imperfections refer to the 'deeper and more resilient aspects of social structure' (Scott, 2004: 1) that contribute to inefficiencies in organizations and nation-states (Meyer *et al.*, 1997; Oliver, 1997). According to Roth and Kostova (2003), in transitional economies, institutional baggage and imperfections proliferate. In the case of China, several factors have accounted for these institutional imperfections. These include: (a) the disconnect between theory and practice in engineering programmes; (b) SOE mentality; and (c) high stay rates of Chinese students in foreign countries. Each of these is briefly discussed:

Disconnect between theory and practice in engineering programmes   While China produces 600,000 engineering graduates annually – the largest amount globally – the country's engineering programmes emphasize theory rather than practice (Iype, 2006). According to Farrell and Grant (2005), of the 1.6 million engineers in China, only one-tenth of them have the practical experience and language facilities to work in FIEs. To become a 'technology superpower', SOEs and indigenous Chinese enterprises also need engineers who can bridge the gap between theory and practice.

SOE mentality   Until its open door policy in 1977, the industrial backbone of China's economy was SOEs. In SOEs, there was no incentive for managers and employees to assume risk since the state was responsible for all profits and losses. This situation is true of other socialist economies as well. According to Jeff Barnes, chief learning officer at GE, China: '(t)he Chinese talent is first-generation. They don't have role models. Their parents worked for state-owned companies' (*The Economist*, 2005). Furthermore, during the Cultural Revolution (1966–76), education and management development were severely disrupted – this has resulted in a lost generation of managers because capitalism was deemed as evil in that tumultuous decade. In addition, under the influence of Confucianism, Chinese education has traditionally emphasized rote memorization rather than analytical thinking. Thus, it is little wonder that Stella Hou of Hewitt Associates bemoaned that: 'The local workforce mainly lacks management skills, leadership, creativity, autonomy or risk-taking, marketing and research' (Sellami, 2005). Besides, the success of the one-child policy in China has meant that there could be a fundamental change to that country's collectivistic orientation. Based on research findings in the west (Hall, 1987; Meredith *et al.*, 1989), some have argued that the lone children in many families could become 'self-centred' and lack 'social skills', thus handicapping them for teamwork that is so essential to success in a knowledge economy (Chandler, 2004; Jiao *et al.*, 1986). Other research (Yang *et al.*, 1995), however, has found no significant difference between only children and those with siblings born after China's one-child policy came into effect.

High stay rates in other countries   The largest source of foreign students in the US is now China, followed by South Korea, Taiwan, India and Canada. The stay rates for recipients of doctorate degrees in science and engineering from China and India were 90 and 86 per cent, respectively (CRA Bulletin, 2005). While this is positive for the US, in the short-term at least, it constitutes a severe brain drain on the native countries of these students.

For this reason, since 2003, Chinese President Hu Jintao has tried to arouse the nationalistic sentiments in overseas Chinese by appealing to them to return home to contribute to economic development at home. The Chinese diaspora is estimated at 55 million worldwide (Kao, 1993). Even though the Chinese diaspora extends to virtually every corner of the world, the bulk of them have settled in Asia. Many members of the diaspora are highly educated and experienced in global business. Combined with their knowledge of Chinese language and culture, they could prove to be an invaluable resource to China's OFDI efforts.

The growing 'boundaryless' nature of the Chinese workforce

Consistent with the Chinese emphasis on learning and education, the country has favoured sending its people overseas to absorb the best and most significant developments in order to regain its former position as 'centre of the universe'. This relentless quest for knowledge has led Charles Zhang (2004: 148), founder of Sohu.com Inc. – one of the largest Chinese internet companies – to remark that: '(I)n the past 150 years, China has been the best student because it has continuously sought to understand' how the country could have suffered a string of humiliating military defeats, beginning with the first Opium War (1840–2), in the hands of foreign powers.

When China re-opened its door to the west in 1977, people who went abroad were financed by the government and therefore were obligated to return home. Beginning in the mid-1990s, however, with relaxation in China's emigration policy and growing affluence in society, more Chinese went abroad to study at their own expense, i.e. financed by their families. As such, there was no obligation to return home upon completion of their studies. Furthermore, some even left to pursue grade or high school education overseas – thus, the average age of Chinese leaving home has decreased over time. According to the Chinese Ministry of Education, between 1978–2002, an estimated 580,000 Chinese went abroad to study. Of these, an estimated 150,000 have returned, resulting in a re-entry rate of roughly 25.86 per cent. While precise statistics are difficult to obtain because of the growing number of Chinese who are studying abroad at their own expense or who emigrated with their families to other countries, the return rate has increased in recent years – some estimates have placed it at 40 per cent between 2004 and 2005.

However, because most returnees have obtained foreign citizenship, an estimated one-half of those who have returned have left again. Thus, whereas in the past it was customary to talk about brain drain and brain gain, perhaps the term 'brain circulation' or 'triangular human capital flows' would be more appropriate to characterize this new phenomenon whereby human talent leaves, then returns, and then leaves again (Devoretz *et al.*, 2002; Saxenian, 2000; Teferra, 2004). This concept of 'brain circulation' is consistent with the emerging trends toward 'boundaryless careers' and 'boundaryless workforce' described earlier.

Based on a study of Hong Kong immigrants to Canada, Devoretz *et al.* (2002) found that immigrants who were more highly educated (or 'high tech immigrants', akin to the term 'human talent' used throughout this paper) had a greater likelihood to leave, i.e. return to Hong Kong after they acquired their Canadian citizenship. This is not surprising because of their ability to secure high-paying positions that offer them better career prospects in Hong Kong, an economy with a more attractive tax structure. Despite their return to Hong Kong, many high-tech immigrants have left their children and sometimes spouse (usually a wife) in Canada. Thus, those who returned to Hong Kong to work are often referred to as 'astronauts' because they maintain homes in both Hong Kong and Canada and shuttle between these two locations on a regular basis to attend to their business and personal lives.

The Canada–Hong Kong connection described above is akin to the trend that Saxenian observed in her study of Asian-born immigrants in Silicon Valley and links to their countries of birth. According to Saxenian (2000: 1), one-third of the engineers in Silicon Valley were born outside of the US. Of the foreign-born engineers, one-half came from Asia. These tend to 'study and work in the US for a certain amount of time and then return or commute regularly between their Asian homes and the Silicon Valley'. Thus, '(I)nstead of draining their native economies of human skills and resources, this new breed of "circulating" immigrants has brought back valuable experience and know-how to their local economies'. Thus, brain circulation has given rise to the emergence of 'transnational and technical communities' (Saxenian, 2000: 3) that span the countries of origin (usually in EEs) of these cosmopolitans and their adoptive countries (usually in advanced, industrialized countries).

In an online survey of 3,097 Chinese students in 49 countries around the world conducted by World HR Lab in 2004, 88 per cent of those surveyed indicated that they planned to return to China in the future, although 53 per cent of them wanted to work overseas for several years before going home (http://www.people.com.cn/GB/jiaoyu/22224/2366926.html). This pattern is consistent with the Silicon Valley–Asia and Canada–Hong Kong connections observed by Saxenian (2000) and Devoretz *et al.* (2002), respectively. The plan by overseas Chinese students to acquire several years of foreign work experience before returning could also be in response to the needs of Chinese companies. Many Chinese companies perceive that a foreign degree is insufficient unless it is accompanied by a successful track record of working abroad.

The findings of the World HR lab survey have several important implications for China's OFDI aspirations. These are:

1   Forty-seven per cent of those who planned to return prefer to work for FIEs, 14 per cent wanted to start up their own companies, 3 per cent chose to work for SOEs, and another 3 per cent preferred to seek employment with indigenous Chinese companies. The reasons for preferring FIEs included better salaries, nicer work environment, and more opportunities for training and development. Many FIEs, such as Microsoft, Siemens, Motorola and B&G, have established corporate universities/training centres

for this purpose. The primary reason for reluctance to work for SOEs is their 'male only' or 'preference for male' policy. In 2004, of the 60,000 people employed in FIEs in Beijing, 46 per cent of were female. This compared to 34 per cent in SOEs with lower representations at management levels (*People's Daily*, 2004). In the case of indigenous Chinese companies, it appears to stem from the latter's unwillingness to hire returnees

2   Nine per cent of returnees have acquired foreign citizenship and wanted to retain options to return to their adoptive homes in the future

3   Of those who planned to return, most preferred to work in Beijing (37.3 per cent) and Shanghai (31.8 per cent) – these are the two most developed cities in China that offer high living standards. The desire to return to the most developed cities is consistent with Tung and Lazarova's (2006) study of returnees to Central and East Europe where those who came from countries that are ranked high on the United Nations' Human Development Index (UNHDI) expressed a greater willingness to return, whereas those whose native countries scored lower on UNHDI, categorized as medium HDI, were reluctant to do so. The UNHDI is an overall measure of a country's well-being, including literacy, life expectancy, poverty, education and childbirth (http://en.wikipedia.org/wiki/Human_Development_Index). In Tung and Lazarova (2006), high HDI countries included the Czech Republic, Hungary, Poland and Slovenia. Medium HDI countries, on the other hand, consisted of Bulgaria, Croatia, Russia and the Ukraine.

While the findings of the 2004 World HR Lab study bode well for FIEs, they present a rather bleak picture for indigenous companies and SOEs as they seek to venture abroad.

Methodology

First study: Chinese students abroad

Sample   A four-page questionnaire was developed to understand the intentions of Chinese students abroad to return to China upon completion of their programme of studies overseas. Specifically, information was sought on the following: (a) their intentions to return to China or remain in Canada/North America, including their reasons for so doing; (b) if they plan to return, the types of companies they prefer to work for; and (c) the most significant challenges to working and/or living in China.

In spring 2006, the questionnaire was distributed to ethnic Chinese students enrolled in computer science and business administration classes at a major university in Vancouver, Canada. Vancouver is a favourite destination for immigrants from around the world; an estimated 40 per cent of its residents are born outside of Canada. The reason for limiting the survey to students in these two disciplines is that graduates from these programmes are in demand in China. A total of 109 usable questionnaires was obtained. The response rate was close to 100 per cent since the questionnaires were administered with the co-operation of the instructors of these various classes although participation was completely voluntary, i.e. students could refuse to complete the questionnaire with no consequence whatsoever.

A total of 38.5 per cent of the respondents were female. About three-quarters of the students (73.4 per cent) were enrolled in the undergraduate programmes. The rest, 15.2 and 11.4 respectively, were studying in the PhD and Master's programmes. A total of 67 per cent have stayed in Canada between two to five years, and another quarter (24.8 per cent) has lived there between 5 to 15 years. On average, the respondents have lived 56.2 months outside of China.

Second study: non-Chinese students

Sample   Another four-page questionnaire was designed to survey non-Chinese students on their willingness to work for (a) a Chinese majority- or wholly-owned company in Canada or North America and the reasons for so doing; and (b) a Chinese majority- or wholly-owned company in China. In addition, the study sought to understand the challenges that non-Chinese students who were willing to work for a Chinese company, regardless of location, would most likely encounter.

In spring 2006, the questionnaire was distributed to non-Chinese students enrolled in computer science and business administration classes at the same university in Vancouver, Canada. In this second study, 102 usable responses were obtained. Again, the response rate was close to 100 per cent for reasons stated in the first study.

A total of 41.4 per cent of the students was female. Almost all (99 per cent) of the respondents were studying at the undergraduate level. The fact that only a very small percentage of non-Chinese students were enrolled at graduate programmes in these fields is consistent with the enrolment patterns in these disciplines at these levels at Canadian universities where an overwhelming majority of the candidates are foreign-born.

The questionnaire surveys of Chinese and non-Chinese students were supplemented by interviews with 40 Chinese who have chosen to remain in Canada and another 40 Chinese who have returned to work in China. These interviews were conducted in summer 2006 and in the language of choice (i.e. either English or Mandarin) of the respondent. Relevant quotations from these interviews are used to support and/or elucidate some of the issues raised in the two questionnaire surveys.

Findings

First study: Chinese students abroad

About one-third (32.1 per cent) of the students indicated that they planned to return to work and/or live in China in the next five years; 29.4 per cent stated that they 'would not'; and 38.5 per cent expressed that they were 'not sure'. There was no significant difference in preferences between male and female respondents.

For those respondents who indicated that they planned to return or were uncertain about returning, they were asked to assess the importance of different reasons for their decision. Table 1a presents these reasons, in descending order of importance. Again, there was no statistically significant difference between the male and female respondents.

Table 1a *Reasons reported by Chinese students for returning to China*

Reasons	Mean (5 = very important)
Better career opportunities for myself	4.32
Better financial remuneration in China	3.77
Standard of living in China has improved	3.69
Other family related reasons	3.56
Quality of life in China has improved	3.55
My elevated social status in China upon return	3.44
Better career opportunities for my spouse/partner	3.16
Better opportunities for my children	3.06
Not used to Canadian lifestyle	2.78
Experienced discrimination in Canada	2.73

In general, it appeared that Chinese students were motivated to return to China because of perceived opportunities for themselves and their families and less so by negative experiences in Canada. Some of the respondents, albeit in the minority, were unable to adapt to the Canadian (Western) lifestyle and/or experienced discrimination in Canada. The average scores of under 3 on both of these items, the neutral value in the scale, suggested that, on balance, their experience in Canada was more positive than negative. However, because the means on both of these items were just slightly below the neutral point, it is important to probe these aspects further.

In-depth interviews with a separate sample of Chinese who have returned to live/work in China helped shed light on these issues. According to one Chinese male, 'I felt that my life (in North America) was the same every day – I felt that I could predict the same lifestyle 20 or 30 years later. I was really bored of that. In addition, even though I spoke good English, ... I never felt that I was part of them'. Another Chinese male echoed this sentiment by stating that despite the fact that he spoke English with no accent, 'I still feel the distance between the local Americans and myself'. These sentiments were echoed by several of those who returned to China. Thus, it appears that while many Chinese might not have experienced overt discrimination abroad, they felt a sense of non-belonging or psychological anomie in their adoptive countries. While psychological anomie by itself might not be a sufficient motivator to lead overseas Chinese to repatriate; however, when it is combined with the allure of participating in the phenomenal economic growth that is occurring back home, it could become a powerful driving force.

Take, for example, the case of Enge Wang, who was a research associate at the University of Houston before returning to Beijing in 1995 to work in the Chinese Academy of Sciences. He is now the director of the Academy's Institute of Physics. In retrospect, Wang indicated that the misgivings his American colleagues and friends expressed about his decision to return were totally unfounded. Wang noted that China's 'research funding is getting much better.... Talented returnees can secure enough backing to build up their own lab and extend their research in one direction for 10 years. It's hard to find such conditions elsewhere' (Chen and Dean, 2006).

For those who planned to return, they did not anticipate major challenges upon repatriation since all the items pertaining to this question recorded means that were below 3, the neutral point. In fact, in-depth interviews with a separate sample of Chinese who have returned revealed that all the interviewees said that they loved China more than before they went abroad. Such positive feelings could stem from the fact that the angst associated with psychological anomie often experienced by immigrants vanished upon return home. This positive sentiment could also be attributed, in part at least, to the fact that all the interviewees who have returned to China now lived/worked in Shanghai, the most cosmopolitan city in China. This finding is consistent with the experience of many returnees to Central and East Europe, particularly the respondents from high HDI countries (Tung and Lazarova, 2006). This positive sentiment among Chinese returnees bodes well for China as Tung and Lazarova (2006) found that there was a correlation between those who experienced problems of reintegration upon return, a phenomenon more common among those from medium HDI countries, and the intention to leave again.

Approximately one-half (45.3 per cent) of the respondents in this study indicated, however, they did not know how long they planned to work in China after their return – this finding reinforces the notion of brain circulation and 'boundaryless' careers discussed earlier.

Of those who planned to return to China, about one-fifth (19.8 per cent) stated that they planned to set up their own companies; another one-fifth (17.4 per cent) planned to work for FIEs; and none chose to work for indigenous Chinese companies. The balance indicated that it 'depends upon the best available opportunity upon return'. The finding that not a single respondent in this study identified indigenous companies as an employer of choice might stem from their perception that Chinese-owned companies may operate along autocratic and/or bureaucratic lines, where promotion and salary could be based primarily on connections rather than competencies. There may be some validity to such misgivings as many returnees to Central and East Europe, former socialist countries, were not able to apply their 'international skills and knowledge at home' (Tung and Lazarova, 2006: 1863).

For those respondents (29.4 per cent) who indicated that they preferred to remain in Canada, they were asked to assess the importance of different reasons for their decision. Table 1b presents these reasons, in descending order of importance. Again, there was no statistically significant difference between the male and female respondents.

Table 1b *Reasons reported by Chinese students for remaining in Canada*

Reasons	Mean (5 = very important)
Quality of life is better in Canada	3.63
Better career opportunities for myself	3.46
Used to the Canadian way of life	3.44
Opportunities in China for returnees are not as good as they were 5–10 years ago	3.31
Better opportunities for my children in Canada	3.21
Better career opportunities for my spouse/partner in Canada	2.87

The observation that the opportunities for *haiguis* (or returnees) were not as good as they were in the mid- to late 1990s merits explanation. In the early 2000s, some *haiguis* have been labelled as *haidai* or 'sea kelp', a derogatory term referring to their lowly status in society. The reasons for the reversal of fortune for some of the returnees are as follows:

1   Unrealistic salary expectations. Since most Chinese are now self-financing their education abroad, they expect to recover the sizable investments in their education as quickly as possible upon return.
2   Perceived arrogance of many *haiguis*: many have a 'sense of superiority ... of their own unique background and experience abroad'.
3   As noted earlier, because some Chinese are leaving home as young as grade or high school, they might have lost touch with the latest developments in China.
4   In the early years of China's open door policy, the government funded the best and brightest to study abroad. With self-financing, anybody who could gain admission abroad can study overseas, thus resulting in a general lowering of the overall quality of those returning (CBIZ.CN, 2004).

In-depth interviews with a separate sample of Chinese who remained in Canada highlighted the importance of two factors (quality of life and children's education) and revealed a situation (brain waste) that was not explored in the questionnaire. Even though the quality of life (QOL) and living standards in China have improved significantly in recent years, environmental pollution is still a major problem. Thus, for those who place a higher premium on QOL issues, it would be very difficult for any Chinese city to compete with Vancouver in this regard. Vancouver has been consistently ranked as one of the most desirable cities to live in the world. In terms of children's education, Vancouver offers a wide selection of high quality private and public schools and post-secondary educational institutions. Given the emphasis that many Chinese place on their children's education, this is an important consideration. In fact, one of the interviewees worked two full-time jobs in order to put her daughter through medical school so that she does not have to obtain student loans to finance her education. Similarly, many Chinese parents saved on other household expenses in order to provide private tutoring in music for their children. In other words, it appears that many Chinese parents were willing to make tremendous sacrifices to accord their children opportunities they themselves were deprived of when young.

Besides QOL and children's education issues, the interviews yielded a disturbing phenomenon: 'brain waste', which refers to a situation where over-qualified immigrants worked in jobs that did not require advanced education and qualifications, thus 'wasting' their skills and talents (Ozden and Schiff, 2006). Examples included: one architect that used to be a designer at a major construction firm in China but who now works in a clerical capacity at a construction company in Canada; a geography lecturer, a software engineer and a human resource manager in China who are now employed as a waiter, chef and sewer at a garment factory, respectively; an embryologist with a PhD in her field of studies who works as an administrative clerk at a day-care centre; and another Chinese with a PhD in Chinese literature who now delivers take-out food orders at a Canadian restaurant. These people could not find jobs in Canada that match their professional competencies because of inadequate English language skills and/or Canadian licensing boards did not recognize their foreign degrees and professional credentials. Unfortunately, brain waste is not unique to Canada or Chinese immigrants alone. Mattoo *et al.* (2005) found that, with some exceptions, this situation was more pervasive for Latin American and Eastern European immigrants to the US, where more 'skilled immigrants end up in unskilled jobs'. In comparison, in the US, brain waste occurred less frequently among immigrants from Asia and other industrialized countries.

For the Chinese immigrants interviewed in this study, a reason for their decision not to return to China despite 'brain waste' was the issue of face. When they chose to emigrate to Canada, their friends and relatives back home admired/envied them as there is still a traditional perception among many Chinese that there are fortunes to be made in North America. San Francisco, for example, is still referred to as the 'old gold mountain' in Chinese – a throwback to the gold rush days when many Chinese migrants went there to 'strike it rich'. As such, the Chinese emigrants to Canada interviewed in this study did not want their friends and relatives back home to suspect that they 'could not make it' abroad and therefore had to return. Thus, many of these immigrants actively hid their current situation from acquaintances back home.

Second study: non-Chinese students

When asked whether they would entertain the idea of working for a Chinese majority- or wholly-owned company in Canada or North America, only 10.8 per cent stated that they would 'definitely not' do so. About a quarter (24.5 per cent) said 'definitely yes' and 64.7 per cent opted for 'maybe/not sure'. Statistically significantly fewer females chose 'definitely yes', however. In general, it appeared that the vast majority of non-Chinese students kept an open mind with regard to working for Chinese companies in Canada and North America. This might stem, in part at least, from the fact that Vancouver, despite its diversity, is a very 'Asian city' in terms of the large settlement of Asians, particularly Chinese, some of whom are affluent.

Table 2a presents the extent to which certain reasons, in descending order of magnitude, have influenced the non-Chinese students' intention to work or not work for a Chinese majority- or wholly-owned company in Canada or North America.

Table 2a *Reasons reported by non-Chinese students for willingness or unwillingness to work for a Chinese majority- or wholly-owned company in Canada/North America*

Reasons	Mean (5 = to a very great extent)
Disagree with Chinese government policies and programmes	3.39
Good career prospects posed by rapid growth of China's economy	3.26
Low status associated with working for a Chinese company	2.67
Limited employment opportunities in other companies	2.51
Fascination with Chinese culture	2.50

In general, it appeared that the most important reason for choosing to work for Chinese companies is the growth prospects associated with China; the most salient factor for not working for Chinese companies is disagreement with Chinese government policies and programmes. Even though the questionnaire pertained to working for Chinese companies, the fact that a primary reason for not working for Chinese companies is 'disagreement with Chinese government policies and programmes' reveals that in the minds of many non-Chinese, Chinese companies in North America are indistinguishable from their government. In other words, there is a perception that Chinese companies are extensions/vestiges of the Chinese government, even though such might not be the case in reality.

There was a statistically significant ($p < .05$) difference between the male and the female students on the career prospects dimension. In general, even though fewer females expressed definite willingness to work for Chinese companies, of those who did, they viewed better career prospects in North American-based Chinese companies than their male counterparts. This might stem from the fact that even though Canada espouses gender equality, because of the relatively lower representation of women at the senior management level, the female respondents were more willing to entertain options or opportunities wherever they arose.

Of those, both male and female respondents, who expressed willingness to work for Chinese companies in Canada, one-fifth (20.6 per cent) indicated that they planned to leave once they have acquired sufficient experience. Less than one-tenth (7.8 per cent) said that they would work 'indefinitely' for a Chinese company and the vast majority indicated that they were 'not sure'.

When the second part of the questionnaire asked about the willingness of non-Chinese students to consider working for a Chinese majority- or wholly-owned company in China, a very different picture emerged. Almost one-half (46.1 per cent) of the respondents said that they 'definitely would not' entertain the idea; an identical percentage chose 'maybe/not sure' and only 7.8 per cent indicated 'definitely yes'. The most serious concerns were with 'lower quality of life, such as pollution', and 'disagreement with Chinese government and policies'. Of those who planned to work for Chinese companies in China, one-third (32.4 per cent) said they would leave once they have acquired sufficient experience and about one-half (44.1 per cent) said they were 'not sure'.

The fact that 7.8 per cent of non-Chinese students expressed willingness to work in China and another 46.1 per cent said that they might do so is consistent with a growing trend where non-Chinese nationals either accept relocation or undertake self-initiated assignments to China because of the prospects for 'excitement, riches and a career boost'. In the words of Ryan Greene, a Dallas Texas attorney: 'What's happening (in China) is so amazing. It's the industrial revolution in early 19th century America all over again' (Yung, 2006).

The non-Chinese students were then asked to assess the challenges they would likely encounter if they were to work for a Chinese company either in Canada or in China. Table 2b presents these challenges, in descending order of significance. The fact that all the dimensions in Table 2b had mean values above the neutral point suggests that while many non-Chinese students were open to the option of working for Chinese companies, albeit more so in their North America-based operations than in China itself, the majority also anticipated major challenges associated with such a career move. This finding has tremendous implications for China's ability to attract highly qualified local nationals to staff their North American operations as they seek to invest abroad.

Table 2b *Challenges reported by non-Chinese students if they were to work for Chinese companies either in Canada/North America or in China*

Reasons	Mean (5 = to a very great extent)
My spouse/partner may object to relocation to China	3.85
Other family-related issues	3.84
Poor working conditions, such as long hours, lower compensation, less job security	3.59
The inability to fully understand the mentality of my Chinese boss and/or colleagues	3.58
Deal with more bureaucracy	3.55
Corruption and other unsavoury business practices	3.48
Perceived influence by the Chinese government in the company's operations	3.48
Glass ceiling, i.e. perception that non-Chinese will have limited opportunities for advancement to the top	3.29
Difficult to transfer experience to other non-Chinese companies	3.16

Moreover, the female students expressed significantly ($p < .05$) higher levels of reservations than their male counterparts on five of the nine challenges, including spouse/partner objection, other family-related issues, glass ceiling, poor working conditions and perceived corruption; and marginally significant ($p < .10$) higher level of reservation as far as perceived bureaucracy is concerned.

This finding of male–female differences is not surprising in light of the fact that women, in general, tend to more sensitive to the needs of their loved ones, in this case the spouse/partner and family, and working conditions, including unsavoury business practices. With respect to the concern over the possible existence of a glass ceiling, as noted earlier, since there is evidence of gender discrimination at the senior managerial ranks in Canada, it is little wonder that the female respondents may harbour fears in light of the attention that the Western media has drawn to gender selection, including alleged cases of female infanticide in China. This finding is also consistent with the experience of returnees to Central and East Europe where female respondents received lower salaries and less support from top management (Tung and Lazarova, 2006). Pollert (2003: 346) asserted that there has been 'widespread post-communism anti-feminism', as witnessed by the plummeting in the Gender-Development Index for the Czech Republic from eighth place in 1990 (just after the Velvet Revolution) to thirty-third place in 1998, for example. Even though China is still a socialist country, since its open door policy and adoption of market reforms, however, there has been growing social inequality, including gender inequity.

This finding of women's concern with possible gender discrimination is consonant with the 2004 World HR Lab survey where most female respondents expressed reluctance to work for SOEs because of the perceived 'male only' or 'preference for male' policy at these enterprises. Given the traditional perceptions of a woman's role in society, Chinese companies, including some FIEs operating in China, apparently consider physical appearance of female job applicants in their selection decision. The *China Daily* reported that: 'Where female graduates are concerned, they are often judged by appearance, stature, and figure. A beautiful face is certainly a plus' (Tao, 2006).

Discussion and conclusion

There are three primary limitations associated with this study. One, the surveys were limited to Chinese and non-Chinese students at one major university in western Canada. However, because the sample sizes were respectable and were supplemented with interviews, the findings did provide useful insights into the human resources challenge that China faces as it pursues its dual objectives of sustaining economic growth at home and expansion overseas. Two, most respondents in this study were ethnic Chinese born and raised in China. Tung (2005) has offered a broader definition of ex-host country nationals (EHCNs) to encompass 'ethnic Chinese (a) who were born and raised abroad; (b) born in China and raised/educated abroad; and (c) born and raised in China and who have lived/worked extensively abroad'. In other words, most of the respondents in this study fell into category (c). In the case of China, since many members of the Chinese diaspora who could play an important role in facilitating China's OFDI aspirations as well as economic growth at home would fall into the first and second categories of EHCNs, future studies should examine the attitudes and intentions of these Chinese as well. Three, the two studies reported here gauged students' willingness and intentions to work for Chinese companies. Willingness and intentions do not always result in actual relocations. However, as revealed in the staffing decisions at most multinationals discussed earlier in the literature review section, willingness to relocate is typically the first step and, sometimes, the primary criterion in the selection decision.

In line with other published literature, the findings of this study suggested that there are many endogenous and exogenous factors, from the human resource perspective, that could facilitate China's OFDI aspirations. These include:

- The willingness of many Chinese who are living and/or working abroad to return.
- Many non-Chinese nationals also entertain the idea of working for Chinese companies, albeit more so in North American-based operations than in China itself.
- The Chinese government is cognizant of the need to rectify some institutional imperfections to alleviate the 'shortage among plenty' paradox, including:
  o the provision of incentives for overseas Chinese to return
  o the announcement of a 'go west' policy to nurture human talent in the lesser developed parts of the country to broaden the labour supply pool (French, 2005)
  o the upgrading of English-language proficiency among its population (China Daily, 2005) and
  o the establishment of Western-style MBA programmes throughout the country. In 2004, an estimated 18,500 students were enrolled in 90 Chinese MBA programmes in the country (*BusinessWeek*, 2006).

At the same time, however, there are many challenges, principal of which are: (a) the preference of Chinese to work for FIEs; (b) the 'male only' or 'preference for male' policy at many SOEs; (c) the deteriorating conditions for *haigui* upon return; and (d) the image problems that non-Chinese nationals have of China. Each of these issues is elaborated below.

In this study, none of the Chinese students in Vancouver chose to work for indigenous companies in China. The finding here is even more dismal than the results obtained in the 2004 World HR Lab survey. In the 2006 Towers Perrin study of 86,000 middle managers around the world, they compared the profile of different countries on the top attraction and engagement drivers. In the case of China, they found that the top attraction drivers, in descending order, were: 'learning and development opportunities, competitive base pay, and career development opportunities'; while the top engagement drivers were: 'improved my skills and capabilities over the last year, senior management's actions are consistent with our values, and good collaboration across units' (Towers Perrin, 2006: 17). FIEs, in general, provide more training, higher salaries and better work environment. In addition, because many FIEs are committed to localization where promotion is based on merit, many cosmopolitans find them more attractive. 'Localization' refers to the objective of eventually staffing top positions in their organizations with Chinese rather than foreign expatriates (Sellami, 2005). Furthermore, because many Chinese have acquired foreign citizenship and want to retain the option of returning to their adoptive countries in the future, experience acquired at a foreign multinational tends to be more portable – this is consistent with the 'brain circulation' phenomenon discussed earlier in the paper.

Despite the Chinese government's attempts to bring about gender equality in the country, such as the Constitutional provision of equal pay for equal work and women retaining their surnames after marriage, it is difficult to eradicate several millennia of discrimination against women, at least from the perspectives of what their proper roles in society should be and what the most cherished attributes in women are. This explains why many Chinese women prefer to work for FIEs. In the present study of non-Chinese students in Vancouver, females were significantly more concerned about many aspects of working in China, the possible existence of glass ceiling in Chinese companies being one of them.

With regard to the deteriorating conditions for *haigui*, i.e. from *haigui* to *haidai*, while the returnees have to bear some of the responsibilities for this turn of events – such as unrealistic salary expectations, lack of knowledge of current Chinese conditions and perceived arrogance at work – if such conditions were to worsen, it could negatively impact the willingness of Chinese to return in the future, particularly those who are in high demand in foreign countries.

The final, but certainly not least, important challenge that China faces in the 'war for talent' is in terms of poor image that the non-Chinese students in Vancouver have of China. Even though the non-Chinese students, in general, kept an open mind with regard to the possibility of working for Chinese companies, they were more receptive to employment in North American-based Chinese operations as opposed to relocation to China. This is particularly depressing in light of the fact that, as mentioned earlier, Vancouver is a very 'Asian' city. Perhaps, there is truth to the maxim that 'familiarity breeds contempt'. The non-Chinese students perceived major challenges in working for Chinese companies whether in North America or China. Their concerns about career opportunities upon return and their family's adaptability to living and working in China, a culturally distant country, are not unique to China and are consistent with those articulated by expatriates toward international assignments, in general. However, their perception that Chinese companies are extensions of the Chinese government can severely hamper China's OFDI aspirations because of the generally negative attributes associated with the investor country, including corruption, excessive bureaucracy and other unsavoury business practices. Whether and how the Chinese government and Chinese companies could overcome such negative perceptions, however inaccurate, certainly merit attention. If China is unable to improve its image with non-Chinese nationals, it may be difficult for Chinese companies to attract and retain highly qualified talent to work for them both at home and abroad.

In summary, from the practical implications' perspective, it appears that while China has been able to transform itself into the fastest growing economy in the world in a short two and a half decades, in order to attain its objective to become a 'technology powerhouse', it has to, first and foremost, confront head on this human resource challenge. Its failure to do so could stall or frustrate that country's attempt to graduate from the ranks of an EE to become an advanced, industrialized nation.

From the theoretical perspective, the findings of this study highlight the need to broaden the field of international human resource management to encompass brain circulation and the growing war on talent. Increasingly, the focus should go beyond the mere traditional identification of appropriate selection criteria, provision of cross-cultural training, and compensation for cost-of-living differentials. Future research should look at the willingness and intentions of Chinese and non-Chinese students in other countries to work for Chinese companies. In fact, this research should be broadened to students and managers from other EEs so as to provide a more comprehensive understanding of the human resource challenge likely to be encountered by these countries as they seek further growth and development. In addition, future research should track the extent to which willingness or intention to work for investors from EEs translate into reality. Besides, new research should also address the factors that could contribute to brain circulation, i.e. under what conditions are cosmopolitans more willing to accept or undertake self-initiated assignments to their native countries or return to their adoptive countries; and what should governments and corporations in both the countries of origin and adoptive countries of these cosmopolitans do to minimize the negatives and accentuate the positives in order to win this battle for brainpower.

In short, from the theoretical perspective, in light of the emerging dynamics of 'boundaryless' careers and 'brain circulation', the time is ripe for greater exchange of ideas and collaboration with scholars in other fields, such as global migration, for example. Within the field of international management itself, this study points to an even greater need to merge the research on cross-national with intra-national diversity called for in Tung (1993) because the lines between what constitutes domestic and international workforce are increasingly blurred. Greater cross-fertilization of concepts and research paradigms in these two areas could advance significantly our understanding of the dynamics and processes pertaining to international human resource management, and thus facilitate the development of more comprehensive models in the field that can truly capture the complexities associated with the management of people in a global economy.

Acknowledgement

An earlier version of this paper was presented at the Annual Meetings of the Academy of International Business, Beijing, China, 23–6 June 2006. This research is made possible by a generous grant from the Social Sciences and Humanities Research Council of Canada, Project # 639560.

References

Accenture (2005) 'China Spreads its Wings – Chinese Companies Go Global'. Online at: http://www.accenture.com

Asia Pacific Canada Foundation and China Council for the Promotion of International Trade (2005) 'China Goes Global: A Survey of Chinese Companies'. Outward Direct Investment Intentions',

Asia Pacific Canada Foundation and China Council for the Promotion of International Trade. Online at: http://www.asiapacific.ca

Barboza, D. (2006) 'Labor Shortage in China May Lead to Trade Shift'. *New York Times*, 3 April. Online at: http://www.nytimes.com/2006/04/03/business/03labor.html?th = &emc = th&pagewanted = all

Battat, J. and Aykut, D. (2005) *Southern Multinationals: A Growing Phenomenon* FIAS. October.

Beebe, A., Hew, C. and Liu, S. (2006) 'Trends and Lessons Learned from Cross-border M&A by Chinese Companies', presentation at the American Chamber of Commerce, Beijing, China, 23 February.

BusinessWeek (2006) 'China's B-school Boom', *BusinessWeek Online*, 9 January. Online at: http://www.businessweek.com/magazine/content/06_02/b3966074.htm

Casson, M. (1987) *The Firm and the Market*. Cambridge, MA: MIT Press.

CBIZ.CN (2004) 'Managing Returnees', CBIZ.CN, October. Online at: http://www.cbiz.cn/news/showarticle.asp?id = 2082

Chandler, C. (2004) 'Little Emperors', Online at: http://money.cnn.com/magazines/fortune/fortune_archive/2004/10/04/8186784/index.htm

Chen, K. and Dean, J. (2006) 'Low Costs, Plentiful Talent Make China a Global Magnet for R&D', *Wall Street Journal*, 14 March. Online at: http://yaleglobal.yale.edu/display.article?id = 7123

China Daily (2005) 'Brown Announces Export Push in China – for English'. *China Daily*, 22 February. Online at: http://www.chinadaily.com.cn/english/doc/2005-02/22/content_418449.htm

CRA Bulletin (2005) 'Stay Rates of Foreigners Earning US S&E Doctorates Increase'. Online at: http://www.cra.org/wp/index.php?p = 31

DeFilippi, R. and Arthur, M.B. (1996) 'Boundaryless Contexts and Careers: A Competency-based Perspective'. In Arthur, M.B. and Rousseau, D.M. (eds) *The Boundaryless Career: A New Principle in a New Organizational Era*. New York: Oxford University Press.

Desvaux, G. and Ramsay, A.J. (2006) 'Shaping China's Home Improvement Market: An Interview with B&Q's CEO for Asia', *McKinsey Quarterly*: 83–91.

Devoretz, D.J., Ma, Z. and Zhang, K. (2002) 'Triangular Human Capital Flows: Some Empirical Evidence from Hong Kong and Canada'. Working Paper Series 02-17, Research on Immigration and Integration in the Metropolis, Vancouver, Canada.

Drucker, P.F. (1994) 'The Age of Social Transformation', *The Atlantic Monthly*, 274(5).

Dunning, J.H. (1988) 'The Theory of International Production', *The International Trade Journal*, 3(1): 21–66.

Economist, The (2005) 'China's People Problem'. *The Economist*, 14 April. Online at http://www.economist.com/business/displayStory.cfm?story_id = 3868539

Economist, The (2006) 'The Battle for Brainpower'. *The Economist*, 7 October. Online at: http://web.ebscohost.com/ehost/detail?vid = 6&hid = 5&sid = 37c2940e-813a-4930-8f3b-c975762a8d8b%40sessionmgr3

Farrell, D. and Grant, A.J. (2005) 'China's Looming Talent Shortage', *McKinsey Quarterly*, Online at: http://www.mckinseyquarterly.com

French, S. (2005) 'Go West – Going, Going, Gone'. *CBIZ.CN*. Online at: http://www.cbiz.cn/news/showarticle.asp?id = 2307

Fuller, T. (2005) 'China Feels a Labor Pinch', *International Herald Tribune*, 20 April. Online at: http://iht.com/articles/2005/04/20/news/costs.html

Hall, E. (1987) 'China's Only Child', *Psychology Today*, July: 44–7.

Harris, H. and Brewster, C. (1999) 'The Coffee-machine System: How International Selection Really Works', *International Journal of Human Resource Management*, 10(3): 488–500.

Harvey, M. (1989) 'Repatriation of Corporate Executives: An Empirical Study', *Journal of International Business Studies*, 20: 131–43.

Human Development Index. Online at: http://en.wikipedia.org/wiki/Human_Development_Index

Iype, G. (2006) 'Engineering Education: Can India Overtake China?' 9 June. Online at: http://ia.rediff.com/money/2006/jun/09bspec.htm?q = tp&file = .htm

Jiao, S., Ji, G. and Jing, Q. (1986) 'Comparative Study of Behavioral Qualities of only Children and Sibling Children', *Child Development*, 57: 357–61.

Kanter, R.M. (1995) *World Class: Thriving Locally in a Global Economy*. New York: Simon and Schuster.

Kao, J. (1993) 'The Worldwide Web of Chinese Business', *Harvard Business Review*, March–April: 24–36.

Kindleberger, C.P. and Andretch, D.B. (eds) (1983) *The Multinational Corporation in the 1980s*. Cambridge, MA: MIT Press.

Lemon, S. (2006) 'China Sets National R&D Goals for Next 15 Years', *InfoWorld*, 9, February. Online at: http://www.infoworld.com/article/06/02/09/75218_HNchinaranddgoals_1.html?BUSINESS%20PROCESS%20MANAGEMENT

Liu, C.Z. (in press) 'Lenovo, an Example of Globalization of Chinese Enterprises', *Journal of International Business*.

Lohr, S. (2006) 'Microsoft and Google Waging "War for Talent"', *New York Times*, 10 May. Online at: http://www.iht.com/articles/2006/05/09/business/titans.php

Luo, Y. and Tung, R.L. (in press) 'International Expansion of Emerging Market Enterprises: A Springboard Perspective', *Journal of International Business Studies*.

Mattoo, A., Özden, C. and Neagu, C. (2005) 'Brain Waste? Educated Immigrants in the US Labor Market'. World Bank Policy Research Working Paper No. 3581. Online at: http://ssrn.com/abstract = 722925

Meredith, W.H., Abbott, D.A. and Zhu, L.T. (1989) 'A Comparative Study of Only Children and Sibling Children in the People's Republic of China', *School Psychology International*, 10: 251–6.

Meyer, J., Boli, J., Thomas, G. and Ramirez, F. (1997) 'World Society and the Nation-state', *American Journal of Sociology*, 103(1): 144–81.

Minder, R. (2005) 'EU Fears China's Rising R&D Spending'. *Financial Times*, 9 October. Online at: http://www.ft.com/cms/s/3a7563b0-38fa-11da-900a-00000e2511c8.html

Ministry of Commerce of the People's Republic of China (2006) 'China's Overseas Direct Investment Statistics 2005', Ministry of Commerce of the People's Republic of China, 26 July. Online at: http://english.mofcom.gov.cn/aarticle/statistic/foreigninvestment/200607/20060702705397.html

Oliver, C. (1997) 'Sustainable Competitive Advantage: Combining Institutional and Resource-based Views', *Strategic Management Journal*, 18(9): 697–713.

Ozden, C. and Schiff, M. (eds) (2006) *International Migration, Remittances and the Brain Drain*. New York: Co-publication of the World Bank and Palgrave Macmillan.

People's Daily (2004) 'Chinese Females Increasingly Find Jobs in Multinationals', 5 April. Online at: http://english.peopledaily.com.cn/200405/02/eng20040502_142271.html

Pollert, A. (2003) 'Women, Work and Equal Opportunities in Post-communist Transition', *Work, Employment and Society*, 17: 331–57.

Porter, M.E. (1990) *The Competitive Advantage of Nations*. New York: The Free Press.

Root, F.R. (2001) 'International Trade and Foreign Direct Investment'. In Tung, R.L. (ed.) *The IEBM Handbook of International Business*. London: Thomson Press, pp. 366–81.

Roth, K. and Kostova, T. (2003) 'Organizational Coping with Institutional Upheaval in Transition Economies', *Journal of World Business*, 38(4): 314–30.

Saxenian, A.L. (2000) 'Brain Drain or Brain Circulation? The Silicon Valley-Asia Connection'. Harvard University Asia Center, 29 September. Online at: http://www.ischool.berkeley.edu/~anno/speeches/braindrain.html

Schifferes, S. (2006) 'Poor Nations Push Investment Boom', BBC news website, 17 October. Online at: http://news.bbc.co.uk/2/hi/business/6054866.stm

Scott, W.R. (2004) 'Institutional Theory: Contributing to a Theoretical Research Programme'. In Smith, K.G. and Hitt, M.A. (eds) *Great Minds in Management: The Process of Theory Development*. Oxford: Oxford University Press.

Sellami, H. (2005) 'Expatriates in China: Changing the Package'. Online at: http://www.cityweekend.com.cn/en/beijing/cib/2005_07/story.2005-06-29.1657349458

Selmer, J. (2001) 'Expatriate Selection: Back to Basics?', *International Journal of Human Resource Management*, 12(8): 1219–33.

Stahl, G.K., Miller, E.L. and Tung, R.L. (2002) 'Toward the Boundaryless Career: A Closer Look at the Expatriate Career Concept and the Perceived Implications of an International Assignment', *Journal of World Business*, 37(3): 1–12.

Tan, W. (2005) 'Culture Conflicts in Sino-Foreign Ventures', *Beijing Review*. Online at: http://www.bjreview.com.cn/En-2005/05-25-e/bus6.htm

Tao, J. (2006) 'To Be Employed? Get Sweet Voice First'. *China Daily*, 5 January. Online at: http://www.chinadaily.com.cn/english/doc/2006-01/05/content_509577.htm

Teferra, D. (2004) 'Brain Circulation: Unparalleled Opportunities, Underlying Challenges and Outmoded Presumptions'. Paper presented at the Symposium on International Labor and Academic Mobility: Emerging Trends and Implications for Public Policy. 21–2 October. Toronto, Canada: World Education Services.

Towers Perrin (2006) *Winning Strategies for a Global Workforce*. New York: Towers Perrin.

Tung, R.L. (1981) 'Selection and Training of Personnel for Overseas Assignments', *Columbia Journal of World Business*, 16: 21–5.

Tung, R.L. (1993) 'Managing Cross-national and Intra-national Diversity', *Human Resource Management Journal*, 32(4): 461–77.

Tung, R.L. (1998) 'American Expatriates Abroad: From Neophytes to Cosmopolitans', *Journal of World Business*, 33(2): 125–44.

Tung, R.L. (2005) 'China's Future Role in International Business', Paper presented at the AIB Fellows Panel, Annual Meetings of the Academy of International Business, Quebec City, P. Q., 9–12 July.

Tung, R.L. and Lazarova, M.B. (2006) 'Brain Drain versus Brain Gain: An Exploratory Study of Ex-host Country Nationals in Central and East Europe', *International Journal of Human Resource Management*, 17(11): 1853–72.

Tung, R.L. and Varma, A. (in press) 'Expatriate Selection and Evaluation'. In Smith, P.B., Peterson, M.F. and Thomas, D.C. (eds) *Handbook of Cross-Cultural Management Research*. Thousand Oaks, CA: Sage.

UNCTAD (2005) *Transnational Corporations and the Internalization of R&D. World Investment Report*. New York and Geneva: UNCTAD.

UNCTAD (2006) *FDI from Developing and Transition Economies: Implications for Development*. World Investment Report, New York and Geneva: UNCTAD.

Vernon, R. (1966) 'International Trade and International Investment in the Product Life Cycle', *Quarterly Journal of Economics*, 81(2): 190–207.

World HR Lab Survey (2004) Online at: http://www.people.com.cn/GB/jiaoyu/22224/2366926.html

Yang, B., Ollendick, T.H., Dong, Q., Xin, Y. and Lin, L. (1995) 'Only Children and Children with Siblings in the People's Republic of China: Levels of Fear, Anxiety, and Depression', *Child Development*, 66: 1301–11.

Yung, K. (2006) 'Execs See China as Place to Boost Career', *The Dallas Morning News*, 21 March. Online at: http://www.dallasnews.com/sharedcontent/dws/bus/stories/032106dnbuschinawork.296484f.html

Zhang, C. (2004) 'China's Leading Internet Guru Charles Zhang, Chairman of Sohu.com Inc., on How the Internet Has Changed the World's Most Populous Nation', *Academy of Management Executive*, 18(4): 143–54.

Zhang, K. (2005) *Going Global: The Why, When, Where and How of Chinese Companies' Outward Investment Intentions*. Vancouver: Asia Pacific Foundation.

The prospect for gender diversity in Japanese employment

John Benson, Masae Yuasa and Philippe Debroux

Introduction

The rapid economic growth of Japan in much of the second half of the twentieth century only served to widen the gap in wages and employment conditions of women workers compared to their male counterparts. While women's participation rate in the labour force increased significantly over this period this was due to the rapid growth in the manufacturing and service sectors. Yet, unlike their male colleagues who enjoyed lifetime employment, seniority promotion and on-the-job training, women workers occupied a peripheral position in the labour market. The male-dominated nature of enterprise unions served to reinforce these practices.

With changes in Japan's business environment, these employment practices have now contributed to a shortage of well-qualified labour. This raises the question as to whether skill shortages will provide the impetus in the long term for increasing employment opportunities for women. It is this question that is explored and analysed in this paper. The paper begins by detailing the current state of women's employment in Japan. The next section explores the changes in the nature of the internal labour market and why such changes are taking place. This is followed by a section that outlines the gender bias inherent in the work organization in Japanese companies and discusses how company practices reinforce these biases. The penultimate section examines whether the changes to the internal labour market will be able to overcome the discriminatory work practices are that are embedded in the way work is organized. A short conclusion completes the paper.

Women's employment in Japan

The participation rate of Japanese women in the labour market was 48.5 per cent in 2002 (MHLW, 2004a). This was down slightly from the peak of 50.0 per cent in 1995. This figure is substantially less than the 75 per cent participation rate in Sweden, 70 per cent in the Netherlands and 59.5 per cent in the United States (ILO, 2004). This rate varies by age: for those in the age range 25–9 the participation rate is 74.0 per cent, for the 35–9 age group, the rate falls to 62.2 per cent and then rises to 73.0 per cent for those women in the 45–9 age group (JILPT, 2005c: 17). In each age category, the participation rate for women is well below that of men, which for the age groups mentioned above is in excess of 90 per cent (JILPT, 2005c: 17). By 2002, Japanese women made up 41.0 per cent of the labour force – up from 31.0 per cent in 1960 (Yuasa, 2005: 196).

In 2003, the average monthly wage of Japanese women employees was 239,400 yen, well below the 368,600 yen earned by their male counterparts. The average Japanese woman worker thus earned 64.9 per cent of the average male workers' earnings (JILPT, 2005c: 46). While this gap has narrowed slightly in recent years (JILPT, 2005c: 46), it remains one of the largest wage differentials among the developed countries (WEC, 2003: 49). Part of the reason for this gap is the shorter tenure of Japanese working women, and the concentration of women in low-paid service and manufacturing sectors. In addition, in 2004 some 40.4 per cent of working women were employed on a part-time basis (JILPT, 2005c: 35–6) and thus earned considerably less than this average. Japanese women workers were more likely to work part time compared to their counterparts in the US, UK, Germany, France and Italy.

These figures suggest that systematic forms of gender discrimination exist in Japanese companies. By the 1980s, demographic changes were placing pressure on the Japanese government to provide some encouragement to women to enter the workforce. Nevertheless, it was only after pressure from the International Labour Organization (ILO) that Japan enacted its first equal opportunity legislation in 1986, the much-criticized Equal Employment Opportunities Law. This legislation, an extension of the earlier Female Welfare Law, encouraged companies to provide equal treatment to male and female employees but contained no penalties for any breaches of the legislation. This law was revised in 1999 and discrimination in recruiting, training, promotion and remuneration was forbidden. However, there is no mention of the inferior working conditions of part-time employees, notwithstanding that women dominate this category. In the same year, the Childcare Leave Law was also revised to provide better working conditions for women workers. The increasing global competition facing Japanese companies will force them to better utilize their female employees, although the response to date has been to employ casual workers with substantially less rewards and benefits. Many of these workers are women.

In advanced industrialized economies, three major reasons are given to explain women's disadvantaged status at work (see Yuasa, 2005). First, companies are reluctant to invest in the training and development of women, as management believes there will be fewer prospects for an adequate return on this investment. Second, the heavy burden of domestic work for many working women often results in the unfavourable treatment of women at work. Third, the way tasks are allocated at work and the male dominant cultures in the workplace lead to significant discrimination against women. In Japan's case, the presence of a strong internal labour market in a company with internal promotion, seniority pay and a complex grading system is a further significant barrier to equality.

The breakdown of the internal labour market?

The characteristics of the Japanese employment system are often described in terms of the internal labour market, which provides a career ladder within the company and restricts candidates for anything other than an entry-level job to those already working for the company. Consequently, the reliance on an internal labour market means that decisions regarding an entire working career are made early in an employee's life and does not allow for periods of time away from work. However, the distinctive features of Japanese employment practices go beyond this general concept (Dore, 1997). As Lam (1992: 28) suggested, 'Discrimination against women constitutes an important basis for the employment practices characterizing Japanese companies'. There are, however, a number of pressures on the internal labour market that may have major consequences for the Japanese employment system and women workers in particular.

The erosion of the grading system

The distinctiveness of Japanese employment is well illustrated by the concept of the traditional 'grading system' (Miyamoto, 1998: 34–5). Underpinning this system are the institutional norms of 'lifetime employment' and 'seniority' promotion, although it should be noted that neither of these practices are widespread outside large companies or are uniquely Japanese (Imada and Hirata, 1996: 2; Miyamoto, 1998: 30). The grading system establishes a range of job grades with a commensurate range of pay rates and effectively rewards the acquisition of skills. These skills make work organization functionally flexible, accommodating a certain degree of environmental changes and effectively utilizing the rigid employment system based on norms of lifetime employment and seniority (JILPT, 2005a: 4). The grading system is thus a sophisticated incentive mechanism that encourages the majority of workers to commit themselves to the long-term process of skill formation (Imada and Hirata, 1996: 62–3). A grading system, however, is not the only effective incentive mechanism for the development of skills but it serves to institutionalize the internal environment of the Japanese company (Miyamoto, 1998: 34).

This high functional linkage cannot now be sustained by the same institutional arrangements for three reasons (Tominaga and Miyamoto, 1998: 17). First, the external business environment of Japanese companies has substantially changed since the 1990s; the emerging cost-effective Chinese and other Asian manufacturers and the relocation of Japanese companies to those Asian neighbours have forced many companies in Japan to restructure so as to become more globally competitive. Second, the rules of capital financing have significantly changed under the radical restructuring of Japanese banks. The long-term-ism of silent shareholders, which is a precondition for the Japanese employment system, is no longer available for the majority of Japanese companies. Third, demographic changes in Japan directly challenge the traditional employment system. The post-war baby-boom generation has made the wage pyramid structure unsustainable and their pending retirement will impact significantly on work organization in Japanese companies. These factors have undermined the current employment practices of Japanese companies and have led to an erosion of the grading system.

Flexible restructuring

The Japanese government has reacted to the structural problems facing Japanese industry with a series of deregulation efforts since the 1990s. The amendments to commercial and antitrust laws in the latter half of the 1990s enabled flexible restructuring of corporate governance. The restructuring started in 1997 with the lifting of the ban on pure holding companies and simplifying the procedures to enable joint ventures. Furthermore, in 2000, a corporate divestiture system was created. A survey on labour union activity (*Roudou Kumiai Katudou Jittai Cyousa*) conducted in 2000 by the Ministry of Health, Labour and Welfare (MHLW, 2001) revealed that 45.7 per cent of companies had restructured or eradicated a division in the past three years (Hisamoto, 2005: 87). In terms of restructuring, a 2001 survey of Japanese companies (JILPT, 2002) found that 14.5 per cent of companies had reorganized their corporate structure within the past three years. These radical changes in company structure and the possibility of more changes have undermined the long-term career development process inherent in the internal labour market.

The decline in commitment to lifetime employment

With the increasing flexibility of company structures, a key factor underpinning the internal labour market, namely 'lifetime employment', is becoming increasingly difficult to sustain. In 2002, the Japanese unemployment rate hit a record high of 5.4 per cent (Benson, 2005a: 42). Although the situation has improved to 4.1 per cent by October 2006 (MIAC, 2006), a number of important long-term trends is noticeable. From 1990 to 2003, a period of economic decline and loss of manufacturing jobs, non-voluntarily unemployment increased 560 per cent and was especially applicable to men over 45 years of age (Hayagami, 2005: 1). In this same period, voluntarily unemployment also increased by 220 per cent and was especially noticeable among women and younger workers (Hayagami, 2005: 1).

In a study of manufacturing companies in Japan over the period 1991 to 2001, Benson (2005b: 68–9) found that the number of companies willing to decrease the number of regular employees when faced with 'a decrease in demand for their major product' more than doubled in the period. By 2001, nearly four in ten companies indicated they would adopt such a strategy. Such reactions, however, may be a short-term response to the difficult economic circumstances facing the firm. Therefore, companies were asked how they would respond to 'an increase in demand for their major product'. By 2001, less than one in four companies (24. 4 per cent) indicated that would increase their number of regular employees. In 1991, the comparable figure was 54.6 per cent. In both cases, the shift was to part-time and temporary workers. Clearly, the commitment to lifetime employment has declined significantly over this period and supports the trends suggested by earlier studies by Lincoln and Nakata (1997) and Takahashi (1997).

In 2003, 30 per cent of workers in the 25–9 years age range quit their first job and 40 per cent of 30–4 year olds did the same (*The Nikkei*, 21 November 2005). This finding, coupled with the results presented above, highlights a major problem for the Japanese company in that long-term skill formation and its incentive mechanisms are no longer sustainable not only because of the high cost to the company but also because of the changing attitudes of workers. In 2004, a survey on workers motivation and personnel management found 54 per cent of workers older than 35 years old supported long-term employment. In contrast, only 37.3 per cent of workers younger than 35 years of age supported such a system (JILPT, 2005b: 72).

Mainstreaming of atypical workers

The deregulation of labour law has resulted in an increased number of atypical workers in Japanese workplaces since the second half of the 1990s. These revised laws included the Labour Standards Law (1998), the Worker Dispatch Law (1999), the deregulation of restrictions on women's late night work (1999), and the enactment of a new discretionary labour system (2000). This deregulation has encouraged competition among different categories of workers and has downgraded general working conditions by creating jobs with little job security and other regular employment conditions (Nakano, 2001; Wada, 1999: 100).

Much of the move towards atypical employment has been prompted by the need to compete in the global market place against countries where labour costs are substantially lower. Recent statistics clearly illustrate these changes. From 1997 to 2002, three million regular jobs were lost, while a slightly larger number of non-regular jobs were created. According to the latest Ministry of Health, Labour and Welfare employment survey, in 2003 part-time and temporary workers comprised 34.6 per cent of the workforce. This was an increase of 7.1 per cent from 1999 (Naikakufu, 2004). In 2004, 53 per cent of working women were atypical workers of some kind. Some of these workers have been dispatched from their regular jobs to other, often smaller, companies where wages are considerably lower. Moreover, the conditions for these workers have been deteriorating; in 1994, the average hourly wage of dispatched workers was 1,704 yen; by 2004, it had fallen to 1,430 yen. The average duration of the contracts is also falling. In 2004, more than 60 per cent of dispatched workers were working on contracts of three months or less. Moreover, a significant decline in job offers for dispatched workers older than 35 years has occurred and there are almost no opportunities for women with young children (Haken Rodo, 2005).

The competitiveness and performance of many Japanese companies is now increasingly dependent on atypical workers whose ability and commitment is questionable (Sato, 2003: 3). Moreover, the trend towards atypical forms of work have placed further pressure on the internal grading system as they increasingly represent pay for the 'job' rather than 'merit' for both part-time and full-time workers (Honda, 2004: 82). The employment of women atypical workers, at substantially lower wages than their regular male workers, has significant implications for all workers and has created further pressure on companies to reorganize their employment system.

The move to external training

There is some evidence emerging that companies are retreating from an internal training strategy, at least in some job categories. A survey of 216 unionized companies who employed more than 300 employees, and whose unions belonged to the Japanese Electrical Electronic and Information Union, found that while the majority of companies in 2002 developed their employees through in-company programmes 14 per cent of companies used mainly externally trained workers for general office work and 9 per cent used externally trained workers for manufacturing parts, assembling products, system engineering, and software development (Turu and General Research Center of Japanese Electrical Electronic and Information Unions, 2005). The survey also asked companies to consider the likely situation in five years time. Less than 50 per cent of companies responded that they would utilize internally trained workers in general office work, manufacturing parts and product assembly (Uemura, 2005: 139–40).

Based on this data, Uemura (2005: 145) analysed the relationship between company strategy and the demise of the internal labour market. Companies that had adopted either a 'selective concentration' or a 'selective contraction' strategy were retreating from the internal development of workers in the areas of general clerical work, parts manufacturing and product assembling. Those strategies were driven by the new global business environment where companies will only invest in human capital where they are an essential part of the high-value creating sections of their value chains. This can be seen by the finding that the large majorities of Japanese companies will maintain the internal labour market for such areas as research and development where intellectual property rights are important and a strategic aspect is present. In short, the past practice of cultivating company-specific intellectual skills for all workers is no longer appropriate and internal training will now depend on the strategic value of the work to the company's value chain (Uemura, 2005: 141).

Increase in performance-related pay

One key characteristic of the Japanese internal labour market is that pay is based on years of service and, when coupled with internal training, represents an experience-ability based remuneration system. The trend now, however, appears to be towards performance-related pay. According to the *General Survey on Working Conditions* conducted by the Ministry of Health, Labour and Welfare, 53.2 per cent of companies have introduced performance-related pay. It is more widely practiced in large companies with more than 1,000 employees where 83.4 per cent of companies have adopted such a system (JILPT, 2005b: 4). In a survey on performance pay and work satisfaction, 75.3 per cent of the 1,278 companies surveyed indicated that they have recently instituted mechanisms to reward employees according to their performance (JILPT, 2005b). In the same survey, 57.8 per cent of companies have a performance-related pay system that recognized performance over age or seniority (JILPT, 2005b).

A number of reasons has been advanced to explain this rapid change in remuneration policy. First, the loss of flexible financial support from the main banks has meant that companies now have to manage labour costs in more direct ways. Second, the aging of the workforce, when coupled with seniority pay, has meant that labour costs have risen disproportionately to the company's performance. Third, the necessity to retrench workers over the past 15 years due to the prolonged economic downturn required companies to select good workers at an earlier stage of their career than was normal under the traditional grading system (Tatumichi, 2004: 41). Fourth, the grading system was unable to respond to the increasingly sophisticated skills that were required and so was incapable of rewarding advanced skill acquisition. Fifth, the rapid development of information technology has changed work organization and collaborative practices that further separated the grading system from individual performance. Finally, the lack of clear measurement standards for assessment in the grading system created insufficient incentives for workers (Sato, 2006: 64).

A survey by the Japanese Institute of Labour Policy and Training of 1,066 companies with more than 100 employees (JILPT, 2005b) found that companies that had introduced a performance-related pay system had tended to introduce it alongside a strategy of individual differential treatment of workers in their task allocations from an early stage of their careers ('earlier selection'), active utilization of atypical workers, and a clearly planned education and training strategy. Thus, performance-related pay was not an isolated practice but part of a bundle or package of new employment practices (JILPT, 2005b: 24). This suggests a systematic erosion of the grading system with its long process of selection of workers with a wide range of job experiences, an emphasis on full-time workers, and the process of skill formation based on on-the-job training.

Changing worker expectations

The direction of change, such as the move towards performance-related pay, seems to be welcomed by the workers. The survey on performance-related pay referred to earlier (JILPT, 2005b) also asked 7,828 workers in the sample companies about their work satisfaction and then analysed the relationship between worker satisfaction and the employment practices of the companies. The results indicated that the practices of 'earlier selection' and targeted on-the-job or external training were factors significantly and positively related to the satisfaction of workers (JILPT, 2005b: 49). The survey also explored the specialist orientation of the workers: more than three-quarters of respondents had a specialist orientation while only one-quarter had a generalist orientation (JILPT, 2005b: 77). A specialist orientation was most common among full-time workers less than 35 years old with 86.1 per cent aiming to become a specialist (JILPT, 2005b: 77). For these workers, 'earlier selection' and career development schemes were important and underpinned their general acceptance of performance-related pay schemes. Only 26.5 per cent of these workers hoped for lifetime employment (JILPT, 2005b: 72).

The changing nature of Japanese labour markets

The changes identified above appear to be driven by the changing business environment brought on by the prolonged economic downturn, globalization, the aging population and the changing orientations and expectations of young workers. This altered business environment has clearly undermined the internal labour market with its emphasis on 'lifetime' employment for male employees. Yet, while these changes may present opportunities for women workers it is likely that for a smaller, select group of (male) employees the internal labour market will continue to dominate their working lives for some time. Nevertheless, the emphasis on an internal labour market will continue to decline as the grading system is no longer the driving force for productivity and performance in this new business environment.

The competitive environment facing Japanese companies, coupled with the changing expectations of workers, means that human resource management (HRM) will need to adopt both short and long-term objectives (Kudou, 2004: 2). In the short term, increased workers' contribution to the company's strategic objectives will be required and one possible avenue for this will be an increase in individualized schemes such as performance-related pay. In the long term, there will be the need to cultivate and improve the ability to construct the strategy (Kudou, 2004: 2). These higher-level skills cannot be developed in a system that focuses solely on in-company training and common rewards. To do so will only increase the severe mismatch that now exists between the demand and supply of skilled labour.

Gender bias in Japanese work organization

It has been argued that the internal labour market has had negative consequences for women's employment in Japanese companies (Nohata, 1997: 112). The most cited reason why this might be the case has been the lack of a transparent and objective measurement of performance. The ongoing changes in the nature of the grading system outlined in the previous section may contribute to the development of a more gender-fair assessment system, although the impact may go well beyond simply increasing the objectivity in assessment. The reason for this is that the grading system, and all that it entails, is the core of a logically coherent, interlocking set of institutionalized practices that serve to maintain the employment and work practices in Japanese companies. This section will explore gender bias inherent in the work organization in Japanese enterprises and how such biases are reinforced by managerial practices.

Increasing objectivity in assessment?

The lack of objective performance measurements in the Japanese company, coupled with vague job descriptions, has allowed gender discrimination to flourish while making it difficult to detect (Lam, 1992: 63). *Satei,* or Japanese individual assessment, is used for scaling tacit 'skill' and is said to have three elements: performance, merit and personality or attitude. Kumazawa (1997: 11, 19) claimed that supervisors normally assess workers' 'abilities' by their attitude and willingness to accept unlimited overtime, and to sacrifice their life for the company. The level of expectation is often so high that workers who have to take care of children find it virtually impossible to meet these expectations. Kumazawa (1997) further argued that these managerial practices coerce positive attitudes from workers and form the basis of indirect gender discrimination. While many regard this merit rating and its incentives as the 'reality' of the productivity of the Japanese companies (Ito, 1994: 238), it clearly marginalizes women workers and more recently has created problems for management.

A survey conducted by the Japanese Institute for Labour Policy and Training (JILPT, 2005c: 4) found among the companies that had introduced a performance-related pay system 59.8 per cent of respondents reported that a major reason for doing so was to increase the legitimacy of assessment. Nevertheless, Tatumichi (2004: 44) found the introduction of performance-related pay increased concerns over objectivity and fairness in its measurement, and over the increasing pay gap among workers. Where a grievance system is in place, however, workers tended to be more satisfied with their work (JILTP, 2005b: 52). The anxiety of workers over assessment is also shared by managers. In a survey of managers concerning important future HRM strategies, 51.6 per cent felt it was important to establish fair assessment procedures (JIWE, 2005a).

Length of service

The short length of women's service traditionally has been regarded as an important reason for their low status level in Japanese companies. Primarily, this was because the adherence to an internal labour market policy meant that 'merit' promotion was implemented according to skill acquisition and experience, which are both closely related to seniority (Imada and Hirata, 1996; Kumazawa, 1997: 61, MHLW, 2002; Uehara, 2003; Tatumichi, 2004: 28). Various recent surveys have now shown a decrease in the importance of seniority as the key criteria in promotion (Tatumichi, 2004: 46; Sato, 2006). This change has come about partly as a result of the high cost of the seniority system and partly as a product of the need to increase the company's skill base.

According to a survey conducted by the Japan Institute of Worker's Evolution on women managers, half of the 409 companies predicted an increase in the number of women managers within five years (JIWE, 2005a). Among those respondents who did not predict an increase, the most cited reasons were a 'lack of job experience' (54.7 per cent), a 'lack of decision-making, planning and negotiation ability' (34.7 per cent) and a 'lack of length of service' (30 per cent). In a much larger survey conducted by the Ministry of Health, Labour and Welfare on women's employment, a similar result was found (MHLW, 2004b). Among the companies with few or no women managers, the major reasons for this were a lack of the required level of knowledge, experience and decision-making ability (48.4 per cent); their short length of service (30.6 per cent); and a recognition that there were some talented women candidates but that they did not have the required length of service (27.6 per cent).

These findings indicate that length of service does matter for promotion despite the decreasing importance of seniority as a measurement of performance. Consequently, women with their shorter tenure are unlikely to gain the necessary core skills of decision making, planning and negotiation that Kudou (2004: 3) argued were the key objectives for HRM in long term. Moreover, it is very unlikely that women would have developed these types of skills in their family or within the Japanese education system. It is also the case that external training programmes that are currently available to women workers are not well enough developed or accepted by management. Consequently, the continued emphasis on in-house training and task allocation in work organization continues to be a major constraint on achieving some measure of gender equality in Japanese companies. This argument is supported by the findings of a survey on the career development of managers (JIWE, 2003). In that study, the most important factor among 695 female and 815 male managers in promoting excellence in performance was the individual's 'experiences in jobs'.

Task allocation and job recruitment

The report on gender wage differences (MHLW, 2002) argued that task allocation and the loosely used appraisal system were the main factors underlying the low status of women workers in Japanese companies. An earlier survey on the employment and management of women workers (MHLW, 2000) showed that a significant number of jobs was dominated by men and the rate of domination increased with a rise in the required skill level; in 20 per cent of the companies, tasks that required more than six years of skills and experience were held only by male workers.

Kimoto (2003) demonstrated that the gender-different task allocations in the same job categories, coupled with a lack of female 'model' managers, contributed to a general lack of desire for promotion among Japanese women workers. Women workers became afraid of, or had little confidence in, promotion because they had neither the training nor enough experience for the position. Furthermore, without promotion, many women had to struggle with 'boredom', 'emptiness' and little autonomy in their work (Kimoto, 2003: 70, 78). Task allocation thus became a significant influence on 'marriage retirement' and hence on the short length of women's service. In turn, this was regarded by many as 'natural' behaviour or the 'choice' of women (Kimoto, 2003: 198).

This situation has changed little over the past few years. In a survey on the employment of women workers (MHLW, 2004b), half of the companies had at least one section that recruited only male workers. In the sections of planning/survey/public relations, research and development, and sales and service, the ratios of workplaces that had both male and female workers had slightly increased from 2000, but overall little improvement can be discerned. In a survey focusing on the development and appointment of women managers (JIWE, 2005a), 39.1 per cent of companies claimed that they consciously gave women a wide range of job experiences. However, the majority of companies recognized that this practice was less important than constructing clear measurements for the appraisal system (59.6 per cent). The same tendency was observed in the survey of women workers referred to above (MHLW, 2004b). Among the companies that claimed to have introduced at least some gender neutral policies, 64.1 per cent of companies stated that there was a need to clarify the standards for pay-rises and promotion. On the other hand, only 29.6 per cent of companies were committed to education and training for women, although this was an improvement from the

18.8 per cent of companies that responded in this way in 2000. Clearly, without access to adequate training, an objective and transparent performance evaluation system will have little effect.

Women managers

The number of women managers in Japanese companies has remained rather static over the past decade and there is strong evidence to suggest it is not likely to change in the foreseeable future. The latest survey on the employment of women workers (MHLW, 2004b) found that the number of companies with a positive action programme for the promotion of women had decreased from 40.6 per cent in 2000 to 21.4 per cent in 2003. There were, however, some positive signs notwithstanding the unwillingness of Japanese companies to promote women at the present time. The survey found that in the same time period the number of companies that were going to 'investigate the gender problem' at workplaces increased from 17.2 per cent to 23.9 per cent and that companies which had 'a plan for gender equality' had increased from 14 per cent to 23.9 per cent.

Some companies have recognized the need to have female role models especially for managerial positions. In the survey focusing on the development and appointment of women managers (JIWE, 2005b), 21.6 per cent of companies claimed they developed 'model' women workers, 11.3 per cent of companies individually trained women candidates for managerial positions, and 8.8 per cent prepared a special training programme for women. Overall, however, these figures show that the vast majority of companies did not have such plans.

The male-dominated organizational culture

There is little evidence that the male-dominated organizational culture of Japanese companies has changed significantly in recent years. A survey on affirmative action (JIWE, 2002) demonstrated the predominance of a widespread male-centred corporate culture among responding companies. Specifically, 72.1 per cent of the companies were trying, or going to try, to prohibit male workers from calling women workers 'our girls'; 61 per cent had recently stopped or were going to stop requiring uniforms only for female workers; 80.3 per cent were trying, or going to try, to share tasks such as making tea and cleaning; and 61.6 per cent were trying, or going to try, to teach managers to regard women workers as useful human assets. A more recent survey on harassment at work (JIWE, 2004) reported that around the half of the 638 companies admitted that there were gender-based task allocations. For example, 55 per cent of companies reported an organizational culture that regarded tea servicing and cleaning as jobs for women workers. These figures clearly show a gender-biased culture, yet the 2003 Basic Statistical Survey on Employment and Management of Women Workers found that the number of companies willing to reform their organizational culture had decreased from 39 per cent to 26 per cent.

Japanese women's employment prospects

The shortage of skilled employees has significantly affected the internal labour market structure of Japanese companies. These changes include the erosion of the grading system, the decline in commitment to lifetime employment, the mainstreaming of atypical workers, a shift to external skill development and the linking of pay to performance. These factors in the past served to restrict women's employment and promotional opportunities. Do such changes now provide opportunities to improve employment opportunities for women? It is our contention that the impact of these changes on women workers will be extremely limited. While some objectivity is being incorporated into the appraisal system, it is still the case that in most firms appraisals are not based on objective and transparent criteria. In addition, length of service remains the key criteria for advancement and job tasks continue to be allocated along gender lines. While there are signs that companies are addressing some of the barriers to women's advancement, it is equally clear that the predominant work organization and culture remains heavily biased towards male workers.

What, then, are the likely prospects for gender diversity in Japanese employment? The breakdown of the internal labour market has been an important but not sufficient force to the creation of a fairer employment system for Japanese working women. The three primary factors mentioned earlier in this paper – management's unwillingness to invest in skill development, domestic work and task allocation – still stubbornly resist the changes. Nevertheless, there are pressures that are developing against these obstacles. One is the politics of the decreasing birth rate and the other is the emerging concept of diversity management. The former might reduce the burden of housework on working women and the latter, if it works effectively, can reduce stereotypical views and radically undermine the male-centred culture in Japanese companies.

When the Koizumi government took power in 2000, fiscal reform became the top agenda. Nevertheless, policy makers could not deliver the desirable reforms with the ever-decreasing birth rate. This led them to renew their commitment to improve the birth rate and to examine their previous policy measures that encouraged women to stay at home during their child-rearing years (Oosawa, 2003). The policy direction has now changed and encourages both men and women to work and to take care of children through reformed tax and pension systems and the introduction of new legislation (Imada, 2003). In 2003, the Basic Law on the Society with Fewer Children and the Law of Promoting Helping Measures for Bringing up Future Generations passed the Japanese Diet (Parliament). Based on these laws, Outlines of Provisions for the Society with Fewer Children was approved by the Cabinet in 2004. This provision includes a number of concrete support programmes for childcare including numerical targets to be reached. Furthermore, the second Basic Plan for Gender Equality passed the Diet at the end of 2005. This plan, through various measures and numerical targets, aims to significantly decrease the burden on working women by 2020. The strong commitment of the government to these measures can be seen in the 2007 budget request: the funding of measures to counteract the effects of the decreasing birth rate was increased 10 per cent from the 2005 figure (*Asahi Newspaper*, 2006). These initiatives will go some way to reduce the heavy burden of childcare for women.

The second factor that will affect the future of women workers in Japan is the emerging concept of diversity management brought on by a shortage of skilled workers and the increasing numbers of foreigners working in Japan. Although diversity management is a developing concept in Japan, elsewhere it is increasingly being accepted as an important HRM strategy (Litvin, 1997) that is superior to 'affirmative action' (Ng and Burke, 2005: 1196). The difference between affirmative action/equal employment opportunities and diversity management is significant: the former is driven by a sense of justice and equality, while the latter is being driven by commercial implications, organizational efficiency and effectiveness (McLeod *et al.*, 1996) in new business environments, such as those caused by a changing labour market or a globalized economy (Benschop, 2001: 1168). The superiority of this approach for women workers is twofold: first it is more likely to encourage executives to devote resources to help the company capitalize on the benefits of a diverse work force and second it promotes awareness of the value of individual differences.

Diversity management will present serious challenges to many Japanese companies where homogeneity or oneness have been highly valued and encouraged (Yasumoto, 1998: 141). There are, however, some signs of the increasing influence of diversity management in Japan. The Japan Federation of Employers' Associations set up a research group on diversity management in 2000. In 2004, the Japanese Committee for Economic Development published a report titled 'Utilizing Diversity and Living in Diverse Ways', which proposed diversity management as a new model for work. In the same year, the Kansai Employers' Association issued a Diversity Report. A report on pioneering cases of work–life balance by the Cabinet Office (2006: 22) argued that the 'inevitable' diversity management is the reason for pioneering provisions for work-life balance among large multinationals.

Clearly, diversity management will have some utility to large multi national Japanese companies due to their global interests and increasing world-wide mergers and alliances. For domestic companies diversity management may be important in their endeavours to mainstream atypical workers. Moreover, as pointed out by Subeliniani and Tsogas (2005: 836), diversity management can be beneficial to knowledge-based innovative activity and so those Japanese companies whose competitiveness depends on their innovativeness may be attracted to diversity management. With little legal enforcement, the majority of Japanese companies have not treated equal employment legislation seriously. The imperatives underpinning diversity management, however, may induce the necessary cultural changes and contribute to the reduction of stereotyping views that exist about women in Japanese companies.

Are Japanese companies moving towards some form of diversity management? A survey on the development and appointment of women managers (JIWE, 2005a) asked 409 personnel managers about their most important future personnel strategies. The most cited issues were the need to construct a fair and convincing evaluation (85.3 per cent), securing diverse human resources (75.6 per cent), expanding performance evaluation (72.2 per cent), and utilizing and appointing women workers (68.8 per cent). This data indicate a high degree of interest towards the key issues underpinning diversity management. While many of the respondents regarded the utilization of women as strategically important, few had any well-developed strategies in their own company. The popular strategies for the utilization of women among the respondents were the need to clarify evaluation measurements (59.6 per cent), clarifying the standards for promotion (55.5 per cent), and providing women workers with a wide range of job experiences (39.1 per cent). Notwithstanding the above, only 4.4 per cent of respondents reported that their company had set a numerical target for the number of women managers.

For those Japanese companies that are interested in diversity management, what form could it take? Diversity management maintains significant managerial rights (Subeliani and Tsogas, 2005: 837) and for many it may simply mean moving away from dealing with racial and gender equality to a mere recognition of diversity (Wrench, 2002). This approach, for example, is indicated in the report by the Nomura Research Institute (Morisawa and Kihara, 2005: 70). The report argued that diversity management is good for creating schemes and institutions for the core workers, although typical programmes for utilizing women workers in Japan fail to accommodate the needs of core women workers and the vast majority of women who work outside of the core. In this case, it is unlikely that diversity management will bring about gender equality. Indeed, it may well widen the gap with male workers and other Japanese working women.

Notwithstanding the positive prospects of these developments, the organizational and societal constraints mean that women's prospects at work will depend heavily on organizational support. Such support does not appear to be forthcoming, at least for the vast majority of women workers. In the survey of 409 companies referred to earlier, 67.5 per cent of those companies employing more than 5,000 employees regarded the full utilization of women workers as an important HRM objective. These figures dropped significantly as the companies fell in size: among the companies whose employee numbers were between 1,000 and 4,999, the percentage was 30.5 per cent; for companies employing less than 1,000 employees, the percentage was slightly less than 20 per cent (JIWE, 2005a: 3). In 2005, about 80 per cent of women employees worked in companies with less than 500 workers (MIAC, 2006). On these figures, it would appear that the prospects for achieving gender equality at work for the majority of women in the immediate future appear slim.

There are other barriers to achieving gender equality in Japanese companies. First, some obvious but indirect gender-discriminatory practices are still legally allowed in Japan. One example is the dual-track system where women have the choice to nominate whether they wish to pursue a career with the company. Notwithstanding the operational problems of such a system, most companies do not offer such a choice. A recent survey on the treatment of women workers found only 18 per cent of companies use the dual-track system (JIWE, 2005b: 2–3). This system was most pronounced in the finance and insurance sector (39.7 per cent) and large companies with more than 1,000 employees (30 per cent). Among small companies with less than 300 employees, the figure was only 10 per cent. Given that the vast majority of employees work for smaller companies, it is likely that most women workers are employed in companies that do not offer such a scheme.

Yet, even when companies offered such a scheme, most women employees opt out of the system. In a survey conducted on the practice of the dual-track system (MHLW, 2005: 3) the percentage of women workers that opted for the career track was only 5.1 per cent among the 180 companies surveyed. In addition, it is more competitive to get a career track position for women than for men: only 0.7 per cent of women are successful compared to 3.3 per cent of men. The survey did note, however, that 64.1 per cent of companies, at some time, had transferred workers from the general track to the career track. Interestingly, of those companies that use such a system, 26.9 per cent will re-examine its use (JIWE, 2005b: 5). The most cited reason was the need to react to the 'changing attitude of workers and changing business environment'. More recently, some firms have been offering an 'in-between' career track ('area professional career track') with limits placed on relocation (*The Nikkei*, 27 March 2006). While this addresses some of the relocation problems for women, the trade-offs are reduced promotional prospects, wage rises and responsibility.

A second barrier or threat to gender equality at work is the increase and/or mainstreaming of atypical workers. According to Weathers (2005), these part-time workers are posing a threat to the dual-track system as the general work category is increasing being filled with atypical workers. The number of regular women workers has decreased in recent years while the number of atypical women workers has increased. On this latter employment mode, the percentage of atypical women workers has increased from 30.7 per cent in 1997 to 50.7 per cent in 2002 (MIAC, 2002). In addition, part-time workers in many companies have been subdivided into core and ancillary employees. The new employee categories are often based on the willingness to accept transfers involving relocation, and the willingness to accept irregular work schedules. The higher-ranking categories have better pay and promotion opportunities. Supermarkets are in the vanguard of these changes since about 80 per cent of their employees are part-time workers. Some of them have low-level managerial functions but at lower pay than the regular employees. These practices penalize working women with children and maintain corporate control over employees, as any employee who wants a full wage must necessarily agree to be constantly available to work and ready to accept transfers involving relocation.

A third constraint facing women at work is the disinterest of Japanese enterprise unions in the atypical worker. Enterprise unions basically share the opinion of management concerning the use of low-cost workers as a buffer to protect regular employees that make up the bulk of their members. Facing a dramatic decline in membership, enterprise unions have acknowledged the necessity of eliminating gender differentials and strengthening their position among non-regular workers. At the peak confederation level, bold initiatives have been suggested but the eventual decisions are taken at the company level (Rengo, 2001). This lack of interest partly explains why the membership rate of part-timers in 2003 was estimated at only 3 per cent (Weathers, 2005). The unions have been successful in protecting minimum work standards and preventing management abuses but they have found it difficult to get significant wage raises or improved benefits for part-time workers. This generates a circular effect as it reinforces the doubts among part timers, often women workers, of the value of union membership that in turn places less pressure on unions to work in the interests of part-time workers.

Interestingly, change may come about from an unexpected source, namely younger male and female workers. In a recent survey on work satisfaction, the attitudes of younger workers were found to be more supportive of a work–life balance (JILPT, 2005b). Workers were broken into two groups: younger workers (less than 35 years of age) and older workers (those older than 35 years of age). Some 77.2 per cent of younger workers considered that workers ought to have the right to take time off for raising children and taking care of parents. In addition, 63.6 per cent of the younger workers felt they should be able to choose their style of work according to their life style and to their life stage (JILPT, 2005b: 73). Less of the older workers emphasized personal life although the gap was only a little more than 10 per cent. While 13.4 per cent of the older workers regarded 'sacrificing family life for work' as unavoidable, only 6.0 per cent of the younger workers agreed (JILPT, 2005b: 72).

Conclusion

This paper assessed the prospects for gender diversity in Japanese employment. While a major constraint on employment equality was the internal labour market that operates in most Japanese companies, the erosion of this market over the past decade has not provided the expected opportunities for women. This was primarily due to the gender bias inherent in Japanese work organization. In particular, the lack of objectivity in assessment, the continued reliance on in-house training (and hence the use of length of service as a key promotion criteria), the bias in the allocation of tasks and in recruitment for certain jobs, the lack of female role models and the entrenched male-dominated culture that exists in many Japanese companies all served to restrict the opportunities available to women workers. These factors served to reproduce the discriminatory work practices, even in the absence of a strong internal labour market.

There were some signs that change was occurring both from government and from managers seeking to move to some form of diversity management. While we would concede that these developments may produce some tangible benefits, the employment prospects of Japanese women will be determined ultimately by the contest between the forces that have worked to erode the internal labour market and the forces that continue to maintain the current discriminatory forms of work organization. The outcome of this contest between these contradictory forces is not clear or pre-determined. The growing skill shortages in Japan, the changing attitudes of young workers and the increasing labour turnover rates may have an important effect on reducing gender biases. This will, however, depend on the degree that Japanese companies are prepared to embrace globalization and government policies designed to counter some of the important demographic changes taking place in Japan.

References

Asahi Newspaper (2006) 'Budget for policy measures relating decreasing birth rate is 1 trillion 674 billion yen, approximate budget request for the next consecutive year', 1 September, Online at: http://www.asahi.com/life/update/0901/010.html

Benschop, Y. (2001) 'Pride, Prejudice and Performance: Relations Between HRM, Diversity and Performance', *International Journal of Human Resource Management*, 12(7): 1166–81.

Benson, J. (2005a) 'Unemployment in Japan: Globalisation, Restructuring and Social Change'. In Benson, J. and Zhu, Y. (eds) *Unemployment in Asia*. London: Routledge, pp. 39–57.

Benson, J. (2005b) 'Employment and Human Resource Management Developments in Japan', *The Journal of Comparative Asian Development*, 4(1): 55–76.

Cabinet Office (2006) *Syōshika sykai taisaku nikansuru Senshinteki Jirei Kenkyū* [A Research on Pioneering Cases which Take Measures for Decreasing Number of Children]. Online at: http://www8.cao.go.jp/shoushi/cyousa/cyousa17/sensin/index.html.

Dore, R. (1997) 'The Distinctiveness of Japan'. In Crouch, C. and Streeck, W. (eds) *Political Economy of Modern Capitalism*. London: Sage, pp. 19–32.

Haken Rodo (2005) 'Haken Rodo Hokoku' [Enquiry on Temporary Staff]. Tokyo: Haken Rodo.

Hayagami, K. (2005) 'Tensyoku to Chingin Henka' [Changing Jobs and Changing Wage]. JILPT Discussion Paper No. 05-004.

Hisamoto, N. (2005) 'Kigyou Soshiki Heno Taiou' [Response to Reorganization of Company Organization]. In Nakamura, K. and Kenkyuusyo, R.S.K. (eds) *Suitai ka Saisei ka* [Declination or Rebirth]. Tokyo: Keisou Syobo, pp. 85–102.

Honda, K. (2004) 'Pāto Taimā no Jinzai Manejimento' [Human Resource Management of Part Timers]. In JILPT 'Kigyou no Keiei Senryaky to Jinji Syoguh Seido ni Kansuru Kenkyu no Ronnten Seiri' [Issues of Researches on Management Strategy and Personnel Treatment]. *Report of Labour Policy Research*, No. 7, pp. 69–90.

ILO (International Labour Organization) (2004) *Yearbook of Labour Statistics*. Geneva: International Labour Organization.

Imada, S. (2003) 'Tomobataraki to Ikuji no Chōwa wo Motomete' [Seeking the Consonance between Dual Income and Child Care]. *Business Labour Trend*, 346: 2–5.

Imada, S. and Hirata, S. (1996) *Howaitokarā no Syōshin Kōzō* [The Structure of Promotion of White-collar Workers]. Tokyo: Japanese Labour Institute.

Ito, H. (1994) 'Japanese Human Resource Management from the Viewpoint of Incentive Theory'. In Aoki, M. and Dore, R. (eds) *The Japanese Firm*. Oxford: Oxford University Press, pp. 233–64.

(JILPT) (The Japanese Institute for Labour Policy and Training) (2002) 'Kigyou Soshiki Saihen ni Tomonau Roudou Mondai no Jittai Cyosa' [Field survey on Labour issues caused by Corporate Reorganization]. Online at: http://www.jil.go.jp/jil/happyyou/020719/saihen.PDF

JILPT (2005a) 'Henbou Suru Jinzai Manejimento to Gabanansu/Keieisennryaku' [Changing Human Resource Management and Governance /Management Strategy], *Report of Labour Policy Research*, No. 33.

JILPT (2005b) 'Seika Syugi to Hataraku Koto no Manzoku Do' [Pay for Performance System and the Degree of Satisfaction of Work], *Report of Labour Policy Research*, No. 40.

JILPT (2005c) *Japanese Working Life Profile 2005/2006*. Tokyo: Japan Institute for Labour Policy and Training.

JIWE (Japan Institute of Workers' Evolution) (2000) 'Sōgō Syoku Josei no Syūgyō Jittai Cyōsa'. [Survey on Employment of Women Workers in 'Career Track']. Online at: http://www.jiwe.or.jp/gyomu/21/shinbun2.html

JIWE (2002) 'Pojitibu Akushon ni kansuru Ankeito Chōsa' [Questionnaire Survey on Affirmative Action]. Online at: http://www.jiwe.or.jp

JIWE (2003) 'Kanrisyoku no Kyaria Keisei ni Tuiteno Anketo Kekka Gaiyo' [Summary of Result of Questionnaire on Career Development of Managers]. Online at: http://www.jiwe.or.jp/jyoho/chosa/car_anq.html

JIWE (2004) 'Shokuba Niokeru Harasumento Nikansuru Anketo Kekka Nikansuru Houkokusyo' [A Report on Result of Questionnaires on Harassment at Workplaces]. Online at: http://www.jiwe.or.jp/jyoho/chosa/h1609sexhara.html

JIWE (2005a) 'Jyosei Kanri Syoku no Ikusei to Touyou ni Kansuru Anketo Kekka Hokukokusyo' [Report on Result of Questionnaire on Developing and Appointing Female Managers]. Online at: http://www.jiwe.or.jp/jyoho/chosa/h1706kanrisyoku.html

JIWE (2005b) 'Josei Roudou Sya no Syoguu Nado ni Kannsuru Cyousa Kekka Houkoku Syo' [Report on Result of Survey of Treatments of Female Workers]. Online at: http://www.jiwe.or.jp/jyoho/chosa/h1706syogu.html

Kimoto, K. (2003) *Josei Rōdō to Manejimento* [Women's Labour and Management]. Tokyo: Keisou Syobou.

Kudou, T. (2004) ''Gaiyou' [Summary]'. In JILPT 'Kigyou no Keiei Senryaky to Jinji Syoguh Seido ni Kansuru Kenkyu no Ronnten Seiri' [Issues of Research in Management Strategy and Personnel Treatment], *Report of Labour Policy Research*, No. 7: 1–10.

Kumazawa, M. (1997) *Nouryoku Shugi to Kigyō Shakai* [Meritocracy and Corporate Society]. Tokyo: Iwanami.

Lam, A. (1992) *Women and Japanese Management*. London: Routledge.

Lincoln, J. and Nakata, Y. (1997) 'The Transformation of the Japanese Employment System: Nature, Depth, and Origins', *Work and Occupations*, 24(1): 33–55.

Litvin, D. (1997) 'The Discourse of Diversity: From Biology to Management', *Organization*, 4(2): 187–209.

McLeod, P.L., Lobel, S.A. and Cox, T.H. (1996) 'Ethnic Diversity and Creativity in Small Groups', *Small Group Research*, 27: 248–64.

MHLW (Ministry of Health, Labour and Welfare) (2000) 'Josei Koyō Kanri Kihon Chōsa' [Basic Statistical Survey on Employment and Management of Women Workers]. Online at http://www.mhlw.go.jp

MHLW (2001) 'Roudou Kumiai Jittai Cyosa' [Survey on Labour Union Activities]. Online at: http://wwwdbtk.mhlw.go.jp/toukei/kouhyo/data-roul1/data12/08.xls

MHLW (2002) 'Danjo Chingin Kakusa Mondai ni kansuru Kenkyū Hōkoku' [Reports on Gender Wage Difference]. Online at: http://www.mhlw.go.jp/shingi/2002

MHLW (2004a) 'Heisei 16 Nenkan Hataraku Josei no Jijo' [2004 Actual State of Working Women]. Online at: http://www.mhlw.go.jp/houdou/2005/03/h0328-7a.html#zu1-23

MHLW (2004b) *Result of 2003 Basic Statistical Survey on Employment and Management of Women Workers*. Online at: http://www.mhlw.go.jp/houdou/2004/07/h0723-2a.html

MHLW (2005) *Situation of Practices of and Guidance to Dual Track System*. Online at: http://www.hlw.go.jp/houdou/2005/08/h0808-1.html

MIAC (Ministry of Internal Affairs and Communications) (2002) *Summary Result of 2002 Basic Survey on Employment Structure*. Online at: http://www.stat.go.jp/data/shugyou/2002/kakuhou/youyaku.html

MIAC (2006) *Labour Force Survey*. Online at: http://www.stat.go.jp/data/roudou/sokuhou/nen/ft/zuhyou/054bh01.xls

Miyamoto, M. (1998) 'Nihon Gata koYou Sisutemu ni Towareteiru Mono' [What is Questioned in the Japanese Style of Employment System]. In Tominaga, K. and Miyamoto, M. (eds)

Mobirithii Shakai heno Tenbō [A Prospect for the Society Where People Move]. Tokyo: Keio University Press, pp. 28–52.

Morisawa, T. and Kihara, Y. (2005) 'Diversity Management as a Management Strategy', *Chiteki Shisan Souzou* [Creating Knowledge Resource], 9: 70–83.

Naikakufu [Cabinet Office] (2004) *Heisei 16 Nenkan Shoshika Shakai Hakusho* [2004 White Paper on Declining Birth Rate]. Tokyo: Cabinet Office.

Nakano, M. (2001) 'Kaisei Rōdōsya Hakenhou to Haken Rōdō no Genzai' [Changes in Temporary Work under the Reformed Temporary Worker Law], *The Bulletin of the Society for Study of Working Women*, 40: 17–26.

Ng, E.S.W. and Burke, R.J. (2005) 'Person–organization Fit and the War for Talent: Does Diversity Management Make a Difference?', *International Journal of Human Resource Management*, 16(7): 1195–210.

Nikkei, The (2005) 'Shanai Kyaria Kouchiku Unagasu' [Encouraging Career Construction Within a Company], 21 November, p. 15.

Nikkei, The (2006) 'Thenkin Nashi ni Atui Shisen' [Female Job Seekers Give 'No Relocation' the Eye], 27 March, p. 32.

Nohata, M. (1997) 'Josei no Gawa Kara Mita Syokugyo Syakai' [Seeing Business World from Eyes of Women]. In Inuzuka, S (ed.) *Atarashii sangyo shakai gaku* [New Industrial Sociology]. Tokyo: Yuhikaku, pp. 103–29.

Oosawa, M. (2003) 'Nihon Hukushi Kokka to Jenda' [Japanese Welfare State and Gender], *Gendaishisou*, 31(1): 80–5.

Rengo [Japanese Trade Union Confederation] (2001) *Vision for the 21st Century*. Tokyo: Japanese Trade Union Confederation.

Sato, A. (2006) 'Nihon Kigyou no Jinji Kaikaku to Jinji no Keizai Bunseki wo Yomu' [Reading 'Transforming Incentives' and Economic Analysis of Personnel Management], *The Japanese Journal of Labour Studies*, 547: 58–67.

Sato, H. (2003) 'Pāto no Kikan Rōdō Ryokuka to Aratana Kadai' [Making Part-time Workforce as Core Worker and New Issue], *The Japanese Journal of Labour Studies*, 45(9): 2–3.

Suabeliani, D. and Tsogas, G. (2005) 'Managing Diversity in the Netherlands: A Case Study of Rabobank', *International Journal of Human Resource Management*, 16(5): 831–51.

Takahashi, Y. (1997) 'The Labour Market and Lifetime Employment in Japan', *Economic and Industrial Democracy*, 18(1): 55–66.

Tatumichi, S. (2004) 'Hataraku Koto no Manzoku do to Kojin/Kigyou no Zokusei' [The Degree of Satisfaction in Work and Attributes of Individuals and Companies]. In JILPT (2005b) 'Seika Syugi to Hataraku Koto no Manzoku Do' [Pay for Performance System and the Degree of Satisfaction in Work].

Tominaga, K. and Miyamoto, M. (1998) *Mobirithii Shakai heno Tenbō* [A Prospect for the Society where People Move]. Tokyo: Keio University Press.

Turu, T. and the General Research Center of Japanese Electrical Electronic and Information Unions. (2005) *Sentaku to Syucyu* [Selection and Concentration] Tokyo: Yuhikaku.

Uehara, K. (2003) 'Oote Ginkou Niokeru Howaitokarā no Shoushinn Kōzō' [The Promotion Structure of White-Collar Workers for Large Banks in Japan], *The Japanese Journal of Labour Studies*, 45(10): 58–72.

Uemura, Y. (2005) 'Sentaku to Syucyu to Koyou Shisutemu' [Selection and Concentration and Employment System]. In Turu, T. and General Research Center of Japanese Electrical Electronic and Information Unions (eds) *Sentaku to Syucyu* [Selection and Concentration]. Tokyo: Yuhikaku, pp. 105–62.

Wada, H. (1999) *Hatarakikata no Chie* [Wisdom for How to Work]. Tokyo: Yuuhikaku.

Weathers, C. (2005) 'Equal Opportunity for Japanese Women – What Progress?', *Japan Focus*, October: 3.

WEC (Women's Education Center) (2003) *Danjo Kyōdō Sankaku Tōkei Deita Bukku* [Statistical Data Book for Equal Opportunities]. Tokyo: Gyousei.

Wrench, J. (2002) 'Critical Analysis of Critiques of Diversity Management', paper presented at Seventh International Metropolis Conference 'Togetherness in Difference: Citizenship and

Belonging', Oslo, 9–13 September: 1–30. Online at: http://www.international.metropolis.net/events/7th_conf_norway/papers/91_Metrop2002-wrench.doc

Yasumoto, M. (1998) 'Tensyoku to Kigyou-Roudousya Kankei' [Career changes and the relation between companies and workers]. In Tominaga, K. and Miyamoto, M. (eds) *Mobilithii Shakai heno Tenbo* [A Prospect for the Society Where People Move]. Tokyo: Keio University Press, pp. 140–70.

Yuasa, M. (2005) 'Japanese Women in Management: Getting Closer to 'Realities' in Japan', *Asia Pacific Business Review*, 11(2): 195–211.

The impact of culture on HRM styles and firm performance: evidence from Japanese parents, Japanese subsidiaries/joint ventures and South Asian local companies

M. Khasro Miah and Allan Bird

The choice of what HRM practices to implement in their subsidiaries in emerging economies is an issue of central concern to multinational corporations (MNCs). On the one hand, a company may want to capitalize on labour costs and locational advantages that these economies may offer. On the other hand, the nature of emerging economies with relatively poorly defined managerial systems and little experience of elaborate, sophisticated human resource management (HRM) practices create a potential obstacle to success in such economies.

With the arrival of the age of globalization and the spread of MNCs, interest in the selection of human resource management systems has grown as managers and scholars alike have sought to identify what HRM styles and practices in overseas subsidiaries of MNCs will be most effective. This is of particular concern for MNCs operating in South Asia where traditional, autocratic practices are often viewed as working against productive subsidiary operations (Habibullah, 1974; Miah, 2000; Miah *et al.*, 2001).

The HRM practices of a given foreign subsidiary are developed in response to influences from its parent company and from its host country environment, suggesting that there is the potential for a cultural gap to exist. Some MNC subsidiaries and joint ventures prefer to transfer their HRM system to all of their subsidiaries; others prefer to trust the locals with the development of their own HRM system, one they believe best suits the local environment and cultural situation (Bird *et al.*, 1999). Recently, it has become evident that MNCs can adopt hybrid approaches as a means of accommodating these competing influences (Bird *et al.*, 1999).

The contrast between the sophisticated, highly elaborated HRM systems of MNCs and the traditional, often simple, but evolving systems found in the domestic companies of emerging economies is perhaps best characterized as a contrast between participative and autocratic approaches to HRM (Miah *et al.*, 2003). Thus, the central research questions we address are: (1) what types of HRM systems do firms in South Asia employ and (2) does a participative HRM system lead to high performance in South Asia?

A controlling assumption underpinning this study is that, given the substantial empirical support (cf. Likert, and Likert, 1976), a participative style is, *ceteris parabis*, more likely to be effective than an autocratic style. Nevertheless, there may be certain conditions under which participative approaches are less effective. The suitability of any HRM system depends on variables such as institutions within the host country, the age of company, the size of company, and the overall economic development of the country, among other contingency variables (Budhwar and Spraw, 2001). Our intent is not to suggest a universal recipe for all companies in South Asia. Rather, by comparing HRM styles, we hope to better understand how firms in South Asia can use their HRM systems to improve firm performance.

Based on the above background information, the present research on companies operating in South Asia (regardless of origin) provides us with a unique opportunity to elaborate extant theory in the HRM field by examining firm behaviours in the context of emerging economies, specifically in the management of firms in South Asia. The overarching objective of this study is to explore and assess national cultural influences on the choice of participative HRM style and firm performance.

Literature review and hypotheses

In this section, we review the research literature on HRM systems and firm performance, with a particular focus on the effectiveness of participative systems. With this as a foundation, we propose seven hypotheses relating to the use and efficacy of different types of HRM systems in South Asia and their relationship to performance.

HRM styles and firm performance

HRM styles and their effects on company performance have been investigated extensively in several ways, including experimental laboratory, case methods, and a quantitative survey approach. According to House and Baetz (1990), Lock and Schweiger (1990), and Strauss (1990) nearly 200 of these studies have been carried out to date. However, research on the effectiveness of participative styles in emerging economies has not been well studied (Miah, 2000; Miah and Kitamura, 2005).

Participative management style refers to the attitude of a superior who, except in unusual circumstances, makes decisions by consensus and then issues organizational goals only after all members involved are consulted, and their opinion thoroughly considered. When this style is applied, employees enjoy good communication flows, a freedom of voice, and so forth (Arthur, 1994; Levine and Tyson, 1990; Miah *et al.*, 2001). In addition, employees take an active role in their own performance appraisal and have positive regard for their colleagues and subordinates. As a consequence of applying these participatory mechanisms, organizations will enjoy high organizational and operational performance (Arthur, 1994; Cutcher-Gershenfeld, 1991; Delaney and Huselid, 1996).

In contrast, under an autocratic HRM style, employees have few ways of voicing their concerns or contributing other than through highly proscribed behaviours. The employee role is reduced to the mere execution of superiors' orders. Additionally, employees are looked upon with suspicion and are generally distrusted; and lower than expected performance is treated in a punitive manner (Likert, 1961, 1967; Statt, 1991).

Previous research (Huselid and Becker, 1994; Levine and Tyson, 1990; MacDuffie, 1995; Pfeffer, 1994) in North America and elsewhere (Boliko, 1997; Kanungo, and Jaeger, 1990; Miah *et al.*, 2001, 2003) has found that a participative style is associated with higher levels of firm performance than an autocratic style. It is noteworthy that prior research examined this relationship in the context of developed economies, leaving open the question as to whether or not a participative style is also relatively more effective in emerging economies. Given this, we are led to the following hypothesis:

Hypothesis 1: Companies with high participative human resource management style will experience better firm performance in South Asia.

HRM practices and their effects on HRM style

A number of leading Western researchers argue (e.g. Beer *et al.*, 1984; Brewster and Bournois, 1991; Guest, 1989a) that whatever models or perspectives on HRM are used, recruitment and selection policies and practices can be perceived as integral. Recruitment and selection practices not only seek to attract, obtain and retain human resources the organization requires to meet its strategic goals, but also they may have a significant impact upon the composition of the workforce, the ultimate fit with the organization's needs and culture, and upon long-range employment stability (Beer *et al.*, 1984). In two relevant and recent comparative studies, the research findings of Easterby-Smith *et al.* (1995) and Lawler *et al.* (1995) provided support for the culturally relativist (divergence) view of HRM with recruitment and selection practices being found to be culturally sensitive and to vary across national borders.

Regarding the effects of training experiences, a previous study indicated that managers engaging in more self-study and training programmes give more support to the participative management style and high performance relative to other colleagues (Miah *et al.*, 2001). On the other hand, high rates of unemployment place employers in a position of power, deteriorate the influence of trade unions and lower the importance employers attach to training their employees. It may be easier, in fact, to hire a better worker from outside the company than to spend extra money to train a current worker or spend extra time in collective bargaining. Spending on training is perceived much more as a current burden rather than as an investment in the quality of people for future gain. Given such logic (Pieper, 1990: 5) excludes third world countries from his international comparisons of HRM systems, because developing countries face very specific problems that cannot be compared to those of industrialized nations. The main problem of developing countries is *not* gaining a competitive edge in international management competition through the sophisticated application of HRM concepts.

In addition, a sizeable literature exists on the determinants of employee turnover, long considered an important outcome for both individuals and organizations. Most of such research has focused on individual-level variables, such as employees' satisfaction with their jobs and their organizational commitment (e.g. Cotton and Tuttle, 1986).

Prior findings have also found support for proposition that organization-level of human resource characteristics are also significantly related to employee turnover in organizations. The expectation is that employee turnover in organizations with autocratic systems will be higher than in those with participative systems. Under autocratic HRM systems organizations with minimum amounts of training and experience can perform such tasks while reducing wages and costs associated with hiring, selecting and training. The above discussion leads to the following hypotheses:

Hypothesis 2: Higher levels of participative HRM style will be associated with higher levels of merit-based hiring.

Hypothesis 3: Higher levels of participative HRM style will be associated with higher levels of training and development.

Hypothesis 4: Higher levels of participative HRM style will be associated with lower levels of employee turnover.

HRM style and firm performance based on national and corporate culture

Ownership plays an important role in the development of a company's HRM style and practices. There are differences in HRM style and practice approach for different forms of ownership. A number of previous research findings shows that there are significant differences between HRM practices in local and foreign companies operating in developing countries. Foreign subsidiaries and joint ventures tend to utilize the advanced (participative) HRM style of the parent companies and introduced more modernization in their management system (Shetty and Prasad, 1971). Shetty and Prasad (1971) found that foreign subsidiaries operating in developing countries utilized more modern management philosophies and practices, employed more participative structures and operated better employee development systems than comparable local firms. Furthermore, the extent of management participation was greater in foreign companies.

In general, learning the techniques of a participative HRM system is very important for the attainment of an industrial efficiency; however, most South Asian managers are traditionalists and prefer their current ways (e.g. Jaeger and Kanungo, 1990; Miah, 2000; Razzaque, 1991). They tend to resist changes and develop culture-based, traditional superior/subordinate relationships based on local customs. South Asian managers do not believe in the development of human resources. Moreover, they believe that plant and equipment, i.e. the machinery of the factory, are more important than the humans in the factory. Thus, the following hypotheses can be constructed:

Hypothesis 5: Japanese companies will demonstrate higher levels of participative HRM style and higher levels of firm performance.

Hypothesis 6: Japanese subsidiaries/joint ventures will demonstrate moderate levels of participative HRM style and moderate levels of firm performance.

Hypothesis 7: South Asian domestic companies will demonstrate the least participative HRM style and the least level of firm performance.

Research methodology

Sample

The sample was drawn from three sources: 150 Japanese companies in Japan (JCs), 150 Japanese subsidiaries/joint ventures in South Asia (JVCs) (i.e. India = 60, Pakistan = 50 and Bangladesh = 40) and 150 South Asian local companies (i.e. India = 60, Pakistan = 50 and Bangladesh = 40 companies). Questionnaires were mailed to the human resource managers of each company with a cover letter soliciting co-operation, and requesting that questionnaires be randomly distributed to managers including those in five functional areas (general administration, personnel, production, factory and quality control). Data were collected during the period of July to September 2004 from JVCs and SACOs and during August to November, 2004 from JCs in Japan. In total, 512 out of 2,200 questionnaires were returned for an overall response rate of 23.3 per cent. This return rate is higher than is common for international survey research (Paxson *et al.*, 1995). Due to missing items or other deficiencies, 15 responses were dropped, leaving 497 responses available for analysis: JCs = 139, JVCs = 176 and SACOs = 182. The response rate for usable data from the JCs, JVCs and SACOs respectively were 18.5 per cent, 23.5 per cent and 24.3 per cent respectively.

Dependent variables

HRM style   Tagiuri and Litwin (1968) defined the organizational environment as 'a relatively enduring quality of the internal environment of an organization that is: (a) experienced by its employees, (b) influences their behaviors and (c) can be described in terms of the values of a particular set of characteristics (or attitudes) of the organizations' (1968: 27). Accordingly, we employed Likert's Profile of Organizational Climate (POC) measure (Likert and Likert, 1976) to measure each firm's managerial system on an autocratic-participatory continuum in which a high score indicates a participative HRM system and low score indicates an autocratic HRM system.

Firm performance   Firm performance in Japan and South Asia was measured using an 8-point scale in which: 1 = Loss; 2 = breakeven; 3 = 1–5 per cent growth; 4 = 6–10 per cent growth; 5 = 11–15 per cent growth; 6 = 16–20 per cent growth; 7 = 21–25 per cent growth; and 8 = more than 25 per cent growth.

Independent variables

HRM practices   We measured the major HRM functional areas of hiring and recruiting, training and development, and employee turnover. Specific items used in the questionnaire can be found in Appendices 1 and 2. HR practices were measured by obtaining responses to items assessing the extent of use of specific HRM practices using a 5-point Likert scale ranging from: 1 = 'not at all', 2 = 'to a small extent', 3 = 'to a moderate extent', 4 = 'to a considerable extent' and 5 = 'to a great extent'. Scales were confirmed using Principal Components factor analysis, as reported in Appendices 1 and 2.

The merit-based hiring and recruiting scale included three items, with a .70 alpha coefficient. The training and development scale included seven items with an alpha co-efficient of .85. Employee turnover was measured using an 8-point scale to assess percentage of employees who left the company voluntarily. The scale was: 1 = none; 2 = less than 5 per cent; 3 = 5–9 per cent; 4 = 10–14 per cent; 5 = 15–19 per cent; 6 = 20–24 per cent; 7 = 25–29 per cent; and 8 = more than 30 per cent.

Control variables

To capture the national cultural effects as reflected in the location or ownership of the company, we measured type of company by using three dummy variables: assigning '1' to Japanese companies operating in Japan, and others '0'; '1' to Japanese subsidiaries/joint ventures operating in South Asia and others '0'; '1' to South Asian local companies operating in South Asia and others '0'. Next, following the convention for capturing the size of company and scale effects on HRM styles and firm performance, we used the log of the number of employees as a measure of company size (Log COSIZE). In the same manner, we used the natural log of company age in years (Log COAGE) assess organizational longevity and maturation effects (e.g. Delaney and Huselid, 1996). The country GDP (Log GDP) variable was used to measure the country business climate of the respective companies in Japan and South Asia.

Results

Tables 1 and 2 provide descriptive statistics and correlation coefficients of all variables used for the present analysis (n = 497). Hypothesis 1, that a participative HRM style will have significant positive influences on firm performance was supported. The participative HRM style was positively correlated with the firm performance for all managers (r = .63, p < . 001). Additionally, this relationship was found to hold for each type of company: Japanese companies (r = .47, p < . 001), Japanese subsidiaries and joint ventures (r = .66, p <. 001), and South Asian domestic companies (r = .42, p < .001).

Tables 1 and 2 also provide evidence of regarding for the next three hypotheses for the sample of all managers. The positive relationship (r = .15, p < .01) between merit-based recruiting and participative HRM supports H2. Similarly, the positive relationship between participative HRM and training and development (r = .25, p < .001), H3, is also sustained. Finally, H4, positing a negative relationship between participative HRM and turnover was also significant and in the anticipated direction for the full sample (r = .13, p < .01).

In order to examine the data in a more comprehensive manner, we conducted multiple regressions of the relevant variables. These are shown in Table 3. There are several

Table 1 *Correlation coefficients for all variables for full sample (lower triangle, N = 497) and SACO managers (upper triangle N = 182)*

Variables	1	2	3	4	5	6	7	8
1. Participative HRM style (PHRMS)	–	.06	.42***	.09	.09	– .01	– .02	.82***
2. Employee turnover (TURNOVR)	– .13**	–	– .03	– .10	.09	– .07	.01	– .07
3. Firm performance (FMNCE)	.63***	– .15***	–	.01	.24**	– .04	.09	– .13
4. Merit-based hiring (MBHING)	.15**	– .04	.13**	–	– .01	.10	.08	.10
5. Training and development (TDENT)	.25***	– .13**	.37***	.06	–	.29**	– .03	.01
6. Log GDP (1990–2002)	– .50***	.36***	– .55***	– .26**	– .31**	–	– .03	– .07
7. Log COAGE	– .08	.12**	.01	.03	– .07	.24**	–	.01
8. Log COSIZE	.77***	– .07	.04	.09*	.06	– .24**	– .11*	–

Note: *p < .05, **p < .01, ***p < .001 (two-tailed).

Table 2 *Correlation coefficients among all variables JC managers (lower triangle, N = 139) and JVC managers (upper triangle, N = 176)*

Variables	1	2	3	4	5	6	7	8
1 Participative HRM style (PHRMS)	–	.02	.66**	−.08	.21**	–	.02	.76***
2 Employee turnover (TURNOVR)	−.05	–	−.05	−.01	−.02	–	.04	−.02
3 Firm performance (FMNCE)	.47***	−.01	–	−.07	.41***	–	.01	.06
4 Merit-based hiring (MBHING)	.16	−.01	.22**	–	−.08	–	.08	−.04
5 Training and development (TDENT)	.16	.01	.18*	.13	.02	–	.09	−.01
6 Log GDP (1990–2002)	–	–	–	–	–	–	.02	.01
7 Company age (COAGE)	−.12	−.06	.10	−.06	−.17	–	–	.02
8 Company size (COSIZE)	.80***	.11	−.13	.02	.04	–	−.21**	–

Note: *p < .05, **p < .01, ***p < .001 (two-tailed).

interesting findings. First, the results show that only company size variables affect participative HRM style and firm performance consistently across all three managerial groups. But Country GDP and Company Age do not show any significant effect with regard to participative HRM style and firm performance results thereby suggesting that the effects of control variables on participative HRM style and firm performance are moderated by national and corporate cultural differences among the organizations where managers work.

Second, Table 3 demonstrates that, as predicted in Hypothesis 1, participative HRM style consistently affects firm performance positively across each of the managerial groups: $\beta = .47 (p < .001)$, $\beta = .66 (p < .001)$, and $\beta = .42 (p < .001)$ for JC, JVC and SACO managers respectively. These findings clearly indicate that the participative HRM style is positively associated with effective firm performance in all sample organizations. In addition, the incremental increase in R-square when adding firm performance was significant, $\Delta R^2 (2-3) = .18 (p < .001)$, $\Delta R^2 (2-3) = .32 (p < .001)$, $\Delta R^2 (3-2) = .13$ $(p < .001)$, for PHRMS. This indicates that the use of firm performance had an independent and significant effect upon participative HRM style, beyond the effect of performance variables combined in the regression. This result provides support for Hypothesis 1, which predicted a direct positive effect for firm performance on participative HRM style. In addition, the overall contribution of performance combined reached $R_3^2 = .40 (p < .001)$ and $\Delta R^2 (3-2) = .36 (p < .001)$ for PHRMS (see Table 3). Moreover, this result suggests that the effect of performance variables on a participative HRM style would be significant when it is evaluated in the context of cross-national comparisons.

Table 3 *Hierarchical regression results on participative HRM style and firm performance*

	JC n = 139						JVC n = 176						SACO n = 182						Overall n = 497					
	PHRMS			FMNCE			PHRMS			FMNCE			PHRMS			FMNCE			PHRMS			FMNCE		
	β	(SE)	t	β	(SE)	t	β	(SE)	t	β	(SE)	t	β	(SE)	t	β	(SE)	t	β	(SE)	t	β	(SE)	t
Step 1 Control variables																								
SACO																			−.34	(.19)	***	−.53	(.08)	**
Saco = 1, others = 0																								
Log GDP		−			−			−			−		−.01	(.01)		−.04	(.01)		−.02	(.01)		−.08	(.01)	
Log COAGE	.06	(.20)		.07	(.08)		.01	(.21)		.01	(.11)		.04	(.16)		.08	(.07)		.03	(.13)		.05	(.06)	
Log COSIZE	.81	(.23)	***	−.11	(.09)		.76	(.25)	***	−.07	(.16)		.82	(.14)	***	−.12	(.06)		.72	(.12)	***	−.10	(.05)	*
R^2_1	.64			.02			.58			.01			.67			.02			.74			.31		
ΔR^2_1	.64		***	.01			.57		***	−.01			.67		***	.01			.75		***	.30		***
Step 2 HRM practices																								
TURNOVR	−.05	(.25)		−.03	(.06)		−.02	(.10)		−.04	(.05)		−.06	(.10)		−.02	(.04)		−.10	(.05)		−.10	(.03)	*
MBHING	.14	(.39)	*	.20	(.09)	*	.09	(.39)	†	−.11	(.10)		.10	(.21)	†	.01	(.06)		.12	(.18)	*	.09	(.05)	*
TDENT	.14	(.41)	*	.15	(.06)	*	.22	(.18)	**	.42	(.06)	***	.09	(.18)	†	.24	(.05)	**	.22	(.12)	***	.35	(.04)	***
R^2_2	.05			.07			.14			.18			.06			.06			.06			.15		
ΔR^2_2	.03		*	.05		*	.12		***	.16		***	.04		*	.05			.04		*	.15		***
$\Delta R^2_2 - \Delta R^2_1$	.61		***				.45		***				.63		***				.49		***			
Step 3																								
Firm performance	.47	(.31)	***				.66	(.18)	***				.42	(.24)	***				.63	(.12)	***			
R^2_3	.22						.44						.17						.40					
ΔR^2_3	.21		***				.44		***				.17		***				.40		***			
$\Delta R^2_3 - \Delta R^2_2$	.18		***				.32		***				.13		***				.36		***			

Notes: 1 ΔR^2_1, ΔR^2_2, and ΔR^2_3 denote the adjusted R^2 generated by the first, second and third step regression respectively.

2 * p < .05, ** < .01, ***p < .001 and † < .10 standardized coefficients (β) are presented.

3 SACO (South Asian domestic companies = 1 and others = 0)

4 JC = Japanese companies, JVC = Japanese subsidiaries and joint ventures, SACO = South Asian domestic companies, Log GDP (1990–2002), Log COAGE = Company age, Log COSIZE = Company size, TURNOVR = Employee turnover, MBHING = Married-based hiring, TDENT = Training and development, PHRMS = Participative HRM style, and FMNCE = Firm performance.

Further consideration of Table 3 indicates that Japanese subsidiaries and joint ventures (JC) have the most participative HRM style among the three-managerial groups. By comparison, JVC have a moderate level and South Asian companies (SACO) showed the least participative HRM style, as predicted earlier in Hypotheses 5, 6 and 7 respectively. These findings are consistent with previous empirical work by Haire *et al.* (1966), which found Japanese companies to be more participative than their Western counterparts. In addition, Cole (1989) found that Japanese cultural norms favour participation and reliance on group decision-making, activities associated with participative HRM. In a similar vein, Kriger and Solomon (1992) found that Japanese companies tend to choose a decentralized decision-making style that reflects a much greater degree both of autonomy and delegation of authority, which are also characteristics associated with participative HRM.

Second, to properly investigate HRM practices and its effect on participative HRM style among the three managerial groups in Japan and South Asia, the present study used three HRM practices. Among the HRM practices, Table 3 shows that merit-based hiring (MBHING) ($\beta = .14$, ($p < . 05$); $\beta = .09$, ($p < . 10$) and $\beta = . 10$, ($p < . 10$) and training and development (TDENT) $\beta = .14$, ($p < . 05$) $\beta = .22$, ($p < . 01$) and $\beta = .09$, ($p < . 10$) consistently influenced the participative HRM style positively across the three managerial groups. Also as anticipated, employee turnover (TURNOVR) consistently affected the participative HRM style negatively across the three managerial groups: $\beta = - .05$, (n.s.), $\beta = - . 02$, (n.s.) and $\beta = - .06$, (n.s.) for (PHRMS) in partial support of JC, JVC and SACO managers respectively. Taken as a whole, it seems reasonable to suggest that a participative HRM style leads to lower levels of employee turnover, which may in turn lead to higher firm performance.

The above findings produced partial support for Hypotheses 2 and 3 that there exists a positive effect of HRM practices upon participative HRM style. Employee turnover (TURNOVER) also showed a negative effect as predicted by Hypothesis 4, although the impact of turnover on HRM practice was not significant at the ($p < . 05$) level across three managerial groups. This result suggests that the effect of certain HRM practices (merit-based hiring, and training and development) upon participative HRM style was significant and positive. On the other hand, employee turnover negatively affected participative HRM style. In addition, the overall contribution of HRM practices when combined reached $R_2^2 = .04$ ($p < . 05$) for PHRMS. This result suggests that the combined effect of HRM practices on participative HRM style could be very significant when it is evaluated in the context of cross-cultural comparisons.

The regression results revealed that significant negative correlation between turnover and participative HRM style and firm performance across three sample firms may mean that when these firms followed higher levels of participative HRM, employee's turnover decreases significantly. The finding that the amount of turnover varies with HRM system has important implications for practitioners seeking to manage this process (Arthur, 1994). Additionally, our findings are also consistent with previous research results showing that organizational culture influences employee turnover (e.g. McEvoy and Cascio, 1985; Sheridan, 1992).

Finally, Table 3 reveals that the country dummy was associated with a significant negative effect, indicating that South Asian managers are the least supportive for each of the hypotheses. On the other hand, this finding clearly indicates that SACOs ($\beta = - .34$, ($p < . 001$) significantly and negatively affect participative HRM style, which in turn leads to poorer performance.

Hypotheses 5, 6 and 7 argue for differences in the mean values of participative HRM style (PHRMS), and firm performance (FMNCE) among JCs, JVCs and SACOs. In order

Table 4 *ANOVA results on HRM style and firm performance*

Variables		JC	JVC	SACO	f	JC-JVC	JC-SACO	JVC-SACO
		N = 139	N = 176	N = 182				
	M	8.57	7.44	5.45				
Participative HRM style					51.39c	b	c	c
	SD	2.47	3.31	2.51				
	M	4.10	5.57	6.09				
Employee turnover					27.31c	c	c	c
	SD	2.81	2.58	1.93				
	M	3.85	3.66	2.93				
Firm performance					57.96c	n.s	c	c
	SD	.59	1.04	.70				
	M	4.65	4.61	4.19				
Merit-based hiring					22.36c	n.s	c	c
	SD	.54	.63	.86				
	M	3.98	3.24	3.17				
Training & development					25.71c	c	c	c
	SD	.77	1.36	1.02				

Note: a < .05, b < .01, and c < .001.

to test Hypotheses 5, 6 and 7, we conducted ANOVA tests comparing HRM style, HRM practices, and firm performance variables three managerial groups. The results of the ANOVA test are presented in Table 4 and Figure 1. Table 4 shows that mean values for the participative HRM style and firm performance are highest among JC managers, followed by JVC and SACO managers (F = 51.39, p <. 001) and (F = 57.96, p <.001) respectively. Results of the group difference tests taken pair-wise by the Bonferroni method were all significant, indicating that there exist systematic group differences among JC, JVC and SACO managers concerning their perceptions of the participative HRM style. In the case of merit-based hiring (MBHING) and

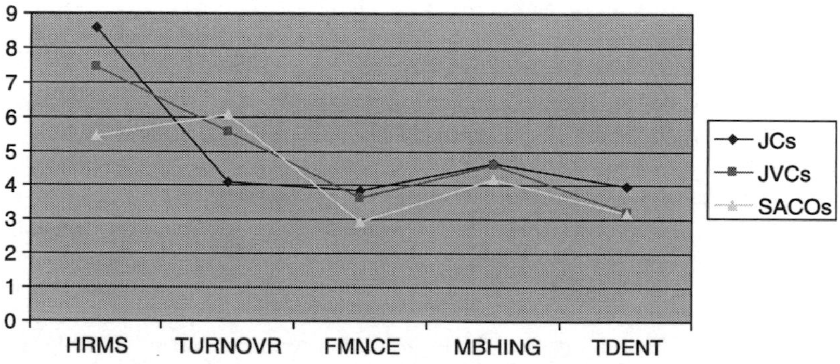

Figure 1 *ANOVA figure on JCs, JVCs and SACOs*

training and development (TDENT), JC managers are highest compared to JVC and SACO managers (F $=$ 22.36, p $<$. 001) and (F $=$ 25.71, p $<$.001) respectively. On the other hand, employee turnover is highest among SACO managers followed by JC and JVC managers (F $=$ 27.31, p $<$. 001).

The ANOVA results in Table 4 and Figure 1 demonstrate that means for participative HRM style and HRM practices for JVC managers occupy the in-between levels, lending support to the possibility that the nature of JVC corporate culture can be explained in terms of the 'third culture' or 'hybrid' HRM concepts (Graen and Wakabayashi, 1994; Wakabayashi and Graen, 1991). In other words, we can say that JVC in South Asia appear to have created adaptive hybrid organizational cultures, which successfully integrated national and multinational corporate cultural attributes into a unique (third) management system. JVC managers in South Asia may have created a mixed HRM style by integrating traditional South Asian culture with participative corporate culture from Japan. Figure 3 graphically presents the results of the ANOVA test where JC and SACO managers find each other in quite opposite positions, while JVC managers occupy just in the middle between the two. This finding is consistent with Hypotheses 5, 6 and 7.

Discussion

The findings derived from this study show support for previous research results (Peters and Waterman, 1982; Pfeffer, 1994) with regard to the significance of human resources as a key variable in achieving effective firm performance. The present research results add to the growing empirical evidence, suggesting that such assertions are credible (cf. Arthur, 1994; Huselid, 1995; Huselid and Becker, 1994; Ichniowaki *et al.*, 1994; MacDuffie, 1995). Overall, and in support of Hypothesis 1, the present study confirms the efficacy of participative HRM styles in contributing to firm performance in developing countries, specifically South Asian countries.

One prospective explanation for these results is that JC management may have more confidence in the participative HRM style compared to JVC and SACO company managers. Extant research findings provide support for this view. Namely, Pascal and Athos (1981) concluded that Japan was the second highest following America with regard to a participative HRM style and supporting the higher capacities of average individuals. In Japanese subsidiaries and joint ventures in South Asia (JVC), there may exist a mixed configuration of effects of both national (South Asian) and multinational (Japanese) corporate cultures, functioning under a third cultural framework for managers (Graen *et al.*, 2000).

Some cross-cultural research on HRM (Bird *et al.*, 1999; Takeuchi, 2001, 2003; Taylor *et al.*, 1996) offer explanations the adjustment processes of HRM practices in Japanese MNCs' subsidiaries, and identified some determining factors that may affect the local adjustment of the parent company's HRM style and practices. One key reliable finding in the literature is that HRM practices shared by managers in JVCs may strongly affect parent firm HRM practices (closed hybrid). On the other hand, SACO strongly affects the style of HRM in the local setting. Our findings demonstrate that in subsidiaries and joint ventures in South Asia, HRM practices are shared among company managers and that the parent company's HRM practices are context generalizable and applicable, i.e. the original HRM template transferred from a Japanese parent firm can be sustained and reinforced in the host country context (Bird *et al.*, 1999; Takeuchi, 2003). However, if a subsidiary's managers believe that the parent company's HRM style and practices are context specific and not applicable then the HRM template is subject to some or significant modifications in the local environment.

The results of the present study indicated that the South Asian company's HRM style is most autocratic in all three categorizations. Many studies (cf. Ahmed, 1974; Habibullah, 1974; Razzaque, 1991; Sohban and Ahmad, 1986) find that South Asian managers in general prefer an authoritarian style of HRM, and tend to equate authoritarianism with professional management. Subordinate participation in the managerial decision-making process is seldom seen in practice. Traditionally, managers prefer a 'closed door' policy, thus it is a common practice in South Asian firms that managers put an unnecessarily greater emphasis on rules and protocols to support the power of one's office.

It is noteworthy, however, that a participative HRM style found to be effective in this cultural milieu, a conclusion supported by variables drawn from three levels, i.e. individual, organizational and contextual. These variables were found to be positively associated with an enhanced participative HRM style: namely, a training and development programme and merit-based hiring criteria. However, employee turnover was found to be negatively associated.

It is clear from the regression analysis that JC managers revealed higher levels of participative HRM style and firm performance. This participative HRM style appears to be deeply rooted in Japan's industrial tradition that is, in itself, a part of Japanese corporate culture. However, managers may face a very autocratic HRM management style in South Asian companies. In SACOs, whatever individual behaviour managers may have, it only helps support the autocratic HRM style and firm performance of the company.

A number of current cross-cultural HRM scholars (Negangdi and Reimann, 1973; Peters and Waterman, 1982; Pfeffer, 1994; cf. Arthur, 1994; Huselid, 1995; Huselid and Becker, 1994; Ichniowaki *et al.*, 1994; MacDuffie, 1995) has reported a positive relationship between participative HRM style and firm performance. The relationship between participative HRM style and firm performance in this study was far larger than that reported in other studies. These robust relationships suggest that the particular set of circumstances found in South Asia at the present time creates different problems and opportunities from those found in other contexts, particularly in the more industrialized countries.

In South Asian companies, managers are least participative in their HRM practices, perceptions, and managers seem philosophically less oriented to employee freedom and participation. The prevailing traditional cultural pattern of behaviours in South Asia manifested a strong tendency to resist delegation and a marked proclivity toward non-participation, centralized and paternalistic management. From the examination of SACO managers' HRM practices and their management perceptions, we can conclude substantial training and experiences should be made available for South Asian managers by working and interacting with Japanese managers and HRM styles so that they can learn more about participative HRM and can best utilize existing human resources for the improvement of South Asian firms' performance.

We conclude by noting several limitations of the study. First, the present study was carried out on three different kinds of firms, namely Japanese companies in Japan, Japanese subsidiaries/joint ventures (JVCs), and South Asian companies (SACOs). The selection of companies was not random, although carefully guided by prior knowledge about the population of firms in each of the three countries. It was felt that such an approach would increase the potential generalizability of the present findings. Results from each of the three firms demonstrated that variation exists between organizations in terms of participative HRM style, practices and performance. In addition, specific variables in the path model varied greatly, suggesting further caution in applying the conclusions of the model to other kinds of organizations. This is not to suggest, however, that generalization of the model is not possible. Table 3 shows that some of background variables (later control variables) do not influence participative HRM style and performance across all three organizations, suggesting that background variables may have cultural influence on participative HRM style, HRM practices and firm performance in Japan and South Asia. For this reason, a series of cross-national comparisons was undertaken and some attractive results were identified. Nonetheless, cultural differences were only implied to explain the results obtained. More straightforward examinations of cultural differences and their effect on HRM style are clearly needed.

Second, Hofstede's (1980a) conclusion regarding the importance of cultural values when implementing United States-based management initiatives in foreign affiliates still applies: it may not be suitable in countries high in power distance. Our findings on cultural value differences not only support Hofstede but also echo his conclusions by suggesting that employees do resist management initiatives when these clash with their cultural values (Kirkman and Shapiro, 2001). Attention to, and respect for, differences in cultural values remains a high priority for international managers (Adler, 1997). Our results found SACO managers were least participative in their HRM style compared to Japanese and Japanese subsidiaries/joint ventures. Clearly, the research results indicate that in overseas subsidiaries and joint ventures firms, the culture of the corporate headquarters often exerts a stronger influence over the subsidiary than does the local context. Similarly, the presence of foreign partners in international joint ventures should influence the functioning of that firm. The expatriation of employees by the parent company to the joint venture, combined with local partner concerns in harmonizing their HRM practices, may lead to the development of a real 'federative' or 'unifying' culture, sometimes quite distant from that of the parent firm back home. This line of reasoning, based on a theory of cultural congruence or 'fit' between the international joint ventures partners or parents, is questioned by Peretti *et al.* (1990). Our findings provide texture to this ongoing debate.

References

Adler, N.J. (1997) *International Dimensions of Organizational Behavior*, 3rd edn. Cincinnati, OH: South/Western.

Ahmed, E. (1974) *Bureaucratic Elites in Economic Growth: Pakistan and Bangladesh*. Bangladesh: Dhaka University Press.

Arthur, J.B. (1994) 'Effects of Human Resource Systems on Manufacturing Performance and Turnover', *Academy of Management Journal*, 37: 670–87.

Beer, M., Spector, B., Lawrence, P., Mills, D. and Walton, R.E. (1984) *Managing Human Assets*. New York: Free Press.

Bird, A., Taylor, S. and Beechler, S. (1999) 'Organizational Learning in Japanese Overseas Affiliates'. In Beechler, S.L. and Bird, A. (eds) *Japanese Multinational Abroad: Individual and Organizational Learning*. New York: Oxford University Press, pp. 235–59.

Boliko, M. (1997) 'Participative HRM and Business Success in Japanese and Zairean SMEs'. *Journal of Association of Japanese Business Studies*. Best Paper Proceedings, 10th Annual Meeting, Washington, DC: 13–15.

Brewster, C. and Bournois, F. (1991) 'A European Perspective on Human Resource Management', *Personnel Review*, 20(6): 4–13.

Budhwar, P. and Sparrow, P. (2001) 'An Integrative Framework for Determining India and British HRM practices: An Empirical Study', *Management International Review*, 38(2): 105–21.

Cole, R.E. (1989) *Strategies for Learning: Small Group Activities in American, Japanese, and Swedish Industry*. Berkeley, CA: University of California Press.

Cotton, J.L. and Tuttle, J.M. (1986) 'Employee Turnover: A Meta-analysis and Review with Implications for Research', *Academy of Management Review*, 11: 55–70.

Cutcher-Gershenfeld, J. (1991) 'The Impact on Economic Performance of a Transformation in Industrial Relations', *Industrial and Labor Relations Review*, 44: 241–60.

Delaney, J.T. and Huselid, M.K. (1996) 'The Impact of Human Resource Management Practices on Perceptions of Organizational Performance', *Academy of Management Journal*, 39(4): 949–69.

Easterby Smith, M., Malian, D. and Yuan, L. (1995) 'How Culture Sensitive is HRM? A Comparative Analysis of Practice in Chinese and UK Companies', *International Journal of Human Resource Management*, 6(1): 31–59.

Graen, G.B. and Wakabayahsi, M. (1994) 'Cross-cultural Leadership Making: Bridging American and Japanese Diversity for Team Advantage'. In Dunnette, M.D. and Hough, L.M. (eds) *Handbook of Industrial and Organizational Psychology*, 2nd edn, Vol. 4. Palo Alto, CA: Consulting Psychologists Press.

Graen, G.B., Wakabayashi, M. and Chun, C. (2000) 'Third Culture Issues and Two Culture Business Ventures in the United States and the People's Republic of China', *Japanese Journal of Administrative Science*, 13(3): 87–98.

Guest, D. (1989a) 'Personnel and HRM: Can you tell the Difference?', *Personnel Management*, 21(1): 48–51.

Habibullah, M. (1974) *Motivation Mix*. Bureau of Economic Research, University of Dhaka, Bangladesh.

Haire, M., Ghiselli, E.E. and Porter, L.W. (1966) *Managerial Thinking: An International Study*. New York: John Wiley & Sons.

Hofstede, G. (1980a) 'Motivation, Leadership and Organization: Do American Theories apply Abroad?', *Organizational Dynamics*, Summer: 42–63.

House, R.J. and Baetz, M.L. (1990) *Gaijin Kaisha: Running a Foreign Business in Japan*. Tokyo: Ch.E. Tuttle Co.

Huselid, M.A. (1995) 'The Impact of Human Resource Management Practices on Turnover, Productivity, and Corporate Financial Performance', *Academy of Management Journal*, 38: 635–70.

Huselid, M.A. and Becker, B.E. (1994) 'The Strategic Impact of Human Resource: Results from a Panel Study'. Working paper, Rutgers University, New Brunswick, NJ.

Ichniowski, C., Shaw, K. and Prennushi, G. (1994) *The Effects of Human Resource Management Practices on Productivity*. Working Paper, Columbia University, New York.

Jaeger, A.M. and Kanungo, R.N. (eds) (1990) *Management in Developing Countries*. London and New York: Routledge.

Kanungo, R.N. and Jaeger, A.M. (1990) 'Introduction: The Need for Indigenous Management in Developing Countries'. In Jaeger, A.M. and Kanungo, R.N. (eds) *Management in Developing Countries*. London and New York: Routledge, pp. 1–9.

Kirkman, B.L and Shapiro, D.L. (2001) 'The Impact of Team Members' Cultural Values on Productivity, Cooperation, and Empowerment in Self-Managing Work teams', *Journal of Cross-Cultural Psychology*, 32: 597–617.

Kriger, M.P. and Solomon, E.E. (1992) 'Strategic Mindsets and Decision-making Autonomy in US and Japanese MNCs', *Management International Review*, 32: 327–43.

Lawler, J.J., Jain, H.C., Venkata Ratnam, C.S. and Atmihanandana, V. (1995) 'Human Resource Management in Developing Countries: A Comparison of India and Thailand', *International Journal of Human Resource Management*, 6(2): 319–46.

Levine, D.I. and Tyson, L.D. (1990) 'Participation, Productivity, and the Firm's Environment'. In Blinder, A.S. (ed.) *Paying for Productivity: A Look at the Evidence*. Washington, DC: Brookings Institution, pp. 183–243.

Likert, R. (1961) *New Patterns of Management*. New York: McGraw-Hill Book Co., Inc.

Likert, R. (1967) *The Human Organization: Its Management and Value*. Tokyo: McGraw-Hill.

Likert, R. and Likert, J.G. (1976) *New Ways of Managing Conflict*. New York: McGraw-Hill Book Co., McGraw-Hill Kogakusha Ltd.

Lock, E.A. and Schweiger, D.M. (1990) 'Participation in Decision-making: One More Look'. In Cummings, L.L. and Staw, B.M. (eds) *Leadership, Participation and Group Behavior*. London: JAI Press Inc., pp. 137–211.

MacDuffie, J.P. (1995) 'Human Resource Bundles and Manufacturing Performance: Flexible Production Systems in the World Auto Industry', *Industrial and Labor Relations Review*, 48: 197–221.

McEvoy, G.M. and Cascio, W.F. (1985) 'Strategies for Reducing Employee Turnover: A Meta-analysis', *Journal of Applied Psychology*, 70: 342–53.

Miah, A.R. (2000) 'Cross Cultural Management and Productivity: Case Studies in Bangladesh'. Basic Research Report. In Sinha, J.B.P. (ed.) *Managing Cultural Diversity for Productivity – The Asian Ways.* Asian Productivity Organization. Tokyo, 9: 17–46.

Miah, M.K. and Kitamura, Y. (2005) 'How Organizational Culture Affects HRM Strategy in India, Pakistan and Bangladesh: A Comparative Case Study between Japanese Joint Ventures and Local Companies', *6th Asian Academy of Management Conference*, Emerging Asian Economy: Local Strategies, and Global Impact 2: 700–6.

Miah, M.K., Wakabayashi, M. and Takeuchi, N. (2003) 'Cross-cultural Comparisons of HRM Styles: Based on Japanese Companies, Japanese Subsidiaries in Bangladesh and Bangladeshi Companies', *Journal of Global Business Review*, International Management Institute, India 4(1): 77–98.

Miah, M.K., Wakabayashi, M. and Tomita, T. (2001) 'A Study on HRM Philosophies and Managers' Beliefs about Human Resources: Comparison Based on Japanese Companies in Japan, and Japanese and Bangladeshi Companies in Bangladesh', *The Japanese Journal of Administrative Science*, 15(2): 131–44.

Neghandhi, A.R. and Reiman, B.C. (1973) 'Correlates of Decentralization: Closed and Open System Perspectives', *Academy of Management Journal*, 16 (December): 570–82.

Pascale, R.T. and Athos, A.G. (1981) *The Art of Japanese Management.* New York: Warner Books, Inc.

Paxson, M.C., Dillman, D.A. and Tarnai, J. (1995) 'Improving Response to Business Mail Surveys'. In Cox, B., Binder, D., Chinnappa, B., Christianson, A., Colledge, M. and Kott, P. (eds) *Business Survey Methods.* New York: Wiley-Interscience, pp. 303–15.

Peretti, J.M., Cazal, D. and Quiquandon, F. (1990) *Vers le Management International Des Resources Humanitie.* Les Editions Liaisons: Paris.

Peters, T.J. and Waterman, R.H. (1982) *In Search of Excellence: Lessons from American's Best Runs Companies.* New York: Harper & Row.

Pfeffer, J. (1994) *Competitive Advantage through People.* Boston, MA: Harvard Business School Press.

Pieper, R. (1990) *Human Resource Management: An International Comparison.* Berlin: Walter de Gruyter.

Razzaque, M.A. (1991) 'The Evolution of Management in an Islamic Society- Bangladesh'. In Jospeh, M.P. (ed.) *Management – Asian Context.* Singapore: McGraw-Hill Book Co., pp. 113–29.

Sheridan, J.E. (1992) 'Organizational Culture and Employee Retention', *Academy of Management Journal*, 35: 1036–56.

Shetty, Y.K. and Prasad, Y. (1971) 'Ownership, Size, Technology and Management Development: A Comparative Analysis', *Academy of Management Journal*, 14: 439–49.

Sohban, R. and Ahmad, M. (1986) *Public Enterprises in an Intermediate Regime.* Bangladesh Institute of Development Studies: Dhaka.

Statt, D.A. (1991) *The Concise Dictionary of Management.* London: Routledge.

Strauss, G. (1990) 'Workers Participation in Management: An International Perspective'. In Cummings, L.L. and Staw, B.M. (eds) *Leadership, Participation and Group Behaviour.* Greenwich, CT & London: JAI Press Inc., pp. 213–305.

Tagiuri, R. and Litwin, G.H. (1968) *Organizational Climate: Explorations of a Concept.* Boston, MA: Harvard University, Boston Division of Research, Graduate School of Business Administration.

Takeuchi, N. (2001) 'Strategic Transfer of HRM Practices for Competitive Advantage: Implications for Sequential Transfer of Japanese HRM to China and Taiwan', *The Japanese Journal of Administrative Science*, 15(2): 109–30.

Takeuchi, N. (2003) 'Effects of Strategy – HRM Alignment on Business Performance: A Test for Japanese Business Firm'. Association of Japanese Business Studies, Best Paper Proceedings, 5–8 June, Conference Montreal, Canada.

Taylor, S., Beechler, S. and Napier, N. (1996) 'Toward an Integrative Theory of Strategic International Human Resource Management', *Academy of Management Review*, 214: 959–85.

Wakabyashi, M. and Graen, G.B. (1991) 'Cross-cultural Human Resource Management: Japanese Manufacturing Firms in Central Japan and Central US States'. In Trevor, M. (ed.) *International Business and the Management of Change*. Brookfield, VT: Avebury.

Appendix 1 *Summary results of principal components analysis for hiring technique*

	F1	F2	h^2
F1: Merit-based hiring	$a = .70$		
Technical skill	**.81**	.09	.66
Good intellectual potential	**.80**	−.06	.64
Good educational qualifications	**.79**	−.06	.64
F2: Linage based hiring		$a = .41$	
Good personal connections	.02	.39	.15
Good family background	.03	.28	.08
Strong recommendations	−.13	.34	.13
Having right attitudes	.25	−.34	.18
Variance explained	3.16	.57	3.73
Residual items			
Fit with company values	.34	−.19	
Variance explained	34	−.19	
Residual items			
Fit with company values	.34	−.19	

Appendix 2 *Summary results of principal components analysis for training and development*

F1: Training and development	$a = .85$	h^2
Skill training by outside agency	**.77**	.59
Overseas training	**.73**	.53
Job rotation	**.72**	.51
TV and radio courses	**.71**	.50
Lectures and seminars inside the company	**.68**	.46
Coaching by supervisor	**.65**	.42
Self-study programmes	**.53**	.28
Variance explained	3.29	3.29

Introducing the impact of technology: a 'neo-contingency' HRM Anglo-French comparison

Jacobo Ramirez and Marianela Fornerino

Introduction

For many decades, scholars have noted that technological, economic and, more recently, institutional forces provoke homogeneity in practices and even reduce cultural differences between nations. These studies have reported similarities between organizations operating in diverse cultural and industrial settings (e.g. Fröbel and Marchington, 2005; McMillan *et al.*, 1973). Controversially, there is a long tradition of work affirming that nations' cultural and institutional idiosyncrasies outweigh the significance of any similarities in the formal structures and processes of organizations (e.g. Richardson, 1953; Tayeb, 1987; Wade, 1996). These studies have reported considerable differences between organizations operating in similar task environments but different societies, which have been underpinned (implicitly or explicitly) by contingency (e.g. Burn and Stalker, 1961; Thompson, 1967; Woodward, 1965) or divergence (e.g. Child, 1972; Donaldson, 2001; Gallie, 1978; Maurice *et al.*, 1980) paradigms. The purpose of this study is to understand how the level of technology that a firm has and the country where the firm operates shape certain HRM policies and practices. In this paper, we aim to analyse both the contingency and the divergence theories, in an attempt to demonstrate that these two theories do not compete with each other as is commonly assumed. Rather they complement each other. The principal question to be discussed in this paper is whether there are consistent patterns of differences and similarities of firms with the same level of technology operating in different countries. Our proposition is that the level of technology that a firm has affects the way HR managers devise HRM policies and practices; however, the technology impact is regulated by country factors where the firm is located.

The importance of studying the contingency and divergence theories in the area of HRM in a cross-national perspective is justified by the fact that to some extent organizations are forced to find the best HRM fit in different environmental conditions. Therefore, it is important to re-study whether technology, cultural factors or the combination of both affect firms' HRM.

This study is a cross-national comparison between France and Britain of recruitment and selection, training and compensation literature that examines these practices in firms operating in different industrial settings. The French and British educational systems will be used to illustrate the cultural difference between these countries. The following sections present a short revision of the contingency and divergence theories that assisted us in proposing the neo-contingency perspective.

Then it goes on to a neo-contingency analysis of the HRM practices mentioned above between France and Britain and the hypotheses to be tested. Next, we present our methodology, describe our sample and report the results. This is followed by a neo-contingency discussion of the HRM practices selected in this study between France and Britain.

Theoretical background

Contingency theory

Contingency theory is essentially about the need to achieve fit between what the organization is and wants to become and what the organization does (how it is structured, and the processes, procedures and practices it puts into effect). Researchers of organizations have identified a number of contingency factors: task uncertainty (Gresov, 1990), technology (Woodward, 1965), innovation (Hage and Aiken, 1967, 1969), environmental change (Child, 1975), technological change (Burns and Stalker, 1961), size (Blau, 1970) and task interdependence (Thompson, 1967). Some contingency variables are within the organization and others are outside it. Contingency variables that are internal to the organizations have an effect, which in turn mould other internal organizational characteristics, for example, firms' HRM policies and practices.

However, the contingency theory has been challenged almost from its initial proposition by many researchers (e.g. Donaldson, 2001; Mohr, 1971; Pennings, 1975; Schoonhoven, 1981). Two lines of criticisms can be identified in management literature: (1) lack of clarity in the contingency theoretical statements and (2) lack of methods in empirically testing the contingency approach. In the first line of criticism, there is one major specific argument in relation to theoretical aspects: (1) theory founded on assumptions of linearity and as being deterministic, tautology and conservative (Schoonhoven, 1981). This criticism has arisen in academic literature because past studies have used the contingent criterion as a predictor of organizational effectiveness (Pennings, 1975; Schoonhoven, 1981). Furthermore, some of these researchers have failed to demonstrate whether the structural-contingency model was useful for explaining why organizations differ in effectiveness in terms of the contingency variables (Pennings, 1975). Indeed, major proponents of the structural-contingency model have confused or combined technology with the environment (e.g. Hickson *et al.*, 1969).

They show little agreement as to whether organizational environment and/or technology have structural correlations. Thus, no conclusive evidence to support the contingency model has been put forward by their studies.

According to the criteria found in the academic literature, in this paper we propose an empirical measurement of the technology variable. The following section presents a technology definition and the criteria to measure this variable.

Technology

Technology could be defined as: 'the organization and application of knowledge for the achievement of practical purposes. It includes physical manifestations such as tools and machines, but also it includes intellectual techniques and processes used in solving problems and obtaining desired outcomes' (Kast and Rosenzweig, 1985: 208). Additionally, technology means the systematic application of scientific or other organized knowledge to practical tasks (Galbraith, 1972: 31).

Technology is one of the contingency variables that could be more problematic to study at the firm level of analysis. Additionally, in response to the criticisms of the contingency theory, in this paper we propose a *measurement* scale to analyse the technology variable. We propose a technology scale at three levels: high-, mid- and low-tech, with the aim of measuring the impact of the technology variable on HRM policies and practices. This approach analyses technology as a nominal variable that interplays between hardware or technoware, orgaware, humanware and other types of invisible assets (Hagström and Chandler, 1998; Ramanathan, 1994).

Technoware   The word technology brings to mind machines. However, machines are merely the physical artefacts of technology, and the object embodied in technology is called technoware (Ramanathan, 1994). Technoware emphasizes the importance of machines' hardware (non-human) and human-machines interactions (Mintzberg, 1993).

Humanware   Continuing in the logic of a sophisticated technoware, it would imply specialized manpower to operate the activities required in a high-tech environment. Thus, person-embodied technology can be called humanware (Ramanathan, 1994). This technology component refers to experiences, skills, knowledge, wisdom and creativity, among other features required to operate a sophisticated technoware.

Inforware   Document-embodied technology can be called inforware (Ramanathan, 1994). This includes all kinds of documentation pertaining to process specifications, procedures, theories, observations, etc.

Orgaware   Orgaware refers to the support of principles, practices and arrangements that govern the effective use of technoware by humanware. It may be viewed in terms of the technological support for the requisite organizational, administrative, and cultural structures: work rules, task roles, requisite skills, work contents, formal and informal covenants of the workplace, system standards and measures, management styles and culture, and organizational patterns, among other elements (Zeleny, 1986).

The technology components presented facilitate the definition of the measure scale to be used in this paper. In our research, technology is viewed as a variable that could have different levels of technoware, humanware, orgaware and inforware from low levels to a higher level. If a firm presents high levels of the technoware specification, it would affect the other technology components in the same direction. At this point, technology and its components have been discussed. In the following section, we present the three levels of technology to be analysed in this paper.

Levels of technology

A high-tech firm can be defined based on its occupational structures (an above-average share of engineers, technologists and scientists) and the relative amount that it spends on research and development, from 3 to 5 per cent of sales revenue. This definition is widely supported by a significant number of researchers (e.g. Breheny and McQuaid, 1987; Jolly and Roche, 1999; Kleingartner and Anderson, 1987; Stuart and Quinn, 1992). The mid-tech classification involves those firms that are definitely not low-tech but classifying them as high-tech could be controversial. For example, (1) firms that invest in R&D activities, although the percentage invested is less than 3 per cent of sales revenues, and (2) firms that belong to the high-tech industrial sector, but the average number of engineers and scientists does not figure in the total organizational workforce. Finally, according to academic literature, low-tech firms have a workforce of 'non-professional/non-knowledge' workers; specialized knowledge workers are not important for the kind of duties that manufacturing firms demand. Moreover, 'non-professional/non-knowledge' workers deal mainly with repetitive tasks, that most of time are very simple functions that can be learned within a short period of training. 'Non-professional workers possess a common knowledge that can be purchased easily in the labour market' (Leonard-Barton, 1995). Additionally, 'the number of engineers that implement or develop technology in low-tech plants is not more than the 5 per cent of the total workforce' (Jolly and Therin, 1996).

Divergence theory

Different researchers have claimed that HRM policies and practices are better explained by country than industrial sectors. For example, Tremblay and Chênevert (2005) claim that the role of national institutional factors explains better than the industrial sector the formulation of HRM strategies. Similar results were found by Gooderham and colleagues (1999) when they studied a sample of firms from Germany, France, Norway and Great Britain; they concluded that HR practices were explained substantially better by country than by industrial sectors. The Gooderham *et al.* (1999: 527) study found evidence for the need to incorporate country-specific institutional factors in studies of patterns of organizational practices in general and HRM in particular. Their findings indicate that the national institutional embeddedness of firms plays a far more important role in shaping HRM than their industrial embeddedness.

National culture configuration – HRM and educational institution

Most discussions of cross-cultural research begin with a definition of culture. Traditionally, culturalists have defined culture in terms of 'values and norms which, in the final analysis, direct and shape observed behaviour' (Maurice *et al.*, 1986: 227). In the same direction, the GLOBE project defines culture as shared motives, values, belief, identities, and interpretations or meaning of significant events that result form common experiences of members of collectives that are transmitted across generations (House *et al.*, 2004).

Cultural differences can be found at many different levels, such as professional, class and regional, but it is particularly potent at the national level because of generations of socialization in the national community. Additionally, researchers such as Hofstede

(1993) have suggested that while acknowledging the role of contingency factors, a more complex culture-bound argument must be applied in organizational practices. Indeed, management practices including HRM are not universal but '*socially constructed*' in each society (e.g. Boxall, 1995). Cultural and societal factors in each nation make a qualitative difference in organizations. Their internal processes tend to vary across nations (Maurice *et al.*, 1980). Country-related factors such as societal and economic policy, and the labour market and educational system account for the differences found in the study developed by van der Klink and Mulder (1995) when comparing HRM practices between four European countries (Germany, the United Kingdom, the Netherlands and France).

We can conclude that culture is operationally defined by the use of indicators reflecting two distinct kinds of cultural manifestations: (a) the commonality (agreement) among members of collectives with respect to the psychological attributes specified; and (b) the commonality of observed and reported practices of entities such as families, schools, work organizations, economic and legal systems, and political institutions (e.g. House *et al.*, 2004). Thus, acknowledging the different approaches to define culture and the challenges to measure it together with the nature of our research, we propose in this paper to assess the impact of culture at the firm level of analysis through the institutional approach.

Institutions play an important role in determining a society. They can be political, legal, financial systems, as well as educational institutions. Calori *et al.* (1997) argue that the administrative behaviours of a nation are strongly influenced by the primary socialization that its people receive at school during their youth. They based their argument on the theory of socialization (Berger and Luckmann, 1967), which posits that the schemas learned during an individual's formative years are deeply internalized, and therefore greatly influence later behaviours. Hence, management education influences management practices (Locke, 1985). This is not to say that other background institutions (Whitley, 1992) are not as important as educational institutions. Family and religion also play an important role; however, it is the educational system that tends to be the most nationally bonding. Educational institutions effectively produce a convergence of beliefs, values and eventually administrative practices among members of one nation, which in turn distinguish that nation from others (Calori *et al.*, 1997). Education is a vast topic; therefore, this study investigates the French and British national education systems and their relation to certain HRM.

Neo-contingency perspective

The contingency (technology) and divergence (national culture) theoretical perspectives present grey areas in their definition and the operationalization of their variables. The debate between the contingency and divergence theories continues today. Mainly, it is about the extent and explanation that they can give to management studies (Harzing and Sorge, 2003). At the more general theoretical level, the national culture to firms' internal organization relation expresses a fundamental tension in management studies (Nelson and Gopalan, 2003).

Table 1 presents an outline of the contingency and neo-contingency perspectives. In an attempt to resolve some the contingency limitations presented, we propose to examine empirically a neo-contingency approach (Donaldson, 2001; Miles and Snow, 1978; Sorge and Maurice, 1990). Testing the neo-contingency approach, we suggest analysing the contingency and divergence perspectives together, which would enrich management studies.

Table 1 *Comparison of the contingency theory and neo-contingency perspective*

Contingency theory	Neo-contingency perspective
• Determinism of certain variables on management processes (Donaldson, 2001) • Unidirectional interaction (Donaldson, 2001) • Universal effect (e.g. Blau, 1970; Kerr et al., 1964; Pugh et al., 1969) • Seeks to understand (1) the interrelationships within and among subsystems as well as between (2) the organization and its environment and (3) to define patterns of relationships or configurations of variables Kast and Rosenzweig (1985) • Organizational effectiveness results from 'fitting characteristics of the organization, such as its structure, to contingencies that reflect the situation of the organization' (Burns and Stalker, 1961; Lawrence and Lorsch, 1967; Woodward, 1965) • Situational approach and non-prescriptive (Haimann et al., 1978: 37)	• Reciprocal interaction and functional equivalence (Swan et al., 1999) • Placing emphasis on the cultural factors of a firm's location (Sorge and Maurice, 1990) • Fitting link-up of the societal effect framework, which roughly maintains that organizational structures and processes are interdependent with the business strategy and the market segment into which a firm launches itself (Donaldson, 2001) • Helps to revolutionize the static assumption of the traditional contingency theory, which could be analysed through a realistic and dynamic approach (Miles and Snow, 1978) • Tries to respond to such criticism of the traditional thinking of the contingency theory (Donaldson, 2001)

The neo-contingency approach that we propose seeks to show the functional equivalence, reciprocal interaction instead of the additive effects of the two variables. Thus, in this study we are integrating an analysis of a contingency variable: level of technology that a firm has and the divergence dimension: a social-cultural variable illustrated by the educational system. They and their inherent perspectives can supplement each other in a fruitful way and thereby lead to further development of our understanding of outer contexts that may influence HRM policies and practices functioning in different environments.

Interaction between the variables levels of technology and country would indicate that the impact of the levels of technology is not the same between France and Britain. This signifies that an understanding of HRM will be accomplished by analysing the country and technological factors together. This paper does not intend to claim primacy for either the contingency or the divergence approaches. It claims that in order to understand the different forms of HRM configurations, it is necessary to analyse the national-culture and technology factors together. Thus, we propose the following.

General proposition

National culture will moderate the relation between levels of technology and HRM policies and practices. National culture and the levels of technology will interact to predict the operation of HRM policies and practices.

This research attempts to find out what types of HRM policies and practices will be effective under different technological and national setting conditions. In doing so, it offers a way of understanding the complexities of large organizations, which can be helpful in making more sense of some of the current management theories. The following section will present an analysis of the different approaches to HRM under the neo-contingency approach, in order to derive the specific hypotheses to be tested in this paper.

Neo-contingency and HRM policies and practices

Recruitment and selection

Employee selection is a fundamental aspect of HRM and assumes that individual differences make a meaningful difference in job performance. Therefore, what is needed to maximize performance is a good match between personal characteristics and job requirements (Cardy and Krzystofiak, 1991). After the domain of performance is examined, the type of personal characteristics that might tap these characteristics must be identified. Selecting the most qualified persons to fill job vacancies seems to be a universal goal for both human-resource and line managers around the world, as a mismatch between jobs and people could dramatically reduce the effectiveness of other HRM functions (Huo *et al.*, 2002). The following sections present an analysis that shows how past researchers have demonstrated the differences between France and Britain in the recruitment and selection processes in firms operating in different levels of technology.

The methodology of personnel selection has never been internationally uniform. Past researchers have demonstrated the differences in the selection tools used in France and Britain (e.g. Winch *et al.*, 2000). For example, Shackleton and Newell (1991) developed an Anglo-French study, which was based on comparing the methods used to select managers in 73 Britain and 52 French organizations. They found that the utilization of assessment centres for selection purposes was greater in Britain than in France: 58.9 per cent of the British sample reported using them, as opposed to 18.8 per cent in France. Another finding was the common use of interviews (93.2 per cent in Britain and 94.3 per cent in France) and the inclusion of line managers in these interviews. In France, 92.4 per cent of the respondents say that they resort to more than one interview, compared with 60.3 per cent in Britain. Thus, to be seen by more than one person in France, and hence to spread the responsibility of the decision, candidates have to attend a number of interviews. In Britain, by comparison, there is a greater tendency to use panel interviews so that one interview permits the candidate to be seen by all concerned.

Maurice *et al.* (e.g. 1980, 1986) investigated the production departments of manufacturing plants in France, Britain and Germany (at that time West Germany). They found that French middle management grades are generally recruited from the higher levels of general academic education, which then is customized in the firms as a *formation maison*. Higher managers possessing diplomas from the elite engineering schools *grandes écoles* may well be capable of deploying their abstract expertise with brilliance to those problems reserved for their attention. Furthermore, it could be argued that the stronger value given to formal education in France is a reflection of the French employment system. These results reflect societal differences between France and Britain.

Recruitment and selection differences according to technology specificity

Recruitment and selection could be analysed through two essential aspects: employee profile and recruitment and selection tools. The first refers to the capabilities, skills that employees need to demonstrate in order to be hired for a certain position. The second aspect refers to the tools that HR managers use in order to test if a candidate possesses the profile of the open position.

Employee profile According to academic literature, employee profile is characterized by three key differences between high-, mid- and low-tech firms. The first, intangible skills, refers to a workforce with tacit or difficult to measure capabilities, such as the ability to work in a team-based system, innovation, flexibility, problem solving capability and good interpersonal relations (Cutcher-Gershenfeld *et al.*, 1998). The second global scope stresses the importance of the recruitment of *'suitable'* employees for the job, without any differentiation based on their nationality. A major premise supporting international recruitment is that technology-oriented firms tend to hire employees with the desirable capabilities related to the specific job's description. A direct result of this practice is that the importance of employees' nationality diminishes while merits increase (Jolly and Roche, 1999). The last key difference is age. According to field literature, technology-oriented firms tend to hire new employees who are under 35 years old (Bowman and Farr, 2000).

Recruitment and selection tools Methods of recruiting employees can be a good indicator of management style and, at the very least, can tell us something about the formality of the employment relationship (Cully *et al.*, 1999: 60). Therefore, in terms of recruitment tools, the Internet and assessment centres were the primary means analysed. The Internet was chosen because it has become a leading recruitment tool for potential employees and employers searching for high-technology positions within the industry (e.g. Buckley *et al.*, 2004). At the same time, traditional assessment centres have also proven to be a suitable tool for evaluating candidates' personality and job skills (Coombs and Rosse, 1992). The following hypotheses were derived from the above discussion:

Hypothesis H1.1. High-tech, mid-tech and low tech firms will present a difference in the recruitment and selection process; high-tech and mid-tech will present more sophisticated processes than low-tech firms.

Hypothesis H1.2: The relation between level of technology and the recruitment and selection processes will be moderated by the national-culture factors.

Training

One of the biggest factors influencing training and development is the labour market in which organizations operate and the level of training and skills available in that market (Tregaskis and Dany, 1996). Different educational systems play an important role in the shaping of training and development systems in different countries (Calori *et al.*, 1997). It is argued that educational systems shape the skills and knowledge of the workforce, who in turn shape the training systems as a result of the requirements for training and their career aspirations (Rose, 1985).

France and Britain have shown an inherent complexity and relative autonomy of educational institutions (Ambler, 1987). In France, formal qualifications are common in both small and large firms, while in Britain there are very few formally qualified workers in small plants (Senker, 1992: 99). A report by the OECD (1997) found French schools to be excessive in their emphasis on deduction and abstraction. In contrast, British pragmatism is a less analytical, more inductive and more action-oriented way of thinking about cause and effect that encourages individuals to search for solutions outside the dominant paradigm, reflecting a greater willingness to accept, rather than avoid, uncertainty (Lessem and Palsule, 1999). Additionally, the Calori *et al.* (1997) findings support the argument that the science and social values that are explicitly and implicitly communicated at school in France (pre-school through early secondary school) are different from the values that are communicated at comparable British schools. Specifically, the French learn to construct reality in terms of orderly hierarchies, while the British learn to do so in a less controlling, more individualistic way (*ibid.* 687).

Training according to technology specificity   The content of training is clearly important. For instance, initiatives such as total quality management require people to be trained in so-called 'soft' skills rather than technical skills (Collinson *et al.*, 1998). High-tech firms tend to be proactive for training purposes; they try to anticipate the training needs for their workforce (Cascio, 1990). High-tech firms commonly view training as employees' development and personal growth (*ibid.*). Training programmes in high-tech environments tend to focus on problem solving, communication, technical skills, job rotation and mentoring relationships (Cutcher-Gershenfeld *et al.*, 1998; Lepak and Snell, 1999). On the other hand, employees in low-tech environments do not receive much training, because the skills and abilities that they need to perform their daily repetitive activities are not unique to a particular firm but are public knowledge (Lepak and Snell, 1999). Therefore, low-tech firms tend to develop training programmes for a specific task, or even just to complete legal requirements (Towers, 1992).

The above discussion provides a perspective in which high-technology firms tend to present a different approach to training and development than low-tech firms; this perspective will derive the following hypotheses:

> *Hypothesis H2.1:* High-tech, mid-tech and low-tech firms will present a difference in the training practices, high-tech and mid-tech will present a more sophisticated approach than low-tech firms.
> *Hypothesis H2.2:* The relation between Level of Technology and the training practices will be moderated by the national-culture factors.

Compensation

Employees' total compensation is the package of quantifiable rewards employees receive for their labour. This concept includes three elements: (1) base compensation, the fixed pay that employees receive on a regular basis, either in the form of a salary or as an hourly wage basis; (2) pay incentives programmes, designed to reward employees for good performance; and (3) benefits, which includes a wide variety of programmes -health insurance and vacations, among others (Gomez-Mejia *et al.*, 1998: 298). It could be argued that the best method of managing people who work 'consists of paying people and not positions'. Each person's wages are fixed as far as possible according to the skills and energy with which he/she performs his/her work, and not according to the position that he/she fills.

In Anglo-Saxon countries (especially in Britain), the salary tends to be closely related to the nature of the job, its responsibilities and the results obtained (Edwards *et al.*, 1992). Therefore, the use of pay systems related to individual and organizational performance: merit pay, profit-sharing share-ownership show considerable growth in Britain (*ibid.*). Indeed, in Britain there is a law that obligates the employer to share returns with an employed inventor in production to the commercial return of the patented invention, and special relocation benefits to bring technical employees on board (Gomez-Mejia *et al.*, 1990). The explanation for this pattern is the Hofstede-type argument (1980) of high-individualism in Britain. The dominant characteristics of this pattern are: personal accomplishment, independence, individual attitudes and utilitarian contractual relationship. On the contrary, France is linked to a high-power distance (Hofstede, 1980), which suggests a hierarchical compensation strategy. In this scenario, differences in pay and benefits reflect job and status differences. Also, large differences between upper and lower echelons could be found (Sparrow and Hiltrop, 1994). In addition to this, the French compensation system has more to do with the individual's credentials, in particular his or her qualifications, but also age, experience and even contacts (Barsoux and Lawrence, 1997).

Compensation according to technology specificity   High-tech firms tend to determine wages based on skills, personal attributes and contributions to the firm, rather than job evaluation procedures, which focus on daily work tasks, a strong tendency seen in low-tech firms. (Gomez-Mejia *et al.*, 1990; Saura Diaz and Gomez-Mejia, 1997) Another characteristic is that the compensation system tends to be flexible and adaptable and offers: sign-on bonuses, stock options and profit sharing, among other incentives; another focus is the R&D group incentive compensation (Balkin and Gomez-Mejia, 1992; Jolly and Therin, 1996; Stuart and Quinn, 1992). High-tech employees are younger, more fluid and more likely to be compensated with stock rather than cash. High-tech organizations offer this benefit in order to ensure that their employees become real stockholders in the company they work in (Saura Diaz and Gomez-Mejia, 1997).

On the contrary, low-tech firms design their compensation systems in such a way that they rely heavily on traditional job evaluation procedures. For example, the payroll assigned to security employees is just short-term oriented (Balkin and Gomez-Mejia, 1992; Saura Diaz and Gomez-Mejia, 1997).

Hypothesis H3.1: High-tech, mid-tech and low-tech firms will present a difference in the compensation system, high-tech and mid-tech will present a more sophisticated systems that low-tech firms,
Hypothesis H3.2: The relation between Level of Technology and the compensation system will be moderated by the national-culture factors.

The proposed model and the hypothesis are presented in Figure 1.

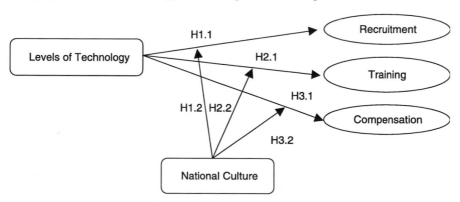

Figure 1 *Neo-contingency approach: the proposed model and the hypotheses*

Method and research setting

The evaluation of the neo-contingency perspective on HRM requires a study in which technology can be measured according to the three levels of technology (low, mid and high-tech) and national-culture can show some varieties. As mentioned, France and Britain were chosen for the setting of this research because, on comparing these countries, similarities in the level of technology in companies located in both countries could be ensured. France and Britain are countries that present a relative homogeneity in size, level of development and historical experience among other factors (Cassis *et al.*, 1995). At the same time, France and Britain present historical, religious, educational and political factors that are decisive in causing cultural differences between them (Crouzet, 1990).

Britain and France were the pioneers of industrial revolution and modern economic growth. However, from World War II to the present time, the rise of the USA and Japan as world leaders and Germany in Europe has not completely diminished the importance of France and Britain in the world's economy and technological development. Further comparisons with America, Germany and Japan have taken precedence. Nonetheless, the object of this research is to explore the potential for comparison in Anglo-French business, because of the significance that France and Britain businesses play in the world and particularly within the EU. Such a comparison should show more clearly which of the factors that are peculiar to Britain and France may have determined the unique and 'universal' phenomenon in these countries' HRM policies and practices that could be applied in countries with similar economy and technology development.

We will assess the magnitude and detail of the level of technology that a firm has in the operation of the selected HRM policies and practices. This analysis will be developed by integrating country and levels of technology as two independents variables. However, we do not seek to measure a country viewed throughout the national institutions directly, specially the educational institution. We have highlighted for France and Britain the influence of the national educational system on shaping HR managers' behaviour. Thus, we will delineate the educational institution through a description of the salient characteristics of the French and British systems. We will use educational institutional description as a foundation for country-specific predictions of firms' adoption of the HRM polices and practices studied in this paper.

Sample and data collection

The sample organizations chosen from France and Britain present the following characteristics: (1) they were engaged in manufacturing – the firms that were eventually selected in each country operate in the following industries: chemical, pharmaceuticals, electronics, IT and software, automotive, telecommunications, metal, food and services; (2) they operated in the private sector; and (3) size – the average size of the organizations (number of employees) ranged from 400 to 1,000 employees. Different sources were consulted in order to compile the sample: in France, *KOMPASS-France* (2000) and Les Echos (2000); in Britain, *KOMPASS-UK* (2000), Scoreboard Report (2001) and British Business Ranking (1995).

A total of 1,200 firms were selected from these sources in both countries. Two rounds of mailed questionnaires were conducted between October 2001 and January 2002. In total, 650 questionnaires were mailed from France and 550 questionnaires from Britain. Up to April 2002, 172 usable questionnaires were received: 76 questionnaires for France with an 11 per cent response rate; and 96 questionnaires from Britain with a 17 per cent response rate. Although the response rate is not equivalent to those in North-American studies, we consider our final sample adequate given the nature of our study. This apparently low response rate reflects the cultural aspects of France and Britain in business academic queries. France has shown low response rates in mailed questionnaires (e.g. Lubatkin *et al.*, 1998).

Sample classification and representativeness   The 172 firms in the sample were analysed individually to assess their levels of technology, based on the three criteria discussed previously: (1) industrial sector; (2) turnover spent on R&D; and (3) organizational structure, number of engineers and technicians in relation to the overall numbers of employees in the organization. It is important to highlight that high-tech and mid-tech firms can be clustered as technology intensive firms. However, within this cluster there are certain features which make a differentiation in the technology intensity between high- and mid-tech firms that is important to analyse.

Forty-eight British and French firms from the sample were categorized as high-tech. The sample presents forty-eight firms that could not easily be coded as high-tech or low-tech; the mid-tech classification was therefore kept for those firms that were definitely not low-tech but classifying them as high-tech could be controversial. Sixty-seven firms in the sample fall into the low-tech classification. Because of the space limit in this paper, a full explanation of the database classification cannot be provided here. Further details can be obtained from the authors. We developed an χ^2 test to validate the representativeness of the sample. As a result, nine questionnaires from the sample (six from France and three from Britain), were discarded by a random procedure. The outcome of the firms' classification is presented in Table 2.

Measurements

Independent variables

The HRM were assessed under the analysis of two independent variables: (1) country, which was defined as a dichotomy variable 1 = France and 2 = Britain; and (2) level of technology was defined as a nominal variable 1 = low-tech, 2 = mid-tech and 3 = high-tech.

Dependent variables

The different HRM policies and practices were conceptualized and measured in a questionnaire using a five-point Likert-type scale ranging from 'Strongly Disagree' to 'Strongly Agree'. The items in the questionnaire cover several dimensions of HRM on the following topics:

1   Recruitment and selection (five items)
2   Training (four items)
3   Compensation (six items).

Table 2 *Sample distribution*

Countries	High-tech	Mid-tech	Low-tech	Total
France	19	18	33	70
Britain	29	30	34	93
Total	48	48	67	163

For each HRM, we established a list of items based on the literature review as presented earlier. Items are listed fully in Appendix 1. The questionnaires were designed in English and translated into French. Several back-translation runs were developed in order to avoid problems of equivalence in terms of concepts, idioms and grammar (Brislin, 1986).

We developed the classical method for instrument validation that consists of a principal component analysis with a varimax rotation to group the different items of the dependent variables: recruitment and selection, training and compensation into different factors. The alpha Cronbach coefficient was calculated for each obtained factor in order to measure its reliability. The following sections present the results divided into three sections: (1) recruitment and selection, (2) training and (3) compensation.

Results

Recruitment and selection

The principal component analysis performed with the five recruitment and selection items resulted in two orthogonal factors (eigenvalues > 1) that explain 57.037 per cent of the total variance. Please refer to Table 3 for the details.

Factor 1: recruitment technical policies   The items that integrate this factor are: (1) global scope, (2) Internet and (3) soft skills. This factor was named 'recruitment technical policies' ($\alpha = 0.5586$) because it refers to the technology-oriented capability and skills that employees working in a fast moving industry might require.

Factor 2: psychological tools   The items that integrate the second recruitment and selection factor are: (1) age and (2) assessment centre. These items provide a tool for evaluating workforces' profile; therefore, this factor was named 'psychological tools' ($\alpha = 0.3882$).

Training   The principal component analysis performed with the training items resulted in one factor with an eigenvalue greater than 1, which explains 53.609 per cent of the variance. The items that integrate this factor are: (1) soft skills, (2) career development, (3) integral career, and (4) international training. The loading factors and communalities for the training items are shown in Table 4. This factor is labelled long-term approach to training ($\alpha = 0.6980$) because the training practices concerned enhance employees' skills for their career development.

Table 3 *Factor analysis recruitment and selection*

Factor	Eigenvalues	Percentage of cumulated explained variance	Items	Loading factors	Alpha
Recruitment technical policies	1.803	32.106	Global scope	0.757	0.5586
			Internet	0.744	
			Soft-skills	0.658	
Psychological tools	1.049	57.037	Age	0.843	0.3882
			Assessment centres	0.715	

Table 4 *Factor analysis training*

Factor	Eigenvalues	Percentage of cumulated explained variance	Items	Loading factors	Alpha
Long-term approach to training	2.144	53.609	Soft-skills	0.765	0.6980
			Career development	0.755	
			Integral career	0.706	
			International training	0.701	

Compensation   The principal component analysis developed in the compensation items, resulted in one factor with an eigenvalue greater than 1, which explains 60.025 per cent of the variance. The items that integrate this factor are (1) compensation based on performance, (2) importance of capabilities for compensation purposes and (3) compensation based on the short-term. The loading factors and communalities for the retained items are shown in Table 5. This factor was labelled compensation based on performance ($\alpha = 0.6310$), because employees' capabilities and performance are valuable criteria that managers appear to reward.

Globally, four factors were obtained from the principal component analysis. Three factors present an acceptable Cronbach α: (1) recruitment technical policies ($\alpha = 0.5586$), (2) long-term approach to training ($\alpha = 0.6980$), and (3) compensation ($\alpha = 0.6310$). The psychological tool factor does not present a satisfactory Cronbach Alpha to guarantee the reliability. Thus, the psychology tools factor was dropped from the analysis. The remaining variables will be analysed in the following section.

General testing approach

The model set forth in Figure 1 was tested by means of a *multivariate analysis of variance* (MANOVA). MANOVA is a technique that allows the researcher to test the influence of two or more independent variables on a set of dependent variables.

Table 5 *Factor analysis compensation*

Factor	Eigenvalues	Percentage of cumulated explained variance	Items	Loading factors	Alpha
Compensation based on performance	1.801	60.025	Compensation based on performance	0.868	0.6310
			Importance of capabilities	0.786	
			Compensation based on short term	0.656	

MANOVA has the specific advantage of being able to test for interaction effects, where the dependent variables are changed as a result of an interaction between two or more of the independent variables. An interaction between national-culture and level of technology was tested.

Multivariate analysis of variance – MANOVA

The MANOVA test was conducted to examine the global effects of country and levels of technology on the three dependent variables through one factor by variable: (1) recruitment and selection: recruitment technical policies; (2) training: long-term approach to training; and (3) compensation: compensation based on performance. Table 6 shows the results. The multivariate F statistics using a lambda Wilks criterion present a global interaction between the independent variables (λ Wilks $= 0.914$, $F = 2.128$), which are statistically significant at the 0.05 level. This interaction signifies that the two countries do not present the same combinative effect of the independent variables on the HRM variables.

Given the positive MANOVA findings for the interactions, Univariate Analyses were performed by country on each variable.

ANOVA test –hypotheses validation

Three univariate analyses of variance tests (ANOVA) were conducted in order to examine the main effect of country and levels of technology on the three factors; Table 6 presents the results.

Recruitment technical policies   Table 6 suggests that there is an interaction between country and levels of technology for the recruitment technical policies factor ($p < 0.05$). This result indicates that the impact of the levels of technology on this variable is not the same in France and Britain. H1.2 is supported. Therefore, in order to test the H1.1 hypothesis, each country is analysed separately. The ANOVA test performed in Britain does not present sufficient statistical evidence of the impact of the levels of technology for this variable $F = 0.776$ d.f. (2.92) ($p = 0.46$). Thus, hypothesis H1.1 that states that technology-oriented firms will recruit employees with a more sophisticated profile and tools than low-tech firms is not supported in Britain. Nonetheless, the ANOVA test performed on the French sample presents a statistically significant effect of the levels of technology on this variable $F = 10.158$, d.f. (2.67), ($p < 0.001$). The *post hoc* Scheffé test shows that high- and mid-tech French firms present higher mean values than low-tech firms ($p < 0.05$). This result indicates that the variable levels of technology mould recruitment and selection in France; therefore hypothesis H1.1 is supported in France. Figure 2 illustrates the results presented.

Long-term approach to training   The long-term approach to the training variable presents an interaction between the independent variables country and levels of technology ($p < 0.05$), Table 6. Thus, the intensity of the impact of levels of technology on the training variable is not the same in France and Britain. This result supports hypothesis H2.2. Therefore, each country was analysed separately. The ANOVA test performed in Britain presents a statistically significant difference between the three levels of technology $F = 2.629$, d.f. $= 2.90$, ($p < 0.10$). The post hoc Scheffé shows a statistically significant difference between high-tech and low-tech firms ($p < 0.10$). Figure 3 shows higher means values for the high-tech firms. Thus, the hypothesis H2.1, which predicts that there is a difference in the training practices between technology

Table 6 *Overview of variance analysis*

Independent variables	Dependent variable	MANOVA results			ANOVA results	
		Wilks' λ	F	p	F	p
National culture	Recruitment technical policies	0.942	2.856	0.039	0.104	0.748
	Long-term approach to training				3.843	0.052
	Compensation based on performance				5.578	0.020
Levels of technology	Recruitment technical policies	0.835	4.335	<0.001	8.152	<0.001
	Long-term approach to training				11.090	<0.001
	Compensation based on performance				1.205	0.303
National culture * levels of technology	Recruitment technical policies	0.914	2.128	0.049*	3.065	0.049*
	Long-term approach to training				3.207	0.043*
	Compensation based on performance				0.638	0.530

Notes: *p < 0.05.

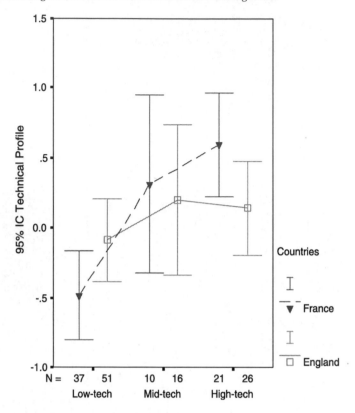

Figure 2 *Recruitment technical policies factor*

intensive firms and low-tech firms, is validated in Britain. The ANOVA test performed on France shows a statistically significant effect of the levels of technology $F = 10.179$, d.f. $= 2.68$ (p < 0.001) on the factor long-term approach to training. The post hoc Scheffé test shows two statistically significant differences: (1) high- and low-tech firms (p < 0.05); and (2) mid- and low-tech firms (p < 0.05). Higher means values are observed for the technology-oriented firms than for low-tech firms. Please refer to Figure 3 for details. Thus, this result validates hypothesis H2.1 in France. Hypothesis H2.1 is completely validated.

Compensation based on performance   The last variable, compensation based on performance, does not present a statistically significant interaction $F = 0.638$, d.f. $= 2.150$, (p $= 0.530$). Additionally, the independent variable levels of technology does not present a statistically significant difference $F = 1.205$, d.f. $= 2.150$, (p $= 0.303$) (Table 6). Thus, hypotheses H3.1 and H3.2 are not supported. These hypotheses predict that technology intensive firms will present a more strategic approach to the compensation system than low-tech firms and that the intensity of this impact will not be the same in France and Britain. According to these results, the technology intensive firms and low-tech firms studied in France and Britain tend to present a similar tendency in the compensation based on performance variable. Country is statistically significant $F = 5.578$ d.f. (1.150) (p $= 0.02$). The ANOVA tests performed between

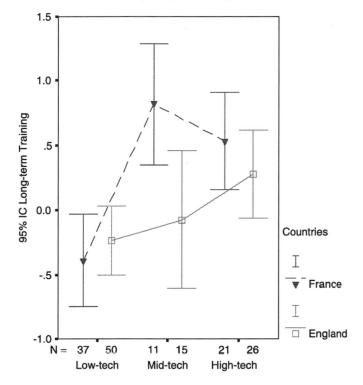

Figure 3 *Long-term approach to training factor*

the two countries for each level of technology in the sample show two statistical differences between the two countries for low-tech and mid-tech firms F = 2.963, d.f = 1.77 (p = 0.089); F = 6.121 d.f. (1.25) (p = 0.021) respectively; France shows a higher mean score, see Figure 4 for details. Table 6 presents a summary of the results of the tests.

Discussion

The debate between the contingency and divergence theories on their impact on management continues today. The findings presented in this paper support our proposition that the contingency and divergence theories do not compete with each other. Rather, analysing these theories together in the form of the neo-contingency approach could help to reconcile them by the introduction of the impact of the technology and national institution variables on HRM policies and practices.

According to the results presented, the moderator effect of the national culture on the relation between the Level of Technology and the HRM was validated for two variables: (1) recruitment technical policies and (2) long-term approach to training. Hypotheses H1.2 and H2.2 are supported. Nonetheless, only France shows a significant statistical difference between the technology intensive firms and the low-tech firms for the variable recruitment technical policies, hypothesis H1.1 is supported only in France. Britain shows no significant statistical difference. On the other hand, France and Britain present a statistically significant difference between the technologically intensive firms and

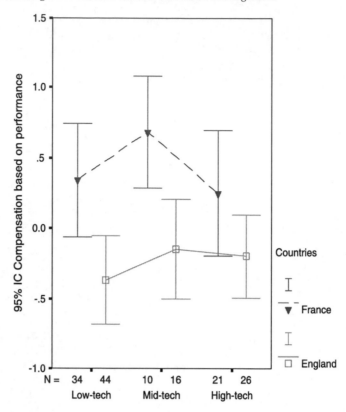

Figure 4 *Compensation based on performance factor*

low-tech firms for the factor long-term approach to training; thus, hypothesis H2.1 is supported. Finally, the moderator effect of the national culture was not supported for the Compensation Based on Performance; hypotheses H3.1 and H3.2 are not supported, see Table 7.

The differences presented between France and Britain in their education systems illustrate the variations found between these two countries. Thus, it is not surprising that technology intensive firms will recruit employees with a more sophisticated profile than low-tech firms in France. This evidence also gives support to the fact that technology intensive firms would place more emphasis on soft-skills training than low-tech firms, which is statistically supported in France and Britain. On the contrary, low-tech firms do not require high levels of investment in these HRM because their workers possess a public knowledge that can be purchased in the labour marketplace. The results presented demonstrate how both national culture and technology have an influence on managers' behaviour. Thus, this research has modestly validated the neo-contingency proposition.

Implication for theory

The tentative interpretation of the evidence for neo-contingency helps to explain the emergence of a comparative advantage on the basis of HRM, organizational patterns and the embeddedness of types of firms in the French and British social structures.

Table 7 *Synthesis table of the hypothesis and the results of tests*

Name	Label	Results of tests
H1.1	High-tech, mid-tech and low-tech firms will present a difference in the recruitment and selection process; high-tech and mid-tech will present more sophisticated processes than low-tech firms	Supported only in France
H1.2	The relation between level of technology and the recruitment and selection processes will be moderated by the national culture factors	Supported
H2.1	High-tech, mid-tech and low-tech firms will present a difference in the training practices, high-tech and mid-tech will present a more sophisticated approach than low-tech firms	Supported
H2.2	The relation between level of technology and the training practices will be moderated by the national culture factors	Supported
H3.1	High-tech, mid-tech and low-tech firms will present a difference in the compensation system, high-tech and mid-tech will present a more sophisticated systems that low-tech firms	Not supported
H3.2	The relation between level of technology and the compensation system will be moderated by the national-culture factors	Not supported *Indirect effect of the national culture on the compensation system is observed*

The difficulties of the traditional contingency theory being static and without a relation between the contingency variables and HRM have been partly resolved by the empirical result presented in this paper. The high- and mid-tech firms investigated give evidence that R&D is a source of new products and processes, large investments that will promote greater external change and variability for an organization in a given industry. A higher level of R&D effort creates a wider and more complex range of relevant knowledge, and employs the services of a greater variety of disciplines and more specialized personnel, it will also add to the complexity of the environment, especially the national location where a firm operates. The point is that the HRM that support the neo-contingency approach are not only important to managers in both Britain and France, but they are culturally rooted in the educational traditions of each country, and the effect they have on managerial and organizational adaptability differs at the corporate and operational levels according to the firm's internal and external contextual-factors.

Implications for practitioners

One of the challenges of this paper is to communicate effectively to practitioners the findings discussed here and their implications for managers' day-to-day challenges in workplaces. At the macro level, this paper draws the attention of managers to potential and actual advantages of national context for their business, as well as to the technology context within their organizations. It also enhances the managers' awareness of the significant roles of the educational systems that mould certain HRM. This awareness helps managers to understand their workforce better and devise appropriate means of handling its diversity at the micro level. For example, it would pointless for a low-tech firm to apply a policy of a long-term approach to training their employees. However, according to the results presented here, this practice could be acceptable in both French and British high-tech firms.

Nonetheless, a difference is also observed between these two countries. Mid-tech firms present higher mean values in France than in Britain. These differences are grounded on the school education system that differs between these countries. The French system presents a close governmental control. Additionally, paternalism in France is observed as professors tend to lecture to their students under a high power distance and exercise close control (e.g. Hofstede, 1991; House *et al.*, 2004; OECD, 1998, 1999). These French patterns are contrary to the British system.

Additionally, the results presented in this paper could be also be applied to high- and mid-tech firms located in the Anglo, or Latin European culture cluster (House *et al.*, 2004). One course of action would be to build up a strong organizational culture and create a more or less homogeneous values system to which employees will be encouraged to subscribe. Selection procedures can be devised to recruit new employees with the kind of values and preferences that are compatible with the prevailing high-tech and mid-tech organizational environment. For example, utilizing net-recruitment and training employees in soft-skills capabilities that would lead employees to build an integral career development within the firm, as well as ensuring that the firm has an equal career development plan, could create an organizational culture that high- and mid-tech firms in the Anglo and Latin European cultural cluster seek to obtain.

Limitations and future research

This study presents certain limitations. First, although the sample was tested for internal validation with respect to the database, it undoubtedly presents a limited number of cases (163 firms). However, to some extent this may reflect inadequacies in the measurement employed or the variables investigated. Future work on refining methods for the relation between HRM under the neo-contingency approach proposed in this paper would be useful. Additionally, the HRM questionnaire did not include legal differences between France and Britain, which may influence HRM in a particular firm. Therefore, the findings must be interpreted cautiously.

It would be important for future studies to present a more sophisticated way of operationalizing the neo-contingency perspective with revised research instruments. Perhaps firms' size and strategy could be studied together with their level of technology taken from here with quantitative data on the social-cultural environment to triangulate results and provide new insights.

Additionally, future research should study if the firms that adapt the HRM policies and practices according to the neo-contingency approach proposed here positively affect their financial performance. It could be also interesting to test if the HRM policies and practices suggested to be more appropriate for the high- and mid-tech firms that are adopted in low-tech firms will also enhance positive financial performance.

Finally, in this study we did not test whether the cultural impact on HRM is a phenomenon that the firms aim to obtain. Perhaps it is phenomenon that is intrinsic to the national culture where the firm operates, which in turn shapes managers behaviour without their noticing why they adopt a certain pattern in designing the HRM policies and practices.

Nevertheless, despite the limitations, the findings presented in this paper encourage further testing of the importance of both contingency-technology and divergence-institutions shaping HRM policies and practices. We hope that this research will highlight the possible ways in which national and organizational variables might interrelate and offer some directions for future research.

Conclusions

In this research, we found that HRM is a dynamic function, which requires managers to be inventive and creative when applying them according to the contextual and environmental circumstances in which a firm operates. This general finding, which needs more research and corroboration, lends more weight to the view that societal institutions constitute 'different but equal' practices. From this picture, a notion of universal state-of-the-art HRM policy and practice cannot be ascertained and demonstrated. Societal context and domestic economic strengths appear to define a particular 'rationale' of HRM that a firm puts into practice.

Based on the findings and their interpretation, there is a strong need for more empirical research into the neo-contingency approach proposed in this paper. A lack of systematic empirical research in cross-national research on HRM under the neo-contingency views has created several myths. The field of international management is, unfortunately, full of partial insights blown up into conclusions that exceed the methodological foundations on which they stand (e.g. Harzing and Sorge, 2003). A firm's level of technology and the particularity of the national educational system where a firm operates appear to be stronger than suggested in their effect on certain HRM. These nexus through more detailed research could be on the agenda for the future.

Acknowledgements

The authors are grateful to Professor Stephen Procter and Professor Michel Leber for their encouragement and helpful comments.

References

Ambler, J.S. (1987) 'Constraints on Policy Innovation in Education: The Thatcher's Britain and Mitterrand's France', *Comparative Politics*, 20(1): 85–105.

Balkin, D.B. and Gomez-Mejia, L.R. (1992) *Compensation, Organizational Strategy, and Firm Performance*. Cincinnati, OH: College Division South-Western Publishing Co.

Barsoux, J.-L. and Lawrence, P. (1997) *French Management Elitism in Action*. London: Cassell.

Berger, P.L. and Luckmann, T. (1967) *The Societal Construction of Reality – A Treatise in the Sociology of Knowledge*. Harmondsworth: Penguin Press.

Blau, P.M. (1970) 'A Formal Theory of Differentiation in Organizations', *American Sociological Review*, 35(2): 201–18.

Bowman, B.A. and Farr, J.V. (2000) 'Embedding Leadership in Civil Engineering Education', *Journal of Professional Issues in Engineering Education and Practice*, 126(1): 16–20.

Boxall, P. (1995) 'Building the Theory of Comparative HRM', *Human Resource Management Journal*, 5: 5–17.

Breheny, M.J. and McQuaid, R.W. (eds) (1987) *The Development of High Technology Industries. An International Survey*. London: Croom Helm.

Brislin, R.W. (1986) 'The Wording and Translation of Research Instruments'. In Lonner, W.F. (ed.) *Field Methods in Cross-cultural Research*, Vol. 8. London: Sega, pp. 137–64.

British Business Ranking (1995) *Key British Enterprises*. London: Dun and Brandstreet's.

Buckley, P., Minette, K., Joy, D. and Michaels, J. (2004) 'The Use of an Automated Employment Recruitment and Screening System for Temporary Professional Employees: A Case Study', *Human Resource Management*, 43(2&3): 233–41.

Burns, T. and Stalker, G.M. (1961) *The Management of Innovation*. London: Tavistock Publications Ltd.

Calori, R., Lubatkin, M., Very, P. and Veiga, J.F. (1997) 'Modelling the Origins of National-Bound Administrative Heritages: A Historical Institutional Analysis of French and English Firms', *Organization Science*, 8(6): 681–96.

Cardy, R.L. and Krzystofiak, F.J. (1991) 'Interfacing High Technology Operations with Blue Collar Workers: Selection and Appraisal in a Computerized Manufacturing Setting', *The Journal of High Technology Management Research*, 2(2): 193–210.

Cascio, W.F. (1990) 'Strategic Human Resource Management in High Technology Industry'. In Gomez-Mejia, L.R. and Lawless, M. (eds) *Organizational Issues in High Tech Magazine*, 2: pp. 179–98.

Cassis, Y., Crouzet, F. and Gourvish, T. (eds) (1995) *Management and Business in Britain and France: The Age of the Corporate Economy*. Oxford: Oxford University Press.

Child, J. (1972) 'Organizational Structure, Environment and Performance: The Role of Strategic Choice', *Sociology*, 6: 2–21.

Child, J. (1975) 'Managerial and Organizational Factors Associated with Company Performance, Part 2: A Contingency Analysis', *Journal of Management Studies*, 12: 12–27.

Collinson, M., Rees, C., Edwards, P. and Inness, L. (1998) *Involving Employees in Total Quality Management: 123*. London: Department of Trade and Industry.

Coombs, G. and Rosse, J. (1992) 'Recruiting and Hiring the High-Technology Professional: Trends and Future Directions', *Advance in Global High-Technology Management*, 1: 91–107.

Crouzet, F. (1990) *Britain Ascendant: Comparative Studies in Franco-English Economic History*. Cambridge: Cambridge University Press.

Cully, M., Woodland, S., O'Reilly, A. and Dix, G. (1999) *Britain at Work. As Depicted by the 1998 Workplace Employment Relation Survey*. London: Routledge.

Cutcher-Gershenfeld, J., Nitta, M., Barrett, B.J., Belhedi, N., Sai-Chung Chow, S., Ishino, I., Lin, W.-J., Moore, M., Mothersell, W.M., Palthe, J., Ramanand, S., Strolle, M.E. and Wheaton, A.C. (eds) (1998) *Knowledge-Driven Work. Unexpected Lessons from Japanese and United States Work Practices*. New York: Oxford University Press.

Donaldson, L. (2001) *The Contingency Theory of Organizations*. London: Sage.

Edwards, P., Hall, M., Hyman, R., Marginson, P, Sisson, K, Waddington, J. and Winchester, D. (1992) 'Great Britain: Still Muddling Through?'. In Ferner, A. and Hyman, R. (eds) *Industrial Relations in the New Europe*. Oxford: Basil Blackwell.

Fröbel, P. and Marchington, M. (2005) 'Teamworking Structures and Worker Perceptions: A Cross-national Study in Pharmaceuticals', *International Journal of Human Resource Management*, 16: 256–76.

Galbraith, J.K. (1972) *The New Industrial State*. London: Penguin Books.

Gallie, D. (1978) *In Search of the New Working Class – Automation and Social Integration within the Capitalist Enterprise*. Cambridge: Cambridge University Press.

Gomez-Mejia, L.R. and Welbourne, T.M. (1990) 'Influence of Venture Capitalists on High Tech Management', *The Journal of High Technology Management Research*, 1(1): 103–18.

Gooderham, P.N., Nordhaug, O. and Ringdal, K. (1999) 'Institutional and Rational Determinants of Organizational Practices: Human Resource Management in European Firms', *Administrative Science Quarterly*, 44(3): 507–31.

Gresov, C. (1990) 'Effects of Dependence and Task on Unit Design and Efficiency', *Organization Studies*, 11: 503–29.

Hage, J. and Aiken, M. (1967) 'Program Change and Organizational Properties: A Comparative Analysis', *American Journal of Sociology*, 72: 503–19.

Hage, J. and Aiken, M. (1969) 'Routine Technology, Social Structure and Organizational Goals', *Administrative Science Quarterly*, 14: 366–76.

Hagström, P. and Chandler, A.D. (1998) 'Perspectives on Firm Dynamics'. In Hagström, C.A.D. and Sölvellö, P. (eds) *The Dynamic Firm. The Role of Technology, Strategy, Organization, and Regions*. Oxford: Oxford University Press, pp. 1–12.

Haimann, T., Scott, G.W. and Connor, P.E. (1978) *Managing the Modern Organization*. Boston, MA: Houghton Mifflin Co.

Harzing, A.W. and Sorge, A. (2003) 'The Relative Impact of Country of Origin and Universal Contingencies on Internationalization Strategies and Corporate Control in Multinational Enterprises: Worldwide and European Perspectives', *Organization Studies*, 24(2): 187–214.

Hickson, D.J., Pugh, D.S. and Pheysey, D.C. (1969) 'Operations Technology and Organization Structure: An Empirical Reappraisal', *Administrative Science Quarterly*, 14: 378–97.

Hofstede, G. (1980) *Culture's Consequences – International Differences in Work–Related Values. Cross-Cultural Research and Methodology*. Beverly Hills, CA: Sage.

Hofstede, G. (1991) *Culture and Organizations: Software of the Mind*. New York: McGraw-Hill.

Hofstede, G. (1993) 'Cultural Dimensions in People Management'. In Pucik, V., Tichy, N.M. and Barnett, C.K. (eds) *Globalizing Management*. New York: Wiley, pp. 139–58.

House, R.J., Hanges, P.J., Javidan, M., Dorfman, P.W. and Gupta, V. (2004) *Culture, Leadership, and Organizations: The GLOBE Study of 62 Societies*. London: Sage.

Huo, Y.P., Huang, H.J. and Naiper, N.K. (2002) 'Divergence or Convergence: A Cross-National Comparison of Personnel Selection Practices', *Human Resource Management*, 41(1): 31–44.

Jolly, D. and Roche, L. (1999) 'La GRH dans les Enterprises a Fort Contenu Technologique', *Management and Conjoncture Sociale*, (556): 25–32.

Jolly, D. and Therin, F. (1996) 'Technology Strategy: Towards a Resource-Based Approach', *Les Cahiers du Management Technology*, (16).

Kast, F.E and Rosenzweig, J.E. (1985) *Organization and Management: A Systems and Contingency Approach*, 4th edn. New York: McGraw-Hill.

Kerr, C., Dunlop, J.T., Harbison, F. and Myers, C.A. (1964) *Industrialism and Industrial Man. The Problems of Labor and Management in Economic Growth*. New York: Oxford University Press.

Kleingartner, A. and Anderson, C.S. (eds) (1987) *Human Resource Management in High Technology Firms*. Los Angeles, CA: Lexington Books.

Kompass France (2000) *Répertoire général de la production Française*. Paris: Dafsa Kompass.

Kompass UK (2000) *Register of British industry and commerce*. East Grinstead: Kompass Publisher.

Lawrence, P.R. and Lorsch, J.W. (1967) *Organization and Environment. Managing Differentiation and Integration*. Boston, MA: Harvard University.

Leonard-Barton, D. (1995) *Wellsprings of Knowledge. Building and Sustaining the Source of Innovation*. Boston, MA: Harvard Business School Press.

Lepak, D.P. and Snell, S.A. (1999) 'The Human Resource Architecture: Toward a Theory of Human Capital Allocation and Development', *Academy of Management Review*, 24(1): 31–48.

Les Echos (2000) *Enjeux-Les 500 premiers groupes Français et Européens*. Paris: Les Echos Novembre, Hors-série, p. 130.

Lessem, R. and Palsule, S. (1999) *From Management Education to Civic Reconstruction. The Emerging Ecology of Organizations*. London and New York: Routledge.

Locke, R. (1985) 'The Relationship between Educational and Managerial Cultures in Britain and West Germany: A Comparative Analysis of Higher Education, from an Historical Perspective'. In Joynt, P. and Warner, M. (eds) *Managing in Different Cultures*. London: Global Book Resources Ltd, pp. 166–214.

Lubatkin, M., Calori, R., Very, P. and Veiga, J.F. (1998) 'Managing Mergers Across Borders: A Two-Nation Exploration of a Nationally Bound Administrative Heritage', *Organization Science*, 9(6): 670–84.

Maurice, M., Sorge, A. and Warner, M. (1980) 'Societal Differences in Organizing Manufacturing Units: A Comparison of France, West Germany, and Great Britain', *Organization Studies*, 1(1): 59–86.

Maurice, M., Sellier, F., Silvestre, J.-J. and Goldhammer, A. (1986) *The Social Foundations of Industrial Power. A Comparison of France and Germany*. Cambridge, MA: MIT Press.

McMillan, C.J., Hickson, D.J., Hinings, C.R. and Schneck, R.E. (1973) 'The Structure of Work Organizations across Societies', *The Academy of Management Journal*, 16(4): 555–69.

Miles, R.E. and Snow, C.C. (1978) *Organizational Strategy, Structure, and Process*. New York: McGraw-Hill.

Mintzberg, H. (1993) *Structure in Fives: Designing Effective Organizations*. Englewood Cliffs, NJ: Prentice Hall, Inc.

Mohr, L.B. (1971) 'Organizational Technology and Organizational Structure', *Administrative Science Quarterly*, December: 444–59.

Nelson, R.E. and Gopalan, S. (2003) 'Do Organizational Cultures Replicate National Cultures? Isomorphism, Rejection and Reciprocal Opposition in the Corporate Values of Three Countries', *Organization Studies*, 24(7): 1115–52.

OECD (1997) 'OECD Economic Survey 1996–1997 France: Special Features Labor Market Corporate Governance: 167', Paris: OECD.

OECD (1998) 'OECD Economic Survey: United Kingdom: Implementing Structural Reform: A Review of Progress towards a Better Integration of Work and Welfare Corporate Governance: 186', Paris: OECD.

OECD (1999) 'OECD Economic Surveys: France Special Features: Structural Policies Research and Innovation: 174', Paris: OECD.

Pennings, J.M. (1975) 'The Relevance of the Structural-Contingency Model for Organizational Effectiveness', *Administrative Science Quarterly*, 20(3): 393–410.

Pugh, D.S., Hickson, D.J., Hinings, C.R. and Turner, C. (1969) 'The Context of Organization Structure', *Administrative Science Quarterly*, 14: 91–104.

Ramanathan, K. (1994) 'The Polytrophic Components of Manufacturing Technology', *Technological Forecasting and Social Change*, 46: 221–58.

Richardson, S.A. (1953) 'Organizational Contrasts on English and America Ships', *Administrative Science Quarterly*, 1: 189–207.

Rose, M. (1985) 'Universalism, Culturalism and the Aix Group: Promise and Problems of a Societal Approach to Economic Institutions', *European Sociological Review*, 1(1): 65–83.

Saura Díaz, M.D. and Gomez-Mejia, L.R. (1997) 'The Effectiveness of Organization-Wide Compensation Strategies in Technology Intensive Firm', *The Journal of High Technology Management Research*, JAI Press Inc., 8(2): 301–15.

Schoonhoven, B.C. (1981) 'Problems with Contingency Theory: Testing Assumptions Hidden within the Language of Contingency "Theory"', *Administrative Science Quarterly*, 26: 349–77.

Scoreboard (2001) Department of Trade and Industry (DTI) (web address: innovate.gov.uk). 10 July.

Senker, J. (1992) 'Automation and Work in Britain'. In Adler, P.S. (ed.) *Technology and the Future Work*. Oxford: Oxford University Press, pp. 89–110.

Shackleton, V. and Newell, S. (1991) 'Management Selection: A Comparative Survey of Methods Used in to English and French Companies', *Journal of Occupational Psychology*, 64: 23–36.

Sorge, A. and Maurice, M. (1990) 'The Societal Effect in Strategies and Competitiveness of Machine Tools Manufacturers in France and West Germany', *The International Journal of Human Resource Management*, 1(2): 141–72.

Sparrow, P. and Hiltrop, J.-M. (1994) *European Human Resource Management in Transition*. New York: Prentice Hall.

Stuart, L.H. and Quinn, E.R. (1992) 'Executive Leadership and Performance: Comparing High- and Low-Technology Firms', *Advance in Global High-Technology Management*, 19–32.

Swan, J., Newell, S. and Robertson, M. (1999) 'Central Agencies in the Diffusion and Design of Technology: A Comparison of the UK and Sweden', *Organization Studies*, 20(6): 905–31.

Tayeb, M. (1987) 'Contingency Theory and Culture: A Study of Matched English and Indian Manufacturing Firms', *Organization Studies*, 8(3): 241–61.

Thompson, J.D. (1967) *Organizations in Action*. New York: McGraw-Hill.

Towers, B. (1992) *The Handbook of Human Resource Management*. Oxford: Blackwell Publishers.

Tregaskis, O. and Dany, F. (1996) 'A Comparison of HRM in France and the UK', *Journal of European Industrial Training*, 20(1): 20–30.

Tremblay, M. (2005) 'The Effectiveness of Compensation Strategies in International Technology Intensive Firms', *International Journal of Technology Management*, 32(3&4): 222–39.
van der Klink, M. and Mulder, M. (1995) 'Human Resource Development and Staff Flow Policy in Europe'. In Harzing, A.W. and Van Ruysseveldt, J. (eds) *International Human Resource Management and Integrated Approach*. London: Sage, pp. 157–78.
Wade, R. (1996) 'Globalization and its Limits: Reports on the Death of the National Economy are Greatly Exaggerated'. In Berger, S. and Dore, R.P. (eds) *National Diversity and Global Capitalism*. Ithaca, NY: Cornell University Press.
Whitley, R. (1992) *European Business Systems, Firms and Market in their National Contexts*. London: Sage Publications.
Winch, G., Clifton, N. and Millar, C. (2000) 'Organization and Management in an Anglo-French Consortium: The Case of Transmanche-link', *Journal of Management Studies*, 37(5): 663–86.
Woodward, J. (1965) *Industrial Organization: Theory and Practice*. London: Oxford University Press.
Zeleny, M. (1986) 'High Technology Management', *Human Systems Management*, 6: 109–20.

Appendix 1

Items of the dependent variables HRM

1   Recruitment system with a global scope.
2   Tendency to employ a workforce with intangible skills.
3   Net-recruitment.
4   Use of Assessment Centres in the selection process.
5   Preference for employing a workforce younger than 35 years.
6   Training programmes designed by focusing on the development of soft-skills/capabilities.
7   Training as an integral part of the employee's career development.
8   Firm provides all its employees with career development plans.
9   Training programmes designed to follow strict operational procedures.
10 Firm provides international training.
11 Firm provides its employees with opportunities to learn new skills from other departments.
12 Scientific employee working in R&D area could have a salary scale equivalent to that of a manager.
13 Compensation system based on individual performance.
14 Importance of employee's capabilities for the compensation system.
15 Freedom for the personnel staff to develop, for their units, their own payment system.
16 Compensation system based on employee's short-term accomplishment.
17 Flexibility of the compensation system.

INDEX